AUGUSTINE THE THEOLOGIAN

Eugene TeSelle

AUGUSTINE
THE THEOLOGIAN

HERDER AND HERDER

1970
HERDER AND HERDER NEW YORK
232 Madison Avenue, New York, N.Y. 10016

Library of Congress Catalog Card Number: 75–87772

Contents

TO MY PARENTS

Preface

I WISH HERE to express my appreciation to some of those with whom my recollections of the work on this volume will always be bound up:

The students in the Yale Divinity School and in several departments of the Yale Graduate School who, during the four years that I conducted a seminar on the theology of Augustine, have forced me to clarify my own ideas and suggested many new ones; and James M. Gustafson and George A. Lindbeck, who first encouraged me to undertake the seminar;

Raymond P. Morris, Helen B. Uhrich, and Jane E. McFarland of the Yale Divinity School Library, who not only maintain a well-stocked library as a matter of course but have been helpful in extraordinary ways as well, securing out-of-the-way works and granting the use of materials through the summer months;

The members of the United Church of Christ in Monterey, Massachusetts, together with their present minister, Virgil B. Brallier, in whose midst my family and I spent several happy summers and who made available the cool and quiet study space in which most of the writing was done;

And above all my wife, Sallie, who not only lived with the process of study and writing but kept me at the task and was an encouragement in all seasons.

EUGENE TESELLE

New Haven, Connecticut

Chronological Table Of Augustine's Works

De Gen. ad litt.	*De Genesi ad litteram* (*Literal Commentary on Genesis*)	402–413
Tr. in Joann. ev./ep.	*Tractatūs in Joannis evangelium/epistulam* (*Expository Sermons on the Gospel and First Epistle of John*)	406–407 (ev., tr. 1–16; ep., all)
De Trin.	*De Trinitate* (*The Trinity*)	407 (book VIII)
De pecc. mer.	*De peccatorum meritis et remissione* (*The Merits and the Remission of Sins*)	411
De spir. et litt.	*De spiritu et littera* (*The Spirit and the Letter*)	412
De civ. Dei	*De civitate Dei* (*The City of God*)	413–426
De Trin.	*De Trinitate* (*The Trinity*)	413–416 (books V–VII, IX–XII)
De nat. et gr.	*De natura et gratia* (*Nature and Grace*)	415
De perf. iust. hom.	*De perfectione iustitiae hominis* (*Man's Perfecting in Righteousness*)	416
De gest. Pel.	*De gestis Pelagii* (*The Proceedings of Pelagius*)	417
De gr. Chr., De pecc. orig.	*De gratia Christi et de peccato originali* (*The Grace of Christ and Original Sin*)	418
C. serm. Ar.	*Contra sermonem Arianorum* (*Against the Sermon of the Arians*)	418
De Trin.	*De Trinitate*	418–421 (books XIII–XV)
In Joann. ev.	*Tractatūs in Joannis evangelium* (*Expository Sermons on the Gospel according to John*)	418–421 (tr. 17ff.)
De an. et or.	*De anima et eius origine* (*On the Soul and its Origin*)	419
De nupt. et conc.	*De nuptiis et concupiscentia* (*Marriage and Concupiscence*)	420
C. duas ep. Pel.	*Contra duas epistulas Pelagianorum* (*Against Two Letters of the Pelagians*)	421
C. Jul. Pel.	*Contra Julianum Pelagianum* (*Against Julian the Pelagian*)	421
Ench.	*Enchiridion ad Laurentium* (*A Handbook Concerning Faith, Hope, and Love*)	423

Abbreviations

AM	*Augustinus Magister. Actes du Congrès international augustinien.* 3 volumes (Paris, 1954)
BA	*Bibliothèque Augustinienne* (Paris)
CC	*Corpus Christianorum* (Turnholt)
CSEL	*Corpus Scriptorum Ecclesiasticorum Latinorum* (Vienna)
DTC	*Dictionnaire de théologie catholique* (Paris)
KpS	Berthold Altaner, *Kleine patristische Schriften* (Berlin, 1967)
PG	*Patrologiae cursus completus. Series Graeca,* ed. J.-B. Migne (Paris)
PL	*Patrologiae cursus completus. Series Latina,* ed. J.-B. Migne (Paris)
RA	*Recherches augustiniennes* (Paris)
REA	*Revue des études augustiniennes* (Paris)

AUGUSTINE THE THEOLOGIAN

Introduction

I. ON APPROACHING AUGUSTINE'S THEOLOGY

AUGUSTINE ATTRACTS OUR INTEREST in many ways—as the personality exhibited in the *Confessions*, as a bishop and a champion of the Church, as a saint—but he has remained an abiding presence in the subsequent history of the West chiefly as a thinker, and its theology, both Catholic and Protestant, is largely a series of annotations to his work. He may have even greater relevance today than in the past, for when theological edifices built during the Middle Ages and since are being threatened, if they have not already crumbled, a new creativity, as we are often told, is demanded; and if we are not to start out lightheadedly elaborating our latest fancies, we would do well to dismantle the later edifices and look again at the original components from which they have been built, the insights that gave impetus to the whole development.

My purpose is to consider Augustine as a theologian and trace the course of his reflections, not with the expectation of assenting to his conclusions in every case, but in order to learn, first of all, something about the way in which he, in his situation, approached the problems of theology, and then how we in our own situation might think through the problems again with some measure of the breadth and originality exemplified in him. The task is primarily one of "historical theology," therefore; but throughout there will be an interest in learning more about the nature of the theological enterprise, and a concluding chapter is expressly devoted to asking after the lessons that can be drawn from his achievement and noting those points at which some of the most treasured assumptions of theology since the Middle Ages, often shared by traditionalists and radicals alike, may be qualified or supplemented or in some cases called into question by his thought.[1]

In order to catch Augustine the theologian at work we shall approach his thought not as a finished product, a "system" or at least a single complex of ideas, but as a process of reflection and discovery. And such a method is suited to the subject matter, for Augustine's thought proceeds by way of ceaseless inquiry; he often refrains from making final judgments, and even when he makes them he is prepared to modify them in the light of fresh examination. Consequently each stage in his thinking must be examined in and for itself in the attempt to discover its exact pattern and framework: what is taken for granted, what is a problem to him, what options lie at hand, what resources he has for bringing a problem to its resolution. There will be a continuity in his thought, but it will be the continuity of a process of becoming; there will be coherence, but it will be a coherence that is always changing. The method of study, then, must be "cinematic," as it has recently been put in one of the most successful achievements along these lines[2]—Augustine's thought must be seen as a constantly changing whole.

Augustine knew how much his mind had changed. From time to time he reflected on his development, and in the *Retractationes*, written toward the end of his life, he furnished a catalogue, in chronological order, of all his major writings. The task of tracing his development still is not an easy one, however, for his greatest works took many years to complete and he said little about the course of their production; and we are left almost entirely without guidance concerning the sermons, including the important series on the Psalms and on the Fourth Gospel. Chronological study of Augustine's writings has gone on since Erasmus and the Maurists,

[1] It will be noted that I am using the word "theology" in its broad modern sense. It is a term that was not often used in the patristic period, and when it was used it had more specialized meanings. In that day what we call theology was more often called philosophy, and Augustine considered Christian thought in its fullness the "one true philosophy" (*C. Jul. Pel.*, IV, 14, 72).

[2] Olivier du Roy, *L'Intelligence de la foi en la Trinité selon saint Augustin. Genèse de sa théologie trinitaire jusqu'en 391* (Paris, 1966), p. 19.

but it is only in the twentieth century that the research has become sufficiently subtle in its methods and detailed in its findings to enable us to see the general outlines with some clarity, though many puzzles remain and some new ones have come to light.[3] My purpose here is not to engage in further study of chronology, which is a specialized discipline of its own. This is an essay not in history but in historical theology: that is to say, I am attempting to follow the reflections of Augustine as a theologian, utilizing the chronological studies that have been made, but with the purpose of gaining a better glimpse of him at work on the problems themselves. Nevertheless a few important points of chronology have emerged in the course of my own investigations, especially in chapter 4, and I have tried to indicate their importance to the understanding of his thought.

The study of the chronology of Augustine's writings has gone along hand in hand with another undertaking, the study of the influences upon him and the sources he used. One hypothesis leads to another; the query whether this or that motif is to be found only after a certain date leads to a search after the cause, and if it can be shown that a writing of some philosopher or theologian could have come into his hands at that time the two hypotheses will reinforce each other. My purpose is not to trace sources; for that, a very different and far more technical mode of procedure is required. But I find it necessary to proceed with an awareness of sources, especially in the case of Augustine, for he seems to have been aroused to his best reflections when challenged by something from beyond himself: a philosophical writing, a biblical passage, a query or a controversy. Indeed, his life was so busy that he wrote little that was not called forth by some such challenge; and even when his literary undertakings were self-motivated, so to speak, and were governed by some large speculative design—*The Trinity*, for example, or *The City of God*—then as well he seems to have sought out the stimulation of other

---

[3] This may be the appropriate point at which to mention that guidance through the mass of material written on all the varied topics of Augustine research can be found in Tarsicius van Bavel, *Repertoire bibliographique de saint Augustin* (Louvain, 1954), and *Repertoire bibliographique de saint Augustin, 1950–1960* (Hague, 1963); Carl Andresen, *Augustinus-Gespräch der Gegenwart* (Köln, 1962); and the annotated bibliography published each year in the *REA*.

works, toward which he was sometimes antagonistic, and which at other times served to instruct him, but to which in every case he reacted with fresh and independent reflection.

Augustine was not really an occasional *thinker*, though he produced many occasional *writings*. Each new challenge is met out of the resources of what he has already come to affirm, and though it often leads to a modification of his understanding of some topic there is a sovereign independence of mind and continuity of conviction that keeps his thought from ever becoming merely a passive response. Still an awareness of sources and influences is important for our purposes, for it safeguards us from the altogether uninteresting temptation to attribute everything in Augustine's thought either to an unbroken and perfectly unified Catholic tradition or to his own personal genius and sanctity. To be sure, Augustine did take tradition seriously, and often the presence of an opinion in his writings will signal its presence in the wider Church. And his achievement does depend in large part upon genius and sanctity, working together. But the tradition of the Church is taken seriously only when one asks in exactly what shape it was presented to Augustine, what opinions were ranged before him, and especially what *changes* it made in his own thinking when he discovered something new in the tradition. And his originality is not diminished but is only given greater definiteness when we can see what he owed to others and how he transformed it through his own insight and power of synthesis. There will be, then, a discussion of sources from time to time, not for its own sake, as a matter of curiosity, but in order to catch a better glimpse of his preferences where he had a choice among alternatives and of his creativity in combining and reworking the materials at hand. If we give lip-service to open-mindedness, to constant inquiry, to the dialogical method, then we must be prepared to examine it at work in Augustine's intellectual career and follow where it leads.

Since my purpose is to consider Augustine the theologian, little can be said about the externals of his career, and in any event they have been treated well in books recently made available in English. The general outlines of his life and thought are traced by Gerald Bonner in *St. Augustine of Hippo: Life and Controversies* (Philadelphia, 1963), the character of his day-to-day life as a churchman is examined with great sensitivity by F. Van der Meer in *Augustine the Bishop* (New York, 1961), and the story of his involvement in the wider life of the times and in the controversies of the Church is told with verve and a good "sense of place" and "sense for the occasion" by Peter Brown in *Augustine of Hippo: A Biography* (Berkeley and Los Angeles, 1967).

Little will be said, furthermore, about Augustine's thoughts concerning society and politics, or the history of the human race as traced in Scripture, or the Church and its sacraments, though all of these topics do belong in some way to his theology. They are omitted in part because they verge more closely on the outward story, and in part because they constitute, even in their more theoretical aspects, a vast field with its own specialists. I am quite prepared to affirm that these topics must be studied if one is to get a complete picture of Augustine and his thought, and that they are well worth the study. But there is sufficient basis in the character of Augustine's own thought for leaving them to one side in discussing his theology. He himself thinks according to distinct topics or problems, and often he discusses them in separate writings. His own deepest interest is clearly in questions about God, man, and the cosmos; when he is not pressed by his ecclesiastical responsibilities and has the liberty to plan his own work, it always concerns these matters.

I shall attempt to focus attention, then, upon the inward history of a brilliant mind, following out his reflections on those topics that were of greatest importance to him, making use of whatever can be learned about his life, the chronology of his writings, and the possible influences upon his thought—for this is indispensable —but still giving it only a supporting role, for my interest is in the theological problems and the way in which Augustine approaches them.

This study is, by its nature, a general one; lengthy discussion of the history of scholarship or detailed analysis of texts is out of the question. I shall try throughout to be to the point. Where Augustine's meaning is clear or where previous scholarship has cast light on some problem, I shall not belabor the issue. The procedure will not be argumentative but expository. In order to avoid making constant detours I have refrained from quoting Latin passages in the footnotes to substantiate or illustrate assertions made in the text; on the principle that the reader ought in any case to consult Augustine's writings directly, I have simply made reference to the relevant passages, following the standard method of citation (a table of Augustine's major works, with both Latin and English titles and their probable dates, is supplied on pp. 11-14).

My hope is that in approaching Augustine's theology in its entire sweep it will be possible to gain a better articulated and more dramatic understanding of his theology. It is not enough merely to know what statements he happens to have made; the problem is to *construe* them properly, to know what is central and what is peripheral, what stood repeated examination and what was modified, with what degree of certitude and on the basis of what reasons he made this or that assertion. I would hope that the following discussion might furnish a useful handbook to the study of Augustine's theology. But I also recognize that it must be of the nature of an interim report, for every new finding will alter, however minutely, the way in which all else is seen. What finally justifies such a venture is the fact that, though detailed studies are necessary for a proper understanding of Augustine's writings, there is also an advantage in looking at his work in a broader perspective, for in this way some perplexities may be resolved, new questions may arise, new features of his development may come to light. At least that has been my experience in the writing, and I would hope that the reader, thinking through the problems for himself as he goes along, will likewise find himself challenged to restructure his conceptions of Augustine's theology and will be stimulated to return once more to a closer study of his writings with new questions in mind.

Since a year-by-year account of Augustine's intellectual development would be not only unmanageable but foolish, given the state of our knowledge, his intellectual career has been divided into six periods, not arbitrarily, I may say, but inductively, on the basis of the broad continuities and the important breaks, as I have been able to discern them, in his thought. It does seem to me that each period constitutes a unit with certain external circumstances and a certain inward spirit of its own, and though there are noteworthy developments and even changes of course within them (and these will be noted), they can be viewed in most cases as the outworking of the same set of convictions or the investigation of the same set of problems.

But before coming to Augustine the Christian theologian as he can be studied in his own writings, it is necessary to glance at two matters which constitute the "background" of his thought: first, his own life up through his conversion, and second, the influence of the various intellectual currents in the ancient world upon him.

2. AUGUSTINE'S WAY TO CHRISTIANITY

Those who have read the *Confessions*, and many who have never even looked into it, will remember the main features of Augustine's life: that he was born in 354 in the North African town of Thagaste, of middle-class parents, the temperamental Patricius and the more pious Monica; that he was brought up as a nominal Christian, though only as a catechumen, for, in keeping with the common practice of the day, he was not baptized early in life; that his parents' chief ambition for him was that he go through the curriculum of liberal education leading toward one of the careers which brought prestige and often wealth and power in late Roman society; and that he succeeded in this until he abruptly changed course and devoted his life first to contemplation and then to the service of the Church.

The study of Augustine's life as narrated in the *Confessions* and elsewhere, a problem that has taken up whole books,[4] can be considered here only briefly. What is important for our purposes is his intellectual development during those years, the "prehistory," as it were, of his thought as a Christian, and it is important not only because of its enduring influence upon him but because of what it tells of the intellectual and moral appeal Christianity held for him.

The way begins with Augustine's reading of Cicero's dialogue *Hortensius* at the age of nineteen. This work, a typical exhortation to the life of philosophy and probably modeled on similar works by the young Aristotle and by Cicero's own teacher Posidonius,

---

[4] Special mention should be made of Prosper Alfaric, *L'Évolution intellectuelle de S. Augustin. I. Du Manichéisme au Néo-platonisme* (Paris, 1918); Pierre Courcelle, *Recherches sur les Confessions de saint Augustin* (Paris, 1950); Jean-Marie Le Blond, *Les Conversions de saint Augustin* (Paris, 1950); John J. O'Meara, *The Young Augustine: The Growth of St. Augustine's Mind up to his Conversion* (London, 1954); and the notes by Aimé de Solignac in *BA*, vols. XIII and XIV (Paris, 1962).

aroused in him a *magnum incendium*, a burning desire to devote himself to the search for wisdom. From what we know of the work through the surviving fragments we can surmise something of its effect. It urges men to devote themselves wholeheartedly to the pursuit of wisdom, forsaking all other desires; but it disabuses them of any expectation that the way will be an easy one, for Cicero followed the teaching of the Academics that nothing can be known with certitude in the realm of philosophy—at least, he says, during the present life, for he hopes for something better afterward.

Cicero supplied a continuity to Augustine's subsequent development. Not only did the philosophical ideal continue to remain before him, though only as an ideal; much that he knew of philosophical problems and analyses came to him through Cicero's writings. But in one way, Augustine says, the classical exhortation to the philosophic life did not satisfy him: he found in it no mention of the name of Christ or of the Christian religion, with which he had been imbued since infancy (*Conf.*, III, 4, 8; *C. Acad.*, II, 2, 5; *De util. cred.*, 1, 2). It is clear from the narrative in the *Confessions* and from earlier, more sketchy comments that the awakening of a philosophical interest led to a serious encounter with the Scriptures; it is also clear that this study of the Scriptures did not have a satisfactory outcome. In the *Confessions* (III, 4, 9) he says that it was because he did not approach the Scriptures with the proper docility; in the earlier accounts he says more provocatively, once in his own voice and once while reporting the arguments of the Manichaeans (*De beata vita*, I, 4 and *De util. cred.*, 1, 2 respectively), but both times in the very same terms, that he was "frightened away by superstition" from engaging in a search for the truth through the study of the Scriptures. When Prosper Alfaric[5] suggested that this *superstitio* must be the Christian religion in which he was brought up, an anguished cry of rage came from most scholars; but the textual evidence is clear, and Courcelle[6] and Solignac[7] have agreed that the term does refer to Catholic Christianity and that Augustine is reporting the attitude he actually took at the time: his interest in philosophy had been

---

[5] *L'Évolution intellectuelle*, p. 70, n. 7.
[6] *Recherches*, pp. 60–78.
[7] *BA*, XIII, pp. 127–128, n. 1.

aroused, and the insistence of the Catholics that one must first assume the posture of faith did not sit well with his aspirations. Their policy *would* appear superstitious to him, and finding no encouragement among them in his attempt to gain better understanding he would be vulnerable to the rationalistic claims of the Manichaeans.

In the earliest account (an accurate recollection of his own feelings at the time) he says that a childish superstition—not his own but that of others, we may suppose—deterred him from the search for truth (*De beata vita*, I, 4). In a later account (*De util. cred.*, 1, 2), which is probably a fuller report of the circumstances, he puts the statement into the mouths of the Manichaeans, who forswore "awesome authority" (*auctoritas terribilis*) and claimed to lead men to God through reason alone (this is quite in keeping with their attack on the wrathful God of the Old Testament); then he goes on to report their accusation that it is because of superstition that the Catholics are awed by authority, to such an extent that they tell people they must simply have faith, while the Manichaeans do not press anyone toward belief without a full discussion of the matter. Putting the two accounts together we can see the transition that Augustine underwent at the time: the type of Christianity with which he was acquainted in North Africa was one which stressed reverence for divine authority at the expense of rational inquiry and may even have been inclined to counsel blind faith—at least Augustine saw it so[8]; and when the Manichaeans characterized this attitude as *superstitio* and promised something more philosophical, Augustine was ready to agree with them and follow their method for a while. The contrast between authority and reason, which continued to occupy Augustine's attention for many years, could well have been made at that early time either by Augustine or by Manichaeans trained in the classics, for Cicero uses it with some frequency, and in such a way as to reinforce Augustine's drift away from Catholic Christianity: in the dialogue *Lucullus* (II, 18, 60) he suggests that the Academics have veiled their true teachings precisely "in order that those who hear them might be led more by reason than by

---

[8] That he did not exaggerate is proved by a letter from a fellow bishop, Consentius, to Augustine about 412 (*Ep.* 119 in the Augustine corpus), whose point is that "God is not to be sought after by reason but followed through authority."

authority"; in other words, teachings are not to be accepted at face value, for that would be a passive submission to authority, but they are to be taken as an invitation to autonomous rational inquiry.

Augustine considered himself to have been an adherent of the Manichaeans, though only as an *auditor*, for nine years, between the ages of nineteen and twenty-eight, thus from 373 to 382 (*De mor.*, I, 18, 34; II, 19, 68; *Conf.*, IV, 1, 1). During this period Augustine was a disaffected Christian looking for a more adequate form of his childhood religion, and it should be remembered that Manichaeism, though it had originated in Persia, was not just one more exotic oriental sect but had absorbed a considerable amount of Christianity (specifically the Gnosticizing Christianity of Edessa) and was able to present itself as the true faith—with some success, for it seems to have absorbed much of the Marcionite church in the Roman world.[9] The Manichaeism that Augustine knew in Africa was probably quite thoroughly Westernized; it had philosophical pretensions and utilized Stoicism and Pythagoreanism to buttress its claims. It may even be that a leader like Faustus of Milevis took a rather casual attitude toward the writings of the sect and instead stressed, like the Marcionites before him, the epistles of Paul.[10] When Augustine reveals that his reading of Cicero left him with a feeling of disappointment at one point, that it made no mention of the name of Christ (*Conf.*, III, 4, 8), we may suppose that it was precisely because Manichaeism claimed to possess the true and reasonable Christianity that he became interested in it. We should be aware, then, of the positive aspects of Manichaeism, at least as they appeared so to Augustine at the time: its striving for rationality, its criticism of the anthropormorphisms and the wrathful father-figure of the Old Testament, its loftiness of mind, its concern for moral and spiritual

[9] For the Christianity of Edessa, see Walter Bauer, *Rechtgläubigkeit und Ketzerei im ältesten Christentum* (Tübingen, 1934) ch. 1, and Helmut Koester, "ΓΝΩΜΑΙ ΔΙΑΦΟΡΟΙ. The Origin and Nature of Diversification in the History of Early Christianity," *Harvard Theological Review*, LVIII (1965), 279-318.

[10] Paul Monceaux, "Le Manichéen Fauste de Milev. Restitution de ses *Capitula*," *Mémoires de l'Académie des inscriptions et belles lettres*, XLIII, 1. partie (1933), pp. 1-111, esp. 20ff.; W. H. C. Frend, "The Gnostic-Manichaean Tradition in Roman North Africa," *Journal of Ecclesiastical History*, IV (1953), pp. 20-22.

values, its willingness to shun earthly things so that the soul might truly live.[11]

It should not be supposed, therefore, that there was any conflict between Augustine's philosophical passion and his flirtations with the Manichaean sect, for they seemed, at least for the time being, to reinforce each other. His continuing interest in philosophy is manifested by the writing of a treatise *On the Beautiful and the Fitting* (*De pulchro et apto*) about 381. It may be that the treatise, as best it can be reconstructed on the basis of the account given in the *Confessions* (IV, 13, 20—15, 27), contained some themes and images derived from the Manichaean liturgy.[12] But it would be a mistake to suppose that its inspiration was predominantly Manichaean. The treatise, written in Carthage, was dedicated to Hierius, a Greek from Syria who had learned Latin and became a famous rhetor in Rome itself. As Augustine years later inquires into his own motives it is not surprising that he finds he admired Hierius because of his fame and hoped to follow the same course: it is, comments Marrou, the typical gesture of a provincial seeking to curry favor with a great man.[13] The ideas set forth in the treatise are not at all alien to the world of classical culture. The basic theme of the work—that the term "beautiful" is applied to the harmonious appearance of a patterned whole, and the term "suitable" or "fitting" is applied to the harmonious relation of one thing to another or of the parts to the whole—is derived, even down to the illustrations employed, from Cicero's writings, and specifically from those portions which transmit Stoic arguments for the coherence of the cosmos and the purposiveness of all its parts.[14] What is not Ciceronian can in large measure be traced to other classical sources. When Augustine reports having said that virtue is a kind of peace and vice a kind of discord, or that things are loved because of their harmony, it is possible to discern the influence of Varro.[15] And when he speaks of the "monad," the

[11] See Brown, *Augustine of Hippo*, pp. 49–50.

[12] An attempt has been made to demonstrate this in Takeshi Katô, "Melodia interior. Sur le traité *De pulchro et apto*," *REA*, XII (1966), 229–240.

[13] Henri-Irénée Marrou, *Saint Augustin et la fin de la culture antique* (Paris, 1938), p. 163.

[14] Maurice Testard, *Saint Augustin et Cicéron, I. Cicéron dans la formation et l'œuvre de saint Augustin* (Paris, 1958), pp. 55–66.

[15] See section 3 below.

undivided, asexual mind, and the "dyad" which results when it is contaminated by an alien principle, he is only giving a Manichaean twist to a standard Pythagorean theme. Solignac has shown[16] that it is likely that Augustine did make use of a Pythagorean work at the time when he was teaching rhetoric in Carthage, and thus at the time when he wrote *De pulchro et apto*, for the commentary of his own pupil Favonius on the *Dream of Scipio* (the classic statement of cosmology and eschatology for the Roman world which appears at the end of Cicero's *Republic*) manifests similar themes, and the source is the *Introductio arithmetica* of Nicomachus of Gerasa, translated into Latin by Apuleius.

Augustine says that he never really assented to Manichaean doctrine, but only hoped that under the veil of their public teachings there were more profound truths to be uncovered (*De beata vita*, I, 5; *De util. cred.*, 8, 20). And if Augustine's philosophical knowledge for a time seemed to converge with Manichaean doctrine, finally it led him into serious doubts about it, initially, according to his own report, because of scientific difficulties, chiefly in astronomy (*Conf.*, V, 3, 6—5, 9). Augustine never became familiar with the mathematical aspects of astronomy, but he learned enough about the heavenly bodies to see that the science of his day conflicted with the Manichaean picture of the cosmos.

His career as a rhetorician led him first to Rome and then to Milan, and it was at Milan that he was gradually nudged toward Christianity by a succession of events. The sequence can be pieced together from the *Confessions*, books V–IX, and from earlier accounts, written soon after his conversion (*De beata vita*, I, 3–4; *C. Acad.*, II, 2, 4–5) or a few years later (*De util. cred.*, 8, 20–21).

Out of professional interest Augustine went to hear Ambrose's sermons, and Ambrose—not yet in person, but only from afar—began to resolve the difficulties he had had with the Old Testament. Such difficulties were not unusual in the ancient world. People acquainted with philosophical notions of God were uncomfortable with the anthropomorphisms of the Old Testament (not only with its descriptions of God under human form, but its suggestions that God has human emotions, or changes his mind).

---

[16] Aimé de Solignac, "Doxographies et manuels dans la formation philosophique de saint Augustin," *RA*, I (Paris, 1958), pp. 129ff.; cf. his later discussion in *Note complémentaire* 16, *BA*, XIII, pp. 670–673.

Augustine had been inclined to follow the Manichaeans and simply *reject* the Old Testament, but now he learned from Ambrose that its more shocking features could be allegorized and made symbols of a deeper meaning. Augustine says he often heard on Ambrose's lips the verse, "The letter kills but the spirit gives life" (*Conf.*, VI, 4, 6), and since this verse is to be found, among the extant sermons of Ambrose, only in the expositions of Luke (the third, the sixth, and the ninth), it may be these that Augustine heard.[17] As a result he began to recover his basic sense of identity as a Catholic Christian; he thought of the Christian faith as unbeaten, he says, though not yet victorious, and he resolved to remain a catechumen of the Church in which he had been brought up while awaiting further light (*Conf.*, V, 14, 25; *De util. cred.*, 8, 21).

But another more surprising result of Ambrose's influence was, as Testard stresses,[18] to lead Augustine toward a more intense Ciceronianism. For the first time he seriously entertained the Academic view that in all the big questions a firm grasp on the truth is impossible, so that one can only withhold assent and give oneself over to an unceasing inquiry in philosophical questions (in practical matters, where one must do *something*, one can act on the basis of probability). Augustine says that when Monica arrived in Milan she found him holding the Academic philosophy, but was consoled by the fact that he had been led into it through the influence of Ambrose (*Conf.*, VI, 1, 1; *De util. cred.*, 8, 20). What it involved, as his own account suggests, was a clearing out of his earlier convictions and a certain disorientation as to where he might turn next; he was not yet able to rise above his dependence upon sense and imagination in thinking about philosophical problems, but he knew that they are not adequate vehicles of philosophical knowledge.

Now Ambrose came to influence him in another way. In reflecting on Ambrose's sermons, he says, he came to understand the place of authority and belief (*Conf.*, VI, 5, 7-8). This meditation on authority was Augustine's own; he could not have derived from Ambrose himself any clear notion of it.[19] The distinction between

[17] Solignac, *BA*, XIII, 141-142, n. 1.
[18] Testard, *Saint Augustin et Cicéron*, I, 83, n. 4.
[19] Du Roy, *L'Intelligence de la foi en la Trinité*, p. 113, n. 5.

authority and reason came from Cicero, and it had been a problem to Augustine for a long time; he uses those terms in recounting his thoughts at the age of nineteen, when it seemed to him, following Cicero, that authority and reason are opposed and his devotion to philosophy led him to abandon Catholic Christianity in favor of the seemingly more rational religion of the Manichaeans. Now he came to recognize that there may be a place for authority, understood as "authentic" and "authoritative" testimony on the part of others, and for belief in that testimony when one does not have direct experience or rational proof of a matter. During this period in 385 Augustine found that his doubts and difficulties concerning Christianity were gradually subsiding, and his thoughts at the time (into which we cannot look any further) are discussed at length in book VI of the *Confessions*.

About this time Augustine was fired with the project of organizing a community of gentlemen engaged in the philosophic quest. The inspiration came chiefly from Cicero, who often praised the *otium philosophandi*, but there were a few Pythagorean features in the scheme, such as the holding of all goods in common.[20] Augustine seems to have had some success, gathering a group of interested friends and even inspiring a wealthy man from Thagaste, Romanianus, to take a leading role. But the project remained only a dream; Augustine was not able to abandon his hopes for a successful career and marriage into respectable society, and the friends found that their wives would not acquiesce in the plan (*Conf.*, VI, 14, 24; *De beata vita*, I, 3; *C. Acad.*, II, 2, 5).

But Augustine's contacts with high society, as it turned out, had even more fruitful consequences. In 385 he had great success in declaiming panegyrics in honor of Bauto (*C. litt. Petil.*, III, 25, 30) and the emperor Valentinian II (*Conf.*, VI, 6, 9).[21] As he rose in the esteem of influential people he hoped for some kind of civil post. Instead he was brought under new philosophical influences which moved him closer to Christianity.

It was only after he had been in Milan for some time, and probably in the spring of 386, that Augustine became acquainted with a group of Platonists, wealthy laymen in high positions, some of them Christian and some not—Zenobius, Hermogenianus,

[20] Solignac, *BA*, XIII, pp. 566–567, n. 1.
[21] Courcelle, *Recherches*, pp. 78–83.

Celsinus perhaps, and especially Flavius Manlius Theodorus, a
public official and an eloquent orator who had also gained some
stature as a writer of philosophical treatises in Latin.[22] Courcelle
points out that the atmosphere in Milan was, for political reasons,
one of animosity toward the court in Constantinople and toward
everything Greek; thus there was a conscious attempt at what
might already be called a *translatio studii* from Greece to the West,
from the Greek to the Latin language, and even from Greek to
Latin thought-patterns (for Augustine seems to think that there is
a difference: in the third book of *Contra Academicos* he repeatedly
chides the Greeks for their levity and sophistry). As best the
record can be pieced together, Augustine had several conversations with Manlius Theodorus and began to learn how to think
of God and the soul as incorporeal (*De beata vita*, I, 3); on the
basis of this man's interest in neo-Platonism ("I gathered that you
were most interested in it," he says in *De beata vita*, I, 4) he did
some reading in the works the Platonists—and this means specifically Plotinus, whose name is mentioned twice in the early writings
(*De beata vita*, I, 4; *C. Acad.*, III, 18, 41), though Augustine
probably read only a few of the 54 treatises in the *Enneads*, and it
is unlikely that all of them were translated by Marius Victorinus.
The circumstances of Augustine's securing these writings are a
matter of some curiosity to the scholars, for in the *Confessions*
(VIII, 9, 13) he says that they came to him, by divine guidance,
through a certain man who was puffed up with a monstrous pride.
Courcelle has suggested Manlius Theodorus[23]; O'Meara has
suggested Porphyry, the editor of the *Enneads* and an opponent of
Christianity[24]; but the most promising suggestion comes from
Solignac, who argues that it must be someone in the immediate
circle of Platonists in Milan and that the use of "a certain man"
(*quidam*) indicates that it was one of the non-Christians, perhaps
Celsinus, who, according to *C. Acad.*, II, 2, 5, had called these
books *pleni*—copious, pregnant, suggestive.[25]

What Augustine encountered was not always a Platonism
recommended and interpreted by Christian Platonists. There were

[22] See Pierre Courcelle, *Les lettres grecques en Occident. De Macrobe à Cassiodore*
(Paris, 1943), pp. 119–129; Solignac, *BA*, XIV, pp. 529–536.
[23] Courcelle, *Les lettres grecques*, pp. 119–129.
[24] O'Meara, *The Young Augustine*, p. 153.
[25] *BA*, XIII, p. 103. Cf. his note on "*cuiusdam Ciceronis*," *ibid.*, p. 667.

non-Christians among his acquaintances in Milan. Nevertheless he saw from the first that Plotinus could be made to agree with the *mysteria* of the Christian faith—and this means specifically its doctrine of the Trinity (*De beata vita*, I, 4; *Conf.*, VII, 9, 15). It is probably accurate to say, with Gilson and Boyer and most other recent scholars, that Augustine read the *Enneads* in a Christian sense; and Père Hadot has added that if he read the *Enneads* in a Christian sense it was because Marius Victorinus before him had read the prologue of the Fourth Gospel in a neo-Platonist sense.[26] His interest in Platonism, and his confidence that it was consistent with Christianity, were probably reinforced by the sermons of Ambrose which he heard at the same time, if Courcelle is correct: the sermons on Jacob, on the six days of creation, on Isaac, and on the value of death, all of which contain Plotinian motifs.[27] In the account given soon after his conversion he speaks of the passion which the Platonist writings aroused in him, and he says that his childhood religion was again attracting his interest, though still without his knowledge (*C. Acad.*, II, 2, 5).

And yet Augustine in looking back at this intellectual conversion finds much for which to reproach himself. "I was babbling as though I thought myself an expert," he says (*Conf.*, VII, 20, 26), and he thinks that he fell in with those proud men of whom the apostle speaks, who know God but do not honor him as God (*Conf.*, VIII, 1, 2). Courcelle has suggested that he was trying to achieve an ecstatic vision of God, and some passages in the *Confessions* (VII, 10, 16; 17, 23; 20, 26) seem to suggest that he caught a glimpse of God, but only momentarily, and then fell back. But this interpretation is belied by statements in Augustine's writings soon afterward, for he makes no claim to have attained to a direct vision of God and in fact speaks of God as hidden, touched only rarely by the human mind or not at all (*C. Acad.*, I, 8, 22). The experiences which Augustine in the *Confessions* reports himself to have had on reading Plotinus are not thereby devaluated, but we are enabled to understand them correctly as his arriving at the conviction that the Light is there and that it is attainable by the human mind, but his discovery at the same time that when the eyes of the mind are weak or are suddenly opened

[26] Quoted in du Roy, p. 61, n. 2.
[27] *Recherches*, pp. 98–103, 122–124.

we are hesitant (*trepidamus*) to look at the Light (cf. *De beata vita*, IV, 35). Even in the three passages in the *Confessions*, he repeats that he knew there was something to be seen, but that he was not yet the one to see it.

Though Père Henry is right in pointing to Augustine's mystical aspirations,[28] we should not, I think, speak of "attempts at ecstasy" with Courcelle[29] and the many others who have followed his interpretation. What Augustine experienced, if the record can be trusted, was a "trepidation at ecstasy." He was aware of his own limitations, and, far from frustrating him in his attempt to achieve ecstatic union with God, they held him back from even making the attempt. The impression one gains from the writings of the time is that he felt so habituated to the sensory realm that he was overcome with vertigo at the prospect of returning to the intelligible world which is the mind's proper habitat, and therefore preferred to remain in his accustomed haunts.[30] It is not that he tried and failed, then, but that he thought he could gradually make his way toward the goal in the fashion taught in the Platonist writings, not to the exclusion of Christianity (for he did find the Trinity in them, and even the need of purification), but with the assumption that there was a comfortable harmony between Platonism and Christianity (*Conf.*, VII, 20, 26).

Then he eagerly seized (*arripui*, he says in both accounts) the writings of the apostle Paul (*C. Acad.*, II, 2, 5; *Conf.*, VII, 21, 27). It was not, I think, because of an attempt at mysticism and the experience of failure. In the account given soon after the event he says merely that his childhood religion, about which he had thought only incidentally (*tantum...quasi de itinere*) for many years, now attracted him, though without his knowledge, and he began eagerly reading Paul (*C. Acad.*, II, 2, 5).[31] The account in the

---

[28] Paul Henry, *Plotin et l'Occident* (Louvain, 1934), pp. 111–119.
[29] *Recherches*, pp. 157–167.
[30] See the discussions in chapter 1 below.
[31] This phrase "*quasi de itinere*" has caused difficulty to the scholars, but I follow the translation of Jolivet (*BA*, IV, p. 69), which seems most natural. Courcelle (*Recherches*, pp. 168–169) suggests that it means "while on the way"; Testard (*Saint Augustin et Cicéron*, I, p. 167, n. 2) suggests that it means "while away from the road"; O'Meara (*The Young Augustine*, p. 157), that he looked back as from the end of a long journey; and Körner (*Das Sein und der Mensch* [Freiburg-Munich, 1959]), pp. 61–68, 112–134, makes of it a Platonic recollection of the intelligible realm.

Confessions (VII, 20, 26—21, 27) is not a record of his experiences at the time but an interpretation of them with the wisdom of hindsight, for the whole account is permeated with Pauline motifs of the sort that Augustine did not grasp even at the time of his conversion but came to understand only later, in the years just prior to the writing of the *Confessions*—that the only function of exhortation is to show man his need of divine assistance, and that whatever man achieves is the gift of God.[32] According to the earlier narrative what he found in Paul was something else: the record of heroic lives which demonstrated the compatibility of Christianity with the philosophical ideal. "These men could not have lived in this way or have done such things, I thought, if their writings and their thoughts had been contrary to so great a good" (*C. Acad.*, II, 2, 5). The lives of the Platonists began to pale in comparison.

About this time Augustine began going to see Simplicianus, who drove the point home. Simplicianus had all the qualifications needed to commend him to Augustine, for he was a Platonist and many years earlier he had been acquainted with Marius Victorinus, the translator of Plotinus, who, in fact, became a Christian largely at Simplicianus' urging. In his conversations with Augustine Simplicianus probably supplied a pattern by which to bring Platonism and Christianity into meaningful relationship.[33] Solignac points out that Ambrose (*Ep.* 65) praised the inquiring spirit of Simplicianus, a man who kept on asking questions though he had gone through the whole world seeking an understanding of God, who spent much time in reading, who liked to point out the shortcomings of the philosophers; and that Gennadius (*De script. eccl.*, 36) said that in asking questions as though he were seeking to learn, he was able to teach the one who appeared to be teaching.[34] He was a Socratic figure, then, who probably fitted his questioning to Augustine's needs. He showed him the kinship between Platonism and Christianity, remarking, for example, that

[32] See chapter 3, sections 3 and 5, below.

[33] This point is given special attention in Goulven Madec, "Connaissance de Dieu et action des grâces. Essai sur les citations de l'Épître aux Romains, I, 18–25 dans l'œuvre de saint Augustin," *RA*, II (Paris, 1963), pp. 273–309, though I cannot agree that the first chapter of Romans, or even the anti-Christian bias of Porphyry, played any role in those conversations.

[34] *BA*, XIV, p. 531.

a Platonist had once told him that the opening words of the Fourth Gospel should be inscribed in gold in all the churches (*De civ. Dei*, X, 29). But he also pointed up the shortcomings of the Platonists. He told Augustine that Victorinus, in his function as a rhetor, took part in Roman civic religion with its worship of "monstrous deities of every sort, and Anubis who barked like a dog, all the gods who had once borne arms against Neptune and Venus, and against Minerva" (*Aeneid*, VIII, 698ff.), and yet was ashamed of making public profession of Christianity. If we wish to know the impact Simplicianus had upon Augustine at the time, something of a clue is perhaps to be found in the opening chapters of his work *On True Religion*, where the Platonists come under reproach for not having the courage of their own convictions: they knew that there is one God, but they continued to take part in superstitious rituals out of fear of popular opinion (cf. also *De civ. Dei*, IV, 29; X, 1). By contrast the Christians, whom the Platonists scorn for their lack of learning, have actually lived out the implications of monotheism and will reap its benefits. The image employed in the *Confessions* (VII, 20, 26—21, 27) and in other passages (e.g., *De Trin.*, IV, 18, 24), that the Platonists can see the goal in the distance but that only the Christians are traveling along the way that leads toward it, probably represents an accurate recollection of Augustine's thoughts at the time of his conversion even though it is overlaid with later preoccupations, for during the years just before the writing of the *Confessions* he had been studying Paul again, and his use of Romans 1 to criticize the Platonists for their proud refusal of divine assistance is a theological interpretation of his earlier reflections.[35] The opposition which he felt at the time was that between the moral courage of the Christians and the empty professions of the Platonists.

The recognition of this tension between Platonism and Christianity did not by itself resolve his own problem. His hesitations continued, for merely to know that the eternal Light must be sought, and to know that Christian dedication was the way by which to become fit for the vision of that Light, did not lead immediately to willing it. He says, soon after the event, that he was ready to weigh anchor and set forth but was swayed by the

---

[35] See chapter 4, section 4, below.

existimatio of certain men (*De beata vita*, I, 4). This term can be read positively, as the honor and esteem in which he was held, so that he was tempted to remain in a profession in which his talents could be put to successful use, or in a more neutral sense as group opinion, with its pressures toward conformity. But it is just possible that it is to be read negatively, as the *judgment* of certain men, dissuading him from embarking on a new course by suggesting that he might not be able to see it through; in a later passage which has a certain autobiographical intensity about it he interprets the *lingua subdola*, the beguiling tongue of Psalm 119 (120), 4, as the voice of those who implant despair at ever being able to carry through a heroic commitment (*Enarr. in Ps.* 119, 5; 123, 6), and the same passage is applied directly to his own situation in the *Confessions* (IX, 2, 3), though in connection with the days following his conversion, not those preceding it.[36] Whatever the role of others, it is clear that Augustine had difficulty bringing himself to an unambiguous commitment to a new way of life, and this is the problem that occupies him throughout book VIII of the *Confessions*.

What finally tipped the balance? In the early writings Augustine says only that he had developed a pain in his chest, and though he had already decided to enter upon a life in search of wisdom it was this that forced him to give up his activities as a teacher of rhetoric more quickly (*De ord.*, I, 2, 5; *De beata vita*, I, 4; cf. *Conf.*, IX, 2, 3). In the *Confessions* he recounts a series of events to which no allusion is made in the earlier writings. Ponticianus, a high official in the court, happened to be visiting and told him first of Anthony, the father of monasticism, and then of the two young men who had been converted to the monastic life after chancing upon the narrative of his life while they were at Trêves. This account of heroic Christianity seems to be what brought Augustine to the crisis point. After an intense inward struggle he threw himself down under the fig tree and gave way to a flood of tears; he heard a voice saying, "Take up and read," picked up the codex of Paul's letters, read the passage in Romans 13, 13–14, and thereupon experienced a new peace and resoluteness.

[36] The use of this text is noted by Pierre Courcelle, "Source chrétienne et allusions païennes de l'épisode du 'Tolle, lege,'" *Revue d'histoire et de philosophie religieuse*, XXXII (1952), p. 198, n. 104.

Does Augustine contradict himself? Is the account in the *Confessions* largely a fabrication, as some have suggested? It seems to me that a reason can be given for the absence of this episode in Augustine's earlier writings. He was taking precautions lest he dramatize himself too much (*Conf.*, IX, 2, 3), and in any case his primary concern was with the outcome, his devotion to the philosophic life, not with the subjective factors leading to it. A reason can also be given for its presence later in the *Confessions*. In the intervening years Augustine had been reflecting upon the nature of conversion in the light of Paul's epistles, and in his response to one of the questions sent him by Simplicianus (*Ad Simpl.*, I, q. 2), written only a short time before the *Confessions*, he came to a definitive answer: though conversion is indeed an act of the human will, *whether* and *when* a man turns to God is not entirely at his own disposal; it takes place only when he is called in a way suited to his condition (*congruiter vocatur*), and this is a matter of divine prearrangement.[37] Augustine was therefore led to reconsider his own life in the light of his current theological convictions, and what had earlier seemed to Augustine the "philosopher" a minor episode, perhaps too intimate to report, now took on decisive importance.

We must agree, I think, with Pierre Courcelle[38] when he says that the passage has some highly stylized elements. In the chapter preceding the conversion Augustine describes his situation in terms of the Stoic theme of Hercules at the crossroads: he hesitates, wavering between the recollection of his former loves and the call of Continence, who beckons to him and holds up before him the many examples of her sons and daughters. But this feature of the narrative, far from casting doubt on its accuracy, shows that it is very much in keeping with everything else that can be known about Augustine's struggle at the time. It was, quite simply, a matter of deciding between two courses of life; it was even so mundane as to be a choice between two occupations: between a career as a successful rhetor and the life of philosophical contemplation with its usual accompaniment of sexual denial.

It is important to understand precisely what choice Augustine faced in his own mind. He could have become a nominal Christian

[37] See chapter 3, section 5, below.
[38] *Recherches*, pp. 188–202.

easily enough; but this was not his problem, partly because the Church still enforced high standards of behavior in those days and partly because Augustine himself was serious enough in his quest to be satisfied with nothing short of total conviction and dedication. And yet it is not really correct to say that the project which he envisaged for himself, and before which he vacillated, and which he finally chose, was to become a *monk*, for he did *not* then take up the monastic life in any proper sense (even according to the criteria of those beginning days of monasticism, before it became standardized). He knew of monasticism—from Ponticianus' narrative, and from his own acquaintance with communities in Milan and Rome—but he declined to follow it for a full five years. What he had in mind was rather the wholehearted pursuit of wisdom. It involved, to be sure, full-time dedication and celibacy, and in both respects it was something more than the life of an ordinary layman. Like the monks Augustine probably thought of his vocation as neither clerical nor lay but as belonging to a third kind, or perhaps even to a fourth (since he seems not to have classified himself among the monks), for it had tasks peculiar to itself; unlike the clerical life it involved no responsibilities for a parish, and unlike the life of the laity it involved a certain independence of the supervision of the clergy, befitting an intellectual and moral elite. It was even more on the fringes of the Church than the monasticism of that day, for it was dominated by this consciousness of belonging to a select few, and its inspiration came directly from the philosophical tradition of the Stoics, Cicero, the Pythagoreans, and the neo-Platonists, not through ecclesiastical channels. To that extent Alfaric was correct when he suggested that Augustine was converted more to neo-Platonism than to standard Christianity.[39] But to Augustine it now appeared that the life of philosophy could be pursued only along the path marked out by the gospel. He saw no incompatibility between the two, and he only claimed exemption from some of the ordinary duties, arising from the ordinary weaknesses and distractions, of most Christians.

Augustine knew where he wanted to go, but he could not bring himself to get under way. His difficulty, as he analyzes it in a famous passage in the *Confessions* (VIII, 9, 21), was that his will

[39] *L'Évolution intellectuelle*, p. 399.

was divided: he willed contrary things simultaneously, and could not will one of them wholeheartedly. William James has suggested that Augustine's experience is typical of a certain kind of religious experience, the sense of having a divided self until the conflict is resolved by a new and lasting integration.[40] But that, taken by itself, seems to make the problem and its resolution too much a function of psychological mechanisms. To Augustine the struggle was a moral or existential one, and fully conscious. The resolution is more complex than James ever suggests, and Augustine thinks himself able to trace it out in some detail. The malaise does not, by itself, lead toward its own solution; it only drives him deeper into despair. Even when the dam breaks and he gives way to a flood of tears, this yielding in the depths of the heart is not the final resolution; it only leads him to acknowledge his own misery and inability and to throw himself upon God. As though in answer, he hears the call, "*Tolle, lege.*" Augustine professes to be uncertain of its source: it may have been children playing, and yet he knows of no such game. There seems to be a studied ambiguity in his narration of it, for the real point is that it is a command that spoke to him in his own situation, and perhaps, as Courcelle suggests, we are to understand the voices as those of the sons and daughters of Continence.[41] But the voices do not bring a resolution, either; they are not the occasion for Augustine's conversion. They tell him to open the Scriptures and take their counsel to heart, and it may be that in the "*Tolle, lege*" Augustine is utilizing a standard Greek formula for appealing to the testimony of a written text; in any case the import is something like this: "Do you still claim to be uncertain? The solution to your problem is right before your eyes. Pick it up and read." So he takes up the codex of Paul's letters, which he has been reading, and opening it seemingly at random he hears the words of Romans 13, 13–14 as being addressed directly to himself.

It is the words of Scripture that constitute the real divine call and which occasion his conversion. We know that this was Augustine's theory at the time he wrote the *Confessions,* and at the end of book VIII he finds it verified in actual instances. He

---

[40] *The Varieties of Religious Experience,* Lecture VIII.
[41] *Recherches,* 196. Courcelle has defended and modified and elaborated his theory in many subsequent articles.

2*

says first of Anthony that he was converted when he read a passage from the gospels and felt that it was addressed directly to him (*Conf.*, VIII, 12, 29); then that his friend Alypius was given firm resolve and bound to a worthy purpose suited to his own character ("*placitoque ac proposito bono et congruentissimo suis moribus ...coniunctus*") by reading another passage, this time from the letter to the Romans; and then that he himself was turned toward God (by still another passage, as we have seen) in such a way that he would no longer vacillate, still entertaining hopes for marriage and wordly honor (*Conf.*, VIII, 12, 30). The words of Scripture, then, are the means by which God turns men toward himself, in each case by issuing an exhortation or presenting a possibility that is "congruous" with a man's condition.

Though some parts of the narrative may be stylized, its representation of the struggle and its resolution is in keeping with what can be known of Augustine's thoughts at the time, and the theory of conversion that is worked out here, though its emphases reflect Augustine's later assumptions, is well suited to the analysis of the moral conflict he underwent. The tensions under which man labors are internal to the life of the will. It is for rhetorical effect that Augustine asks,

Where, during all those years, was my free will? From what deep and hidden place was it called forth in a moment so that I might bend my neck under thy yoke, which is easy, and take up thy burden, which is light, o Christ, my Help and my Redeemer? (*Conf.*, IX, 1, 1).

His will was there, but it was immobilized by internal conflict. Man cannot bring himself to make a wholehearted commitment to the good because he is attached to many things, past and present, by the bonds of affection and is deeply involved with them because of his concerns and anxieties. The balance is tipped by a factor coming from beyond man. It is not something hidden and mysterious which overpowers the will or gives it some special impulse. The crucial factor is fully apparent, for it is simply the "call" which comes to man. It is something creaturely, and it enters man's inner life through the channel of his understanding; then, by appealing irresistibly to his affections, it liberates them to act wholeheartedly in a single direction.

The "conversion" took place in August, 386. Augustine decided to finish out the term in order not to make a spectacle of himself and then retire quietly from the "windy profession" (*C. Acad.*, I, 1, 3). His friend Nebridius took over his pupils, and he retired with his mother and brother, some close friends, and a few favored pupils to a villa owned by Verecundus at Cassiciacum, in the mountains above Milan. It is there that his career as a dedicated seeker after wisdom, a Christian thinker, and a serious writer begins. But first something must be said about the intellectual equipment he took with him.

3. PHILOSOPHICAL INFLUENCES ON AUGUSTINE'S EARLY THOUGHT

It is difficult to ascertain the extent of Augustine's acquaintance with ancient philosophy, for he himself supplies few clues. Many of the works which he might have read have now perished and are no longer available for comparison, and even when works are extant it is difficult to trace his dependence upon them. The problem of influences upon his thought is thus a matter for careful and detailed study, and here we can look only at the general course of the investigation.

1. The most immediate influence in the months preceding and following his conversion is Plotinus, who is certainly the chief author, perhaps the sole author, of the *libri platonici* Augustine read in Milan. The greatest advance in the study of Plotinus' influence was made by Paul Henry in his *Plotin et l'Occident*, published in 1934. Père Henry abandoned the usual method of pointing out similarities with Plotinus' entire system with the aid of texts drawn indiscriminately from the *Enneads*, and instead tried to demonstrate Augustine's *literary dependence* upon *particular* passages in the *Enneads*. The task was difficult because Victorinus' translation is no longer extant and because Augustine never merely copied a passage but reworked its themes, often giving them a different import. Henry used the device of printing parallel columns and giving emphasis to those words or phrases in Augustine which seemed to reflect, so far as it could be puzzled out, the probable Latin translation of Plotinus' language. Using this method Henry felt that he could demonstrate a literary dependence upon two treatises in the *Enneads*: I, 6 ("On Beauty") and

V, 1 ("On the Three Divine Hypostases"), and a probable dependence upon two more: III, 2 ("On Providence") and IV, 3 ("On the Soul").[42] Since then the method has been used by others and the catalogue of treatises from the *Enneads* has been extended. Robert J. O'Connell has shown convincingly, I think, that Augustine must have read the treatises VI, 4 and 5,[43] and Olivier du Roy has demonstrated an influence of V, 5 on Augustine's earliest conception of the Trinity.[44] But it is necessary to be cautious in this matter and affirm a direct influence only in the case of those treatises which are used extensively and which alone could explain the occurrence of certain ideas or terms in Augustine's writings. Following these criteria, it seems to me that the research thus far demonstrates the use of the following treatises:[45]

I, 6 ("On Beauty")
III, 2-3 ("On Providence")
IV, 3-4 ("On the Soul")
V, 1 ("On the Three Divine Hypostases")
V, 5 ("That Intelligibles Are Not Outside Intelligence")
VI, 4-5 ("How That Which Is One and the Same Can Be Everywhere")

and indicates the possible or probable use of the following:

I, 2 ("On the Virtues")
I, 4 ("On Happiness")
I, 8 ("On the Origin of Evil")
III, 7 ("On Eternity and Time")
IV, 7 ("On the Immortality of the Soul")
IV, 8 ("On the Descent of the Soul into the Body")
V, 3 ("On the Three Hypostases Possessing Knowledge")

[42] *Plotin et l'Occident*, p. 144.
[43] Robert J. O'Connell, "*Ennead* VI, 4 and 5 in the Works of Saint Augustine," *REA*, IX (1963), 1–39.
[44] *L'Intelligence de la foi en la Trinité*, pp. 157–158.
[45] For further references to the mass of work that has been done, see Robert J. O'Connell, "The Plotinian Fall of the Soul in St. Augustine," *Traditio*, XIX (1963), pp. 8–9, 30, etc.; Solignac, *BA*, XIII, pp. 110–111; and du Roy, *L'Intelligence de la foi en la Trinité*, p. 70, n. 1.

V, 8 ("On Intelligible Beauty")
VI, 6 ("On Numbers")
VI, 9 ("On the Good and the One")

As the number of treatises mounts, the question must arise whether they were translated intact or were excerpted by Marius Victorinus, somewhat in the fashion of Porphyry's *Sentences*, which is an adaptation of several treatises from the *Enneads*. But the answer must await a far more exact pinpointing of the passages that were used.

2. A deeper and more mellowed influence upon Augustine's early thought comes from Cicero.[46] Much of what Augustine knew of ethics came from *De legibus* and *De finibus*, much of what he knew about ancient philosophy from *De natura deorum* and the Tusculan disputations, much of what he knew about the problem of knowledge from the *Academics* and *Lucullus*. Cicero tended toward the scepticism of the New Academy, but it was tempered by the influence of two of his teachers, the greatest philosophical minds of the first century B.C.: Posidonius, who transformed Stoicism in accordance with his own vast knowledge of science and history, and Antiochus, who in a somewhat similar way transformed Platonism in the light of Stoic and Aristotelian contributions to the analysis of philosophical problems. From them Cicero derived the cosmology and the eschatology presented in the Dream of Scipio at the end of his *Republic*, which had an enormous influence upon Latin thinkers and helped to prepare the way for a more thoroughgoing Pythagoreanism and Platonism.[47]

3. Varro, a contemporary of Cicero, supplied, by Augustine's own admission, much of the material found in the opening books of *The City of God*, but his nine books on the disciplines exerted their influence at an earlier time as well. The poem of Licentius to Augustine, appended to *Ep.* 26 in the manuscripts and the editions, indicates that Augustine put these books into the hands of

---

[46] The definitive study is Maurice Testard's *Saint Augustin et Cicéron* (Paris, 1958), containing in the first volume a study of Cicero's influence and in the second a catalogue of all of Augustine's quotations from or allusions to Cicero.

[47] Cf. Michel Ruch, "Cicéron et l'Orphisme," *REA*, VI (1960), pp. 1–10.

his pupils. Varro's program was to lead the soul by degrees from the visible world toward the invisible by following the curriculum of the arts,[48] and it was from him that Augustine gained both his conception of their value and most of what he knew about them. During a period of several years following his conversion Augustine tried his hand at writing beginning treatises in several of the disciplines, and those that survive (the analysis of rhythm in *De musica*, I–V, which was to have been followed by an analysis of harmony, and the elements of logic in *De dialectica*) indicate that Augustine had at his disposal a reliable summation of some quite sophisticated developments in Hellenistic culture among the Stoics and others.[49]

As to the bias of Varro's own philosophy the consensus is that he followed his teacher Antiochus of Ascalon, often scorned in modern histories as an "eclectic" but probably an original thinker, in many ways as important as Posidonius in the advancement of philosophy.[50] Antiochus was first a Stoic, it seems; then he studied under the Academic Philo of Larissa, but broke with the scepticism of the "New Academy" and tried to restore the teachings of the "Old Academy," that is, the older tradition of Platonism, now mixed with, or stimulated by, Peripatetic and Stoic elements. It seems to have been he, rather than Posidonius, who transformed the Platonic ideas along Stoic lines and made them practical ideas in the mind of the divine artist.[51] Thus the source of Augustine's own understanding of the doctrine of ideas (as contained in *De div. quaest.*, q. 46, *De civ. Dei*, VII, 28 and XIX, 3, and elsewhere) is Varro, and ultimately Antiochus.[52]

This line of dependence has been further traced in a succession

[48] What Claudianus Mamertus, *De statu animae*, II, 8, says about Varro— "*per corporalia cupiens ad incorporalia quibusdam quasi passibus certis vel pervenire vel ducere*"—fits Augustine's own conception of the liberal arts (Harald Fuchs, *Augustin und der antike Friedensgedanke. Untersuchungen zum neunzehnten Buch der Civitas Dei* [Neue philosophische Untersuchungen, III; Berlin, 1926], Beilage 1, p. 158, n. 1).

[49] B. Darrell Jackson, "The Theory of Signs in St. Augustine's *De doctrina Christiana*," *REA*, XV (1969), 33-49.

[50] See especially Georg Luck, *Der Akademiker Antiochos* (Bern, 1953).

[51] Luck, *Der Akademiker Antiochos*, p. 30.

[52] Willy Theiler, *Die Vorbereitung des Neuplatonismus* (Problemata, I; Berlin, 1930), p. 19; Aimé de Solignac, "Analyse et sources de la question 'De ideis,'" *AM*, I, p. 315.

of German studies.[53] One of the most characteristic themes in Augustine's thought, his stress upon the right ordering of all things, including man's loves, according to the levels of being which establish a hierarchy of values, is from this source.[54] Such a view of things is capable at once of taking into account their dynamic tendencies and of setting them in an objective scheme. From it come such features in Augustine's thought as the contrast between the rightly ordered and the perverse and his understanding of peace and happiness as the proper accommodation or adjustment (*obtemperatio* or *convenientia*, probably the translation of οἰκείωσις) of one being to another or of all the parts to the whole, a vision summed up in a classic passage in *The City of God*, XIX, 13:

The peace of the body is the orderly balance of its parts; the peace of the animal soul is the orderly satisfaction of its appetites; the peace of the rational soul is the orderly agreement of thought and action; the peace of body and soul together is the orderly life and health of the whole animate being; the peace of man with God is an orderly obedience in faith to the eternal law; the peace of men living together in a house or a state is an orderly agreement of those who command and those who obey; the peace of the heavenly city is a most orderly and unanimous sharing in the enjoyment of God and of each other in God. The peace of all things, then, is the tranquility of order, by which each thing is set in its proper place.

4. An important study of Solignac has shown that Augustine's knowledge of the history of philosophy extended well beyond what he could have learned from Cicero and Varro. Scattered throughout Augustine's writings are materials derived ultimately from Theophrastus' *Opiniones physicae* and Sotion's *Successiones*. Solignac suggests that these early doxographies were drawn upon in a work which Augustine himself mentions in the prologue to his *De haeresibus* (written in 428), the six volumes of *Opiniones*

---

[53] Fuchs, *Augustin und der antike Friedensgedanke*; Rudolf Lorenz, "Die Herkunft des augustinischen *frui Deo*," *Zeitschrift für Kirchengeschichte*, LXIV (1952-53), pp. 34–60; Max Zepf, "Augustinus und das philosophische Selbstbewusstsein der Antike," *Zeitschrift für Religions- und Geistesgeschichte*, XI (1959), pp. 105–132.

[54] Fuchs, pp. 31–32; Lorenz, p. 37; Zepf, pp. 114–122.

omnium philosophorum by Celsus, probably identical with the Cornelius Celsus mentioned in the *Soliloquies* (I, 12, 21).[55]

Pierre Courcelle has developed a more complex theory. Cornelius Celsus, he argues, is mentioned in the latter passage not as a doxographer but as a philosopher developing his own opinions. He suggests that a manuscript error has been made in *De haeresibus* and that Celsinus of Castabala, a Greek doxographer mentioned in Suidas, must be the author; and in order to explain its translation into Latin Courcelle suggests that the doxography of Manlius Theodorus, mentioned in Claudian's encomium of him, may be merely a translation of this work.[56] While Solignac does not entirely rule out this theory he thinks it more likely that the Celsinus mentioned in *C. Acad.*, II, 2, 5 is a member of the neo-Platonist circle in Milan, and that Theodorus' work on the history of philosophy, far from being a doxography, was a popularization, and probably an anecdotal one at that.[57]

Whether we accept the simpler or the more complex explanation, it seems undeniable that Augustine was in a position to acquire a knowledge of the history of philosophy that was of the first quality. Though modern researchers have tended to be condescending toward Augustine's ventures into the history of Greek thought in *The City of God* and elsewhere, such as his sketch of the Ionian and Italic traditions (*De civ. Dei*, VIII, 2), it now appears that his statements may be more reliable than many of those preserved in other writings surviving from antiquity. He is often in direct encounter with thinkers of the distant past. When he speaks of Stoicism, for example, it is usually the classical variety of Zeno and Chrysippus, quite different from the Stoicism of Posidonius represented in Cicero's *De natura deorum*, book II.[58]

5. Solignac has also shown that the *Introductio arithmetica* of Nicomachus of Gerasa, translated by Apuleius, is the source of Augustine's "Pythagoreanism": his speculations on the derivation of number from the mind as monad, his stress on the role of numerical proportions in the formation and ordering of all things,

[55] Aimé de Solignac, "Doxographies et manuels dans la formation philosophique de saint Augustin," *RA*, I (1958), pp. 117-118; 126, n. 36; 138-148; cf. his later summary, *BA*, XIII, pp. 88-93.

[56] Courcelle, *Les lettres grecques*, pp. 123, 179-181.

[57] *BA*, XIV, p. 534.

[58] Gérard Verbeke, "Augustin et le stoïcisme," *RA*, I (1958), pp. 67-89.

his interest in the symbolism of numbers. It is also the source of much that Augustine knew about Platonism, such as the contrast between the worlds of change and of permanence, and even of his distinction between "knowledge" and "wisdom."[59]

6. Mention should be made in passing of Aristotle's *Categories*, which Augustine read at the age of twenty (*Conf.*, IV, 16, 28). Though they were not a major influence upon his early thinking, they did become important later on when he was working out his doctrine of the Trinity;[60] and in any event we are reminded again of the diversity of philosophical influences to which Augustine was subjected.

7. It is only after noting all these other influences that we can safely come to the hypothesis that Augustine read some works of Porphyry prior to his conversion. These considerations are offered not to prejudice the case against this theory, but rather to give the theory more precision by setting as many boundaries as possible and eliminating all those "Platonist"-sounding passages which can be ascribed to Plotinus or to other writers. Although Plotinus is the only Platonist writer mentioned by name in Augustine's early writings, enough Porphyrian themes are present in them to keep the question alive.

The classic statement of the Porphyry hypothesis is Willy Theiler's *Porphyrios und Augustin* (1933). It has been influential precisely because Theiler dared to formulate a hypothesis and work it through. His method is at first glance outrageous: on the basis of admittedly problematical evidence (for very little of Porphyry's work survives) he outlines the distinguishing features of Porphyry's philosophy and then attempts to show, chiefly on the basis of one work of Augustine's, *On True Religion*, that the neo-Platonist elements in Augustine's thought are dependent upon Porphyry rather than upon Plotinus, for where the two differed he follows the former rather than the latter. This thesis, however audacious and mistaken it may be, has advanced the discussion by erecting some formidable earthworks that must be traversed by all Augustine scholars.

The responsibility of those who adhere to the Porphyry hypothesis is to prove through literary analysis Augustine's

[59] Solignac, "Doxographies et manuels," pp. 129ff.
[60] See chapter 5, section 3, below.

dependence upon specific works, some of which have been lost—
and to prove that Augustine read them at the time of his conversion.

(a) One possibility is indicated by Augustine himself, for in
The City of God, chiefly in book X but also in books XVIII through
XXII, he mentions what seem at first glance to be two lost
works of Porphyry, *On the Philosophy from Oracles* (mentioned only
in *De civ. Dei*, XIX, 23, and then only by its Greek title, Περὶ
τῆς ἐκ λογίων φιλοσοφίας) and *On the Return of the Soul* (mentioned
far more frequently, and by the Latin title, *De regressu animae*).
O'Meara has argued, convincingly I think, that the two titles
belong to the same work, reasoning that the Greek title was never
translated into Latin because it would have been too unwieldy
and that a different title, or a different part of the original title,
was furnished for the Latin translation.[61] Since the *Philosophy
from Oracles* is quoted extensively in Eusebius' *Praeparatio evan-
gelica*, it is possible to gain some idea of its contents and to trace
parallels in *The City of God*, and O'Meara is convinced that many
of the passages attributed by Augustine to *De regressu animae* are
identical with those attributed by Eusebius to the *Philosophy from
Oracles*.

In an extended review of the book, quite unsympathetic to this
identification of the two works, Pierre Hadot makes some telling
points, but they do not seem to me to require anything more than
an adjustment of some details of O'Meara's thesis. Indeed, Hadot
unwittingly furnishes further evidence in support of it, for it
seems quite uncertain whether the works of Porphyry mentioned
by other ancient writers under the titles *On the Philosophy from
Oracles*, *On the Writings of Julian the Chaldaean*, and *On the Return of
the Soul* (this last mentioned only by Augustine) are three or two
or one in number.[62] It would seem quite possible, then, that something about "the descent and return of the soul" was included in
the subtitle of Porphyry's work on the Chaldaean Oracles. These
oracles, written by "Julian the Theurgist," son of "Julian the
Chaldaean," who lived in Rome between the reigns of Trajan and

---

[61] John J. O'Meara, *Porphyry's Philosophy from Oracles in Augustine* (Paris,
1959), p. 21.
[62] Pierre Hadot, "Citations de Porphyre chez Augustin, à propos d'un
ouvrage récent," *REA*, VI (1960), pp. 214–216.

Marcus Aurelius, contained a philosophical doctrine akin to the Platonism of Numenius, strongly tinged with mysticism and magic and with an intensely anti-Christian bias.[63]

If the *De regressu* which Augustine mentions is indeed identical with the *Philosophy from Oracles*, and if it was written before Porphyry came under the influence of Plotinus, then this work would not furnish an adequate explanation for the neo-Platonic themes in Augustine's earliest writings, and I must say that I do not see, in the materials gathered by O'Meara, any evidence that Augustine read the work until very near the year 400.[64]

(b) Another possibility, recently discussed, again gives opportunity for the most subtle detective work among the scholars, since it concerns another lost work of Porphyry, the *Mixed Questions* (Συμμίκτα Ζητήματα), in particular that concerning the mode of union of soul and body. This question, known indirectly through Nemesius' treatise *On the Nature of Man*, chapter 3, was almost certainly used by Augustine, for it influenced his view of the union of soul and body from an early time, and he later worked out a conception of the union of divinity and humanity in Christ by analogy with it (*Ep.* 137).[65] The problem of the relation of soul and body was much debated among the philosophical schools, and it seems that in answering the Stoic objection that the soul could not be brought into interaction with the body if it were incorporeal Porphyry, working from a suggestion of Ammonius, developed an original solution that went well beyond Plato's own view that the body is a mere garment or instrument of the soul: they must be, Porphyry argued, two distinct substances which are brought together in a union or composition (ἕνωσις, σύνθεδις) without mingling or confusion.[66]

[63] Hans Lewy, *Chaldaean Oracles and Theurgy: Mysticism, Magic, and Platonism in the Later Roman Empire* (*Recherches d'archéologie, de philologie et d'histoire*, XIII; Cairo, Institut français d'archéologie orientale, 1956), pp. 3–5; Hadot, pp. 211, n. 24, 214.

[64] See chapter 2, section 3, and chapter 4, section 4, below.

[65] Ernest L. Fortin, "Saint Augustin et la doctrine néoplatonicienne de l'âme," *AM*, III, 371–380; *Christianisme et culture philosophique au cinquième siècle. La querelle de l'âme humaine en Occident* (Paris, 1959); Heinrich Dörrie, *Porphyrios' 'Symmikta Zetemata'* (Zetemata, 20, Munich, 1959); Jean Pépin, "Une nouvelle source de saint Augustin: Le ζήτημα de Porphyre *Sur l'union de l'âme et du corps*," *Revue des études anciennes*, LXXXVI (1964), pp. 53–107.

[66] Fortin, pp. 112–118; Dörrie, pp. 159–174.

According to Proclus the question began by reporting a debate
between Porphyry's teacher Longinus and the Stoic Medios,
and Dörrie thinks that Porphyry took the Stoic objections
seriously, acknowledging that this was a problem which Platonism had not yet solved and then thinking it through afresh, even
using Stoic terminology.[67] Whereas Plotinus simply repeated the
traditional Platonist position that the soul is undivided in itself
but is truly divided when it becomes embodied, Porphyry argued
that Plato's remarks on the "parts" of the soul belong in the
context of a discussion not of the nature of the soul but of the
virtues, that is, the varying ways in which the soul can be said to
act in relation to the material world, and therefore he claimed
freedom to forge his own vocabulary.[68] He placed the soul unambiguously on the side of the divine rather than the material
world, and taking his departure from the venerable Platonist
emphasis upon unity he argued that the soul not only is undivided
within itself but remains undivided in its union with the material
and thereby has the power to unify that which is beneath it: the
soul is and remains *one* within itself, it *unites* itself with the material
through attention, and it *unifies* the material through this active
presence.[69] All of this, it will be noted, is an ontological analysis,
and it does not obliterate the experienced fact that the soul can
have sympathy with the body and can even be drawn outward
toward it and can be, in a sense, "dispersed" and "divided"
through its commerce with the body. This psychological phenomenon is explained, however, not as an alteration in or an addition
to the *substance* of the soul, but as an attitude or inclination or
intention toward that which is other than itself (σχέσις, ῥοπή,
διάθεσις; in Augustine, usually *nutus* or *intentio*).[70] The soul
animates the body and is present to it not locally but through this
attention and affection, not as a form or entelechy which fulfills
matter by being ingredient in it but as a self-subsisting immaterial
being which goes out of itself through attention and confers
being upon material things through its presence to them.

Augustine knew this discussion and was influenced by it. But

[67] Dörrie, pp. 104–106; 159–161.
[68] Dörrie, pp. 172–173.
[69] Dörrie, pp. 166–174.
[70] Dörrie, pp. 104–106; Pépin, p. 89.

it is doubtful that he read it before going to Cassiciacum, and in any case the question on the union of soul and body does not explain all the Porphyrian elements that were present in his thought at the time. Therefore the search goes on.

(c) Another writing of Porphyry's which Augustine might have used is the *Sentences*, a set of maxims designed to conduct the reader toward intelligible things ('Ἀφορμαὶ πρὸς τὰ νοητά).[71] Most passages are excerpted from the *Enneads*, especially the treatises I, 2, III, 6, and VI, 4 and 5, but they are given a characteristically Porphyrian slant: the interest in the inward dynamics of the mind and the quest for self-awareness is even more intense than in Plotinus, so that the whole work is a kind of "phenomenology of spirit," and the doctrine that emerges is almost a subjective idealism or existentialism, though of course not to the exclusion of other, more objective aspects of Porphyry's thought. Augustine did learn something from Porphyry along these lines, and almost the whole of his *De vera religione* is a statement of his own "phenomenology of spirit," quite similar, as Theiler saw, to Porphyry's. Solignac thinks that the Porphyrian elements in the Cassiciacum writings can be explained by the *Sentences* alone, and he suggests that Victorinus may have added it as an introduction to his translation of the *Enneads*, or that passages from it were used as glosses.[72] From the standpoint of economy of explanation the latter suggestion seems most plausible, for O'Connell has demonstrated in case after case that Augustine read *Ennead* VI, 4 and 5 in the form given it by Plotinus, not as it was excerpted by Porphyry in the *Sentences*, for Porphyry omitted all the vivid images that are found in the original version and were obviously known to Augustine.[73]

The exact identity of the works by Porphyry which influenced Augustine at an early time remains uncertain. In addition to the three that have been discussed, there are other works which are known only from notice in passing by ancient writers: an essay on the saying, "Know thyself," a commentary on *Ennead* I, 8

[71] The standard edition is by Mommert (Leipzig, 1907). Unfortunately he gives the paragraphs a numbering different from that of the older editions, and therefore it is necessary to cite passages according to both schemes.

[72] "Réminiscences plotiniennes et porphyriennes dans le début du 'De ordine' de saint Augustin," *Archives de philosophie*, XX (1957), pp. 461–462.

[73] "*Ennead* VI, 4 and 5 in the Works of Saint Augustine," p. 12 and *passim*.

("On the Origin of Evil"), and so on.[74] And it is always possible
that the Porphyrian influence was more indirect, perhaps through
Manlius Theodorus or another member of the circle of Platonists
in Milan.

The problem, however tantalizing it may be, is not crucial to
the understanding of Augustine's earliest writings, for du Roy
has shown, quite convincingly I think, that the characteristically
Porphyrian themes are to be found not in the passages written at
Cassiciacum but only in those written after Augustine's return to
Milan. But then there must have been a sudden impact from some
work or works of Porphyry, and from that time on Augustine
can be said to be more Porphyrian than Plotinian where the two
differed.[75]

It should be evident that the philosophical influences on
Augustine were numerous and varied, and that they were often of
the highest stature, confronting philosophical problems with
directness and originality. It is no longer possible to view
Augustine as a solitary genius who forged a new way of thinking
and singlehandedly changed the subsequent history of Western
thought. He was the inheritor of philosophical traditions which
had long since taken an interest (to mention only those areas
often thought unique to him) in subjectivity, in the character of
the ideal contents of thought, and in the dynamic tendencies of
living beings. His originality, then, is not that of a radical inno-
vator but the far more persevering originality of one who allowed
himself to be challenged by longstanding problems and who,
learning from others how to go about them, continued their work
of analysis and argumentation. Many of Augustine's ideas are not
as new as they have appeared. But he did think through the
problems once more, and then repeatedly, for himself; and even
where he merely reaffirmed older insights he transmuted them by
bringing them into the different context of Christian belief and

---

[74] Those who wish to try their hand at the problem might consult the list
of works of Rudolf Beutler's article, "Porphyrios," in the Pauly-Wissowa
Real-Encyclopädie der classischen Altertumswissenschaft, XXII (1953), cols.
275–313.

[75] *L'Intelligence de la foi en la Trinité*, pp. 185–196. His judgment is based on
the studies of Pierre Hadot, who has been at work for many years attempting
to characterize what is distinctive in Porphyry's metaphysic and psychology
(see especially his recent study, *Porphyre et Victorinus* [Paris, 1968]).

obedience. Augustine's intellectual furniture at the time of his conversion, let us remember, was that of classical philosophy. He knew nothing about Christian theology except the little he might have gleaned from Ambrose's sermons. He was as much at the "beginnings" of theological reflection as, say, Justin Martyr or Clement of Alexandria long before him. As the years went on he would learn more from the theologians of the Church, supplementing or modifying his first attempts. And yet much that was worked out in those early dialogues remained characteristic of his thought, and they are necessarily the starting point of any examination of Augustine's theology.

PART ONE

The Apprentice

CHAPTER I

Cassiciacum (386–387)

AUGUSTINE'S EARLIEST WRITINGS have not always been served well by later readers, and Augustine himself was among the first to misrepresent them. The discussion of them in the *Retractationes*, though it is valuable as a source of information about the circumstances of their writing, is quite misleading as an interpretation, for Augustine, no longer able to enter into the spirit of these early dialogues, continually felt called upon to express regret at things that had been said playfully by a cultured schoolmaster. What is required of everyone who goes to them is the kind of historical interest, or simply the kind of aesthetic receptivity, that will permit them to speak for themselves and be savored in their own right, apart from our preconceptions of Augustine or our knowledge of his thought gained through other channels.

Perhaps the poorest preparation for the study of the dialogues is a reading of the account of his life in the *Confessions*, with its deeply personal tone. In the dialogues the reader is kept at arm's length by a style that is always self-consciously literate; Augustine discloses little of himself. The passionate, incantatory language of the *Confessions* is lacking, apart from the long prayer at the beginning of the *Soliloquies*, which reveals that Augustine was perhaps capable of writing a *Confessions* even at this time. We may trust that the Augustine of the dialogues is the same as the Augustine presented in the *Confessions*. Why, then, the striking difference in tone?

At Cassiciacum Augustine was concerned to engage in serious

inquiry and if possible arrive at well-founded conclusions; that was his personal need at the time. Furthermore, the dialogues are based upon actual conversations, some of them quite casual, others staged for the instruction of Augustine's pupils.[1] The haphazard course of some of the discussions and the chance interruptions with which they are beset could scarcely have been contrived, even for literary effect. But it is also clear that Augustine worked them over carefully, following the model of Cicero's dialogues, and supplied long concluding orations in which he, the *magister*, gave an exposition of the matter under discussion. The setting is not conducive to the revelation of what is most intimate. But from time to time a more personal note does break through, even in the conversations. And there is even more of personal disclosure in the long dedicatory prefaces, though it may have been intentionally muted, for the dialogues were dedicated to important men—Manlius Theodorus, Zenobius, Romanianus—who, though they all had a deep interest in the philosophic life, were still enmeshed in their private and public affairs and might be disposed to recoil at an account of Augustine's successful struggles with the spirit of worldliness like that contained in the *Confessions*. Augustine himself tells us (*Conf.*, IX, 2, 3) that he did not wish to make a display of himself as a kind of spiritual virtuoso and therefore mentioned only the pain in his chest as the reason for his change of occupation; a similar diffidence or prudence may have led him to do the same in writing to these men of affairs.

We should not look primarily for disclosures made from the heart, then, in these dialogues. Their function is to resolve some of Augustine's perplexities and start him on the way toward a fuller life. The personal element is there, nonetheless, and something can be surmised about its intensities from the themes that are discussed and the passionate language that is occasionally used.

[1] The probable dates of the dialogues, if internal evidence is reliable, are as follows:

Contra Academicos, I	November 10 and following
De beata vita	November 13 (Augustine's birthday)
De ordine	November 16–17
Contra Academicos, II–III	November 18–22
De ordine, II	November 23

The *Soliloquies* come somewhat later.

I. THE QUEST FOR HAPPINESS

The topic that clearly takes priority in the dialogues is the pursuit of happiness and the question in what the happy life consists (at this stage in Augustine's thinking, it should be noted, happiness is assumed to be realizable here and now; only later Augustine will defer all expectations to the life after death). The problem of happiness is the first to be discussed, for it fills a large place in the conversations on the Academics, and it is the express topic of the conversation, held on Augustine's birthday, which breaks into them.[2]

We have seen that Augustine's whole adult life was given direction and continuity by his reading of Cicero's *Hortensius*, and the influence of that work did not diminish even in writings that come late in Augustine's career, such as the work on the Trinity and his replies to Julian, the champion of the Pelagians.[3] Cicero, proceeding descriptively, began the dialogue with the observation that we all desire to be happy (cf. *De beata vita*, II, 10; *C. Acad.*, I, 2, 5; *De Trin.*, XIII, 4, 7). But he went on to ask whether men can be happy simply by living however they please and possessing whatever they desire. That cannot be, he said; to desire and attain what is inappropriate or evil is to be miserable, not happy (cf. *De beata vita*, II, 10). Happiness cannot be defined solely by man's wishes, then, even though it is true that one element of happiness is the possession of what one desires. Cicero then went on to show that beatitude must consist in living according to that which is highest in man, namely his mind (cf. *C. Acad.*, I, 2, 5), and the goal of the dialogue as a whole is to lead men toward a life in quest of wisdom, however difficult it may be.

Cicero is thus following a broad current, almost a consensus, in ancient thought, spread throughout the civilized world by the

---

[2] The major study of Augustine's understanding of beatitude, set against the background of the philosophical traditions of antiquity, is Ragnar Holte, *Béatitude et sagesse. Saint Augustin et le problème de la fin de l'homme dans la philosophie ancienne* (Paris, 1962).

[3] These works are, in fact, among the principal sources of the fragments of the *Hortensius* collected by Müller, Grilli, and others in their editions, which should be consulted in order to get a picture of Cicero's dialogue. See also the catalogue of quotations from Cicero in Testard, *Saint Augustin et Cicéron*, II.

Stoics, which viewed happiness as virtue, the fully developed and properly ordered functioning of man's powers; sometimes the stress fell more upon intellectual activity, sometimes more upon living one's own life with integrity, but there was a confidence that joy could be found in the very enterprise of living as a human being, for what one desired for oneself need not be bound up with the possessing of external goods or the actualization of external states of affairs: one could remain sovereign over these things that are at the mercy of other men or of fortune.

Before analyzing Augustine's judgment about its shortcomings, we should note how strongly he approved of this approach to the problem of happiness and how deeply he was influenced by it. Perhaps the best testimony to his approval of this heroically "humanistic" ethic (humanistic because man, in the center of his free and intelligent existence, is called upon to exercise sovereignty over his own life within the world) is the fact that from first to last the key principle of his conception of man was the authority of the mind and will over all other functions of human life: not merely as the dominance of soul over body (though of course he often used that language) but in a more dynamic sense as a proper relationship among the various aspects of the "soul," man's animate life as a whole (*C. Acad.*, I, 2, 5).

If we wish to see the power it exerted over him at the time of his conversion we must look at the description of the sage in *De beata vita*, IV, 25, where these classical themes are invoked in high rhetorical style.[4] The wise man is completely happy, despite the fact that he has certain bodily needs which still must be met and which may be frustrated, perhaps painfully; for he neither desires anything immoderately nor fears pain and death. What, then, will the sage do about the everyday problem of physical survival, which the common man seems to solve so easily but whose resolution is no longer evident after such brave philosophical affirmations have been made? The sage also will eat and drink and try to ward off pain and death. But he will do it with full awareness and with the proper motives. Augustine quotes Terence (who was

---

[4] The close parallel between this passage and *De Trin.*, XIII, 7, 10 is noted by Grilli in his edition of the *Hortensius* (Milan, 1962), pp. 144–145. The source is probably Cicero's dialogue, for Augustine, who in the earlier writing appropriates the thought so enthusiastically, later refuses to associate himself with it and instead calls it proud and vain.

himself influenced at this point by Stoicism): "What you can avoid, it is foolish to permit." So the sage will avoid pain and death, "so far as he can and should," because to fail to do so would be a sign of foolishness, not wisdom, and suffering and death under such circumstances would be not happiness but misery, misery not because of what is undergone but because of the stupidity of the decision. Augustine sums up the presentation with another, even more characteristically Stoic passage from Terence: "If you cannot do what you wish, desire what you can do." Thus the wise man, Augustine says, will always be happy, for nothing can happen without his willing it; he will refrain from desiring what is unattainable, and he will commit himself to what can be desired with perfect certitude, a course of life always in accord with virtue.

All of this can be said, it will be noted, with none of the drastic asceticism that some modern readers seem to anticipate in Augustine's writings from this period. He is not ready to make a wholesale renunciation of temporal goods; on the contrary, in characteristic Ciceronian fashion he hopes only to remain sovereign over them and utilize them for higher ends. In the *Soliloquies* (I, 11, 18—12, 20) Reason asks him whether he would desire wealth or honors or a wife if they were necessary to his life with his companions in quest of wisdom, and he answers that he would indeed desire them, not, however, for themselves, but only for the sake of this higher purpose. If there was ever any danger that Platonism, with its contrast between soul and body, might lead toward an unhealthy renunciation of all that is bodily—and we shall see that even in Platonism this tendency should not be over-dramatized—it was counteracted by the more down-to-earth ethical theory of Cicero, and those aspects of Platonism which stressed the sovereignty of the self over the world were reinforced.

Augustine thus retains something of the classical conception of happiness as virtue; but he transforms it into something new, or, more accurately, he thinks that he can discern in it hidden resonances often unsuspected by casual readers, though not unknown, he is confident, to Cicero himself. It is all accomplished by means of a play on the etymological overtones of the old Roman virtues so often discussed by Cicero, and all that Augustine needs to do is to follow out Cicero's own suggestions. He had said (*Tusc.*, III, 8, 18) that *nequitia* (profligacy) is the mother of all vices because it is *nequicquam* (in vain, for nothing). And if vice is sterile, virtue is fecund; the chief virtue, then, is *frugalitas* (temperance, orderliness), which of course suggests fruitfulness. Augustine makes use of the passage early in the dialogue (*De beata vita*, II, 8), and with its aid he leads the classical doctrine of the virtues toward the Platonist contrast, first stated in the *Symposium* (203 A–E), between Plenty (Πόρος) and Poverty (Πενία).[5]

The major portion of the dialogue is concerned with justifying this transformation of the doctrine of virtues by showing that there is a perfect correspondence between a succession of antitheses: virtue and vice, fecundity and sterility, happiness and misery, wisdom and foolishness, plenty and poverty, being and non-being. Such a correlation is not self-evident, and Augustine, borrowing again from Cicero's *Hortensius*, takes up as a thought-experiment the case of Sergius Orata: this man has the resources to possess all that he desires, and he experiences no physical deprivations; yet his happiness can still be marred by anxiety lest he lose what he has, through ill fortune. Such anxiety is not only one kind of misery; it is also, as Monica points out, a lack of wisdom, and Augustine gives the final refinement by pointing out that a man would be even *more* foolish and miserable if he did *not* have anxiety over perishable things (*De beata vita*, IV, 27–28). Augustine thinks, then, that all misery and vice and lack of wisdom can in some way be related to "nothingness," to those things that are always changing and perishing and never really have being, for in concerning themselves with them men "squander" themselves (*De beata vita*, II, 8).

It is somewhat more difficult to say in what the fullness of virtue consists. Augustine, again following Cicero, thinks that the names

---

[5] Augustine draws the same contrast between *Plenitudo* and *Egestas* (*De beata vita*, IV, 30) or between *Divitiae* and *Egestas* (*Ep.* 3, written to Nebridius from Cassiciacum in January, 387). It was probably a commonplace in philosophical textbooks, but perhaps he learned of it from Porphyry's *Sentences* (41, Mommert 40), where it is interpreted within the context of the subject's movement toward either being or non-being, or from Ambrose's sermon on the value of death, if Courcelle is correct in thinking that it was preached during Lent, 386 (cf. Courcelle, *Recherches*, pp. 121–125; Solignac, "Réminiscences," pp. 455–461; du Roy, *L'Intelligence de la foi en la Trinité*, p. 150, n. 3).

of the virtues consistently point toward the same configuration of ideas: *modestia* toward *modus*, *temperantia* toward *temperies*, and so on. The virtues involve a certain measure or equilibrium, then, and one which is not susceptible of degrees but is either present or absent. Wisdom is therefore the supreme "measure of the mind," giving it equilibrium so that it is subject neither to excess nor to defect (*De beata vita*, IV, 32–33). But what is this "measure" which gives fullness to human life? The criterion is that it must be something which is not dependent upon or subject to fortune, something, therefore, which abides and can be possessed whenever and as long as one desires (*De beata vita*, II, 11).

The first suggestion to be made is, quite naturally, that it is virtue itself (*De beata vita*, II, 8). But an alternative is soon suggested: God is eternal and abiding, and whoever possesses God through knowledge is truly happy (II, 11). And yet the discussion of it in this dialogue remains vague, almost subterranean, and there is little preparation for the conclusion, in which Augustine, who has been speaking in the customary fashion of wisdom as a virtue, suddenly reverses his perspective: he mentions that the wise man *contemplates* wisdom, that his soul is embraced by God, and then he suddenly says,

What else is to be called wisdom than the Wisdom of God? The man who is happy possesses God. And what is Wisdom except Truth? Truth has being through some Supreme Measure, from which it proceeds and toward which it returns. ... Whoever comes to the Supreme Measure through Truth is happy. This is the soul's possession and fruition of God. Apart from it there is a being possessed by God, but not a possessing of God (*De beata vita*, IV, 34).

The conclusion is arrived at through what seems to be a sudden leap in the argument. Hints of it have been present, it is true, from the very start, especially in the comments of Monica, who represents a Christian piety able to outrun the doctrines of the philosophers (*De beata vita*, IV, 27). It is Monica who even at the beginning sees that the food of the soul consists in knowledge (II, 8); who, without philosophical training, anticipates Cicero's insight that happiness is not merely the possession of what one desires (II, 10); and who preempts a point that Augustine had been saving as his final word in the discussion of unhappiness (IV, 27). But these are only hints strewn along the way, and by themselves they are not a sufficient basis for the conclusion. That conclusion grows rather out of the main line of philosophical analysis in the dialogue, the one which leads the notions of virtue and vice in the direction of the Platonist contrast between Plenty and Poverty.

What animates the entire argument, though it is not brought into the open, is a discontent with the rather narrow stress of those ethical writers influenced by Stoicism upon the internal qualities of the wise and virtuous man. As a Christian and a Platonist Augustine would want any theory of virtue to include the element of contemplation. But his discontent does not come only from the neo-Platonist stress upon contemplation. He has a more pointed criticism of the overemphasis upon virtue. It is made explicitly in his later work *De moribus* (*On the Morals of the Catholic Church and of the Manichaeans*), though, as I will show in a moment, he was probably aware of it at Cassiciacum. To the Manichaeans' boasting about their heroic abstinence Augustine retorts that the important thing is not what is done but the end for which it is done; after all, Catiline could endure cold, thirst, and hunger, and the only thing that differentiates this parricide from the apostles is the end pursued. The Manichaeans themselves discount the multitude of Catholics living continently by saying, "Even the mule is a virgin" (*De mor.*, II, 13, 27–28).

This broadening of the perspective of ethical theory comes, it seems, from Varro and his teacher Antiochus. Antiochus analyzed all willing, and hence even the virtues, in terms of *relation* or *intention* or *right ordering*: the pertinent question to ask is always what is being willed as the principal value to which all else is "referred." The Stoics had already suggested this distinction between what is willed for its own sake and what is willed for the sake of something else, as a way of considering certain things a matter of "indifference" and still making choices involving them; but for the Stoics it all revolved around the inward tranquility of the wise man, while Antiochus broke out of this ethical solipsism and concerned himself with the hierarchy of values that is established by the actual levels of being.[6] There will always be something that is willed to be "enjoyed," and other things will be "used" in relation to it, and the problem is to let the principal

6 Lorenz, "Die Herkunft des augustinischen *frui Deo*," p. 37, n. 11.

value be that which is truly ultimate. Men can desire the enjoyment of many things—material things, bodily health, the soul,
God, in various permutations, adding up to 288 different ends
(Varro is probably the source of Augustine's sometimes facetious
discussions along this line in *De mor.*, I, 3, 4—6, 10 and *De civ.
Dei*, XIX, 1–3)—but the proper end is the enjoyment of God
through knowing him and becoming as much like him as possible.[7]

It is this notion of enjoying God (*frui Deo*) that closes the circle
and draws together the whole complex of themes that have been
discussed throughout the dialogue in a more fragmentary way:
the universal quest for happiness, the enriching and fulfilling
character of virtue, the possession of God through contemplation.[8] The same thing is suggested by the image of a spiritual
embrace (*amplexus*), taken from Plotinus (*Enn.* VI, 5, 10),[9] which
appears with some frequency in the Cassiciacum dialogues and
thereafter. The embrace is mutual, for the subject is sometimes
God, or his Wisdom or Truth (personified as a feminine figure),
and sometimes the soul, masculine or feminine as the imagery
may demand (*De beata vita*, IV, 33; *De ord.*, I, 8, 24; *C. Acad.*, II,
9, 22; *Solil.*, I, 13, 22). The purpose of the image is to suggest,
once more, the immediacy of vision and the joy of attainment,
and at the same time to show the superiority of the spiritual
embrace which takes place through knowledge, for the same
fulfillment can be shared by many lovers without rivalry or
diminishment (*Enn.* VI, 5, 10; *De lib. arb.*, II, 14, 37).

If we wish to use terms with perfect propriety we must say that
what Augustine really means when he describes the goal of the
human quest is not "the happy life" so much as "life in happiness," for virtue and happiness are differentiated, and although it
may be that virtue comes first as part of man's movement toward
the achievement of happiness, the ideal life, which he thinks
attainable by men after long effort, is one in which God is enjoyed
through knowledge and men live virtuously in accordance with
the law shining within them; in either case—whether virtue is on

---

[7] See Lorenz, pp. 42–46, for the development of this theme in middle
Platonism on the basis of *Theaetetus*, 176B.

[8] Cf. Holte, *Béatitude et sagesse*, p. 219.

[9] O'Connell, "*Ennead* VI, 4 and 5 in the Works of Saint Augustine,"
pp. 21–24.

the way toward happiness or follows from it—the primary value is the knowledge of God, and the dialogue on happiness ends with an evocation of the hidden Sun which is the fountain of all truth and an exhortation to thirst after it, for until man drinks from it and is filled he has not arrived at his full measure of wisdom and joy.

Here we already find the essential themes which will character-ize Augustine's thought throughout his career: God's constant presence to the self, even when its attention is directed toward the external world; the divine light as the source of all the truths that men apprehend; the need to "remember" the divine presence and turn within; the goal of immediate vision of God. That these themes are present from the first is not surprising, for they do not depend upon personal experience of the mystical embrace (Augus-tine denies that he has yet attained it) or upon extensive theological reflection of the sort that will come only later; they are drawn from a philosophical tradition with which Augustine was already acquainted, the highest aspirations coming from Plotinus (especi-ally *Enn.* I, 6; V, 1; VI, 5). For the moment Augustine knows it only as a goal to be striven for, and he hastens to prepare himself for it.

The fact is that men as they are cannot reach the goal. To be sure, God is present to them and their minds are capable of appre-hending God. But even when they catch some glimpse of the light shining inwardly upon them they are unable to endure its splendor because of their impurity of mind; afraid to turn toward the light, they fall back into their accustomed patterns (*De beata vita*, IV, 35; *C. Acad.*, I, 1, 3; II, 2, 5; *Solil.*, I, 6, 12). And in the case of most men there is no awareness at all of the divine presence. In their concern with external things they have turned away from God and forgotten him. Thus when Augustine outlines the *possibilities* of human life he can indicate, in the most optimistic way, the knowability of God and the attainability of happiness, even, it should be noted, during earthly life; but when he des-cribes the *actual* human condition, he stresses the universality of alienation from God and the arduousness of the return toward man's proper mode of existence.

In the passages written at Cassiciacum little is said about the circumstances of man's fall into his present predicament, and what Augustine does say is often not Plotinian but Ciceronian. The body is called a "dark prison" (*C. Acad.*, I, 3, 9) or a "cave" (*Solil.*, I, 14, 24) in which the soul is imprisoned; the "region of its origin" is said to be elsewhere (*C. Acad.*, II, 9, 22; cf. *De quan. an.*, I, 1), and it is exhorted to free its wings from all those affections which hold it down, soar into the atmosphere made lucid by the sun, and return to its home in the heavens (*C. Acad.*, II, 9, 22; *Solil.*, I, 14, 24). This theme of *reditus in coelum* appears in the closing passage of *Hortensius* (quoted in *De Trin.*, XIV, 19, 26), and Cicero in that dialogue held forth the possibility, at least, that the soul might be able to return to a higher life from which it had been exiled in punishment. He seems to have been influenced in this partly by the young Aristotle—who, according to a passage in the *Hortensius* quoted by Augustine himself (*C. Jul.*, IV, 15, 78), said that we are living beings yoked with dying, like prisoners of the Etruscans, grossly tortured—but also by his teacher Antiochus and other contemporaries. Orphic and Platonist themes were a commonplace in those philosophical traditions by which Augustine was influenced, and their appearance in Augustine's writings does not always signal the influence of Plotinus or Porphyry.

It is not surprising, then, that for many years Augustine gave credence to the theory of the preexistence of the soul. What is actually more surprising is that through all these years he held to it with something less than unconditional certitude. He knew that the whole matter was obscure, and on his return to Milan, it seems, he sought more light from Manlius Theodorus (*De beata vita*, I, 1). For some time his own assumptions corresponded quite closely with those of Plotinus: each soul chooses its own destiny, true to character, descending at the appropriate time into a body that conforms with its inner dispositions. Divine "sending" coincides with the soul's own "going," for the soul descends according to its own inclinations and yet it all takes place in accordance with divine justice (cf. *Enn.* IV, 3, 12–13).[10] These assumptions could only be reinforced and given the authority of Christian teaching when Augustine began to read some works of Origen in transla-

---

[10] Evidence that this was in fact Augustine's own view has been marshalled by Robert J. O'Connell in "The Plotinian Fall of the Soul in St. Augustine," pp. 5–6.

tion.[11] Yet even while he *assumed* all this, he never devoted any extended reflection to the problem. About 395 the theory of pre-existence became only one possibility among others (*De lib. arb.*, III, 20, 55—21, 59), and it was rejected about 406 (*De Gen. ad litt.*, VI, 9, 15). It seems always to have been only at the margins of his concern, and he probably held it with what Newman called "notional assent," that is, in a hypothetical way, on the condition that the premises on which it is based are true and the philosophical authorities which are followed are reliable.[12]

What Augustine holds with "real assent," that is, on the basis of direct experience or firm reasoning, is not the theory of pre-existence but the Plotinian and Porphyrian theory of the soul's relation to the body. This includes two aspects which should not be confused: first, the soul's animation of the body by forming a portion of matter as an image, an expression or reflection of its inward life, even while it is able, in principle, to remain "within itself" and "outside" all that is corporeal (*Enn.* IV, 3, 9–10); and then the soul's enslavement to the things of the body when it becomes fascinated with the brilliant reflections of the divine that it sees in the material world and, losing sight of itself, "turns" toward them and "goes forth" from itself and becomes "present" not to itself but to the body (*Enn.* IV, 3, paragraphs 9, 12, 17, etc.). Both of these aspects—the power of man's inward life over his bodily actions, and his enslavement by his own affections for the finite—were a matter of experience to Augustine; he could give unconditional assent when he read them in Plotinus (*Enn.* IV, 3) or in Porphyry (perhaps the *Sentences*). He could say along with them but out of personal conviction, for himself, that the soul has gone outside itself (*progressus*) and is poured out (*a seipso fusus*) into the world of multiplicity, from which it needs to return to itself and thereby to God, who is present within the self. And he could say, again with them, that the way of return is through "fleeing sensible things altogether" (*Solil.*, I, 14, 24; cf. *De ord.*, II, 11, 31), without thereby meaning to suggest that the soul must lose all relation to the body.

Augustine himself is responsible for a widespread misunderstanding of his earlier views. When in the *Retractationes* (I, 4, 7) he

[11] See pp. 108–109 below.
[12] *An Essay in Aid of a Grammar of Assent*, chapter 4.

expresses his regret over this exhortation in the *Soliloquies* to "flee sensible things altogether" ("*penitus esse ista sensibilia fugienda*") he says that it seems to incline too much toward Porphyry's erroneous teaching that there is no resurrection of the body. This statement has been taken by some scholars as evidence that Porphyry had an important influence upon Augustine at the time of his conversion. But it actually manifests a concern that arose much later, for it is only toward the year 400 that Augustine indicates any real awareness of Porphyry's polemics against the Christian doctrine of resurrection and only after 405 or 406 that he combats it directly with any vigor.[13] It is true that a similarly worded exhortation to "flee the bodily altogether" ("*corpus est omne fugiendum*") is attributed to Porphyry's work *On the Return of the Soul*; but that work may well be identical with his work *On the Philosophy from the Oracles*, and there is no evidence that Augustine read the latter until close to 400.[14] Perhaps *On the Return of the Soul* is a different work, then, which Augustine read earlier; perhaps the exhortation was also used elsewhere by Porphyry; or perhaps it was an easily remembered catch-phrase used by the Platonists in Milan. The same theme is to be found (though not in the same language) in passages of the *Enneads* which Augustine almost certainly read (I, 6, 7–8; IV, 3, 32; V, 1, 10). And in any case it is the *doctrine* of Plotinus, not that of Porphyry, that Augustine follows without hesitation, for whereas Porphyry thought that the soul could attain lasting beatitude only by becoming disembodied, Plotinus assumed that the soul always has a relation to *some* body (either a mortal body on earth or an invulnerable body in the heavens) and had confidence that it could raise itself above bodily concerns and in turn influence the body for the better (*Enn.* IV, 3, 17; V, 1, 10).

To "flee" sensible things, then, is simply to dissolve the bonds of affection by which the mind is tied to them. Reason tells him,

There is only one precept I can give you; I know of no other. You must flee from these sensible things altogether, for as long as we bear this body we must beware lest our wings be held down by them, as if by birdlime. We have need of healthy, sound wings if we are to fly from this darkness to the light above, which does not deign to manifest itself

[13] See chapter 4, section 4.
[14] See introduction, section 3, and chapter 4, section 4.

to men shut up in this cave unless they are able to break through it and annul its effect and emerge into the air that is their habitat. When you reach the point that earthly things no longer delight you, at that very moment, believe me, you will see what you desire (*Solil.*, I, 14, 24).

This image of the adhesive power of earthly things, arising through their own attractiveness and through men's affection for them, is one which will remain an important element in Augustine's psychological theory (special note should be taken of *Conf.*, IV, 10, 15, and *De Trin.*, X, 8, 11, where love is said to be a *gluten*, a "glue" which holds the mind to the things which it has experienced). The abiding hold of past experiences over present attitudes and decisions through the power of *consuetudo*—not "habit," for in current English usage that suggests too much an automatism, but "custom," becoming familiar with certain things and feeling at home with them through constant contact—is another element of his psychological theory that is already present and will soon take an important position in Augustine's thinking (*C. Acad.*, III, 6, 13; cf. *De quan. an.*, 4, 6; 28, 54; 33, 71). He had probably learned through some philosophical source that custom had been called "second nature" (*De mus.*, VI, 7, 19; cf. *C. Jul. op. imp.*, I, 69), and it will become his own explanation of the inevitability of sin, put forward in opposition to the Manichaean theory of the presence of an evil nature in man (*De fid. et sym.*, 10, 23; *Conf.*, VIII, 9, 21—10, 24).

Augustine's central concern, then, is with the psychological dynamics of the soul's bondage and with the existential task of returning to the life that is appropriate to its capabilities and desires. His interest in the circumstances of the soul's entrance into the body remained only marginal. And in Plotinus he could have found encouragement for this order of priorities, for Plotinus himself effectively "demythologizes" or "existentializes" the traditional Platonist doctrine, not, to be sure, by denying pre-existence or reincarnation, but by interpreting all that occurs in terms of subjective tendencies and by stressing that the divine realm which is the true home of the soul is not to be sought by man somewhere else or in another time, for it is non-spatial, omnipresent, to be sought here and now. If there is a pilgrimage to be taken, it is journey for the affections, and it consists in purifying the soul, making it more like God so that it will become capable of attaining the "beatific vision" (*Enn.* I, 6, 6–8). Whatever Plotinus may have thought about the lasting attainability of this goal during the present life, Augustine did assume it at first; and though he came to abandon this dream as a viable aspiration for sinful humanity and acquired a more Pauline (and coincidentally more Porphyrian) sense for the "eschatological tension" between the present time of purification and the coming time of fulfillment, he never forsook it as a description of the original possibility with which man was created, and it may be testimony to the boldness of Augustine's Christianity that he refused to accept as inevitable either the blinding of the mind by its concern with the finite or the merely momentary character of Plotinian ecstasy.

Nonetheless Augustine did not suppose that he had yet reached the goal, and he knew that the way was difficult. It was to the tracing and the following of the way that he devoted most of his labors at Cassiciacum.

2. AUTHORITY AND REASON

Neither man's impulse toward the philosophic life nor the validity of philosophical knowledge is intrinsically dependent upon faith or historical revelation. The impulse arises from fundamental human desires and capabilities, and it can be given a reliable orientation by the reflections of the philosophers.

Augustine therefore anticipates no incompatibility between Christianity and authentic philosophy; the *mysteria* of the Church, that is, the Trinitarian doctrines transmitted in the Creed, converge with the teachings of the Platonists (*C. Acad.*, II, 1, 1; III, 20, 43; *De ord.*, II, 5, 16; *De beata vita*, I, 4). Though they have come through different channels they emanate from the same source, the eternal Word; there is, so to speak, a preestablished harmony between them, and therefore it is no surprise that they assert the same things, using different words.

When Augustine speaks of true and authentic philosophy ("*vera et germana philosophia*" [*De ord.*, II, 5, 16]) it goes without saying that he has a specific tradition in mind, that stemming from Pythagoras and Plato. It is still a human philosophy, and it has undergone many vicissitudes; but as a result of many centuries of controversy a single valid doctrine has "filtered through" ("*eliquata est*"). That Augustine does not understand it in a narrow way is shown by his mention of Aristotle along with Plato and his belief that the harmony of their views has been demonstrated by certain perceptive men (*C. Acad.*, III, 19, 42). Augustine does not have the neo-Platonists in mind; the source of this statement is Cicero (*Acad.*, I, 4, 17–18; *Lucullus*, II, 5, 15; *De leg.*, I, 13, 18), and the joining of the two traditions is thus the one that occurred during the first century B.C. in Antiochus and others. Despite the all-too-human career of the true philosophy, it is not the "philosophy of this world" that is condemned in Scripture (Colossians 2, 8) for it is derived from the other, the intelligible world (*C. Acad.*, III, 19, 42). (By the "philosophy of this world" Augustine always understands those traditions which are dominated by sense and imagination: Stoicism and, at a much lower level, Manichaeism; his confident use of Scripture in this connection at such an early date may be the outcome of his conversations with Simplicianus, the presbyter and neo-Platonist.)

Revelation and true philosophy converge not only in a common source but in a common goal, the wisdom in which man finds happiness. The focus of attention in Augustine's discussions of faith and reason is rarely upon the cognitive aspect in isolation from the practical or existential; when he mentions the former, he soon looks to the latter: the true philosophy has given men a knowledge of the intelligible world, and to it they strive to return. It is in connection with this practical task, not the cognitive, that Augustine speaks of the indispensable role of authority and the fruitlessness of philosophy if it is not preceded by faith; for men need to be shown the way to return toward God, and God in his "clemency" has made it known, but the philosophers in their pride have scorned the humble form in which God appeared to men (*C. Acad.*, III, 19, 42; *De ord.*, II, 5, 16).

Augustine understands *auctoritas* not in the abstract sense that the word "authority" has in modern political theory, but more in its classical Latin sense of authentic and authoritative *testimony* to or *disclosure* of something that is not directly known. What unmistakably differentiates divine authority from that of men or demons is that it (a) manifests a divine power through miracles, (b) exhibits God's clemency toward men and his purpose of helping them through the lowly form he assumes, and (c) leads them by its precepts beyond these visible signs, not keeping them bound to them but inviting them to seek the divine Understanding itself (*De ord.*, II, 9, 27).[15] Authority is the doorway that must be entered first; but it leads to the further treasures of rational knowledge, and this is the goal aimed at by revelation itself.

Within the life of faith there are really two quite distinct functions of reason, both of them clearly understood in the Cassiciacum dialogues but first formulated a few months later (*De quan. an.*, 15, 25): to *supply arguments* which will give greater certitude about the truths of revelation, and to *exercise the mind* so that it will be capable of beholding spiritual things.[16] The first of these corresponds to what has already been said about the cognitive validity of philosophy (cf. *De ord.*, II, 9, 26 for its place in the life of faith); the second, far more important in Augustine's estimation, is practical in character, "anagogical," leading the mind toward the goal of immediate vision and accustoming it to the intelligible realm so that it will not be blinded by the light of eternity (*C. Acad.*, III, 9, 20; *Solil.*, I, 13, 23 and II, 20, 34; *De ord.*, I, 1, 4; *De quan. an.*, 15, 25).

Augustine can make some astounding claims for the philosophic life and its *exercitatio* of the soul in these early dialogues. In what is perhaps the most notorious passage he says:

> I do not see how those who are content with authority alone, who devote their energies to good works and upright desires but either scorn or are incapable of gaining learning in the liberal disciplines, can ever be called happy while they live here among men, though I firmly believe that as soon as they leave this body they will be liberated, with ease or difficulty in proportion to the degree of righteousness with which they have lived (*De ord.*, II, 9, 26).

The passage becomes less offensive when we recognize the anagogical context of all that is said: the life of reason is here understood not as the study of philosophical opinions for their own sake but as a preparation for the intuitive vision of God, and it involves a triad of activities, not only diligent study but devoted

---

[15] For the interpretation of this passage, see Magnus Löhrer, *Der Glaubensbegriff des hl. Augustinus in seinen ersten Schriften bis zu den Confessiones* (Einsiedeln, 1955), pp. 92–95.
[16] Cf. Marrou, *Saint Augustin et la fin de la culture antique*, pp. 277–327.

worship and virtuous living (*De ord.*, II, 8, 25 and 10, 51; and, much later, *De Trin.*, XV, 27, 49).[17] Beatitude is denied to the simple believer not because he is uneducated in the rational disciplines but because his apprehension of God, based on authority alone, is mediated and thus is held at a distance from the vision of God which constitutes beatitude and which Augustine still thinks attainable during the present life. Augustine readily affirms that the life of faith, hope, and love, without any training in the arts, is an adequate preparation for the vision of God after the soul's separation from the body (*De ord.*, II, 9, 26; *Solil.*, I, 13, 23); and within the dialogues Monica's devotion is repeatedly acknowledged to be a legitimate substitute for learning; indeed, it is affirmed to be almost an alternative form of "philosophy" (*De beata vita*, II, 10; *De ord.*, I, 11, 32; II, 1, 1; II, 17, 45).

There is nonetheless something of a harsh tone of superiority toward Monica in the dialogues, for Augustine has been attracted to the life of philosophy and seeks all that it can offer. But it is not a smug superiority; doubtless following earlier models (for his language is similar to Cicero's) but also disclosing something of his own feelings, he describes the philosophic life in terms that suggest that it is "a dangerous calling, as difficult as it is irresistible,"[18] arising from a kind of compulsion: those who have been seized by the passion to seek truth and gain intellectual enjoyment must go on, come what may (*De ord.*, I, 8, 24; *Solil.*, I, 13, 23). Their way will be long and circuitous; but they will be following the sacred circuits which lead the initiate into the sanctuary itself—for Augustine is probably using *circuitus* (*Solil.*, II, 20, 34; *De quan. an.*, 4, 6 and 7, 12) and *ambulatio* (*De doct. chr.*, I, 10, 10) to suggest a similarity with the mystery cults. It was a commonplace in Greek culture from Pythagoras and Plato onward to view philosophy as an initiation into the true mysteries; the comparison was utilized by Posidonius, and doubtless by Antiochus, for it played an important role in the writings of both Varro (who was confident that the liberal disciplines and philosophy could conduct the soul to the intelligible realm) and Cicero (who, somewhat more hesitant, said at the end of the Hortensius, as quoted by Augustine

---

[17] *Ibid.*, pp. 175–176, 364.
[18] *Ibid.*, p. 369, n. 1.

in *De Trin.*, XIV, 19, 26, that whatever man's end may be—whether it is extinction or return to a better home in the heavens—he should lead a life of virtue and study the liberal arts, for they will facilitate his ascent toward wisdom).

Augustine should be taken quite seriously when he says repeatedly that there are two ways of salvation (*C. Acad.*, III, 20, 43; *De ord.*, II, 5, 16 and 9, 26; *Solil.*, I, 13, 23; *De quan. an.*, 7, 12), for the way of authority alone and the way of reason operating on the basis of authority are different in their methods, their aspirations, and their results, at least during the present life. Nevertheless they are seen within the same framework. They share the same goal; they both accomplish a readying of the mind for the attainment of this goal; they operate together, with faith preparing the way and reason continuing what has been begun. By the time of the *Soliloquies* Augustine has come to view the whole process in an integral way. The human mind (for this is the identity of the mysterious figure of "Reason" in that work) is the medium within which the entire movement toward God takes place. Faith, hope, and love are indispensable to it, for they first purify the mind to make it capable of seeing, then they orient the mind toward God, and even when vision is achieved they sustain the mind's attention in the face of danger and temptation (*Solil.*, I, 6, 12—7, 14). But precisely because the rational mind is the subject presupposed and perfected by these Christian virtues, Augustine naturally anticipates that it will go on to do its proper work of inquiry and elucidation; indeed, without such activity there can be no transition from the second phase of "looking" to the third stage of "seeing," for the spiritual exercises of philosophical activity are needed if the mind is ever to become accustomed during the present life to the direct contemplation of the light (*Solil.*, I, 13, 23). Having some sense of its proper place, we must turn, then, to a consideration of the rational process as Augustine understood it in these earliest writings.

3. THE WAY OF REASON

The dialogue *On Order* (*De ordine*) is perhaps Augustine's greatest *tour de force* from the stay at Cassiciacum. It begins with a discussion in the middle of the night concerning the cause of the alternate rushing and slowing down of the flow of water through the conduits near the house, soon accounted for by the fall of leaves in late November; it continues as a more general discussion of the orderliness, and the providential ordering, of all that occurs within the finite world, and even the numerous interruptions and chance associations of ideas with which the conversation is beset are taken into account as they try to show, with the Stoics and Cicero, that the entire web of finite occurrences is administered in accord with divine justice; the attempt is then made to rise above *ordo* in the merely descriptive sense of the disposition of finite occurrences to the original *ordo* in the divine mind; and finally it is discovered that if one is to grasp this original *ordo* it is necessary to follow still another *ordo*, that of the liberal disciplines, which constitute an *ordo studiorum sapientiae* and make the mind capable of understanding the supreme *ordo* (II, 18, 47).

Some orientation to this last and most difficult problem, which occupies the whole of book II, is given in the prefatory remarks to Zenobius. There Augustine acknowledges the difficulty of seeing the providential order of the world, but he is confident that it can all be drawn into a consistent pattern, just as a mosaic which seems wildly disorganized when one focuses attention on only one tessera takes on a pattern when one looks at the whole (*De ord.*, I, 1, 2). Augustine proposes to show, then, how the whole scheme of things can be construed properly by seeing it as a whole, a "uni-verse," organized by a single unifying principle, and he clearly assumes that it is a whole not in its own being but in the divine Understanding (*Intellectus*), indeed, that it is a "uni-verse" *only* there (*De ord.*, II, 9, 26; cf. II, 16, 44). The problem, consequently, is that the mind, which naturally seeks to unify all that it finds, will not be satisfied in its quest until it comes to know what is in the mind of God; and the function of the rational disciplines is to lead him there step by step.[19]

[19] The stress on unity and the way in which it is stated in *De ord.*, I, 2, 3 and II, 18, 48 seem to be characteristic of Antiochus, and the interest in divine ideas also owes something to him, perhaps even the expression "the two worlds and the Father (cf. *Timaeus*, 28C) of the universe" in *De ord.*, II, 18, 47. See Fuchs, *Augustin und der antike Friedensgedanke*, pp. 157–161; Lorenz, "Die Herkunft des augustinischen *frui Deo*," p. 47; Zepf, "Augustinus und das philosophische Selbstbewusstsein der Antike," pp. 127–128; and with

Augustine is not unaware of another possibility: that man himself might confer unity upon the world through his power to change it, his artistic creativity, or his reasoning activity. But this would still be a structuring and unification of the world from within, not very different, really, from birds' building nests and other such ordering activities found throughout nature. And it would still not solve the problem of bringing order into man's own life; that can come only through his conscious adherence to rational norms. Thus without denying the reality of unifying activities within the world (cf. *De ord.*, II, 18, 48—19, 50), Augustine wishes to show that they point beyond themselves to a supreme ordering principle. Indeed, man's own practical activities are taken as the point of departure for a demonstration that those higher intensities have been present from the first.

In *De ordine* (II, 11, 30ff.) Augustine works out a theory of human life as the life of an animal that is at once rational and mortal, standing as it does between the intelligible and the corporeal worlds. Because man's attention has already "gone forth" toward earthly affairs it is difficult for him to return to himself, and because of the limited scope of these affairs one cannot discern in them *all* that reason can do; nevertheless men always act with the aid of reason, and therefore it is possible to begin by examining reason where it has expressed itself in the sensory world (II, 11, 30). So he looks at the *rationabilia* or *vestigia rationis* (11, 33), which make up the whole of human culture: first, the things produced by reason to be immediately enjoyed, such as good cuisine, or the ordered sounds of music, or the disciplined movements of the theater; then the symbols through which something is communicated from mind to mind; and finally the plans or rules by which reason is guided as man executes his actions (II, 11, 34—12, 35). These are the primitive givens of human life. The rational disciplines then arise through *reflection* upon different aspects of these already established cultural activities. It is only with the rise of these reflective activities that men begin to discover that there is

---

special reference to this dialogue, A. Dyroff, "Über Form und Begriffsgehalt des augustinischen Schrift 'De ordine,'" *Aurelius Augustinus* (Köln, 1930), pp. 15–62; K. Svoboda, *L'esthétique de saint Augustin et ses sources* (Brno and Paris, 1933), pp. 32–40. This is not to deny the presence of Plotinian themes, drawn especially from *Enn.* III, 2 ("On Providence").

another beauty than that which is ingredient in sense and imagination; they begin to emerge from their total involvement with the physical world and rise by degrees toward the intelligible. With Pythagoras in mind, he sees the beginning of the process in reflection upon what strikes the ear: such cultural facts as song, wind instruments, and plucked and percussive instruments; it was discovered that the music which had arisen, quite spontaneously, would have been ugly except for the measured proportion and variety of sounds. It is the same with the visible world, where the mind came to see that whatever pleased the eye embodied intelligible proportions; thus arose geometry and its application to the heavenly bodies in astronomy.

Augustine, it will be noted, is fully aware of the achievements of culture and of the rational disciplines that reflect upon them; he does not discount their usefulness or overdramatize their harmful consequences. His balanced judgment on them is expressed some months later in *De quantitate animae* (19, 33). They do help the soul to "grow" by unfolding its powers, he says. And yet such growth may not always be healthy. Sometimes it is superfluous, like a sixth finger, and this is Augustine's evaluation of "curiosity," the accumulation of facts and rational knowledge for its own sake; it is not harmful, but it is a distraction from man's proper tasks, and, like the piper mentioned by Varro who so charmed the crowds that they wanted to make him king, it may lead man toward the wrong loyalties.[20] Culture becomes definitely harmful, a tumorous growth which ought to be excised, only when it leads the soul directly and unambiguously into the sphere of the senses where it will waste away, as in the "art" of the gourmet who can judge foods by their taste and smell and who knows the best vintages of all the wines. The proper function of culture and of rational reflection, directly opposed to these superfluous or harmful functions, is to lead the soul toward the realm of the purely intelligible.

The critical phase in human development comes when men, having discovered that the rhythms and proportions of all things

---

[20] Cf. *De mus.*, VI, 13, 39; *De ver. rel.*, 29, 52; 49, 94; *De util. cred.*, 11, 25. For a fuller discussion of Augustine's comparatively mild estimate of culture during this period, see Marrou, *Saint Augustin et la fin de la culture antique*, pp. 277ff.

can be measured according to rational patterns, ask about *the mind itself* and its ability to measure and judge all things (II, 15, 43). Philosophy in the proper sense begins when men begin asking about the nature of the soul; its goal is reached only when they come to understand God (II, 18, 47). This sequence—first the self, then God: "*noverim me, noverim te*" (*Solil.*, II, 1, 1), "*in me redeam et in te*" (*Solil.*, II, 6, 9)—is at once a process of rational inquiry and an existential movement of the soul toward God. The aspiration is in large part Plotinian, and this "interior way" to God is probably inspired by passages like *Ennead* V, 1, 1, in which the soul is urged first to know itself in order to learn that its eye is capable of seeing God, or *Ennead* I, 6, 9, in which the mind is led within itself to a solitude uninterrupted by the external world and then is told to look and see God.[21] But the way traveled is not Plotinian but Varronian. The stress on going through a process of reasoning is alien to Plotinus, who relies more upon intuition of God, but it is characteristic of Varro with his interest in all the rational disciplines and his trust that they will lead the mind by degrees toward God. What Varro represents is an authentic Platonism drawn from Plato in his moments of enthusiasm for dialectic, the properly articulated classification of the entire realm of intelligibles (cf. especially the *Phaedrus*, 265D–266B); while Plotinus represents an equally authentic Platonism based upon the more mystical spirit of, say, the *Symposium*. The Plotinian influence was present; but when Augustine says that God is known by the soul only to the extent that it knows how much it does *not* know him (*De ord.*, II, 16, 44; II, 18, 47), he means this not in the Plotinian sense of a vision through immediate presence, surpassing knowledge,[22] but in the far more direct sense of a lack of conceptual knowledge, a lack which is to be overcome through rational inquiry. This *docta ignorantia* about God is Socratic, a fitting humility about the extent of one's knowledge preparatory to a cautious and self-critical investigation of the way toward God, step by step; at least that is the spirit of the opening passage of *De quantitate animae*, in which Evodius recalls that Augustine has

[21] Cf. Gérard Verbeke, "Connaissance de soi et connaissance de Dieu chez saint Augustin," *Augustiniana*, IV (1954), pp. 513–515.

[22] Augustine could very well have read *Enn.* VI, 9, 4, or a modified statement of the same theme in Porphyry's *Sentences*, 25 (cf. Solignac in *BA*, XIII, 703); but he does not understand the words as they do.

often warned him away from certain questions by citing the Greek proverb that we should not look into those things that are above us, but suggests that it would not be at all improper to inquire about man's own soul. Augustine was not about to abandon what he had learned from the Academics, then, for they had shown him the frailty of ill-founded assumptions; what he proposed was to surmount their objections through careful argumentation, building a sturdy framework as he moved toward the contemplation of God.

The point of departure is the soul itself, and Augustine shows a special interest in its activity of reasoning. By this he understands not the "verbal" kind of reasoning which manipulates concepts and propositions but a reasoning which involves "insight" into the contents themselves; reasoning is a movement of the mind by which it construes the contents of apprehension, "discerning" where one thing is really distinct from another, "connecting" where there is genuine unity (*De ord.*, II, 11, 30; 18, 48). Now men are able to *use* reason well enough in their worldly affairs, and they are *aware* of their own reasoning activities; but what Augustine seeks is a correct *understanding* of reason, a knowledge of what it is and what it can do, and *this* is the character of the "return to oneself" as Augustine executes it: it is not a purely immediate self-awareness but a reflexive understanding of the self, aided by clear conceptualizations. Only a few men are capable of accomplishing this, for it is a difficult task that demands the use of —reason itself; reason must circle back upon itself and try to discern itself, just as it has discerned the nature of many things other than itself (*De ord.*, II, 11, 30; *De quan. an.*, 14, 24).

Augustine's beginning is quite straightforward, for he is concerned first to analyze the different moments in the reasoning process (*Solil.*, I, 6, 12; *De imm. an.*, 6, 10; *De quan. an.*, 27, 53). Reason, he says, can mean (a) the "eye" of the mind, (b) the mind's "looking" (*adspectus*), its attending to possible contents of knowledge without yet grasping them; (c) the mind's thinking (*ratiocinatio*), the activity of inquiry as it moves among the data, guided by the rules laid down in the science of dialectic, classifying and distinguishing things through definition and partition, separating them with disjunctive propositions and joining them through formal implication (*C. Acad.*, III; *De quan. an.*, 25, 47;

26, 51—27, 52); and finally (d) the completion of the process either in an immediate vision (*intellectus*), a union of the mind with that which is known (this is the Plotinian way of describing it) or, at a lower level, in a "grasping" of something with unshakable conceptual knowledge (*scientia* [and this is the Stoic and Academic way of describing it]).

But at this point Augustine collided with the Academics' contention that nothing can be known with certainty, that nothing can be grasped so unambiguously that it cannot be mistaken for something else (*C. Acad.*, I, 5, 11; III, 9, 18 and 21). He had to refute the Academics because philosophy as he understood it would be pointless if it were merely an *unending search* for truth, as they contended; its goal must be attainable, and the wise man, if he knows nothing else, must know at least wisdom, indeed, the divine Wisdom. It was a matter of some importance to him, therefore, not for theoretical but for personal reasons, for the Academics had set up an obstacle to precisely that enterprise which had now become central to his life (cf. *C. Acad.*, III, 14, 30 and 20, 43; *Ep.* 1, 3; *Retr.*, I, 1).

It is in this atmosphere of expectation, and without looking ahead to the arguments that are brought forward subsequently, that the conversation between Alypius and Augustine early in the third book of *Against the Academics* should be read. Alypius, perhaps baffled by Augustine's hints, still unfulfilled despite much verbal parrying, that he has some arguments to bring forward against the Academics, says that some such argument may come to light, though it seems as elusive as Proteus, and if it should be found it would "demonstrate" ("prove" or "point toward") the truth (*C. Acad.*, III, 5, 11). Augustine gladly picks up the suggestion, and with a certain playful solemnity he agrees that the figure of Proteus, often depicted by the poets, represents Truth itself; for men repeatedly think they have Truth within their grasp, but then it slips away from them like Proteus if they have allowed their thoughts to be led astray by sensory images (*C. Acad.*, III, 6, 13). He refers to the conversation again a few days later (*De ord.*, II, 15, 43), and Proteus is once more a symbol of the divine principle of Number by which our minds measure all things but which escapes our grasp when our attention is drawn to the things that are measured. (The comparison is not Augustine's own; it was a commonplace in Greek philosophical circles, and Augustine learned it from Varro, as the poem of Licentius, appended to Epistle 26 in the editions of Augustine's letters, makes clear.)

But the discussion of Proteus only raises and does not answer the question how truth can be "demonstrated" (*C. Acad.*, III, 5, 12). In answer there is the epiphany of another mysterious figure who, as Augustine repeats in several passages, "promises to demonstrate" this or that divine matter to him (usually the expression is "*se demonstraturam pollicetur*"). She is sometimes divine Reason (*De ord.*, II, 7, 24), sometimes man's own reason (*Solil.*, I, 6, 12), and finally becomes, in the dedication to *Against the Academics*, philosophy (I, 1, 3), which she probably was to begin with, for in the first day of recorded conversation Trygetius tells Licentius that he has thrown off the yoke of authority for the sake of that liberty into which philosophy herself promises to deliver men (*C. Acad.*, I, 3, 9). The source is doubtless Cicero, who with the same vocabulary often speaks of philosophy or reason making promises to men (*Tusc.*, IV, 83 and V, 20; *De fin.*, V, 87). Cicero could not have heard her promise much, for he thought that truth and wisdom could only be pursued, not attained. Augustine had greater confidence about the extent of Reason's promises.

In Augustine's use of the theme it makes little difference whether this personification is divine or human reason, for in any case the goal is a knowledge of divine things, and on the other hand the whole procedure is executed by human reason. This last assertion, based on the actual character of Augustine's arguments, must be underscored, lest his "Platonism" in this period be misconstrued. Augustine accepts the Stoic and Academic definition of knowledge as a "grasping" of something (*comprehensio*, κατάληψις), and he accepts, furthermore, their criterion of certitude by which knowledge can be recognized: the object must be clearly manifested and must have no features which might lead it to be confused with something else (*C. Acad.*, I, 5, 11; III, 9, 21). With the Academics he criticizes the Stoics for supposing that sensation can yield authentic knowledge; but against the Academics he proposes to show that knowledge is attainable in the sphere of the rational (*C. Acad.*, III, *passim*; *De quan. an.*, 30, 58).

In carrying out his program he makes use of three different arguments:

(a) The first and perhaps the most interesting is an argument based upon the reflexive character of the mind and its activities. The wise man (even as conceived by the Academics, the man engaged in constant inquiry) will know at least the wisdom by which he is wise (*C. Acad.*, III, 3, 5–6); and even if he denies that his wisdom is wisdom, it will be his own wisdom that enables him to say that—and simultaneously refutes him (III, 14, 31). Similarly the Academics' criterion of knowledge, the rule which they follow in their mental operations, will itself be known even if nothing else satisfies it (III, 9, 21). Augustine calls this argument a *complexio*: a statement which includes itself, a definition which is an instance of itself, a designation which also points to itself (III, 9, 21). Perhaps the simplest example is the term "word," which both designates words and is itself a word (cf. *De dialectica*, 5; *De magistro*, 4, 10). But Augustine applies the same pattern to mental acts, presumably on the assumption that the character of words is a fair reflection of the mental acts which they express, for the mind, which is capable of knowing many things, also knows itself; the will, which wills many things, wills its own act of willing. When this pattern of self-inclusion is described by the logical term "*complexio*," it points up an interesting characteristic of at least *some* language about language: even while it stays confined in its function as "second-level" or "reflexive" discourse, it may circle back upon itself and disclose something unexpected about its own character and perhaps about the character of assertions generally.

(b) There is another argument, likewise designed to show that the implications of the Academic position are not what they seem, but this time from *presupposition*. Augustine readily concedes that much of the content of sensation may be mere appearance, but he insists that there would be no dispute if there were *nothing* that "appeared": to speak of false appearances already presupposes that *something* is manifested to us (*C. Acad.*, III, 11, 24). Again, Carneades' principle that in practical matters one can act according to "probability" but without proof (*probatio*) or assent (*approbatio*), or according to "versimilitude" but without any expectation of knowing the truth itself, already presupposes that there *is* a truth; and the Academics themselves have said not that the truth is nonexistent but that it is universally distorted and confused by appearances (*C. Acad.*, II, 5, 12 and 11, 26; III, 18, 40).

(c) In the foregoing arguments Augustine has shown that even the Academics give assent to some propositions and hold them to be true. Now he goes on to show more directly that some things can be known with certitude. He acknowledges that there are many disagreements about the origin and nature of the world; but he surmounts the problem by taking one step backwards and formulating the alternatives in a series of *disjunctive propositions*: either there are many worlds or there is one, and if there are many they are either infinite or finite in number; the disposition of things results either from the intrinsic nature of atoms or from a providence distinct from them; the world either begins in time or it does not; and so on. Similarly a series of connections between propositions (*hypothetical syllogisms*) can be formulated: if there are one and six worlds, there are seven worlds; and so on. We know these purely formal truths whether in our everyday experience we are dreaming or awake, and whether what we call the world can be known or not; and even when it comes to immediate experience we can say many true things, with perfect certitude, about what *seems* to be and how we *feel* (III, 11, 26).

It will be noted that the data for these arguments are taken from the quite concrete activities of the mind in its encounter with the physical world. There are no "timeless contents" like the pure idea of "two" which serve to complicate matters in some of Augustine's later writings. All the instances of certain knowledge come from dialectic, which is, Augustine says, the discipline which he knows best (*C. Acad.*, III, 13, 29). It is perhaps fortunate that his reflections began here, for dialectic, especially in the Stoic form in which, as mediated by Varro, it reached Augustine, was concerned with the rules of relation between propositions, and Augustine was aware of the "hypothetical" character of the *connexio* or hypothetical syllogism (*if* the antecedent is true, that which is implied by it is also true) and of the *disjunctio* (*if* one member is false, the other is true). In the *Soliloquies* dialectic is often described as the discipline which regulates all the other disciplines; it is "true by itself" and is the source of whatever is true in them (*Solil.*, II, 11, 21; 13, 24; 15, 27; 18, 32). But this function belongs to dialectic not because it is identical with divine Truth, nor because all other disciplines are deduced from it, but because of its formal character; it regulates them and makes them genuine disciplines, for the mark of a discipline is its clarity of articulation through the definition and classification of all its parts (*Solil.*, II, 11, 20). The entire argument thus remains within the sphere of human *ratio*, the activity of distinguishing and uniting. No occasion arises for the introduction of a mysterious commerce with the divine. The truth in question is very much within the sphere of the human mind and is not (at least in any *simple* sense) identical with divine Truth. Though it is not under the mind's control (for it is a "rule" according to which the mind ought to operate if it wishes to think well), it is "ingredient" in the mind and dependent upon it to such an extent that Augustine thinks its presence in the mind a decisive proof of the immortality of the soul (*De ord.*, II, 19, 50; *Solil.*, I, 15, 29; II, 13, 24 and 18, 32—19, 33; *De imm. an.*, 1, 1—6, 11).

One may be tempted to suspect that Reason has not fulfilled her promise to disclose God and that Proteus, the divine Truth, has been unmasked as nothing more than the boundlessness of the human spirit. And this seeming failure of the argument should be highlighted lest Augustine be misunderstood, for in fact the context of the argument is an intensely *personal* one: what he seeks is not an inferential proof of God's reality, but a more intimate union with God. The theme of the dialogue *On Order* is that the mind in its reasoning activity of distinguishing and joining *seeks unity* (*De ord.*, II, 18, 48; cf. I, 2, 3): not an understanding of the simplicity of God's nature, attained by negating finite limitations and raising finite perfections to their highest power, but a grasp of the complex unity of the "uni-verse," the intelligible realm held in the divine Understanding, by which the corporeal world, with all its conflicts and divisions, is justly ordered. This seeking of unity is, then, a process of organizing the multiplicity of data of experience into an articulated whole by means of the rational disciplines, presided over by dialectic. It is a "way" toward God not because it proves his reality or clarifies his nature but because by following it the mind is enabled to achieve an increasingly inclusive grasp of rational structures and thereby an identity of content with the divine Understanding; and since this process, though it is "rational" throughout, cannot continue and reach completion unless man internalizes his knowledge and lets it transform his own being, it renders him fit for the intuition of God as the climax toward which it has always been leading him:

All of these things the educated mind continues to consider and discuss within itself.... By degrees it leads itself toward a virtuous life with the certitude of reason; for when one has come to see the power of ordered proportions it will seem unworthy and lamentable to use his knowledge merely for navigation or for playing the harp while his own life goes on aimlessly and is dissonant with vice. When the mind sets itself in order and makes itself harmonious and lovely, it will then dare to look at God [the Spirit?] and the Fountain of all that is true and the Father of Truth. Great God, what those eyes will be! how sound, how suitable, how capable, how constant, how serene, how happy! (*De ord.*, II, 19, 50–51).

A Varronian anagogy terminates in a Plotinian vision.

The same resolution is seen in the *Soliloquies*, where the function of Reason is clarified: she will show him God in the same fashion that the sun is shown to the eyes; that is, beginning with the reflected luminosity of the rational disciplines, and only afterward looking to God, who is its source. Reason "demonstrates" God, it would seem, in the sense that she leads the way and points toward him and then becomes merely the *adspectus*, the attention of the mind as it looks toward God himself. She promises to show him God in the same way that she has shown him the truths of mathematics, that is to say, through an immediate vision in both cases, and she assures him that the difference is not in the kind of knowledge (for in both cases it is an immediate possession) but in the things known (*Solil.*, I, 4, 10—5, 11). Reason herself confesses, however, that she is not always ready to see God: he cannot be shown ("*demonstrari non potest*") to those whose minds are fixed on the concerns of earthly life. If God cannot be shown to man he must be made known in another way, through the authority of revelation; and if the mind in its present condition is unable to see God, it can only trust that it will see him when it is in a better condition (*Solil.*, I, 6, 12).

Thus the assisting role of authority, and of the faith based upon it, makes its appearance along the way envisaged by reason itself. Reason is the medium within which the whole process takes place;

there can be no mistaking that. But reason is not ready for the execution of its task until it is purified by faith and hope and love. When these virtues based on revelation have done their work, reason can go on to complete its own quest, which is not merely to know *about* the truth but to bring man into direct encounter with the Truth itself and thereby to give him the only full and lasting happiness.

CHAPTER 2

Milan, Rome, and Thagaste (387–391)

DURING THE WINTER of 387 Augustine returned to Milan. While he was there he received instruction and was baptized at Easter by Ambrose; but his central concern seems to have been the continuation of his philosophical activities. At Cassiciacum Augustine had manifested nothing but uncertainty about the nature of the soul, and in the dedication of *De beata vita* he entreated Manlius Theodorus to shed some light on this question. Even though he has entered the haven of philosophy, he says, it is still a vast bay, and he does not know where to come ashore in order to reach the life of true happiness (*De beata vita*, I, 5). Courcelle has noted other similarly anguished passages in which Augustine expressed his desire for guidance in this matter by an unnamed "learned and eloquent man" (*Solil.*, II, 12, 26; *De quan. an.*, 33, 70),[1] and one of the more tantalizing questions about Augustine's intellectual development concerns the nature and extent of Theodorus' influence upon him: was it solely through conversation? Or had he completed by this time his work on the soul, mentioned in Claudianus' panegyric? Or did he put the writings of others, perhaps of Porphyry, in Augustine's hands? However it came about, Augustine in Milan became for the first time a follower of Porphyry at those points where the latter disagreed with Plotinus, both in metaphysics and in the understanding of the soul.[2]

---

[1] Courcelle, *Recherches*, pp. 204–210.
[2] Du Roy, *L'Intelligence de la foi en la Trinité*, pp. 185–196.

While he was still in Milan Augustine also began writing a series of textbooks on the liberal disciplines, probably derived almost exclusively from Varro's encyclopedic work on the disciplines, and with the same purpose as Varro, to introduce the soul to the intelligible realm. The remains of this project (*De musica* and a fragmentary *De dialectica*) manifest Augustine's sense of its importance but also his lack of genuine excitement about it and his inability to acquire from the sources available to him an adequate technical knowledge of any of the disciplines.[3] His studies of rhythm were put to good use in his subsequent reflections on the experiencing of time, and his acquaintance with dialectic supplied the data for the theories of knowledge and of signification which he worked out through these years. But his interests and his genius lay in speculation on the great philosophical problems, not in manipulation of the techniques of the preparatory disciplines, and it did not take him long to become aware of that fact.

Perhaps during the summer of 387 he and Monica traveled to Rome, intending to return to Italy. While they were there awaiting passage Monica died suddenly; Augustine prolonged his stay in Rome and while he was there wrote his works *On the Quantity of the Soul*, *On Free Will* (book I and most of book II), and the twin books *On the Morals of the Catholic Church* and *On the Morals of the Manichaeans*. He returned to Africa in 388 and on the estate inherited from his parents set up a community devoted to the *otium philosophandi* and to the more personal task of purification and contemplation.[4] From this period come the commentary on Genesis against the Manichaeans, the sixth book of *On Music*, *On the Teacher*, *On True Religion*, and many of the short discussions "on various questions," perhaps the first fifty.

Augustine's writings from these years are devoted, then, to polemic against the Manichaeans, to direct investigation of philosophical problems, and increasingly to the understanding of the Catholic faith. It is a time of vigorous reflection, of elaborating and consolidating the scattered convictions and insights evoked by his reading in a variety of philosophical traditions. For sheer

[3] See Marrou's rather severe estimate, based on an acquaintance with the best of Hellenistic culture, in *Saint Augustin et la fin de la culture antique*, pp. 247–248.

[4] See Georges Folliet, "'Deificari in otio.' Augustin, Epistula 10, 2," *RA*, II (1962), pp. 225–236, for the varied sources of his program.

intellectual stimulation these writings are perhaps Augustine's most engaging, for there is an attempt to work problems through carefully, taking account of the data of experience. This is especially true of his investigation of the nature of "soul," to which we shall turn first.

1. Psyche

After his first speculations in the sketches *On the Immortality of the Soul*, written in Milan, Augustine seems to have decided upon a slower and more painstaking analysis of the nature of soul. I shall employ terms like "soul," "psyche," "life," "mind," in their abstract or generic form as a designation for a wide range of sensory and conative activities, for this is in keeping not only with the phenomenological method of modern philosophy (with which Augustine's own procedures have a certain similarity) but with the usage of ancient philosophy itself. Plotinus and Porphyry often speak of soul without using the definite article, and see it as infinitely varied in its forms of expression, though always as deployments of the one World Soul. Even more to the point, Varro transmitted to Augustine a theory of ordered degrees of vitality or soul, reaching from the simplest plants to animal life and the human mind, derived from Aristotle and Theophrastus and probably reworked by Antiochus or Posidonius.[5] Thus Augustine was confronted with a tradition very much at odds with the Pythagorean and neo-Platonist influences upon him, and he was doubtless stimulated to do his own thinking about the matter. We should remember, furthermore, that Augustine also felt the force of the Academics' critique of knowledge and would not be disposed to talk loosely about entities merely supposed to exist. Something like a phenomenological method was suggested to Augustine in giving his answer to the Academics ("whatever it is that contains and sustains us, this is what I call the world" [*C. Acad.*, III, 11, 24]; "whether we are dreaming or awake, we know with perfect certitude what *seems* to be and how we *feel*" [*C. Acad.*, III, 11, 26]). In his discussions of soul he makes much use of the immediate awareness of life, feeling, and thought, and

[5] Theiler, *Vorbereitung des Neuplatonismus*, p. 54; Zepf, "Augustinus und das philosophische Selbstbewusstsein der Antike," pp. 114–115, n. 45.

in fact he takes these immediate data of consciousness to be not merely a "symptom" of an underlying entity but the self-transparent reality as such.

At one point in his anxious inquiries about the nature of the human soul Augustine states the problems: "what the soul can do *in the body*, what *in itself*, what *before God*" (*De quan. an.*, 33, 70). We would do well to begin with the first and not move too hastily to the others, for a large part of his analyses (located chiefly in *De quantitate animae* and *De musica*, VI) concern those aspects of soul which man shares with other animals.

His point of departure is a definition of sensation drawn from Plotinus (*Enn.* IV, 3, 23 and 26): it is an awareness of something that is undergone by the body ("*non latere animam quod patitur corpus*" [*De quan. an.*, 23, 41], or "*passio corporis non latens animam*" [*ibid.*, 25, 48]). Then he gives an excellent demonstration in logic as he sets about examining this definition; he asks whether it is in keeping with all the instances which we usually assume to fall under the term, and, conversely, whether only these particulars fall under the definition: in other words, whether the intension and the extension of the definition coincide (*De quan. an.*, 25, 47). He points out that some things undergone by the body—growth, for example—do not lie within the scope of sensation, but that we can become aware of growth in another way, through reasoning about what is given in sensation. He modifies the definition, then, so that it will exclude all such indirect kinds of awareness: sensation is an *immediate and inward* awareness of what is undergone by the body ("*passio corporis per seipsam* [not *per aliud*] *non latens animam*" [*De quan. an.*, 25, 48]). This definition covers not only the five kinds of external sensation but all that we mean by "feeling": sickness, desire, fear, joy (*ibid.*, 23, 41).

With this definition in mind, we may begin at the lowest reaches of awareness and move upward by degrees, considering them in order and observing Augustine's own classifications as they are worked out here and there.[6]

(a) *Feeling*. Augustine's basic understanding of pleasure and pain and the other emotions probably comes through Varro from

[6] The following "key" will help to correlate my own discussion with his two most important classifications:

older Greek sources.[7] The soul in animating the body seeks a harmonious balance of all its parts (*ordinata temperatura partium*), and pain is the awareness of some disturbance of this balance, pleasure of its restoration. Now it is undeniable that material occurrences, external or internal, are the occasion for this psychic feeling. But Augustine rejects the common-sense language which suggests that psyche is subjected to the influence of material occurrences. In a passage introduced with some solemnity he works out an alternative way of speaking: psyche is indeed related to physical occurrences, but always in the mode of noticing, responding to, or attending to changes in bodily state ("*non latent*," "*fit attentior*," "*se accommodat corpori*," etc.). Thus a "passive" disturbance of bodily equilibrium evokes an "active" psychic feeling of pain, pleasure, hunger, satiation, nausea, sickness (*De mus.*, VI, 5, 8). When there is a state of equilibrium in the body psychic feeling is not absent, but it "lounges" ("*iacet*" [*De quan. an.*, 30, 59], "*vegetat*" [*De mus.*, VI, 5, 11]); the equilibrium of the body furnishes a ground-tone against which any physical disturbance can be quickly noted so that an appropriate psychic response can issue forth. But in either case, whether there is harmony or dissonance in the bodily state, the "feeling" is not directly a feeling of the physical state but the immediate awareness of a specific *psychic reaction* to it. The animating action which

		De quan. an., 35, 79	*De mus.*, VI
(a)	feeling		
		animatio, actio de corpore	
(b)	action		
(c)	sensory pleasure		*numeri occursores*
		sensus, actio per corpus	
(d)	intentionality		*numeri recordabiles*
(e)	projects		*numeri progressores*
		ars, actio circa corpus	
(f)	artistry		*numeri judiciales* or *sensuales*
(g)	rational judgment		*numeri moderatores* or *exploratores*
(h)	virtue	*virtus, actio ad seipsam*	
(i)	contemplation	*tranquilitas, actio in seipsa*	
		ingressio, actio ad Deum	
		contemplatio, actio apud Deum	

[7] For an extended discussion of passages in Augustine's writings and parallels in antiquity, see Fuchs, *Augustin und der antike Friedensgedanke*, pp. 143-144.

supplies the ground-tone now feels itself exerted somewhat differently because of the changes undergone in the body (*De mus.*, VI, 5, 11). What all of this suggests, then, is that the most elementary task of "soul," perhaps its essential character, is quite simply the establishing and maintaining of *unity* or *harmony*, in the body or wherever else its sphere of responsibility extends (*De ord.*, II, 18, 48; *De ver. rel.*, 41, 77; *De lib. arb.*, III, 23, 69–70). But Augustine does not assent to the suggestion of some ancient philosophers that psyche is simply equivalent with the harmonious functioning of the body. His argument against it, based on Plotinus (*Enn.* IV, 3, 20), is that a harmony is "in" that which is harmonized, as an attribute is "in" a substance, while soul has a being of its own; that is to say, it is an irreducible fact of experience which must be explained in its own terms and not in terms of changes of bodily state (cf. *De imm. an.*, 2, 2). It is, at the very least, a kind of co-ordinated striving after harmony in bodily state and a reaction against any disturbance of that harmony.

(b) *Action.* Once there is feeling there is action as well. Augustine does not attempt to give soul credit for *everything* that takes place in an action; he gives it a carefully delimited role *alongside* physical processes, as can be seen from his analysis of bodily strength (*De quan. an.*, 22, 38–40). Strength cannot consist merely in bodily weight, for a small man who is well trained can overturn a much heavier man. The muscular system, then, is also important, and its good health and careful training enter into physical ability. But finally psychic elements—attitudes of courage or fear, hopefulness or despair—make their appearance as a factor in what we call strength, not by some occult influence of mind over matter but quite simply by furnishing an inclination (*nutus*) in some definite direction. Thus there is a cooperation of psychic attitude, the leverage of the muscular system, and sheer corporeal bulk. The data upon which Augustine draws are those which man has in common with quite primitive animals, for the psychic factor involved here is not know-how or craftiness, but the same phenomenon of "feeling" which has just been analyzed on its receptive side. But here feeling transcends the mere changes of physical state not only with an awareness of what has been undergone but in addition with a nisus, conveyed to the motor system, toward pursuit or rest or flight.

(c) *Sensory pleasure*. Sensation, as Augustine points out in a number of passages concerning aesthetic experience, may involve a pure sensory pleasure which lies at a more elemental level than the attending to external things which we usually mean by sensation. What gives pleasure to the eyes and ears is not the intrinsic character of the thing seen or heard, for sensory pleasure is indifferent to that. The pleasure comes from the balance of the very colors or sounds that strike the sensory organs: not from their color or sound as such, for these taken singly may be unpleasant or dull, but from their structures and patterns and intensities. Sensory pleasure, then, is a kind of feeling based upon a bodily state induced from without, by colors or sounds that "come to" the sensory organs (Augustine regularly uses terms like "*obiicere*," "*occurrere*," "*accidere*"). But it could not arise unless there were already a readiness in the animate body for certain kinds of stimuli and a capacity for a natural and quite unreflective exercise of "judgment" or "evaluation"; only this can explain the fact that feelings of approval or disapproval will arise spontaneously as colors or sounds enhance or disturb the equilibrium of the sensory organs (note especially in the discussion of *numeri occursores* in *De mus.*, VI, 2, 3).

(d) *Intentionality*. In vision we somehow "feel" another body that is located elsewhere than the feeling itself (*De quan. an.*, 23, 44; 30, 59–60). Augustine's descriptions of this paradoxical fact have usually led interpreters to take him literally when he suggests that in vision there is a radiation of light from the eyes. But he is simply attempting to state the phenomenon of intentionality or (in Whitehead's even darker language) transmutation: what we "see" is the thing in the distance, though we know very well that the immediate occasion of our seeing is the impact of light rays on the retina. To be sure, Augustine uses words like "*lustrare*" or "*collustrare*" (*De quan. an.*, 14, 24; 23, 43)—but their meaning is simply "to survey"; or words like "*emicare*" (*De quan. an.*, 23, 43; *De mus.*, VI, 8, 21; *De Gen. ad litt.*, XII, 16, 32)—but its meaning is simply "to dart forth." Any naïve way of construing his understanding of vision will stumble over his theory of sensory images, for he points out that we can see or imagine or remember vast expanses even though the physical organs involved are very small (*De quan. an.*, 14, 23–24; *Conf.*, X, 8, 12–15). And Augustine is quite capable of speaking unparadoxically and saying that sight (*visus*, the act of looking or attending), even while remaining where it is, directs itself outward to the place where the other thing is (*De quan. an.*, 23, 43). His inability to arrive at an unequivocal formulation comes in part from the difficulty of describing intentionality at all, and in part from the fact that he wants to say something quite specific about it: that it is not a two-stage process of physical reception and psychic projection but an integral union of the two in which the psychic side takes priority. Light rays are always striking the body, but we do not always see them; even when they strike the retina the eyes may still be "unseeing," as we say, if attention has lapsed. It is the same with hearing, as Augustine himself points out (*De mus.*, VI, 8, 21). The crucial factor, then, is attention; this is what enables us to "feel" not our own bodily states but something other than ourselves.

In vision attention is directed toward a field of space and toward focal points within it; in hearing it spans a period of time with the aid of memory, so that the consciousness is "extruded" (*De mus.*, VI, 8, 21) or "distended" (*Conf.*, XI, 26, 33). In both cases Augustine uses the metaphor of "illumination," and what he has in mind is the unifying of the data of sensation within the forms of space and time so that they can be construed as an organized whole; it is only when these data are held by unbroken attention within a single field that they can be "articulated" in meaningful patterns and scanned by the more sovereign eye of reason (*De mus.*, VI, 8, 21). Augustine assumes, by the way, that our measurements of all quantities of space and time are not absolute but *ad aliquid*, always on the basis of our perception of proportions which would remain the same even if the whole pattern were to be expanded or contracted.

Proportion is ingredient in the physical world itself, to be sure; but its apprehension requires a high level of organizing ability (*De mus.*, VI, 7, 19). Because of his Platonism (of both the orthodox and the Academic variety) and because of the incisiveness of his own analyses Augustine was aware of the fragmentary character of spatiotemporal occurrence with an intensity paralleled perhaps only by Whitehead. Purely physical occurrences are drawn tight in the net of localization; they are connected only by immediate contiguity or succession. This isolation is transcended first by corporeal form or proportion (*De imm. an.*, 7, 12—8, 13; *De quan. an.*, 17, 29), which transforms a mere accumulation of matter into a unified "body"; then by life, and the self-awareness of feeling, and the other-awareness of external sensation. But this transcendence of the conditions of space and time is never absolute, for soul always has the task of animating and directing corporeal bodies. Though soul is not "in" the body and is not "contained" in any "place," it is not similarly exempt from time. Perhaps the foundation in experience for these assertions is the difference between our transcendence of the limitations of space in vision (and in imagination and visual memory) and our transcendence of the limitations of time in the awareness of duration and sequence. In the former, our attention is able to leap over the intervening spaces and even times; in the latter we remain immersed within the temporal process, and it is only by undergoing our own temporal experiences and synthesizing them through continuing awareness that we are able to "transcend" time at all. Awareness and attentiveness, we may assume, are essentially the same in both; the difference, then, is rooted in the nature of things and reflects something of the character of life and soul wherever it is found.

(e) *Projects*. Mentality is first exhibited in human practical activity ("making," *poiēsis*, or "doing," *praxis*), in which some plan of action is projected and executed. The paradigm which Augustine usually selects is the recitation of a poem or the delivery of a speech, in which one anticipates what one is going to say and how one is going to say it and then executes it accordingly (see especially the discussion of *numeri progressores* in *De mus.* VI); but the entire realm of human activity and culture is involved. There is an effective sovereignty of the mind over the conditions of bodily life, for a course of action quite different from the immediate situation can be outlined. Nevertheless the action which is envisaged is totally embodied; at this level the mind is concerned only with governing and shaping a sequence of external events. It is an irreducible task of mind within the physical world, but it does not exhaust its potentialities.

(f) *Artistry*. A higher stage in the mind's commerce with matter is in its recognition and appreciation of physical beauty, embodied rationality and order, what he calls in one place the traces or footprints of reason within the world (*De ord.*, II, 11, 31–34). His delimitation of this sphere is accomplished in that passage through a kind of linguistic analysis as he asks what physical things or events we call "reasonable." Clearly we say this of a speech or a painting. But we do not say that a smell or a taste or a texture is reasonable—unless we are speaking of an artifact made to have these characteristics by the skill of a chef or a weaver, sometimes merely for the sake of sensory pleasure, sometimes (especially in the case of the "fine arts") to create a pattern that is intrinsically harmonious and can be enjoyed for itself with a pleasure that is more than an immediate sensory feeling. Indeed, we spontaneously take pleasure in well-structured forms, even though their full appreciation may require training. Therefore he later suggests (*De mus.*, VI, 6, 16—9, 24) that in all human activities there is a spontaneous exercise of aesthetic evaluation: whatever we do, whatever we make, we try to do it with "style." Here something more is involved than the mere carrying out of a plan of action; there is a judging or evaluating of one's own acts not for their effectiveness alone but for the way they are done. This judging, Augustine thinks, can be accomplished only on the basis of intelligible rules which are somehow imprinted on the mind, though often unconsciously, and give it the capability which we call "art" (*De mus.*, VI, 12, 34). Thus the analysis of the phenomena of human activity leads beyond the immediate situation of man's encounter with the world and raises the question of the soul "in itself" and "before God."

In all of these activities, the psychic has not yet "come to itself." Its attention remains directed toward physical occurrences; even in cultural life, despite the creative role of artistry, the concern is chiefly with the shaping of artifacts, whether for technical or for aesthetic purposes. In all these activities, then, the psychic pours itself out in a concern for that which is other than itself and is caught in the net of spatio-temporal occurrences. It is not that these things are intrinsically evil, or that they are alien to the psychic; indeed, its task is to animate and care for them, and in most of its exemplifications the psychic does nothing more than this. But it is capable of something more:

The soul of animals is bound to the body and uses its senses only for satisfying the desires for food and pleasure which are aroused by the body. But the human soul, possessing reason and knowledge, which are far superior to the senses, is able to raise itself above these bodily attachments and enjoy purely inward satisfactions (*De quan. an.*, 28, 54).

It is able to do this as it becomes increasingly less "localized" by concern for the particular set of circumstances that affect the body and comes into closer proximity to the universal perspective of God (*De mus.*, VI, 14, 48). The mind's return to itself is not, however, a simple process that takes place automatically once mind arises. For Augustine the mind *is* as it *thinks* and *acts*. Of course it is always mind, and it is always aware of itself. But its return to itself must be more explicit than that. The sequence which Augustine seems to assume in the writings of this period, especially those concerned with anagogy (*De quantitate animae, De libero arbitrio* II, *De musica* VI), moves from an apprehension of the rational norms by which all activities are judged, to a forming of oneself through virtue on the basis of those norms, then to a complete return to oneself and a "resting" in oneself, and only then to the climactic act of looking toward God (*De quan. an.*, 28, 55).

Aesthetic valuation, as we have seen, is a spontaneous criticism of human actions and works, either in the creative process itself or in subsequent experience of them; but this aesthetic delight is now placed under more explicit scrutiny by reflective reason, not in such a way as to usurp and displace the creative activity of the artist or the critical discernment of the connoisseur, but to accomplish two further tasks: the philosophical one of clarifying the norms of valuation and the ethical one of judging one's own preferences in the light of these rational norms.

(g) *Rational judgment.* Mental activity first begins to look within and above itself in making conscious, reflective judgments about finite things. Augustine does not think that corporeal things are "known," in the proper sense of the word, by the senses; in *De quan. an.*, 26, 49–51, he sets up the sequence *sensus-ratiocinatio-scientia*. This does not mean that either corporeal things or the senses "deceive"; sense is often the occasion of error, but the error occurs only because the mind has interpreted and judged sense incorrectly (*De ver. rel.*, 33, 61—34, 63; 36, 67). The possibility of mistaken judgment arises from the lack of perfect adjustment between the two components of rational knowledge: the physical world is dispersed by space and time, and whatever order and unity it has are eked out in the midst of a rich variety of occurrences, constantly changing; the mind seeks intelligible unities and is tempted to make premature and oversimplified judgments about the physical universe. Augustine's stock example (and it is a good one) was inherited from the Academics: an oar dipped in water appears to be bent. He knows that this phenomenon is to be explained in terms of physical occurrences: air and water are of different densities and somehow affect light differently (*De ver. rel.*, 33, 62). The bending of light rays and the subsequent reception of them by the eye simply *are what they are*, a train of occurrences in physical reality. Difficulties arise only when a psychic element enters the picture. The intentionality of sensation attempts to transcend this complex and sometimes distorted flow of physical occurrences by projecting an external continuum of space or extruding an internal continuum of time, within which to construe sense impressions in a pattern which will interpret the broader environment to the organism. In general it works well; but in cases like this one, in which the propagation of light has been affected by some complex interactions, sensory intentionality is misleading.

The aim of judgment is *truth*—a correspondence or adequation of thought and language to reality, "saying what is the case"— and the corresponding problem is that of *error*. Something like truth is already present in a minimal way in immediate feeling, for there is a certain mirroring of the physical by the psychic; but there is no problem of error because interpretation is not required. One simply feels chilly or happy or sick (*C. Acad.*, III, 11, 26). But when external sensation arises, the contents of awareness present themselves as the manifestation or appearance (*apparere, videri*) of something beyond the percipient. The experience can still be described solely in terms of feeling, that is, in terms of subjective states alone: "I *seem* to see something white" (*ibid.*). If that were all there is to it, the matter could be left there; truth would be easy to come by. But Augustine does not think that we mean to speak merely of our subjective states. External sensation, unlike immediate feeling, is concerned with the environment and not with states of the organism and psychic reactions to them. It suggests to us that there is not mere "seeming," but *something that appears*. And the very fact that self-critical reason is able to see that appearances may lead to mistaken judgment presupposes a concern for the *reality* that appears (*C. Acad.*, III, 11, 24).

It is to be noted that Augustine's chief question is not *whether* there is a reality that appears, but *what* reality it is that appears, its actual character and its similarity to or difference from the appearances. When he uses the term "judgment," then, he is using it primarily with reference to essence, not existence, and modern Thomists, who have perhaps an exaggerated interest in the latter, should not misunderstand him. When we judge that a visual configuration is a tree, and that it is a real tree (*Solil.*, II, 15, 28), or that a pattern of sounds is iambic tetrameter (*De mus.*, VI, 7, 19), or that several figures of different size and texture are all squares (*De ver. rel.*, 30, 56), or that a square is a better balanced figure than a lozenge (*De quan. an.*, 9, 14ff.), or that the stage show which so pleasingly depicts Venus and Cupid is nonetheless immoral (*De ord.*, II, 11, 34), we are judging on the basis of norms: a definition of "tree," a criterion of reality, a standard of equality or proportion, a norm of right and wrong. The role of these rational norms is precisely delimited. They are not the sole source of knowledge, though to know them is to know something important; sensory experience is also needed for knowledge of the realm of contingency. But rational norms are the criteria by which such knowledge is attained; they are not alien to the realm of contingency, but they are, on the contrary, most pertinent to it, for they make it understood clearly for the first time and (in the case of scientific explanation and prediction) enable inferences to be made from one event to another.

There is nothing mysterious about the rational disciplines as such. They consist in human conceptions, definitions, and classifications, derived from reflection on the data of culture and natural history. In order to understand them one need have no commerce (at least in any obvious way) with an intelligible realm hidden in God. Platonism as Augustine encountered it was very far from the naïve visualization it is often thought to be. Probably from Antiochus and Varro he learned that the norms of judgment do not have size and are not picturable in any other way. The criteria by which triangularity, or a proportion of two to one, or a dactylic rhythm, or a logical entailment are judged cannot be visualized, though they *can* be verbalized more or less adequately, usually according to a law prescribing certain mental operations. From the Pythagorean Nicomachus of Gerasa he learned that even numbers, which seem to be ostensive, are generated from unity according to laws of multiplication, series, and the like (*De ord.*, II, 15, 43; *De lib. arb.*, II, 8, 22-24; *De mus.*, VI, 17, 56).

Nevertheless Augustine also pressed the question of the provenance of these norms of judgment and the metaphysical grounding of rational activity. His answer, worked out only gradually, was given first in terms of a kind of innatism or subjective idealism according to which the soul itself is the ground of intelligibles (*Solil.*, II, 18, 32—19, 33; *De imm. an.*, 1, 1—6, 11); then in terms of the old Platonist and Ciceronian (cf. *Tusc.*, I, 58) theory that all learning is somehow recollection (*De quan. an.*, 20, 34); and finally in terms of illumination of the mind by a light constantly present to it (*De lib. arb.*, II; *De mag.*, 11, 38ff.). [8]

Just what Augustine meant by illumination has been a matter of controversy since the Middle Ages. Four basic options can easily be differentiated: (1) the "Avicennan," first put forward by Gundissalinus and William of Auvergne and other early disciples of Avicenna in the West, which sees the divine Word functioning as the *dator formarum*, the separate agent intellect which supplies intelligible species to the mind on the occasion of sensation—an interpretation which can cite numerous passages in which Augustine speaks of an illumination or imprintation of the mind[9]; (2) the "ontologist," according to which all intelligibles are known "in God" through an immediate vision of God himself—an interpretation which can cite those passages in which understanding is called a seeing and the object of this vision is said to be the *rationes* within God's mind[10]; (3) the "Thomist," for which illumination is nothing else than the creation of the

---

[8] For the development of Augustine's views, see especially Johannes Hessen, *Augustins Metaphysik der Erkenntnis*, 2. Aufl. (Leiden, 1960) and Franz Körner, "Die Entwicklung Augustins von der Anamnesis- zur Illuminationslehre im Lichte seines Innerlichkeitsprinzips," *Theologische Quartalschrift*, CXXXIV (1954), pp. 397-447.

[9] This is the interpretation of Portalié in his article on Augustine in the *DTC*, I, 2, cols. 2334-37.

[10] This is the interpretation of the *early* Hessen in *Die Begründung der Erkenntnis nach dem hl. Augustinus* (Münster, 1916).

human mind with its ability to confer intelligibility upon the contents of sensation—an interpretation which can cite those passages in which Augustine, on the basis of Romans 1, 20, says that the invisible things of God are glimpsed through visible things[11]; and (4) the only one which seems fully defensible to me, the "Bonaventuran," which attempts to think through the problem as Augustine saw it and recognizes that he was concerned not primarily with "ideogenesis" (the origin of ideas in the mind, whether by implantation or by vision or by the activity of man's own agent intellect) but with the validity of our judgments and the regulating authority under which our minds act.[12]

When we examine carefully all the things Augustine says about understanding, we find that there are three "moments" to the process. The first is the being of the mind itself, and Augustine calls it *lux creata* (*C. Faust.*, XX, 7) because it is aware of its own rationality and freedom. The mind has reached the limits of the finite; it must either look above itself or become its own master. Considered by itself, it has the capacity for either, and it can succeed to a certain extent in closing itself off and living autonomously. But this is a blind venture, for the mind is by its nature brought into relation with the realm of intelligibles common to all; repeatedly Augustine's formula is that the mind is naturally "connected" to them and "subjected" to their authority (*De lib. arb.*, III, 5, 13; *De Trin.*, XII, 15, 24; *Retr.*, I, 8, 2). The second moment, then, is illumination itself, described with a variety of terms but always in such a way as to suggest the *immediacy* of understanding: it is insight into what is conveyed through words, knowledge by a kind of immediate acquaintance (*nosse*, *notio*), best described with the metaphor of vision; and that which is seen or understood is somehow *present* within or above the mind, touching it (*tangens*), speaking to it (*narrans*), accosting it (*obiectans*), illuminating it (*illustrans*), putting its imprint on it (*imprimens*, *sigillans*). But this immediate acquaintance is not all there is to

[11] This is the interpretation of Charles Boyer in *L'Idée de vérité dans la philosophie de saint Augustin* (Paris, [1]1920; [2]1940), and Fulbert Cayré in *La contemplation augustinienne* (Paris, 1927; 1954).

[12] This is the interpretation of Etienne Gilson in *The Christian Philosophy of St. Augustine* (New York, 1960); Régis Jolivet, *Dieu soleil des esprits, ou la doctrine augustinienne de l'illumination* (Paris, 1934); and Frederick Copleston, *A History of Philosophy*, II (Westminster, Md., 1950), pp. 59–67.

understanding. It gives rise to an activity of thinking (*cogitatio*) within the mind, and the outcome is conceptualization, the shaping of explicit formulations which, at their best, come to have the accuracy and detail of the rational disciplines; these conceptualizations can then be held in consciousness and memory in a way that immediate insight cannot (see especially *De Trin.*, XII, 14, 23). Thus there is a difference between understanding and conceptualizing, between "knowing" and "thinking," between "seeing" and "saying" (*De Trin.*, XV, 10, 19), and only the former belongs to the still rather mysterious moment called illumination.

What makes Augustine's theory of knowledge different from Thomism, with its identification of illumination with the creation of the light of the agent intellect, is *not* that it views illumination as the imprinting of *specific* ideas and rules, but that the mind is seen as constantly responsible before a supreme authority over all its thoughts and judgments and as somehow aware of the presence of this authority as the ground of their validity. The final authority which governs the mind is neither the flux of phenomena (positivism, phenomenalism) nor the historical process (dialectical materialism, pragmatism) nor the mind itself (existentialism, constructivism) nor the principles of reason (idealism)—though any or all of these may play a supporting role—but God himself. This need not mean that all knowledge is based immediately upon God. Augustine, even while he acknowledges that the philosophers have been able to show that all temporal occurrences result from eternal ideas and have been able to gain a knowledge of, say, the genera and species of animals that approximates to the content of those ideas, *denies* that they have gained such knowledge from any direct inspection of the divine ideas; it has come from nothing more exalted than a careful description and classification of empirical facts (*De Trin.*, IV, 16, 21). It is clear even from the earliest writings in which illumination is asserted that it is found on a sliding scale, and Augustine, obviously aware of the difficulties that this admission involves, compares illumination to the radiation from a fire: a fire's light can be seen at some distance, but its heat can be felt only near by; similarly the understanding of number is widespread among men but those who are ready to draw near to the divine Wisdom are rare (*De lib. arb.*, II, 11, 32). And on the way between the one and the other, men may have some awareness of what wisdom and happiness are before attaining them (*ibid.*, II, 9, 26 and 15, 40), and they may understand something of the "rules and guiding lights of the virtues" without being virtuous (*ibid.*, II, 10, 28–29). Illumination at its minimal and most surreptitious level, then, may be experienced as nothing more than a sense of responsibility before higher norms, or a sense of certitude about the validity of one's knowledge and judgments, or even a hesitant *questioning after* their validity (we may recall Tillich, to whom the question about an ultimate ground of meaning itself testifies to an awareness of that ground,[13] and Augustine at least once [*De ver. rel.*, 39, 73] anticipated Tillich's insight).

What makes this theory of knowledge unmistakably Augustinian rather than Thomist is that some intuition of God (perhaps only a "contuition," as Bonaventura put it, in and with the activity of thinking about and evaluating finite things) is seen as an irreducible element in inquiry and judgment and certitude. And this awareness of God does not enter merely as a question about the *cause* of being or certitude or value, *after* they have been affirmed on other grounds; they can be affirmed only *on the basis of* this apprehension of God, dim and unexamined though it may be. Where Thomas says that God is known implicitly in all knowledge of finite things and loved implicitly in all willing of finite values, Augustine would say that they are known and willed in God. The neo-Thomism of Maréchal and Rahner and Lonergan, which makes similar affirmations, is in this crucial respect far more Augustinian or Bonaventuran than it is Thomist; if it has any basis in Aquinas himself, it is not in those passages in which Aquinas set himself in opposition to his contemporaries but in those in which he employed their language and was perhaps influenced more than he thought by their assumptions. I suspect that Karl Rahner, as he has gone on to develop a theory of grace as the immediate illumination of human existence and then an entire metaphysic based on this new insight, has become Augustinian rather than Thomist. It is a rather astounding testimony to the modern relevance of Augustine, then, that his insights are

---

[13] See especially his programmatic essay, "The Two Types of Philosophy of Religion," *Union Seminary Quarterly Review*, I (1946), 3–13, reprinted in *Theology of Culture* (New York, 1959), pp. 10–29.

called into service by many of those philosophers who have felt most deeply the force of the critique of knowledge and many of those theologians who have reflected most thoroughly upon the character of human existence.

(h) *Virtue.* The discovery of the intelligible world of the rational disciplines and of ethical reflection bears fruit, Augustine thinks, only as man discovers that his own value is superior to that of the whole corporeal world, turns within, and seeks himself. He has a certain obligation to himself: he must "give himself back to himself" (*De quan. an.*, 28, 55) by forsaking other things and resting within himself. This is not a self-centered enterprise, an end in itself; it is mentioned only as a stage on the way toward God. It is nonetheless an indispensable stage, for the soul's likeness to God must be restored and safeguarded as the only instrument by which God can be apprehended. Augustine's stress on tranquility and cessation of activity (*De quan. an.*, 28, 55 and 35, 79; *De mus.*, VI, 5, 14; *De ver. rel.*, 35, 65) is reminiscent of the exhortation of Plotinus (*Enn.* V, 1, 2) that the soul, freed from errors and seductions, be silent so that it might then look beyond itself; and the beautification of the soul through virtue, which leads up to this goal (*De quan. an.*, 35, 79), corresponds to Plotinus' image of the forming of a statue by chipping away the excess, straightening what is crooked, and bringing light where there has been shadow (*Enn.* I, 6, 9).

This ideal human state is not disembodied, nor is it a state of pure inwardness, blocking out the body and its needs. Augustine's language sometimes sounds almost like that of a Christian Scientist, or rather (since he has a more robust sense of the reality of the body) like that of a Yogi or a practitioner of psychosomatic medicine. The more man's psychic life is freed from its concern to satiate the desires of the body and its anxiety over the stormy affairs of the world, the more relaxed it becomes, and it transmits a healthier life to the body it rules, presumably by letting all the bodily functions and sensory activities go along naturally, with their proper equilibrium and without interference from the misdirected concerns and anxieties of the spirit (*De mus.*, VI, 5, 13). The goal for this kind of neo-Platonism is not pure spirituality but a multi-dimensional psychic life, letting each aspect go its own way but drawing all together under the guidance of overarching rational purposes. It is not so much an abandoning of the changeable world as a shifting of the point of view, so that the mind gains a balanced perspective and is no longer submerged within that which is localized and always changing.

It is true that such insouciance is difficult to achieve in the face of death, danger, and disease; and Augustine assumes that these hazards belong to man's present condition, for the soul, which was created perfect and with an incorruptible body, sinned through its own free choice and has fallen into the miseries of hardship and mortality as an appropriate penalty (*De lib. arb.*, II, 11, 23—12, 24; *De mus.*, VI, 11, 33; *De ver. rel.*, 20, 38). Such views, commonplace in Platonist circles, were reinforced and given a certain ecclesiastical authority by some writings of Origen which Augustine probably acquired while in Rome. In his interpretation of the "tunics of skin" made for Adam and Eve on their expulsion from Paradise, Augustine takes up the suggestion of Origen (found in his sixth homily on Leviticus, translated by Rufinus) that the expression symbolizes the transmutation of the human body from an incorruptible to a mortal state: because pelts are taken from dead animals, they are an appropriate figure for the mortality and frailty of the body (*De Gen. c. Man.*, II, 21, 32).[14] The resurrection of the body is understood, consequently, as a restitution of its original integrity (*De ver. rel.*, 15, 29; 16, 32; 23, 44; 41, 77; 53, 103), and this means that it is changed from "flesh and blood" into an ethereal body and transported from earth to the heavens (*De fid. et symb.*, 10, 24). Quite naturally Augustine assumed that men before the fall would have no need of sensible media to receive communications from God (*De Gen. c. Man.*, II, 4, 5; *De mus.*, VI, 4, 7); but this does not mean that they would have no use for sensation at all, for it is the normal means of commerce between finite beings. Imagination, fantasy, is, however, the result of mortality (*De mus.*, VI, 11, 33). Augustine also assumes, as he will for many years to come, that sexuality is the result of the fall into mortality, as are all the relationships of domination and submission and all the bonds of special affection

---

[14] Jean Pépin, "Saint Augustin et le symbolisme néo-platonicienne de la vêture," *AM*, I, 293–306; Berthold Altaner, "Augustinus und Origenes. Eine quellenkritische Untersuchung," *Historisches Jahrbuch*, LXX (1951), pp. 26–28 (*KpS*, pp. 236–238).

in the family and society (*De mus.*, VI, 13, 41; *De ver. rel.*, 46, 88). But these beliefs should not be exaggerated or misinterpreted; they are not the projections of neurotic emotion but the conclusions reached by a particular line of philosophical reasoning, and they represent not a total distrust of the body but a carefully focused speculation on the range of its possible states, based on the sometimes hasty judgments of ancient science.

Augustine acknowledges, then, that the man of virtue must contend permanently, while he is living on earth, with the hazards of mortality; he also thinks that "carnal custom," the soul's familiarity with the desires of the flesh, is more easily acquired than overcome (*De mus.*, VI, 5, 14 and 11, 33). Thus there is already a certain Pauline sense of struggle and "eschatological tension." But Augustine is confident that carnal custom, though it cannot be abolished, can be overcome by virtue. Since he gives more extended attention to the vices than to the virtues, and since in any case the way back toward virtue must retrace the way traveled toward vice, we may devote some attention at this point to Augustine's analysis of the vices.

He regularly classifies them according to a tripartite scheme: carnal desire, pride, and curiosity (*De mor.*, I, 19, 36—21, 38; *De Gen. c. Man.*, I, 23, 40; II, 17, 26—18, 27 and 26, 40; *De mus.*, VI, 13, 39–41; *De ver. rel.*, 38, 69—55, 107). Their sequence is based upon the different levels of human activity at which man's development is, so to speak, arrested. Concupiscence is an inordinate concern with bodily feelings, sometimes even a perverse stimulation of desire in order to have more intense and pleasurable feelings. Man slips into it by paying too much attention to the constant change of feeling that is evoked in the course of terrestrial life, and the outcome is that he prefers "care" to "freedom from care" ("*praeponens curam securitati*" [*De mus.*, VI, 5, 14]). Pride as Augustine depicts it during this period is not the deeply subjective and "spiritual" sin that it is usually made in modern discussions of the vices; it is simply the pomp and vain glory of the world, *gloria popularis* (*De mor.*, I, 21, 38). What makes it a "perverse imitation of God," then, is not simply the element of independence but the far more definite desire to rule over all things (*De ver. rel.*, 45, 84). It arises from the wish to appear outwardly to be what one is not (*De Gen. c. Man.*, II, 5, 6), or, even more subtly, from a "love of action" (*De mus.*, VI, 13, 40), for there may come to be a fascination with the struggle itself, apart from any concrete results. The third vice of curiosity is an excessive concern with gaining knowledge of the natural world (especially through astrology) or of the heritage of human culture, but without self-criticism or a genuine desire for understanding, and once more the consequence is that the mind comes to be dominated by sense and imagination (*De Gen. c. Man.*, II, 26, 40).

These three vices are linked from the first (cf. *De mor.*, I, 21, 39) with a biblical passage, I John 2, 16, which speaks of "the lust of the flesh, the lust of the eyes, and the ambition of this world"; but the order followed at first is not the biblical, but one corresponding to the Platonist division of the soul into the appetitive, the irascible, and the rational functions. This suggests, then, that Augustine may have derived them from some philosopher, and Porphyry is the usual nominee.[15] What makes me hesitate to ascribe this list of vices to any neo-Platonist, however, is that it is quite out of keeping with the more subjective focus of the later school; the description of the vices and even the language used (especially in the first discussion in *De moribus*) would seem to be more in keeping with an older Platonist like Varro, living in the golden age of the Republic.[16] They have no integral relationship with the neo-Platonist conception of the origin of sin; Augustine must gradually work that out for himself. In the process he has great difficulty deciding which of them is the chief vice that gives rise to sin, and he ascribes priority to first one and then another. Finally he recognizes that all three vices, as he had described them, only explain the sins that occur in man's commerce with the sensory realm (*De ver. rel.*, 38, 69). In order to account for the dynamics of sin and return he begins to utilize a new theme, and this time it is genuinely neo-Platonist (cf. *Enn.* VI, 5, 12; *Sent.*, 41 [Mommert 40]): one should not say to himself, "I am this and not

[15] Theiler, *Porphyrios und Augustin*, pp. 37ff.; du Roy, *L'Intelligence de la foi en la Trinité*, p. 344, n. 3. For the most recent discussion of the problem and its literature, see du Roy, pp. 343–352.

[16] For parallels in the political literature of the Republic and early Empire, as well as later times, see Endre von Ivánka, "Römische Ideologie in der 'Civitas Dei,'" *AM*, III, 414–415. Ivánka goes on to indicate how such themes could have come through Porphyry, but he acknowledges that the evidence is not compelling.

that," for the grasping of a *part* leads to alienation from the *whole* and dispersal in the realm of the material; in order to return to God one should remove this sense of differentiation and become rejoined with the whole (*De ver. rel.*, 55, 112). It is not surprising, then, that Augustine comes to change his interpretation of the vices and their sequence, partly, perhaps, through the influence of a text like Ecclesiasticus 10, 14–15, which calls pride the beginning of sin (first quoted in *De mus.*, VI, 13, 40), but partly through the logic of this neo-Platonist phenomenology of part and whole. Whatever the cause, at some time between 390 and 395 he came to consider pride a turning to one's own good, curiosity a turning to external goods, and concupiscence a turning to inferior goods (*De lib. arb.*, II, 19, 53). It was only then that the typically "Augustinian" doctrine of the vices and their development began to take shape.[17]

Like the movement away from God, the movement back toward God is a change not of place but of affection (*De mor.*, I, 11, 19; *De mus.*, VI, 13, 40). On the basis of Christian teaching, neo-Platonist psychology, and his own reflections Augustine quickly integrated a doctrine of virtue as rightly directed love. In part this is a matter of having the right ultimate aims, for happiness can be found only in the possession of something which truly makes man happy and which cannot perish or be taken away; the love of God is therefore the only reasonable and feasible kind of love, the only one that can gain what it seeks (*De lib. arb.*, II, 13, 37; *De mus.*, VI, 14, 44). But virtue also has its heroic aspects, and it is specifically in connection with the warfare in man's affective life between earthly cares and adherence to God that Augustine discusses the classical virtues of temperance, fortitude, justice, and prudence (*De mor.*, I, 15, 25; *De lib. arb.*, I, 13, 27; *De mus.*, VI, 15, 50—16, 51; *De ver. rel.*, 15, 29; *De div. quaest.*, q. 30); their function is to sustain the proper balance among the affections and to resist the temptations of the flesh in favor of the higher loyalty to God. This understanding of the virtues is doubtless based upon Plotinus (*Enn.* I, 2, 4; I, 6, 6) or Porphyry (*Sent.*, 34 [Mommert, 32]), who

[17] Du Roy, p. 348; for the dating of the passage, p. 237. See also the tables of passages in which Augustine named all three vices (pp. 350–352), from which it would appear that the transition to this new scheme was a slow one, confirmed only about 398 or 399, and that the older scheme always retained a certain force in Augustine's thinking.

set the virtues in the context of man's task of purification. But when Augustine makes all four virtues modalities of love, he is being influenced by Origen's interpretation of the Song of Songs, as contained in either the homilies translated by Jerome or the commentary translated by Rufinus[18]; there virtue is defined as well-ordered love on the basis of Canticles, 2, 4 ("*ordinate in me caritatem*"), and since that definition appears in a writing begun in Rome (*De mor.*, I, 25, 46), it would seem that Origen helped to stabilize Augustine's thought along these lines quite early. This view of virtue as well-ordered love converged with Augustine's own earlier reflections, suggested perhaps by Varro, on the "structured" character of all willing, for everything is "referred" to one or another ultimate value[19]; and Augustine's doctrine of virtue, though it stretched the classical doctrine in a new direction, was still very much in continuity with it. Like the Stoics, who said that virtue is the only thing that lies fully within our own power and cannot be lost against our will ($\tau\grave{o}$ $\dot{\epsilon}\phi'$ $\dot{\eta}\mu\hat{\iota}\nu$),[20] Augustine asserts that nothing is more within the power of the will than the will itself, so that whoever wishes to love rightly and honourably can achieve it simply by willing it; the *velle* is already the *habere* (*De lib. arb.*, I, 12, 26 and 13, 29). Virtue, though it consists in a directing of the will toward God and a patterning of all other loves around this one, is an act that is rooted in man himself. Unlike beatitude, in which the center of gravity shifts radically to God in contemplation and enjoyment, virtue is the fulfillment of man's own being.

From the confluence of a variety of traditions Augustine was able to mold a doctrine of virtue that is perhaps more intensely voluntaristic and more intensely relational than most, for he saw the problem as one of affection, valuation, personal attitude. It is at the same time more intellectualistic and more objective than most, for Augustine understood that attitudes and loves and a grading of values are evoked by the things one experiences and cannot issue forth without some conviction about real states of affairs. His doctrine locates virtue, then, at the center of man's consciousness and freedom. Man can act both irrationally and per-

---

[18] Altaner, "Augustinus und Origenes," p. 29 (*KpS*, p. 239).
[19] See pp. 66–67.
[20] Cf. Du Roy, p. 240, n. 11.

versely, to be sure. But the restoration of his mind to its proper functioning in virtue is a restoration of both intelligence and freedom. Where he had cut himself off from the perspective of the whole in order to pursue his own narrow interests, he now returns to it and discovers that the understanding of the divine plan is true rationality and the service of God is perfect freedom. Only then is he ready to look toward God himself.

(i) *Contemplation.* In the *Confessions* (IX, 10, 23–25) Augustine claims to have attained to the vision of God, seemingly for the first time, while Monica was still alive, thus in 387. As he and his mother leaned from a window in Ostia, conversing about eternal life, they ascended in thought by silencing created things one by one, moving from the physical world to their own souls and then beyond them, impelled by love and desire for God. In contrast to Augustine's experience in reading the *libri platonici*, when he merely became aware that there was something to see but was unable to see it and hesitated even to look toward it, both of them were now longing for eternal Wisdom, and Augustine claims that they reached out toward it with a total leap of the attention and briefly touched it (*"attingimus...toto ictu cordis"*; cf. the *"ictu trepedantis aspectus"* of *Conf.*, VII, 17, 23). Then their consciousness again lapsed to the realm of everyday experience.

The vision at Ostia leaves no traces in the writings of the time. Though there are expositions of the way of ascent (*De quan. an.*, 33, 70—35, 79) and attempts at anagogy (*De lib. arb.*, II, 3, 7—15, 43), the writings from those years are not confessional or mystical; they are concerned with the investigation of philosophical problems. But one of those problems is the nature of contemplation and the conditions of its possibility.

The exact character of Augustine's "mysticism" has been a matter of some controversy. We must agree, I think, with those who assert that Augustine really meant to claim an immediate vision of God, of the sort that Plotinus (e.g., in *Enn.* I, 6, 7) would have prepared him to expect.[21] But we must also agree with those who deny that it was "mysticism" in the sense which that

[21] Cuthbert Butler, *Western Mysticism* (London, 1922), pp. 87–88; Joseph Maréchal, "La vision de Dieu au sommet de la contemplation," *Nouvelle revue théologique*, LVII (1930), pp. 191–214; Paul Henry, *La vision d'Ostie* (Paris, 1938), pp. 88–103.

term has had since the Middle Ages.[22] The reason is that Augustine did not think it abnormal or the result of any exceptional gifts, as in later mystical theology, but saw it as the proper exercise of man's natural capacities; what makes it exceptional, so that great effort is required, is the mind's distraction by the cares of earthly life and the bondage of the affections to finite things. When these obstacles are overcome the mind becomes aware of God, or of the Wisdom which is the divine principle of self-disclosure, God speaking *per se ipsum* (*Conf.*, IX, 10, 25; *Ep.* 147, 19, 47; *De Gen. ad litt.*, XII, 27, 55), and what differentiates the experience from beatitude in the proper sense of the word is that the contemplation is only momentary: if this brief *momentum intelligentiae* in which the whole attention of the mind is directed toward God were to be protracted, it would be the entry into the joy of the Master (*Conf.*, IX, 10, 25).

Augustine's view, then, is that God is always present to the mind and that the mind is always capable, at least in principle, of apprehending him with immediacy, "*nullā naturā interpositā*" (*Solil.*, I, 13, 22; *De mus.*, VI, 1, 1; *De Gen. op. imp.*, 16, 60; *De div. quaest.*, q. 51, 2; *De util. cred.*, 33; *De Gen. ad litt.*, III, 19–20; *De Trin.*, XI, 5, 8)—and here Augustine is applying to man himself Plotinus' statement that between Psyche and Nous, or between Nous and the One, there is nothing intervening to block the knowledge of the higher by the lower (οὐδὲν μεταξύ [*Enn.* V, 1, 3 and 6]). This immediate apprehension of God is the only proper fulfillment of human life, and God himself is called the true "life" of the soul (*Solil.*, I, 3; *De lib. arb.*, II, 16, 41; *De ver. rel.*, 12, 25 and 49, 97). Why this end alone? Because the very nature of mind is to be open toward all reality and truth and value; it can recognize the difference between the complete and the incomplete, the permanent and the changing, and finally it is satisfied only in seeking and adhering to God in love and possessing him through knowledge. It is in the contemplation of God that man lays hold upon that which can truly be enjoyed, intelligently and gladly, and thus he reaches the happiness he has naturally been seeking for himself. But that is not all. In the contemplation of God, or specifically of the divine Wisdom, the object which is

[22] Ephrem Hendrikx, *Augustins Verhältnis zur Mystik* (Würzburg, 1936), pp. 17–35.

possessed and enjoyed through knowledge in turn influences and forms the mind, so that the mind itself becomes wise "through participation." The participation in divine perfection, it will be noted, occurs through knowledge at this level of finite life; it is man's own act of knowledge, or rather that which he apprehends immediately in the act, that transforms his being.

Because of the incompleteness of man's happiness apart from the contemplation of God, and especially because of the incompleteness of his wisdom and other such qualities apart from participation in God through knowledge, Augustine thinks of this immediate vision of God as the intended goal of man's creation and even as the state in which man was at least provisionally created. Quite naturally he takes up the Alexandrian interpretation of the image of God: when it is said (Genesis 1, 26) that man was created "according to" (κατά) or "to" (ad) God's image and likeness, this is taken to suggest that it is not *man himself* who is the image of God but that man is created in a certain relationship to the true and undistorted Image, the divine Word.[23] Augustine assumes in the writings of this period that the Word is the *only* proper Image and Likeness of God—Likeness because he is in no way unlike the Father, Image because he is derived directly from or expressed by the Father (*De ver. rel.*, 43, 81; *De Gen. op. imp.*, 16, 57; *De div. quaest.*, q. 74). It cannot be said that man *is* the image and likeness of God, therefore; and yet he is set above other created things, for they have been made with only a certain degree of order within their own being, while man is able to look beyond himself and grasp the Likeness himself through knowledge, with perfect immediacy[24]:

[23] See A. Gaudel, "La théologie du Λόγος chez saint Athanase," *Revue des sciences religieuses*, XI (1931), 1–26; Jules Gross, *La divinisation du chrétien d'après les pères grecs. Contribution historique à la doctrine de la grâce* (Paris, 1938); Régis Bernard, *L'Image de Dieu d'après Saint Athanase* (*Théologie*, XXV; Paris, 1952); Th. Camelot, "La théologie de l'image de Dieu," *Revue des sciences philosophiques et théologiques*, XL (1956), 443–471; Walter J. Burghardt, *The Image of God in Man according to Cyril of Alexandria* (Washington, 1957).

[24] For the development of Augustine's views on the *imago Dei*, see Michael Schmaus, *Die psychologische Trinitätslehre des hl. Augustinus* (Münsterische Beiträge zur Theologie, XI, Münster, 1927), pp. 291–297; J. Heijke, "The Image of God according to Saint Augustine (*De Trinitate* excepted)," *Folia*, X (1956), 3–11; John Edward Sullivan, *The Image of God: The Doctrine of Saint Augustine and Its Influence* (Dubuque, 1963), chapters 1 and 2; Alfred Schindler, *Wort und Analogie in Augustins Trinitätslehre* (Tübingen, 1965), pp. 61–74.

Because man is able to participate in Wisdom through the inward man, it is according to the latter that he is said to be created *ad Imaginem*, in order that he might be fully formed by this Image with nothing intervening and in such a fashion that nothing could be closer to God. Thus he would truly know, and live, and be. No created thing could be greater (*De div. quaest.*, q. 51, 2).

In this pilgrimage the Word or Wisdom of God is the principle of intelligibility, both instructing man along the way and illuminating him at the goal. The Spirit is the Gift by which the soul is given integrity (*De ver. rel.*, 12, 25; 55, 112–113), the source of the *caritas* by which man is brought to God by seeking him with all his powers (*De mor.*, I, 13, 23; 16, 29; 17, 31). Man is thus brought to participate in the inward life of God himself through knowledge and love. The Trinitarian problem has been raised in its full intensity, then. And Augustine, almost as soon as he takes note of it, comes to see that the Trinity enters directly into the finite world, not only at the highest point of human aspiration but at every level of finite reality.

2. MANIFESTATIONS OF THE TRINITY

It is during Augustine's years in Thagaste that he seems to have worked out his own quite original understanding of the Trinity, or, more precisely, of the manifestations of the Trinity within finite being. He had a fragmentary notion at best of the inner life of the Trinity, derived from the likewise fragmentary suggestions of earlier writers like Hilary and Ambrose; he speaks of the Word as the Image expressed by the Father or, since he is equal to the Father, the Likeness of the Father (*De ver. rel.*, 43, 81); he knows that there must be one divine substance, and consequently that one person cannot "receive" or "participate" anything proper to another person (*De div. quaest.*, q. 23). But beyond this there is no doctrine of the "immanent Trinity"; indeed, there will be no real progress for many more years, until about 413 he learns the way from the writings of Gregory Nazianzen.

The progress that is made (and it is largely the outcome of his own insight and power of synthesis) is in the working out of a

"Trinitarian ontology"[25] based on the triadic structure of being. Augustine did not operate entirely without suggestions and encouragement from earlier thinkers, both philosophical and theological. But he was the one who succeeded in working through these suggestions consistently and thoroughly.

The first insight, and the one which sets the framework, is a participationist understanding of all finite reality: whatever a thing becomes and however it changes, it lives and moves and has its being "in God" (Acts 17, 28). This theme is given a Trinitarian interpretation by the passage in which Paul speaks of God as the one *a quo, per quem, in quo* all things have their being (Romans 11, 36), a passage used by Augustine for the first time in Rome (*De quan. an.*, 34, 77; *De mor.*, I, 14, 24) and often thereafter.[26] What is perhaps most striking about Augustine's understanding of finite being is the stress on its radical mutability, so that it needs divine support if it is to gain coherence and continuity; God "holds together" (*continet, συνέχει*) all things. This notion, rooted in the cosmology of Plato's *Timaeus* and expressly formulated by Aristotle and the Stoics,[27] could have reached Augustine through many channels: Cicero, Varro, Porphyry. It is employed in a Trinitarian context, using Romans 11, 36, in Ambrose's first homily on the creation narrative (*Exameron*, I, 5, 19)[28]:

From him is the origination of the substance of all things, that is, from his will and power (all things began by his will, for there is one God the Father, from whom are all things; indeed, because he willed and it was done, he can be said to have made them "from himself"); *through him* is their *continuation*; and *in him* is their *end*. From him, then, comes *matter*; through him the activity which *binds together and consolidates* all

[25] Du Roy in his work has exhibited the difference in Augustine's thought between a Trinitarian "ontology" (of all finite being), "analogy" (within man's inner life), and "anagogy" (contemplative movement toward God).

[26] See du Roy, Appendix V, pp. 479–485, for a tabulation of passages in which this text is cited.

[27] Theiler, *Vorbereitung des Neuplatonismus*, p. 47.

[28] Du Roy finds evidence of Augustine's use of this work while still in Rome (pp. 270, n. 1, and 275, n. 1); and Courcelle (*Recherches*, pp. 98–103) thinks that Ambrose preached these sermons in 386, thus within Augustine's hearing. A far-reaching investigation of this cosmological theme, taking Ambrose's first sermon on the creation narrative as its point of departure, is to be found in Jean Pépin, *Théologie cosmique et théologie chrétienne* (Paris, 1964).

things; in him, because and as long as he wills, they *abide and are held together* by his power, so that their end is likewise in God's will and their dissolution is according to his decision.

What is crucial about finite being, according to this perspective, is not its aspect of form so much as its dynamic aspect of striving after the embodiment of form or the preservation of whatever form has been achieved. When Augustine uses the term "*ordo*" it soon loses the Ciceronian and Plotinian meanings it had in the early dialogues and comes to be employed almost exclusively in a rather different sense, probably conveyed through Varro. It is used with reference to this dynamic and volitional aspects of things, and the basis in ordinary speech is the "order of battle," the "array" of an army drawn up with certain ends in view (this is a common meaning of *taxis* in Greek). Order in this sense consists, then, in the "coordination" of component parts or the "right ordering" of one's own attention and affection. The importance of *ordo* for the very constitution of finite being is stated most strikingly in an early passage (*De mor.*, II, 4, 6):

"Being" refers to a certain permanence, . . . and those things which [in becoming] tend toward being tend toward coordination [*ordo*]; when they attain it they have attained being, so far as that can be attained at all by creatures. Coordination [*ordo*] gives some kind of harmony to that which it orders; and since being is nothing else than unity, something *is* insofar as it has unity, and this unity is brought about by a harmonious and coordinated functioning [*operatio*]. It is in this way, then, that composite things have their being, insofar as they have being at all; for simple things, which are already one, have being through themselves, while things that are composite are able to imitate this unity through the harmony of their parts, and insofar as they attain this they have being. Therefore coordination [*ordo*] is what draws a being together, while disorder, perversion, corruption, is what brings about its non-being.

Soon afterward Augustine discovered a passage in the book of Wisdom (11, 21) which said that God has ordered all things according to *mensura et numerus et pondus*. From the first this triad is linked with divine Trinity (cf. *De Gen. c. Man.*, I, 16, 26). The use of this passage in a Trinitarian context is nowhere to be found prior to Augustine; he seems to have come upon it by himself (du Roy thinks that he was giving careful study to the book of

Wisdom during these years),[29] and it doubtless answered to his previous reflections along this line. The text is used repeatedly in his subsequent writings, and he seems eventually to have arrived at a dual terminological scheme, using the more philosophical-sounding triad *modus, species, ordo* with reference to the phenomena within the created world, and the biblical triad *mensura, numerus, pondus* with reference to the causes (both creaturely and divine) manifested in them (*De nat. boni*, 3; *De Gen. ad litt.*, IV, 3, 7).

It is not always easy to see what phenomena are apportioned to each of the three aspects—or at least to the first, for it is clear that any element of movement, directionality, or desire belongs to the third, and that form and proportion of any sort, including the sequential processes of change and growth in the natural world and the correspondence of subject to object in sensation and understanding, belong to the second. What is left to the first, after these phenomena of dynamism and of form are discounted, is the hard to describe but nevertheless unmistakable phenomenon of localization, boundedness, thisness, and thus individuality and even centeredness, the "ipseity" of each occasion of activity or experience. The expression "measure" had the connotation of bounding or giving definiteness to something (*finire*); the Father is said to be the Measure (*Modus*) of divine Truth (*De beata vita*, IV, 34),[30] God is said to be boundless but bounded by himself ("*infinito in se sibi fine*" [*Conf.*, XIII, 11, 12]), and all things are said to be bounded or given a place by the hand of Truth that upholds them (*Conf.*, VII, 15, 21).[31] Often Augustine associates the Father with the creation of matter, and in this imagery of "measuring" and "bounding" there may be something of what Aristotle meant when he called matter the principle of individuation, that which separates this from that, here from there, then from now. Every thing, every event, has its "allotted" measure of space and time, giving it a privileged sphere of its own which constitutes the substratum of any subsequent formation or deformation, rectitude or perversity.

[29] Du Roy, pp. 224–226, 273, 279.
[30] Du Roy (pp. 157–158) demonstrates that the source utilized in this passage is *Enn.* V, 5.
[31] A possible source is *Enn.* I, 8, 2, where God is called the measure and limit of all things.

It should be evident that Augustine had a far more "modern" understanding of finite being than the ontology of substance and accident which has been dominant in many circles. To him a being is constituted (or, in a sense, constitutes itself) in three stages or dimensions: there is a certain allotment of space and time as a base of operations, there is a definiteness and structure which it has or develops according to natural sequence or toward which (in the case of spirit) it is to strive; and there is a coordinated or uncoordinated functioning of the being in its actual operation. This third aspect, which it is difficult to trace yet which is often far more important than the mere morphology of an organism, is the crucial unifying factor. Augustine understands the "compositeness" of finite beings not only statically but dynamically as well, for a thing is finally synthesized by its own functioning, and this may be crucial to its possessing certain characteristics or to its being anything at all.[32]

Toward 390 Augustine began to see the Trinity reflected in these three aspects which every finite thing, if it has being at all, will exhibit:

ut sit	*ut hoc vel illud sit*	*ut in eo quod est, maneat quantum potest* (*Ep.* 11, 3)
est quodammodo	*ab eo quod omnino nihil est, plurimum distat*	*suis partibus sibimet congruit*
esse	*hoc esse*	*sibi amica esse*
quo constat	*quo discernitur*	*quo congruit* (*De div. quaest.*, q. 18)
esse	*species*	*ordo* (*De ver. rel.*, 7, 13)
natura, ut sit quidquid est, appetit unitatem	*suique similis in quantum potest esse conetur*	*ordinem proprium . . . tenet* (*De mus.*, VI, 17, 56)

He also points out that instruction in rhetoric teaches men to discuss three kinds of questions: *whether* something is, *what* it is, and *how* it is and whether it is to be approved or disapproved (*Ep.* 11, 4; *De div. quaest.*, q. 18; *Conf.*, X, 10, 17).[33] It is doubtful that the rhetorical formula was the sole basis of the insight, for it was long

[32] See also the comments on Augustine's later understanding of substance and accident in chapter 5, section 2.

[33] Alfred Schindler, *Wort und Analogie in Augustins Trinitätslehre* (Tübingen, 1965), pp. 56–60; du Roy, p. 386.

in coming and was probably suggested by biblical passages like Romans 11, 36 and Wisdom 11, 21. But a formula like this, or, again, Varro's division of philosophy into natural, logical, and ethical (*C. Faust.*, XX, 7; *De civ. Dei*, XI, 24–28), was important because it furnished his Trinitarian doctrine a reference point in general philosophical knowledge and encouraged him in his belief that all finite actuality is a reflection of the Trinity.

The three dimensions of finite being are then referred to the persons of the Trinity:

Causa naturae	*Species per quam . . . formantur omnia*	*Manentia quaedam in qua sunt omnia* (*Ep.* 11, 3)
ab uno Principio	*per aequalem illi ac similem Speciem*	*divitiis Bonitatis eius, qua . . . Charitate, iunguntur* (*De mus.*, VI, 17, 56)
Deus	*Forma infabricata*	*Salus, Donum* (*De ver. rel.*, 11, 21)
Modus	*Forma*	*Ordo* (*De ver. rel.*, 43, 81)
Unum	*Similitudo*	*Convenientia* (*De ver. rel.*, 39, 72)

Augustine assumes that in all cases the influence of the three Persons is both inseparable and simultaneous (*De ver. rel.*, 7, 13; *Ep.* 11, 3), for he has by this time read Hilary's *De Trinitate* and Ambrose's *De Spiritu Sancto* and knows the current doctrine of the Church. But he never will mean by this what some of the scholastics later supposed, that the influence of the three persons is entirely undifferentiated. For him the triadic structure of finite being is the authentic impress of the Trinity, and the influence of the persons is called undivided not because it is undifferentiated but because there would be no finite being at all without the constant influence of all three persons, supporting it in all its dimensions simultaneously and thereby taking it up, in a sense, into the divine life (*Ep.* 11, 3). Though Augustine took pains to deny Stoic pantheism, about which he knew very well, and wanted to stress that the finite effects are really distinct from God, he felt nevertheless that it could be said with perfect propriety that all things have their being "in God"; therefore when it is said that God disposed all things according to measure, number, and weight, he interpreted this to mean in the last analysis that God disposed all things "in himself," so that all three terms can be applied to him, originally and properly ("*primitus et veraciter et singulariter*"): he is the unmeasured Measure which bounds all things, the unnumbered Number which forms all things, and the unmoved Movement ("*stabilis motus*," as he will put it) which sustains and orients and gives fulfillment to all things (*De Gen. ad litt.*, IV, 2, 7—4, 9). There is still only an analogy between finite measure, number, and weight and the divine Trinity; but the finite analogue is immediately derived from the infinite analogate by participation in what is proper to each person.

The Trinitarian problem in those years, we should recall, was not how God, being one, could be three, but how God, being three, could be one. Against the Arians it had to be shown first of all that the activity of the three persons is not separable, as they supposed, but that there is on the contrary a perfect agreement among them in will and activity; from this agreement in activity it was possible then to conclude to their unity of substance, but it was impossible to obliterate the distinct activities of the persons.[34] Augustine follows the same path. In question 38, written in Thagaste, he juxtaposes three verses from the Fourth Gospel: "No one comes to me unless the Father draws him" (6, 44); "No one comes to the Father except through me" (14, 6); and, "He [the Spirit] will lead you into all truth" (16, 13). He attempts to show that this diversification of functions is compatible with unity of substance, and he does it through comparison with human activity. In the philosophical tradition there was a stock distinction between natural powers, knowledge, and volitional activity, all of them obviously belonging to the same being and often cooperating in the accomplishment of a single task, as in the work of a craftsman (cf. *De civ. Dei*, XI, 25).[35] In some such fashion, then, the threefold influence of God within the world is united in a single substance.

There may be, by the way, an incipient analogy here between

[34] Cf. Didymus, *De Spiritu Sancto*, translated by Jerome (*PL*, XXIII), chapters 16–17, 22–24, 36–37.

[35] For the origins of this distinction and the channels by which it was transmitted, see du Roy, pp. 300–302. Augustine may have learned to apply it in a Trinitarian context from Hilary (*De Trin.*, II, 1 [*PL*, X, p. 51]), who speaks of the Father as the Power *from* whom, the Son as the Offspring *through* whom, and the Spirit as the Gift *in* whom all things subsist, and thus finds in the Trinity the perfection of all three aspects of creative work: "infinitas in Aeterno, species in Imagine, usus in Munere."

the Trinity and the inward life of man, but it is to be noted that the purpose of the comparison is not to gain an understanding of the intra-Trinitarian relations, as in Augustine's later writings, but solely to demonstrate how three distinct things ("*aliud . . . aliud . . . aliud*") can belong to a single substance. Augustine is still feeling his way tentatively through the problems of theology, and although his analyses are original and thorough and far-reaching, as we have just seen, we should not expect to find anticipations of all his later views in his first ventures.

3. TRUE RELIGION

Toward the end of Augustine's stay in Thagaste and at the beginning of his activities in Hippo we find a new interest in the topic of "religion." To Augustine, familiar as he was with classical Latin literature, this term had reference to the traditional beliefs held by a community and the discipline conscientiously observed within it. Religion was a way of life as much *enmeshed* in the historical process as philosophy represented an attempt to take a perspective *independent* of it, and Augustine, who understood well enough the appeal of the latter, wanted to show that the particularity of the religious community with which he had cast his lot was not incompatible with the universal perspective of philosophy. It was not at all difficult for him to find the basic answer. Long since, at the time of his conversion, he had sensed the appeal of the lives Christians had led and he had arrived at a clear conception of the relationship between the authority of revelation and the direct insights of reason. From the first his "philosophy of religion" was that which he stated in 391 in these words: "All religion is for the sake of the soul" (*De util. cred.*, 7, 14). And he knew that the test which proves Christianity the only true and perfect religion is that it successfully reconciles the soul to God (*De quan. an.*, 34, 78 and 36, 80).

Despite this continuity with Augustine's earlier thought, there seems to be a new urgency in the writings about 390 and 391. Fulfilling an earlier pledge to Romanianus (*C. Acad.*, II, 3, 8), but perhaps responding to current challenges as well, he wrote in high rhetorical style an extended protreptic discourse *On True Religion*, a kind of "address to the Gentiles" similar to the writings of the apologists of earlier centuries, in which he discussed the problem of religion within the context of the philosophic quest. In the early chapters he praises the philosophers, especially the Platonists, for their discernment of the truth about the one God, but at the same time he brings them under reproach for not having the courage of their convictions but submitting instead to the pressure to conform with popular religion. Christianity, then, is the true fulfillment of Platonism, proclaiming those same truths about God which the Platonists had already glimpsed, now purged of the superstitions of pagan religion. What Augustine treasures most about the true religion is not that it gives a more certain knowledge of God (in fact, Augustine assumes, on the one hand, that God is knowable to all men and, on the other, that speculation is needed even to complete the knowledge given in revelation) but that in it men have *lived out* their knowledge of God in such a way as to convince others, even the unphilosophical, of its truth and to inspire them to follow the same way of life. What the Platonists only intimated, the true religion has actualized and made available to all.

But the uniqueness of its achievement poses further philosophical problems, and in the writings of these years belief (*fides*, *credere*) becomes the subject of extended analysis for the first time. The problem which Augustine now feels to be the dominant one is no longer the authoritative character of revelation (in the Cassiciacum dialogues this meant, for all practical purposes, the Creed, which converged almost completely with the results of speculative philosophy) but the contingent character of the events narrated in Scripture, the problem, then, of their historicity and particularity and the necessity of giving assent to the reports of others.

Recently the suggestion has been made by du Roy[36] that at least the later portions of *On True Religion* (the prologue and other passages sprinkled throughout the work) are an answer to a challenge issued in Porphyry's work *On the Return of the Soul*, which Augustine had just encountered for the first time. In a passage Augustine later quotes from that work (*De civ. Dei*, X, 32) Porphyry had said, "No one sect has yet drawn together in

---

[36] Du Roy, pp. 311ff.

itself all those things that would comprise the *universal* way of liberation for the soul; at least, if there is such a way, it has not yet been brought to my notice through the historical record." But he added that some such way of salvation must exist, and that divine oracles, especially those transmitted by the Chaldaeans, had indicated something about it. Thus the problem of the one universally applicable way of salvation was raised by Porphyry, though, despairing at ever finding it, he merely reaffirmed the pluralistic and relativistic religious policies of the Hellenistic and Roman worlds.[37] He also supplied a hint about the solution to the problem: there must be some "historical" validation of the true religion (and we should remember that throughout antiquity "history" meant not the *events* which had occurred but the *recounting* of those events, the *historia rerum gestarum*). It may be, then, that Augustine accepted the challenge on the terms offered: "The chief argument for following this religion," he says, "is history" (*De ver. rel.*, 7, 13). Certain things have been done, and they have been attested by writings and other proofs; and beginning from the one region where God was properly worshiped, the word has gone throughout the whole earth and has been believed everywhere (*De ver. rel.*, 3, 4).

There are enough traces of Porphyrian themes in the writings from Thagaste to make this suggestion plausible—not only the interest in the way of salvation and in its historical documentation, but a new concern with the worship of the fallen angels, known to be an important problem for Porphyry as well (*De ver. rel.*, 13, 26—14, 28; 55, 108–112). Nevertheless it is surprising that Augustine's reaction to Porphyry's anti-Christian polemic is much less intense than it will be some years later[38]; far from making any direct refutations, he simply engages in oratory in the exalted manner. This suggests either that *On the Return of the Soul* and *On the Philosophy from Oracles* are two different works, the first of which Augustine read in 389 or 390 and the second of which he read about 400; or that at this earlier time he was responding not to a writing from the past but to the contemporary pagans (*De ver.*

---

[37] For an excellent study of the head-on encounter between Christianity and classical culture over this question, as first formulated by Justin and Celsus, see Carl Andresen, *Logos und Nomos. Die Polemik des Kelsos wider das Christentum* (Arbeiten zur Kirchengeschichte, XXX; Berlin, 1955).

[38] See chapter 4, section 4.

rel., 4, 7) who seek oracles from demons and to the followers of Porphyry in Augustine's own day, like those depicted in Macrobius *Saturnalia*,[39] who denied the incarnation and resurrection and raised objections to the biblical narratives. Some years later Augustine wrote an extended reply (*Ep.* 102) to some questions from Deogratias concerning a friend of theirs who hesitated to become a Christian because of objections said to come from Porphyry himself. It is possible, then, that the fresh challenge from the side of pagan neo-Platonism came from his own contemporaries, and in a form that did not call for a detailed refutation but rather stimulated him to inquire further into the earthly career of the people of God. Indeed, there may have been an equally strong stimulus from within the Christian tradition, for Augustine had probably begun reading some of the literature of African Christianity with its strong emphasis on the Church, such as Cyprian's *On the Unity of the Church* and *On the Lord's Prayer.*[40]

The decisive proof of the true religion, as indicated before, is in the lives of a long succession of men, from the patriarchs and prophets and all the obedient men in Israel, to Jesus of Nazareth and the apostles and martyrs, and on to the Church of Augustine's own day, spread throughout the world (*De mor.*, I, 7, 12). The decisive achievement, of course, is the life of Jesus himself. His whole life, Augustine says, was an "education in morals" (*De ver. rel.*, 16, 32) through both precept and example. He is the exemplar and the first fruits of a redeemed humanity (*De quan. an.*, 33, 76), who, because of his inseparable union with the divine Word, was able to live under the conditions of human life and still despise what sinful men desire and suffer what they dread (*De mus.*, VI, 4, 7; *De ver. rel.*, 2, 3; 16, 31). But similar achievements are found in the Christian people, whose heroic martyrdoms were the seed by which the churches spread and whose continence and renunciation fulfill what remained only a dream in Plato (*De ver. rel.*, 3, 5).

This "moral" argument dominates the writings from Thagaste.

---

[39] Courcelle, *Les lettres grecques en Occident*, pp. 170, 195–209. For a recent discussion of the setting, see Herbert Bloch, "The Pagan Revival in the West at the End of the Fourth Century," *The Conflict between Paganism and Christianity in the Fourth Century*, ed. Arnaldo Momigliano (Oxford, 1963), pp. 193–218.

[40] Hugo Koch, "Cipriano in Agostino," *Ricerche Religiose*, VIII (1932), pp. 317–337, lists the parallels in detail.

It is obviously the kind of argument that can have an appeal to the minds and the passions of reasonable men. But Augustine recognizes that it may not speak to the condition of people who are not yet fit to reflect about divine matters (*De ver. rel.*, 25, 47), and soon afterward, in the work *On the Usefulness of Belief*, he turns his attention to a different set of credentials which supplement it:

Christ, bringing the medicine to heal corrupt morals, through his miracles gained authority, through his authority merited faith, through faith drew together a multitude, through this multitude secured permanence and antiquity, and through this permanence corroborated his religion (*De util. cred.*, 15, 33).

The moral achievement obviously keeps a certain apologetic force of its own; Augustine still mentions "the humanity and teachings of Christ, the journeying of the apostles, the reproaches, crosses, blood, and deaths of the martyrs, the laudable lives of the saints" (*De util. cred.*, 17, 35). But he suspects that good examples are effective more in changing men's opinions than in changing their lives; good examples, no matter how striking, will not be contagious by themselves but need the reinforcement of divinely authorized instruction which can *command* a certain mode of life (*De util. cred.*, 15, 33—17, 35). The function of miracles is to assure a large number of believers, and convinced ones at that, not merely by impressing men with demonstrations of divine power but by doing good to them and evoking their gratitude. And similarly the persistence and vast expanse of the Church function as a sign of divine authorization, helping to convince people in later times, who are not in a position to know Jesus or his achievements at first hand, that the testimony of the Church is reliable. When Augustine makes the notorious statement, "I would not believe except for the authority of the Catholic Church" (*C. Ep. Fund.*, 5), or when he says that the authority of the Church must be given first place (*De util. cred.*, 17, 35), he is simply describing the nature of belief, for it is necessarily dependent upon "authority," that is to say, the testimony of others; what the Church says about Christ in its interpretation of the Scriptures and in its doctrines is, then, the precondition of the belief that will eventually lead to fuller understanding.[41]

Thus Augustine, in justifying the true religion, is led to give

[41] For a more extended discussion of the "motives of credibility," see Löhrer, *Der Glaubensbegriff des hl. Augustinus*, pp. 144-173.

further thought to the nature of belief. In one of the brief discussions "on various questions" (*De div. quaest.*, q. 48), probably written toward the end of his stay in Thagaste, he gives a clear *partitio* of the different functions of belief. It is evident that belief is always a *mediated* acquaintance with something that is not directly knowable, either because of its own character, being separated from the human subject by space or time, or because of the shortcomings of the mind, which is separated by its own impurity from something that is fully accessible. But there are three cases: (1) that of historical accounts of contingent events, which must *always* be believed because they are separated from direct experience; (2) that of the rational sciences, which are learned through human instruction and thus with an initial attitude of giving credence to what is said, but which are immediately understood if there is any insight into what is being conveyed; and (3) that of the divine presence, from which man is alienated by his misdirected affections, and which must therefore first be believed but can later come to be known directly. The third is stressed in the Cassiciacum dialogues. The first—*fides historica et temporalis*—is new. Here belief is not a stopgap, a substitute for a more appropriate mode of apprehension; it is the appropriate means of access to things which we cannot experience personally.

This analysis of belief, though it probably came to Augustine through a Latin writer like Varro, has its source in Plato, specifically in the *Republic* and the *Timaeus*. Augustine, like the Plato of the *Republic*, scorns changeable things as mere *opinionabilia* (*C. Secund. Man.*, 8) or *verisimilia* (*Ep.* 13), for from the standpoint of a Platonist ontology and epistemology neither belief nor its object has a high status. The conditions of knowledge are such that changing things are not fully knowable (though this demeaning judgment applies to them only in their particularity and fleetingness; Augustine always assumes that order is ingredient in the world and that it can be studied exhaustively and with perfect rationality by the various sciences). But like the Plato of the *Timaeus*, who found that he must give to the narrative form and to belief based upon it a more positive force because it is the only way in which the origin and destiny of the temporal world can be apprehended, Augustine, without having read the *Timaeus*, followed the same path, discovering the indispensability and even the appropriateness of belief where becoming, change, and new beginnings are concerned.

The two variant estimates of temporality and of belief can co-exist. From the theoretical standpoint Augustine, as a good Platonist, always gives pride of place to fully rational knowledge, into which the sensory component enters at most as a set of variables. But he also knows that the temporal universe is our own universe, and what is most important to us is usually the all too contingent course and disposition of events; we must live in this universe as best we can, and we must discover something about its actual course. Though its intrinsic value from the theoretical standpoint may not be as great, its practical importance for us and for our destiny is crucial. Augustine believes that the entire disposition and course of events could be known through immediate contemplation of the mind of God, and would be so known had men not forfeited their destined mode of life; but under present conditions a sense of the makeup of the world and where it is going can be gained, humanly speaking, only through the accumulation of experience, not only one's own but that of others, reported by them and received with credence.[42]

But the biblical revelation offers something better—not human records of the past or human prognostications about the future, but divinely revealed narratives and prophecies, reaching backward to the creation and forward to the eschaton (*De ver. rel.*, 25, 46; *De lib. arb.*, III, 21, 59–62). Augustine's estimate of the value of revelation is precisely the reverse of what is often assumed in our own day. He was ready to acknowledge that the philosophers had known the *eternal* things, at least through the use of reason if not through direct contemplation. What seemed far more difficult to him was to discover something about the course and meaning of human history and to accomplish something in one's own life, beset as it is with mutability without and within. Like the Franciscan theologians of the Middle Ages, then, he would make theology—and especially in its distinctively *Christian* aspects—

---

[42] This is the perspective of *De Trin.*, IV, 16, 21, which, though it was written some fifteen years after the period with which we are concerned, has the marks of being influenced by the same philosophical tradition, probably through Varro. In *De mus.*, IV, 16, 30, a work largely cribbed from Varro, he draws a distinction between knowing something and believing it on the basis of report.

5 +

more a practical than a theoretical discipline. The Scriptural record is important chiefly because of what it says about the work of salvation, both as it affects each individual (and Augustine in his interpretation of Scripture always attempts to bring it into relation with existential problems) and on the broad stage of world history.

One of the new elements of Augustine's thought at this time is an awareness of the *dispensatio temporalis* (*De ver. rel.*, 7, 13; 10, 19, etc.; *De fid. et symb.*, 4, 6 and 6, 8; *De div. quaest.*, q. 57, 2), the pattern of God's saving activity from the beginning to the end of the human race. Augustine had never denied the importance of the historical activity of Christ and its indispensability to sinful man. But its function had been interpreted entirely within the Platonist framework of striving to return to the eternal; the temporal was merely the way to the goal, and he hurried along it somewhat impatiently. Now he will not deny those assumptions, for the temporal dispensation still belongs to those things that are to be "used" as means rather than "enjoyed" as an end (*De ver. rel.*, 24, 45; 50, 98; *De doct. chr.*, I, 35, 39); but he will give more reverent attention to the way, for God is encountered not only at the goal but along the temporal way itself, leading man gently, in accordance with his capacities. Augustine now has an enlarged awareness of the span of biblical history, and he interprets it as a kind of education of the human race analogous to the life of an individual, so that it is gradually transformed from the old Adam into the new, first under the hidden signs of the old dispensation, then with the explicitness of the new, and reaching a consummation only in the resurrection (*De ver. rel.*, 27, 50—28, 51).

Faith has two different aspects, then, one directed toward the eternal Trinity ("*fides spiritalis et aeterna*"), and the other directed toward the temporal dispensation ("*fides historica et temporalis*" [*De ver. rel.*, 50, 99; cf. *De fid. et symb.*, 4, 6; *De lib. arb.*, III, 21, 60; *De ag. chr.*, 17, 19]).[43] Augustine retains his earlier interest in seeking an understanding of what is believed; but the outcome of this new awareness of the *dispensatio temporalis* is an enlarged conception of that task. As before he thinks of the eternal realm, even the Trinity, as fully accessible to understanding. But the temporal dispensation is not knowable in the same way as God himself or the timeless structures of the intelligible realm, for it is

[43] Löhrer, *Der Glaubensbegriff des hl. Augustinus*, pp. 195ff.

a free enactment on God's part and involves much that is contingent. Even here it is possible to reason about and arrive at a fuller understanding of the things that are believed, but only in such a way as to manifest their *possibility* and *suitability*, not their *certainty* (*De ver. rel.*, 8, 14). Augustine thus points the way for the medieval theologians, from Anselm on, who were concerned to discover, starting in faith, the perfect coherence of God's purposes and the appropriateness of each detail. He forestalls the temptation, to which he sometimes yielded in his earlier writings, to abandon the temporal in the attempt to transcend mere belief, for God himself is concerned with the temporal, and to transcend mere belief is to begin to understand even the temporal from within God's own counsel.

Perhaps it was because of these new interests in the people of God and the history of salvation that Augustine came to rethink his vocation as a Christian. Perhaps it was because of a crisis in his own life, brought on by the deaths of his friend Nebridius and his son Adeodatus.[44] In any case he now had second thoughts about his life spent in *otium philosophandi* on the fringes of the Church and decided to edge closer to its organized life. His plan, he says, was to transform his little community into a monastery devoted to the study of Scripture, and he began looking about for a suitable locale (this is the story told both in *Ep.* 21, 3, soon after the event, and in Sermon 355, 1, 2, toward the end of his life). He avoided the places he knew to be without bishops, lest he be pressed into service as a cleric, but he was drawn to Hippo in order to see a friend who seemed a good prospect for the monastic life; when he went into the basilica he was noticed and was detained by popular acclaim to become a presbyter and the successor designate to the aged bishop Valerius.

[44] Brown, *Augustine of Hippo*, pp. 135–136.

CHAPTER 3

Hippo (391–396)

AUGUSTINE PROBABLY EXPERIENCED a certain "cultural shock" in returning from Italy to Africa and especially in assuming ecclesiastical responsibilities there. He had set out to lead a life in search of wisdom, in a Christian form, to be sure, but with a sense of the superiority of this mode of life to that of the ordinary Christian. The tone of the early writings is invincibly classical. Where Christian dogma enters in, it is usually rephrased in language akin to that of philosophy. Popular Christianity is at the margins of his vision, occasionally noted, but only as an empirical fact to be cited for the purposes of argument against the Manichaeans (as in *De moribus*) or the Platonists (as in *De vera religione*). One could not guess from the writings of Rome and Thagaste that Augustine attended church at all, and there is little to indicate the nature of his relationship with the broader Christian community.

The African Church was an old spectre in his memory. He stated openly that its obscurantism, its *superstitio*, had been a hindrance to his development as a Christian. He might have continued to drift, intellectually at sea, had it not been for the Platonism he encountered in Milan. Now Augustine, who had become accustomed to the free air of philosophical inquiry, was plunged back into the life of the African Church with its heritage of authoritarianism (regional synods were constantly being held to make and enforce a common discipline) and its traditional insistence upon the necessity of baptism and physical membership in the visible Church. Plinval is correct in suggesting that such things were "in basic contradiction to the open nature of his spirit," or at least to the intellectual convictions at which he had arrived (for one must always acknowledge the possibility that his deepest inclinations were different, as those with a flair for psychoanalysis have alleged); he is also correct, at least with respect to the broad pattern of Augustine's development, in saying that his thought came to bear "the stamp of African particularism."[1] Something of the general situation is suggested in Peter Brown's characterization of Augustine in Milan (and he is fully aware of the qualifications that have to be made):

He would have been like a Westernized Russian in the nineteenth century, established in Paris. But he will soon return home to spend the rest of his life as a recluse, then as a priest, and later as a bishop, among simple men in Africa: like the "Holy Russia" of the nineteenth century, this world will close in around him; and, as is very often the case with educated men, it will close in all the more effectively for having once been rejected.[2]

We have a genuine problem here, for Augustine did slip steadily into the spirit of African Christianity. But it took place slowly, one stage at a time, even hesitantly and after many years of inquiry, though not reluctantly, for he took authority seriously, and not blindly, for he was always able to penetrate the deliverances of authority with the light of understanding. There was no sacrifice of intellect, for he did not take a firm step until he had good reasons. He even succeeded in pursuing his own way, both as a presbyter and as a bishop, and he did not feel restrained from engaging in polemics with the self-assuredness and often the contemptuousness of a superior mind. The very fact that he and his friends were tolerated suggests that the stereotype of North African Christianity—the extravagances of the Donatists, the authoritarianism of the bishops, the vestiges of primitive paganism in much of popular piety—does not tell the whole story. Augustine's resistance to the characteristic traditions of the African Church continued until he left the relatively isolated and carefree life of a contemplative, then of a local presbyter, and

[1] Georges de Plinval, *Pour connaître la pensée de saint Augustin* (Paris, 1954), p. 89.
[2] Brown, *Augustine of Hippo*, pp. 33–34.

assumed responsibility as a bishop, and an important one at that, a man to whom his colleagues looked for intellectual and tactical leadership in the affairs of the Church. His case confirms once again the insight of the "group dynamics" people—if you want to change someone's opinions, get him involved in a problem situation and give him responsibilities in it.

During his first years in Hippo as a presbyter, Augustine devoted himself especially to the study of Scripture and searched out whatever commentaries produced in Latin or translated from the Greek could be found. This did not exactly involve a narrowing of his vision, for he did not revoke any of his philosophical opinions, but there was a focusing of his attention upon the life of the Christian community and the teachings of Scripture and tradition. With such a constant stream of new influences he may have experienced some disorientation in his intellectual convictions, but it would be wrong to overdramatize his subjection to authority; his earlier "rationalism" was not completely displaced, though certainly it was modified by his new interest in the literal meaning of the biblical text and the events reported in it.[3] He read widely in ecclesiastical writings, chiefly exegetical, and doubtless honored the authority of tradition in them, but he retained his own right of judgment in both theology and exegesis and increasingly tried to work out guidelines of his own in both those areas.

Without his stay in Milan, Augustine would not have broken free of the simple and authoritarian spirit of the Christianity he knew in his youth. And yet, without his return to Africa and his assumption of ecclesiastical duties the Christian philosopher would not have been in a position to run the course that he did. During his years in Hippo he was forced to think about new and unexpected problems. He did not forget what he had learned from Cicero and Varro, Plotinus and Porphyry; his philosophical aims remained the same. But he had to deal with new materials, and they were only gradually elucidated and brought into the framework of what Augustine could hold as his own reasoned understanding of the matter. In the process what had at first

---

[3] Alberto Pincherle, *La formazione teologica di Sant'Agostino* (Rome, 1947), pp. 150, 190–193, seems to draw too much of a contrast between his attitudes in Hippo and those taken previously.

seemed alien to his perspective was gradually absorbed and recast by it.

1. THE STRUCTURE OF FINITE BEING

This is perhaps the most appropriate point at which to discuss Augustine's metaphysic. There are, to be sure, anticipations of all its essential features even earlier, throughout the period covered in the foregoing chapter, and its fullest exposition comes just beyond the close of the period with which we are dealing, in book XII of the *Confessions*; but it was during these first years in Hippo that he began to work it out systematically for the first time. His activities as a presbyter and his interest in the study of Scripture did not suppress his concern for philosophical problems. It was during these years that he again took up a work that he had begun in Rome, *On Free Will*. He says (*Retr.*, I, 9, 1) that he worked on it from time to time as he was able, in the midst of his other activities; thus it serves as a repository of his philosophical reflections during the period, and the work as a whole gives a stratigraphic record of the course of Augustine's thought between 388 and 395 or 396. The earlier portion probably extends through II, 16, 43,[4] for the atmosphere is that of other early writings, strongly focused on the inward life, while from II, 16, 44 on there is a new interest in generalizing about all created things, corporeal and incorporeal, in the same categories, and he does it with a sureness of touch which suggests that he had a sense of the direction he wanted to move. But not only in a philosophical work like this one, but even in an ecclesiastical address like *On Faith and the Creed*, delivered before a synod meeting in Hippo in 393, and an exegetical writing like the unfinished "literal commentary on Genesis," written about 393 or 394, he manifests his interest in the problem of matter and form which is central to his metaphysic.

In these years, then, Augustine's metaphysic was worked out in what is essentially its finished form (what will be added later is not a "metaphysic," in the sense of an account of abiding structures, but a "cosmology," a detailed account of the exact character

---

[4] I am in agreement with du Roy's judgment on this (*L'Intelligence de la foi en la Trinité*, pp. 237–238).

of the cosmos and its development; this will be discussed in chapter 4, section 2). It is undeniably based upon what he learned of Platonist philosophy from Cicero and Varro, Plotinus and Porphyry, and the Pythagorean Nicomachus; but it is a Platonism that is checked against, and in some important instances modified by, Scripture and the doctrines of the Church.

The most important insight, and one which came only in this period, is that the same set of concepts can be applied to material and immaterial being. The time can be pinpointed accurately, I think, for the doctrine is first put forward in the unfinished Genesis commentary. Like other ancient men Augustine was disturbed at the absence of any clear reference to the creation of the angels, who played such an important role in the administration of the cosmos, and he was receptive to the suggestions of Origen in his first homily on Genesis[5] that the angels are designated in the mention of the heavens in verse 1 or of the waters above the firmament in verse 7.

The imagery of the waters above the firmament reminded him (*De Gen. op. imp.*, 8, 29) of something he had read in Plotinus concerning "spiritual matter" (*Enn.* V, 1, 5, which Augustine certainly read, and also V, 3, 8 and 11; V, 4, 2). Plotinus, following out Aristotle's correlation of matter and form with potentiality and actualization, applied them to the mental realm as well as the corporeal (as did Aristotle himself in *De anima* 430a 10–25). The basis of comparison is that in the act of knowing there is a distinction between knower and known; the knower is made a knower only by the act of knowing, and this actuality, this being a knower, is dependent upon that which is known. There has been, then, an *actualization* of the subject by the object, a passage into act, which presupposes some element of potentiality within the knower. Before or apart from actual vision, "sight seeing," there would be only looking, "sight not yet seeing." Thus when Plotinus speaks of a material principle within the spiritual realm, he means to suggest that the mind is an indeterminate substratum which becomes fully actualized only in knowing definite objects. Even when this potentiality is ceaselessly being actualized (as he thinks it is in the case of the divine hypostases), there is still potentiality and actualization, and the material principle is

---

[5] Altaner, "Augustinus und Origenes," pp. 23–25 (*KpS*, pp. 233–236).

constantly dependent upon the object of knowledge and desires to adhere to it.[6]

Given Augustine's assumption that the angels are mentioned somewhere in the creation narrative and his predisposition to find resonances of the highest philosophy in the biblical text, it is not surprising that he would look for metaphors which might designate the angels and would take this notion of materiality, extended to the whole of created reality, as the key to their discovery and interpretation. In the waters of the deep, mentioned in verse 2 (*De Gen. op. imp.*, 4, 17), and then in the waters above the firmament, mentioned in verse 7 (8, 29), he sees an intimation of the intrinsic instability and vacillation, the *fluitatio*, which characterizes the life of created spirits when they live from their own resources alone. They are capable, however, of gaining knowledge of God and his Truth, and then they come to be "formed" by virtue and wisdom so that their mutability is restrained and held under control ("*cohibetur atque constringitur*" [8, 29]).

I have suggested that this connection was first made when Augustine began reflecting on the Genesis account, but the same universal hylemorphism then appears in other than exegetical contexts, especially in the sections of *On Free Will* written in Hippo. He stresses that all finite things, both body and mind, are mutable and thus "formable"; that they cannot form themselves but must be formed by the unchangeable and eternal Form; that form is the basis of whatever being they have, and that the loss of form is what reduces them to nonbeing (*De lib. arb.*, II, 16, 44—17, 46). He calls the intrinsic powers of the soul "*media bona*," good things of which either a good or a bad use can be made through the

---

[6] See René Arnou, "Le thème néoplatonicien de la contemplation créatrice chez Origène et chez saint Augustin," *Gregorianum*, XIII (1932), pp. 124–136, and "Platonisme des Pères," *Dictionnaire de théologie catholique*, XII, 2, cols. 2355–59; Joachim Ritter, *Mundus Intelligibilis. Eine Untersuchung zur Aufnahme und Umwandlung der neuplatonischen Ontologie bei Augustinus* (Philosophische Abhandlungen, VI; Frankfurt am Main, 1937); J. Wytzes, "Bemerkungen zu dem neuplatonischen Einfluss in Augustins 'de Genesi ad literam,'" *Zeitschrift für neutestamentliche Wissenschaft*, XXXIX (1940), pp. 137–151; Jean Pépin, "Recherches sur le sens et les origines de l'expression 'caelum caeli' dans le livre XII des 'Confessions' de saint Augustin," *Bulletin du Cange. Archivum Latinitatis Medii Aevi*, XXIII (1953), pp. 185–274; Hilary Armstrong, "Spiritual or Intelligible Matter," *AM*, I, pp. 277–283; Eugene TeSelle, "Nature and Grace in Augustine's Expositions of Genesis I, 1–5," *RA*, V (1968), pp. 102–103.

soul's free exercise of them, and the problem is to use them in a way that is unqualifiedly good by obeying the divine rules of virtue and cleaving to God as the unchanging Good (II, 19, 50–53). There is nothing radically new in all of this; the association of being in the proper sense of the term with form and order and union with God, and of nonbeing with loss of form, disarray, aversion from God, is part of his earliest inheritance from Plotinus and Porphyry, and the view that the various dimensions of finite being are reflections of the Trinity comes from his first ventures in theological reflection. What is added now is a more explicit attempt to draw all levels of being together.

At the heart of this metaphysic is what one might call a two-stage understanding of creation as first the positing of "matter" (corporeal and spiritual) and then the formation of this material substratum by the influence of the Word and its stabilization by the Spirit; there is, to use Augustine's own later terminology, first *existence*, the coming forth of matter as something other than God, and then *conversion*, not always a conscious "turning" but matter's being changed for the better and becoming similar to God in some respect (*Conf.*, XII, 3, 4; *De Gen. ad litt.*, I, 5, 10). This is, of course, the familiar neo-Platonic scheme of πρόοδος and ἐπιστροφή, developed by Plotinus to describe the career of the soul, but extended by Augustine (perhaps following Porphyry, who believed in the creation of matter, or Marius Victorinus) to the corporeal world as well.

It is clear that conversion is far more important than the mere coming forth. Therefore Gilson is correct in calling Augustine's metaphysic "essentialist," and despite his obvious preference for the "existentialist" metaphysic that he ascribes (correctly or not) to Aquinas his analyses of the precise character of this metaphysic are sympathetic and quite penetrating.[7] By an essentialist ontology two distinct things can be meant, and both of them apply to Augustine's thought. The first is merely grammatical. From the time of *On the Immortality of the Soul* he calls God *Essentia*. The expression should not be understood along the lines of the Thomist distinction between *esse* and *essentia*, actuality and that

[7] Gilson, *The Christian Philosophy of St. Augustine*, pp. 200–205, and also 21–23; "Notes sur l'être et le temps chez saint Augustin," *RA*, II (1962), pp. 205–223.

which is actualized. Augustine inherited the term from Cicero, who coined it as an equivalent of the Greek οὐσία, "being-ness," "being itself." Augustine's own participationist understanding of the term becomes unmistakable in the passages in which he contrasts beautiful things and Beauty itself (*pulchra* and *Pulchritudo*), or similar things and Likeness itself (*similia* and *Similitudo* [*De div. quaest.*, q. 23; *De ver. rel.*, 43, 81; *De Gen. op. imp.*, 16, 57–59]); God, then, is being itself (*Essentia*), through whom finite things have being (*esse*). Thus far the term is equivalent with the more Thomistic-sounding "*ipsum esse*." What sets Augustine's metaphysic apart from Aquinas's is not mere terminology but the substance of what is asserted. For Aquinas the fundamental distinction within finite being is between that which is (*essentia*) and that *by* which it is (*esse*); for Augustine it is between the *existentia* of an already real material principle, which furnishes the substratum of potentialities, and the *esse* in which those potentialities are fulfilled as much as they can be and in a way appropriate to them ("*pro suo modulo*," as he usually says) through becoming formed and coordinated and directed toward an end. The experienced world of regulated and orderly sequence stands, so to speak, "between" the sheer mutability and indeterminacy of matter and the perfect stability of God. Any degree of form and order that is attained comes about when matter, which has "gone forth" as other than God, "turns back" by undergoing a change for the better and participates to some degree in his perfection of being. But however much it comes to be "like God," it is always with a difference, for within the finite there is always a composition of matter with form, of the indeterminate substratum of activity with the definiteness which it acquires from God through participation, while God is identical with all the perfections of being and intelligibility and right orientation.

That which is unique to the finite, then, is "materiality," whether corporeal or spiritual. It is clear that Augustine thinks it possible to give some description of materiality, for it is one component of our experience and it can even be considered by itself, leaving out of account for the moment the element of form which must also be present if anything is to be experienced at all. Physical occurrences are always characterized by separation or externality in both space and time. An event occurs and perishes, giving way to another; but it has occurred in its own place and time, differentiated from all others. Now materiality is not identical with space and time as we experience them; space and time represent the overcoming of sheer materiality to a considerable degree by formation and unification, both in physical processes, where the continuity of time and space is created by communities of form and discreteness is a function of the differentiation and variation of forms (*Conf.*, XII, 9, 9: 11, 14; 12, 15), and in our own experience, where we surmount the isolation of sheer privacy by "projecting" or "extending" our attention toward the things which have occasioned some new modulation in our sensory organs to construe spaces, and surmount the fleeting present by "protracting" or "distending" our attention through a succession of well-defined occurrences to create duration and measure periods of time. Thus whatever definiteness or continuity the finite possesses is the outcome of form or intention. Matter by itself is only the principle of mutability and extensivity, the unordered flux which is always hastening on, the indeterminate spreading out which isolates event from event. It is only through the introduction of form or intention that materiality is "pinched off" into well-defined events and sequences and structures.

But materiality is a precondition of there being any finite world at all. God is perfectly self-identical and perfectly stable, neither divided into parts nor changing, neither *alter* nor *aliter* (*Conf.*, VII, 20, 26).[8] If finite things are to be something more than a phantasmagorical play of ideas in the simplicity of the divine intellect they must have an "existence" of their own, and they are differentiated from God ("*non quod ipse est*") precisely through their lack of perfect simplicity and self-identity (*Conf.*, VII, 11, 17; *De nat. bon.*, 10). To say that matter is *other* than God is not to say that it is totally *opposed* to him or in every way unlike him; Augustine resisted this implication in Plotinus (especially in *Enn.* I, 8) as being too close to Manichaeism and instead followed Porphyry in granting to matter a minimal degree of being and even goodness (*De ver. rel.*, 18, 35–36).[9] Matter does have an aspect of "nothingness," but in the familiar and quite undramatic sense of *descriptive negation*: if something is here it is not there, if

[8] Gilson, "Notes sur l'être et le temps," pp. 214–215.
[9] Du Roy, *L'Intelligence de la foi en la Trinité*, pp. 194–195.

it exists now it does not exist then, if it is this it is not that. Non-being in this sense is prerequisite to the rise of definiteness in the realm of the finite: if there is to be *something*, it must be set apart from something else that it is *not*.[10] Matter as the basis of change and pluralization prior to all form is designated by Augustine as "*nihil aliquid*" or "*est non est*" (*Conf.*, XII, 6, 6), expressions reminiscent, of course, of Plato's "that which is always becoming and never is" (*Tim.*, 28A).

It is much the same in the case of finite spirit. Here Augustine is concerned to distinguish between what is intrinsic and what is adventitious to the life of spirit, for the experiencing of physical space and time belongs to it only in its aspect of animating the body and being concerned, properly or improperly, with sensible occurrences. Leaving these aside, there is one phenomenon that is intrinsic to the life of the mind, and that is the successiveness of its own inward acts. It is mutable through and through. Being indeterminate, it is under the necessity of directing its attention and affection freely toward one or another of the data of experience (itself, finite things, God). Being changeable, it is always faced with a fresh future; its acts last only for the moment and its attention will be flitting constantly from one thing to another. Thus finite spirit does not arise fully constituted; it has the character of a *task*, for it is aware of itself and its own freedom, and of the wider field of reality within which it stands, and of its responsibility for setting itself in relation to all these things, moment by moment. Even then it is capable of transcending the flow of temporality through its own consciousness, not by a mere collation of images, for this would never create duration, but through the inclusion of one inward act in another through remembrance and anticipation, self-identity and steadiness of purpose. Indeed, it cannot help transcending the flow of physical occurrence, even the flow of its own acts. But this is not sufficient by itself either to give satisfaction or to draw it entirely above the hazards of time, and the greater part of Augustine's analysis of consciousness in the *Confessions* (books X and XI) and elsewhere is concerned

---

[10] Jules Chaix-Ruy, *Saint Augustin. Temps et histoire* (Paris, 1956), p. 105, works out on Augustinian principles a "transcendental deduction of space and time" as "the application of the principle of non-contradiction to the realm of existence."

with the mind's loss of control, its dispersion and self-alienation in the vastness of space and the variability of time.[11] A full integration of consciousness comes, to be sure, through steadiness of vision and constancy of purpose; but these are finally secured only in relation to God, who unifies in himself the whole of time and space.

If you wish to escape unhappiness, love your own desire to *be*. If you wish to gain more and more being, you will draw near to him who is supremely. . . . The more fully you love being, the more you will desire eternal life, and you will then hope so to be "formed" that your affections are not temporal, bearing the impress of love for temporal things . . . . He who loves being will approve of finite things insofar as they are, but he will love that which is eternally. If he was always drifting about in the love of those things, he will become strong in loving this; if he was dispersed in the love of transient things, he will become stable in loving that which abides, he will himself abide, and thus he will possess in himself that being which he desired when he feared nonbeing but was not able to stand firm, ensnared as he was by love for fleeting things . . . . If, starting with this desire to be, you add more and more being, you will strive upward and build toward that which is supremely, and in this way you will also be safeguarded from the ruin with which lower things pass away, undermining the powers of him who loves them (*De lib. arb.*, III, 7, 21).

I am divided by times whose order I do not know, and my thoughts, the inmost organs of my soul, are torn apart by the confusion of change, and so it will be until, purified and melted by the fire of your love, I flow into you. Then I shall become stable in you and be set firm in the mold of your Truth (*Conf.*, XI, 29, 39–30, 40).

Although all finite things bear within them the stigmata of changeability and disparateness, matter nonetheless has a positive capacity to receive form and to be drawn into organized wholes (*De ver. rel.*, 18, 36; *De fid. et symb.*, 2, 2; *De nat. bon.*, 18), and it can even be brought to a kind of perfection when it is fully formed and stabilized—in this contemplation of the eternal God in the case of "spiritual matter," in the perpetual circular motion of the heavenly bodies, imitating eternity, in the case of corporeal

[11] See the discussions of Augustine's phenomenology of the disintegration of consciousness in fallen man in Chaix-Ruy, pp. 39, 74–75, 109–112, etc.; and Jean-Marie Le Blond, *Les Conversions de saint Augustin* (*Théologie*, XVII; Paris, 1950), pp. 269–272.

matter (*De mus.*, VI, 11, 29). There is not a radical dualism of matter and form as alien principles brought into tragic conflict; that is precisely what Augustine had encountered and rejected in Manichaeism. For many years he refrained from using the Greek term *hyle* at all because of its Manichaean associations, and when he did use it he noted that he understood it in the sense given it by the *antiqui*, as referring to that which is without form or quality (*De nat. bon.*, 18).[12] Matter thus has the character of indeterminate potentiality, of "meontic" nonbeing, of that which is "not yet" what it can become. Of course the development comes from God and not from within matter itself. But the stress on matter's capacity for quality and form and harmony suggests that it supports and does not hinder the process of formation and stabilization, that it has a readiness to become the vehicle of a definiteness and a continuity that are based elsewhere, that form really becomes ingredient in matter. And if any uncertainty remains about Augustine's assumptions concerning corporeal matter, there can be none when it comes to spiritual matter, for he could not be more explicit in his assertions about the mind's capacity for the knowledge of God in which it becomes fully formed.

But matter, though it has a capacity for form, does not form itself; its intrinsic tendency is not toward form but toward dispersion and disruption. Unformed matter, if it existed by itself, would not even exhibit time and space in the usual sense (though it is the principle of mutability and extensivity), because times and spaces are functions of orderly continuities and variations of form (*Conf.*, XII, 9, 9; 11, 14; 12, 15). This complete obscurity and randomness and disparateness may be what Augustine was referring to when he said that God made all things from that which is "nothing else than nothingness" (*De ver. rel.*, 18, 35), or when he described form as that by which a thing is kept from nothingness (*De div. quaest.*, q. 18). Here we have nothingness as the opposite of ordered being, the scattering and nullification of form, sequence, or coordination. Matter, functioning by itself, "tends, by its formlessness, toward nothingness" (*De Gen. ad litt.*, I, 4, 9); that is, it does not permit the rise of pattern and order. And nothingness in the sense of the dispersion and disruption of

[12] For Augustine's various discussions of corporeal matter, see du Roy, pp. 273–276.

whatever order has been achieved is the abyss over which every composite being is suspended.

This is the point at which the problem of evil enters, for Augustine understands evil as disruption of form or perversity of orientation. In the corporeal world, despite the facts of disaster, starvation, predation, and disease, all those occasions which are usually called "natural evils," Augustine persists in calling everything unequivocally good (*Conf.*, VII, 13, 19), not because it is good in each individual case, but because the nexus of action and reaction—the inevitability of physical processes, the adaptation of organisms to their environment and the appropriateness of their instincts to their needs and abilities, the symbiotic or hierarchical relationships among species—together constitute a balanced whole.[13] In the spiritual realm, by contrast, the threat of disruption is not arrested by natural form; everything is left to the free activity of finite spirit, and there is always the possibility that it will forfeit its proper destiny. The only "evil" that deserves the name, Augustine thinks, is that introduced by sin, whether it be the sin itself or the consequences and penalties of sin.

Augustine argues, against the Manichaeans, that evil has no existence as a separate principle but that it is produced by finite freedom in its defection from the higher good to the lower and that the basis of this freely enacted defection is not an actual thing but "nothingness," not an efficient cause but a "deficient cause" (*De lib. arb.*, II, 20, 54; *De civ. Dei*, XII, 7). One is first tempted to suspect that Augustine is merely being clever. But he repeats this turn of phrase enough times and with sufficient solemnity to suggest that he has something in mind.

It is hard to pin it down, however. At the heart of evil is an act of defection, the turning away from the higher good for a lesser good. But it is never a direct willing of evil. However malicious it may appear to be (as in Augustine's own youthful escapade of stealing a neighbor's pears), willing is always for the sake of *some* value, though that value may be insignificant or inappropriate (*Conf.*, II, 4, 9—8, 16). And however foolish or disastrous a course of action may be, nothing can be willed which appears contrary to one's own happiness, though the understanding of happiness may

---

[13] See especially Régis Jolivet, *Le problème du mal d'après saint Augustin* (Paris, ²1936), pp. 52ff.

be shortsighted and influenced by the passion of the moment (*C. Jul. op. imp.*, VI, 11–12). Even suicide is not for the sake of death itself but to be rid of intolerable sufferings or disappointments (*De lib. arb.*, III, 8, 23).

Where, then, does nothingness enter into the evil act? In the instability of finite life, I think, in the constant possibility that what has already been attained will be disrupted and what could be attained will be forfeited by the attraction of lesser values. Freedom is ceaselessly thrown out over the abyss of "nothingness" in the sense that its capacity to be fully formed by divine Wisdom is threatened by its own mutability and defectibility. And it is here that God's final work is done; for if Augustine sees the work of the Father in the bare existence of finite spirit, and the work of the Word in calling man to virtue and holding out the possibility of wisdom and beatitude, he sees the work of the Spirit in giving a right orientation to the will and sustaining it despite the will's own instability.

I have tried to outline in some detail how the same metaphysical schema, and one which is centered on dynamic process rather than permanent substance, is applied to both the physical world and man's inward life, doubtless in an analogical way, bending the coordinates in keeping with the differing character of various levels of being. Such a method, though it is alien to some types of philosophy, is not unfamiliar in our own day, for it is the one chosen by Whitehead and Teilhard (to name only two of the more comprehensive attempts in the twentieth century), as it was by Leibniz before them: if one wishes to have a total framework of interpretation, they would argue, he must take his departure from, and keep constantly in view, our own experiences and activities, for these, after all, are fully as "actual" as the things we apprehend by external sensation and because of their accessibility and greater complexity are far more instructive. Something of the same concern animated Augustine and those from whom he learned his philosophy.

Because of the breadth of applicability of his metaphysical schema, it has always been possible for "Augustinians" to make an easy crossing between philosophy and theology and back again, pressing their quest for understanding farther into the mysteries of faith and at the same time approaching all of knowledge assisted by insights derived from faith. Their methods have always seemed suspect to the followers of other, more cautious schools, and they themselves have often stood to profit from the careful criticisms of others when their speculations soared too high; but the Augustinian tradition indicates at least one of the things meant by "Christian philosophy": here, at least, the two terms are held together without final tension, for, leaving aside whatever use may be made of metaphysics within theology as such, the Christian faith is assumed to be compatible with general knowledge and even to call for the making of connections between the two—and on the other hand to demand of any metaphysic that it at least take into account the phenomena of inward experience and specifically those of the Christian life.

2. SON OF GOD AND SON OF MAN

Augustine mentions in the *Confessions* (VII, 19, 25) that for a time prior to his conversion he thought of Christ along lines which he later discovered were equivalent to the Photinian heresy: that is, as a man born of a virgin, of greater wisdom than all others, and deserving an authoritative position as a teacher of divine truth, but not the Truth in person.[14] He mentions in addition that Alypius was under the impression that the Catholic Church—the opponent of the Photinians in those days—taught that Christ was "God clothed in flesh," without a human soul or mind; and that he later discovered that this was not the Catholic teaching after all, but the heresy of the Apollinarians.[15] Both of them, he says, recognized that the things narrated about Christ in the gospels could not be true if he did not have a human soul and mind; for he is said to have eaten, spoken, walked, slept, rejoiced, and sorrowed, and such intermittent activities and passivities, as Augustine knew from his readings in philosophy, are proper not to the

[14] Solignac (*BA*, XIII, 693–695) disposes of the suggestion that this view of Christ came from Porphyry. If it was not the outcome of Augustine's own reflections, it must be an echo of a Photinian brand of Christianity in Milan.

[15] Robert J. O'Connell, "Alypius' 'Apollinarianism' at Milan (*Conf.*, VII, 25)," *REA*, XIII (1967), 209–210, has put to rest the common assertion of the scholars (based on a surprisingly inattentive reading of the text) that Alypius' own views were Apollinarian. Augustine clearly says that a misconception of the Catholic teaching *held him back* from giving assent to it.

divine Word (or Understanding, as he would have said then), which is immutable, but to "soul," which changes in time and mediates between the divine Understanding and bodies. The point, then, is that Alypius, to his own despair, supposed that Catholic doctrine denied any mediating principle; and Augustine, perhaps more daring, thought of Christ as a complete man, but in such fashion that he could be only a wise man participating in the Word, not the Word incarnate. They soon found that the Catholic faith avoided both errors, teaching both that Jesus had a complete humanity, body and soul and mind, and that he was nonetheless one person with the Word.

Augustine's closing comment should not be overlooked. "Surely it is the process of refuting heretics," he says, "that brings to light the mind of your Church and the content of sound teaching. There must be heresies, in order that those who are tested and proved genuine might be manifested in the midst of the weak (cf. I Corinthians 11, 19)." This is not, I think, merely a moral added at the end but a comment on the actual situation of that day. In 386 the doctrinal controversies with the Photinians and the Apollinarians had just come to a resolution; tendencies toward the one side or the other were still present, and the positive doctrine of the Church had not been made entirely clear.

Augustine's Christology, to be sure, was "orthodox" by the standards of his day, and probably by the standards of a later day. He affirmed clearly enough that the Word and the man were united in one person and that what is said of one can be said of the other, not because of a confusion of natures but because of their conjunction in one person; that Jesus did not first exist as a man and then come to be assumed into unity with God, but that he was assumed from the first moment of his existence; that his uniqueness consists not merely in a moral purity resulting from virginal conception but in a singular assumption into unity with God. In his first venture in preaching, shortly before Easter, 391, Augustine already had a well-worked-out Christology:

A complete man, that is, a rational soul and a body, was assumed by the Word, in such fashion as to be one Christ and one God the Son of God, not the Word alone, but the Word *and* the man [or as he puts it more explicitly in the next paragraph, Word and soul and flesh], and this whole [*totum hoc*] is the Son of God the Father according to the Word and the son of man according to the man. . . . He is not only man but Son of God, but according to the Word, by whom the man is assumed; and he is not only the Word but the son of man, but according to the man, who is assumed by the Word (*Serm*. 214, 6).

But the most interesting question, surely, is not whether Augustine's views fall within the pale of orthodoxy but what precisely his views are. And in answering this question it is most misleading to take the point of view of the period after the Council of Chalcedon in 451 or after Cyril's challenge to Nestorius in 428. Augustine lived in an earlier epoch, one in which other problems were being debated, and it is important, for both historical and theological reasons, to appreciate them in their own right.

Augustine adhered to what must be called an "Origenist" Christology—the doctrine, given classic statement in Origen's *De principiis*, II, 6, that the soul of Christ is the medium of union between the Word and the flesh and that it is inseparably united to the Word with such an intensity of affection and immediacy of intuition that it becomes like the Word in every respect, as iron heated in fire becomes fiery itself. For a century following the condemnation of Paul of Samosata in 268 this Christology was temporarily obscured, for it looked too much like adoptionism; theologians generally assumed that the Word directly assumed flesh without a human soul or, if with an animal soul, then without a human mind.[16] But the Origenist Christology had a brief reflowering during the controversy with Apollinaris after 377; a series of councils, beginning with one held in Rome under Damasus, declared against the view that anything was lacking in Christ's humanity, and theologians like Gregory Nazianzen and Gregory of Nyssa rehabilitated Origen's language, weaving it into a more fully developed doctrine.

---

[16] For the Christology of that period see Charles E. Raven, *Apollinarianism: An Essay on the Christology of the Early Church* (New York, 1923); Friedrich Loofs, *Paulus von Samosata. Eine Untersuchung zur altkirchlichen Literatur und Dogmengeschichte* (Texte und Untersuchungen, 3. Reihe, XIV, 5; Leipzig, 1924); Henri de Riedmatten, *Les actes du procès de Paul de Samosate. Étude sur la Christologie du IIIe et IVe siècle* (Fribourg en Suisse, 1952); Alois Grillmeier, "Die theologische und sprachliche Vorbereitung der Christologischen Formel von Chalkedon," *Das Konzil von Chalkedon* (Würzburg, 1951), pp. 1–242 (translated separately under the title *Christ in the Christian Tradition* [New York, 1965], pp. 183–237).

Augustine was the inheritor of that period of theological renaissance, and in the writings that come from his first years as a presbyter in Hippo he indicates his knowledge of, and assent to, its Christology. He echoes the famous statement of Gregory Nazianzen (*Ep.* 101), "What is not assumed is not healed," in a number of his writings (*De ver. rel.*, 16, 30; *De fid. et symb.*, 4, 8; *De ag. chr.*, 19, 21).[17] He describes the soul or mind or spirit of Jesus as the intermediary of the union between Word and flesh, even between Word and animated body, usually with the purpose of showing how the Word can remain free from the desires and fears of the body even while assuming a human life into unity with himself (*De fid. et symb.*, 4, 10; *De div. quaest.*, q. 73 and q. 80; *De ag. chr.*, 18, 20); he speaks, furthermore, of the human mind of Jesus being joined to and mixed with (*copulatus, commixtus*) the Word in unity of person (*De div. quaest.*, q. 73, 2; *C. Faust.*, XXII, 40; *De Trin.*, IV, 13, 16 and 20, 30). And both of these, once more, are a special emphasis of Gregory Nazianzen in his letter to Cledonius (*Ep.* 101).[18] The difference between the union of Jesus and that of other men with the Word is described as one between the unique assumption of a human life to "bear the person" of the Wisdom of God and the mere reception of the benefits of that Wisdom (*De ag. chr.*, 20, 22), between possession of the Wisdom of God *naturaliter* and merely *participatione* (*Exp. ep. ad Gal.*, 27; cf. *Enchir.*, 12, 40). This contrast between physical and participated union could again be derived from Gregory Nazianzen, who in the same letter said that in Christ there is a union in being, a συνάψις κατ᾽ οὐσίαν, while in the prophets there was merely a gracious activity of God, an ἐνεργεία κατὰ χάριν.[19] It is known that this epistle of Gregory existed in a Latin translation, at least at a later time, and the striking parallels in Augustine suggest that it was already available.[20] It would not be surprising to find it circulating in the West, for there was regular contact between

[17] Tarsicius J. van Bavel, *Recherches sur la christologie de saint Augustin. L'humain et le divin dans le Christ d'après saint Augustin* (Paradosis, X; Fribourg en Suisse, 1954), p. 51, n. 130.

[18] *Ibid.*, p. 181.

[19] Cf. *ibid.*, p. 14, n. 2.

[20] Altaner, "Augustinus und Didymus der Blinde," *Vigiliae Christianae*, V (1951), 118 (*KpS*, p. 299), calls attention to the fact of this translation but leaves open the question whether the letter was already translated in Augustine's day.

Rome and the East during the Apollinarian controversy, and Gregory's own letters (101 and 102) show that he knew of the proceedings of the Roman synods of 377 and 382.

For a time, between 393 and 395, Augustine used the expression "*dominicus homo*" with reference to Christ as man. This expression has a confused history. It was used by Athanasius and other writers, then it was taken over by the Apollinarians. Gregory Nazianzen disliked the term, for to him it carried Apollinarian connotations (*Ep.* 101, 2). But it was used by Damasus in an anti-Apollinarian sense in a letter to Paulinus about 377, and again in the draft of an anti-Apollinarian document prepared for him by Jerome following his arrival in Rome in 382. Jerome says in his *Apology* (II, 20) that the Apollinarians led by Vitalis challenged the term, and when he took them to his library to show them the passage in which Athanasius had used it he found that they had already tampered with the manuscript to make it look like a forgery. Augustine probably derived it from none of these sources, however, but from Jerome's translation of Didymus' work *On the Holy Spirit*, translated about 389.[21] In chapters 51 and 52 the expression is used with reference to the man assumed by the Son and filled with the Holy Spirit; and in the translation, at least (the original does not survive), its import is clearly anti-Apollinarian.

Although Augustine soon abandoned the expression "*dominicus homo*" because of what seemed to him its adoptionist overtones, he never ceased to speak of "the man" assumed by the Word. And I think enough has been said about the Christology of Augustine and of his age to indicate that it gave somewhat more stress to the human being and intellect and will of Jesus than the position widely assumed today to be the "orthodox" doctrine. Therefore it cannot be assumed, as beyond all doubt, that they viewed the Word as the "personal center" of Jesus' consciousness and activity and his human mind as purely instrumental to it. Something more is ascribed to the human intellect and will than that, and they had no fear of using the expression "the man."

It may be objected that Augustine speaks of the humanity being assumed into unity of person with the Word. But this term "person" was an extremely fluid one in that era, not yet reduced to

[21] Altaner, "Augustinus und Didymus der Blinde," 117–118 (*KpS*, pp. 298–299).

any standard doctrinal or theological meaning. Very often Augustine is employing it in its older Latin sense, drawn from the usage of the legal profession and the grammarians, of office or function; he can speak of angels "bearing the person" of God in doing miracles or otherwise acting in God's behalf (*De Trin.*, II, 13, 23; III, 10, 19), or he can say that among the evangelists Luke is the one who describes Christ more "in his person as priest" (*De cons. ev.*, I, 2, 3), or he can suggest that in Scripture Christ sometimes speaks "in the person of his body [the Church]" and sometimes "in his own person as head" (*Enarr. in Ps.* 40).[22] If Augustine's language often stresses the *unity* of function between the Word and the man, often enough it stresses just the opposite, a *difference* between them in one respect or another. The notion of person does not by itself offer any solution, therefore.

It may also be objected that Augustine thought of Christ as having perfect knowledge throughout his life, and as having a certain imperturbability or impassivity of mind. But these are part of his picture of an ideal humanity which he thought all men should have and which, for part of his career, he thought attainable by them even during the present life. Many of the statements found in patristic Christology, we must remember, are affected by the general anthropology of that period, and those today who wish to modify that anthropology must at the same time take seriously the necessity of making corresponding adjustments in their Christology. This is precisely what has been done in Protestant theology since Schleiermacher, and recently in Catholic theology with Rahner and others, to give more of a place to Jesus' growth both in wisdom and in stature.

Now it is obvious that Augustine wanted to say that the Word, remaining in the form of God, assumed the man into unity of person with himself. But it is just as clear that Augustine thought in terms of two minds, human and divine, and two wills, joined, to be sure, without any possibility of falling away, but still with a distinct human life, even a "private" life (*Enarr. II in Ps.* 32, serm. 1, 2), and experiencing all the temptations arising from it, though always being sustained because of the unity with God.[23]

---

[22] For texts see Otto Scheel, *Die Anschauung Augustins über Christi Person und Werk* (Tübingen, 1901), pp. 185–186.

[23] Van Bavel, pp. 135–145.

And any simplistic doctrine of a "Logos hegemony" in the person of Christ stumbles over the fact that Augustine always believed that all three persons of the Trinity are operative in the assumption of the humanity, and doubtless in the continuation of its union with God as well.

This is clearly his view throughout *The Trinity*, and it appears as early as 390, in a letter written in reply to some questions of Nebridius (*Ep.* 11). Nebridius had asked why the Son and not some other person of the Trinity became incarnate. Augustine began by arguing at some length that the persons always act simultaneously and inseparably, and he proved it from the three dimensions of finite being, all of which must be present if there is to be anything at all. The same must apply to the man Jesus: all three persons must be operative in him. Why, then, is he said to be the incarnation of the Word in particular?

Form, which is attributed specifically to the Son, pertains to instruction, and to artistry (if we may use that term in this connection), and to understanding, in which the soul is formed by knowledge. And because in his case the assumption of a man insinuated into our minds, through the majesty and clarity of the thoughts conveyed to them, instruction in living and at the same time an example of those same precepts, it is not without reason that all of this is attributed to the Son. In many matters, which I leave to your own reflection and insight, there may be a number of factors and yet only one of them so stands out that everything can, without absurdity, be ascribed to it in particular. In this case the primary purpose was to exhibit a certain rule or norm of instruction. That was accomplished through the dispensation of the man who was assumed, and it is to be attributed properly to the Son, in order that there might be knowledge *of the Father*, the one Source from whom all things exist, *through the Son*, and an inward, unutterably sweet enjoyment in remaining in this knowledge and shunning all mortal things, which is a gift properly attributed to the *Holy Spirit*. Therefore even though all things are done inseparably, in supreme harmony, still they needed to be exhibited distinctly because of our lack of perception; for we had fallen from unity into diversity and change (*Ep.* 11, 4).

This is not yet a complete Christology. Its focus is more upon the way to be travelled by other men than upon the character of Jesus' union with God. But it does serve to reinforce two points: that the persons of the Trinity are operative, distinctly but inseparably, everywhere, in all things and in all men, and that the case of Jesus is no exception. Though Augustine in his subsequent writings through the years said much more than this, he never reversed the basic principles stated here. Thus a *problem* is posed to us, and we must work it through honestly if we wish to interpret Augustine's Christology in an adequate way.

The problem was discerned by August Dorner, the son of Isaac August Dorner, one of the major nineteenth-century theologians, in a monograph devoted to the systematic structure of Augustine's thought, and Dorner's interpretation was taken up by Adolf von Harnack in his *History of Dogma*.[24] They pointed out that Augustine always affirmed that the activity of incarnation or assumption is distributed among all persons of the Trinity, and therefore the uniqueness of Jesus cannot be explained as an exception to the usual mode of divine operation. Furthermore, Augustine thinks of God—Father, Son, Spirit—as present everywhere, and present everywhere in his fullness, with *all* of his being concentrated at every point ("*totus ubique*"), and therefore the uniqueness of Jesus cannot be explained as a localization of the Word in him.

How, then, can his uniqueness in the midst of creaturely reality be accounted for? The only answer is that there is a singular kind of receptivity in him to God's presence and influence. The divine activity is focused upon him in a special way, to be sure, and is the cause of this singular receptivity from the first, even before any human activities could arise. But that divine activity is completed and takes effect only when there is a finite being capable of receiving it and actually receiving it. And since Augustine located the focal point of the union in the human mind of Jesus, it must be *there*, in its abiding receptivity to the Word and its abiding intuition of the Word, that the union is realized. It would not be improper, therefore, to speak of a human mind and to make it a "psychological center," though without detriment to the language of the Church, long since

---

[24] August Dorner, *Augustinus. Sein theologisches System und seine religions-philosophische Anschauung* (Berlin, 1873), pp. 87–107; Adolf von Harnack, *Lehrbuch der Dogmengeschichte*, reprint of the last edition (Darmstadt, 1964), III, 124–139; in the English translation, V, 125–134.

standardized by Augustine's day, which spoke of the Word assuming the man into unity of person with himself. The kind of union Augustine envisaged, a unity mediated by a human mind, could involve, given his strongly Platonist psychology and epistemology, a perfect responsiveness of the human under- standing and affections to the ideal plans contained in (indeed, equivalent with) the Word, and consequently a perfect coincidence between "the Word" and "the man."

I know that this interpretation of Augustine is almost every- where spoken against. The arguments of Dorner and Harnack were soon attacked by Otto Scheel in 1901, and most subsequent writers on Augustine's Christology, assuming that what is later is probably better, have only read his book and let Dorner's lapse into obscurity. Scheel assumed—understandably enough, but still erroneously—that Dorner and Harnack were influenced too much by their own opinions in Christology and were reading them back into Augustine; he could not imagine that Augustine did not adhere to what he, Scheel, thought was the traditional and orthodox Christology. He himself could not hold to that traditional Christology, but he thought in all honesty as a historian that it was what he read in Augustine. Several genera- tions of Roman Catholic scholars, imbued with the Christology of the schools, have been disposed to accept Scheel's interpreta- tion as a plausible one. But it is time to rehabilitate Harnack's reputation as a historian of theology in this matter, dust off Dorner's volume, and judge Scheel's study, for all its assemblage of texts, as an unperceptive reading of Augustine's views.

Scheel is unable to dismiss the point that the operations of the Trinity are inseparable, for it is clearly in Augustine; but he repeatedly scoffs at the importance of the other fundamental point, that God is present everywhere and that his more intensified presence in Jesus is due to a unique receptivity of his humanity to the Word.[25] Augustine did take this problem seriously, however, and he had a well-worked-out doctrine of divine "presence," beginning with the Cassiciacum dialogues and culminating in Epistle 187, a whole "treatise on the presence of

---

[25] Scheel, pp. 46ff., 225ff., 242, etc. For what it is worth, Harnack took note of these criticisms in the later editions of his *History of Dogma* and felt that they did not affect the points he had made.

God," written in 417 or 418.[26] God, by his essence, is indivisible, and therefore *all* of God is present *everywhere* (*totus ubique*). And yet distinctions can be made. He is "present to" all things, and he is "with" them in giving them existence and form and direction; but he "dwells in" or "inhabits" only those beings which have understanding and volition, and he dwells in them only to the extent that *they* are "with" *him*, oriented toward him with affection and attentiveness (*De ord.*, I, 2, 4; II, 7, 20). According to the later discussion in Epistle 187 (13, 38–41) God dwells in only those men who are influenced by his grace, and they are able to possess him (*capere*) to greater or lesser degrees, according to their readiness. But in Christ the *fullness* of deity dwells bodily (Colossians 2, 9); he is set apart from the others because he has been made one person with the Word. His uniqueness does not mean, however, that the mode of indwelling is entirely unlike that found in other men: the difference is comparable to that between the head, which possesses all five senses, and the body, which has only the sense of touch (this illustration reinforces the suggestion that the unity of person is sustained, from the *human* side, by apprehension of the Word); and the indwelling of God in the man Jesus, though it is unique, is effected by grace just as much as the indwelling of God in other men—indeed, more than in the case of other men, for here there is a "singular grace" of assuming him into unity of person with the Word (*Ep.* 187, 13, 40).

This, I think, is the actual character of Augustine's Christology. Doubtless it is not the only Christology of the early Church. But a strong case can be made that it was the Christology generally assumed to be true during the first few centuries, until it appeared to have been condemned as adoptionism (perhaps through misunderstanding or partisanship) in the affair of Paul of Samosata. But during a crucial period in the development of doctrine, the period between the condemnation of Apollinarianism about 380 and the Council of Ephesus in 431, it came to constitute the main line of development, until once more it fell under suspicion as too close to Nestorianism. What is paradoxical about it—and this is its

[26] For an excellent treatment of the theme of divine presence, though unfortunately thin when it comes to presence in Christ, see Stanislaus J. Grabowski, *The All-Present God* (St. Louis, 1954).

value for the reconciling of apparently incompatible concerns—is that it can keep the integrity of both the divine and the human, to the extent of speaking unabashedly of "the Word" and "the man," and still bring them so closely together that it is possible to speak of "one person." This can be achieved only by placing the emphasis upon *mind* or *spirit* as the medium of union, for it can be at once active and closely conjoined to another. What is asserted here is not any less a theory of "real" or "hypostatic" union; but the reality involved is mind, and its actuality is gained through enactment, not through bare subsistence alone. That, at least, is the view of the Platonists among the fathers; and their true successors in modern theology are men like Schleiermacher and his successors on the Protestant side (up through Karl Barth, certainly), or men like Karl Rahner on the Catholic side, all of whom recognize, in their diverse ways, that human being is intentional, volitional being, and that this character of human being must be respected even in Christology.

3. SIN AND GRACE

A sudden surge of interest in the epistles of Paul becomes apparent about 394. In quick succession Augustine wrote an *Exposition of Eighty-Four Propositions on the Epistle to the Romans*, then an *Exposition of the Epistle to the Galatians*, then an unfinished *Exposition of the Epistle to the Romans*, as well as discussions of Pauline problems in questions 66 through 68 of the collection of responses to various questions. Then he broke off his inquiries for a time, either because he had become satisfied in his own mind or (what is more likely) in order to state his findings in another genre, for this is the atmosphere in which the latter portions of book III of *On Free Will* were written, certainly from 18, 50 on.[27]

It was not all Augustine's own achievement. He learned from others, and the study of the influences upon Augustine during these years has been the special domain of a succession of

[27] Pincherle, pp. 93–94; 111, n. 29. For discussion of these writings see, in addition to Pincherle, Karl Janssen, *Die Entstehung der Gnadenlehre Augustins* (Rostock, 1936); P. Platz, *Der Römerbrief in der Gnadenlehre Augustins* (Würzburg, 1937); Löhrer, *Der Glaubensbegriff des hl. Augustinus in seinen ersten Schriften bis zu den Confessiones.*

Italian scholars: Buonaiuti, who first surmised that the unknown writer whom Erasmus named "Ambrosiaster" was responsible for a change in Augustine's views of sin and grace, then Casamassa, who, though he denied the influence of Ambrosiaster, helped to make the chronology of Augustine's development more precise, and finally Pincherle, who, after an extensive study of the writings of the period, showed that the influence Buonaiuti had sensed was really a double one, first from Ambrosiaster and then, even more decisive, from Tyconius.[28]

The commentaries of Ambrosiaster on the Pauline corpus (omitting Hebrews, which the West still thought to be non-Pauline authorship) are generally acknowledged to be the most impressive literary and historical study of those writings prior to the Renaissance. (In this case as in others, Augustine had the good fortune to be standing in the way of important and suggestive influences.) The same author also wrote a series of questions on the Old and New Testaments. One curiosity is that both works have survived in several different recensions, probably emanating from the author himself.[29]

Internal evidence makes it clear that the author wrote in Rome during the papacy of Damasus (366–384) and probably before 382. He was acquainted with high society, and he had probably held administrative posts in the government, for he had a knowledge of law but of the kind that an administrator rather than a lawyer would have. He had probably lived in a number of parts of the Empire, and somewhere had become deeply interested in the Jews, for he was aware of the features of synagogue worship taken over by the Church. But it has been difficult to establish the identity of the author. On the basis of an oblique attack on his commentary by Jerome, Isaac the Jew, a convert known to have been the center of some controversy in Rome, has been suggested. Because Augustine once quotes the commentary as that of "Hilarius," it has been thought that the author was Decimius Hilarianus Hilarius, an important layman who held various posts in Africa and Italy. In the end Souter suggested Evagrius of

[28] Ernesto Buonaiuti, "Agostino e la colpa ereditaria," *Ricerche Religiose*, II (1926), 401–427; Pincherle, pp. 178ff.

[29] Both works are printed in *PL*, XVII. The only critical editions are of the *Quaestiones*, edited by Souter (*CSEL*, L (1908), and of the commentary on Romans, edited by Vogels (*CSEL*, LXXXI (1966).

Antioch, whose earlier career matches that of Ambrosiaster, who then became a presbyter in 373, was acquainted with Basil and Jerome, but in 388 or 389 became the schismatic bishop of Antioch (at least from the standpoint of Rome and the Paulinian faction), thus calling forth Jerome's comment about "one from the Hebrews who simulated belief in Christ at Rome."[30]

The influence of Ambrosiaster upon some of the teachings most characteristic of the later Augustine is plain. Perhaps the fundamental influence is in the interpretation of Romans 5, 12. The ambiguous Greek expression ἐφ᾽ ᾧ is understood to mean *in quo*—in Adam all sinned, as though *en masse*. In what sense? Ambrosiaster thinks that all men "sinned" in Adam in that they are counted unworthy to eat of the tree of life and are removed from it by the imposition of the penalty of bodily death; the body is subjected to death and the soul, separated from the body, is exiled to the "underworld" (*infernus*). This is not really a doctrine of original sin, for neither guilt nor sinful desire is transmitted. In Ambrosiaster's language, only the "first death," the dissolution of the body, is the result of Adam's sin; the "second death" in Hell is the result of each man's own sins, and consequently righteous men are exempt from this second death though they must remain in the uppermost portions of the underworld "*quasi in libera*," under house arrest, unable to ascend to the heavens prior to the coming of Christ (*In Rom.* 5, 12).

This, without the detail about the underworld, is Augustine's view of the matter after 394. He now thinks in terms not only of a transcendental fall of the soul but of the sin of Adam and Eve. Because of it all men are born in a condition of mortality, ignorance, and difficulty (*De lib. arb.*, III, 18, 51ff.). This predicament can be called "sin," he acknowledges, and men can be said to be "by nature" children of wrath (Ephesians 2, 3), but all that is meant is that man's present state is the consequence of the first sin in Adam (III, 19, 54). It is "equitable," he thinks, that Adam should not beget children purer than himself. Their condition at birth is penal. But they themselves are without guilt, and even this penal state is to be viewed positively, as an

[30] Alexander Souter, *A Study of Ambrosiaster* (New York, 1905), pp. 164ff.; *The Earliest Latin Commentaries on the Epistles of St. Paul* (Oxford, 1927), pp. 48–49.

admonition to, and a suitable point of departure for, a steady process of improvement (III, 20, 56; 22, 65; 25, 76). Men are able to rise above the state in which they are born, and the only "guilt," in the proper sense, that accrues to them is due to their own ratification of the weaknesses of their nature and their failure to confess their shortcomings and rely upon divine aid.

Is the position stated in these writings tantamount to what will later be known as "Pelagianism"? Pelagius and his defenders thought so, and thought that they could cite passages from the earlier Augustine against the later Augustine. Augustine, however, defended himself vehemently. Many scholars have given some degree of support to Pelagius' contention, but when all the evidence is sifted Augustine's judgment, I think, must be supported. The difficulty is that the later Augustine is sometimes approached through caricatures; when he is understood correctly one finds that his later position is not far distant from the earlier. Though there were significant changes, his earlier views are kept from being "Pelagian" in two important ways: mortality, ignorance, and difficulty are viewed as a penal state, a consequence of sin, quite different from the state of Adam before the fall; and Augustine explicitly denies that man is able by his own powers to overcome sin and do God's will.

There is not yet a doctrine of "original sin," to be sure, for Augustine consistently draws a distinction between *mortality*, with its ensuing concerns and inclinations, and *consent* to those inclinations. But he obviously assumes that all men yield, and that they quickly become so accustomed to sin that a new kind of necessity is added to their lives. Thus men live under two quite distinct burdens:

naturale vinculum mortalitatis	*consuetudo carnalis* (*De div. quaest.*, q. 66, 5)
tradux mortalitatis	*assiduitas voluptatis*
ex poena originalis peccati	*ex poena frequentati peccati* (*Ad Simpl.*, I, q. 1, 10)

This conception of the consequences of Adam's sin suggests, on the one hand, that in their fall into sin men are not subjected to fate, but, on the other, that once having fallen they are incapable of recuperation by themselves. And that is precisely the view that is worked out in detail.

In Ambrosiaster's complex interpretation of Romans 5, 13–14, Paul's statement that sin was not counted as sin prior to the revealed law is taken to mean that *men* did not count their deeds culpable *before God*; they knew the natural law, but thought it only a law governing human relationships, not a law according to which God would judge their deeds. Thus when Paul says that death reigned from Adam to Moses, it is because men, with their knowledge of God obscured, thought they could sin with impunity. This is the sin "in the likeness of the sin of Adam," for Adam was the first man to deny God and succumb to idolatry. There were others who did *not* sin like Adam, for there were faithful men even before Moses; even they sinned, however, and had to wait in the underworld for Christ (*In Rom.* 5, 13–15). The function of the revealed law, then, is to convict men of their sin and induce them to struggle against it; but the law is not fulfilled until the giving of the Spirit. While the law of Moses is "spiritual," calling men to life with God, it still consists merely of external words; only the Spirit, God himself, gives the inward reality (*In Rom.* 8, 2).

This is the basis of Augustine's classification of the four ages (*De div. quaest.*, q. 66, 3; *Prop. ad Rom.*, 13–18): *ante legem*, when men were ignorant of their sin, *sub lege*, when they were aware of it but unable to conquer it, *sub gratia*, when they believe in the Redeemer and struggle against sin with divine aid, and *in pace*, when for the first time the body will be brought fully into subjection to the spirit. What makes the difference between law and grace is that only the latter gives man the power to struggle successfully with sin. In man prior to grace there is enough freedom to *will* not to sin, but there is not the ability to avoid sin in actual practice (*Prop. ad Rom.*, 18). The law is fulfilled only through *caritas*, which gives the mind a delight in the good and opposes the delight that is taken in temporal things (*De div. quaest.*, q. 66, 6).

Clearly the crucial problem will be Augustine's understanding of the interaction between free choice and divine influence throughout this process. His analysis of the sequence corresponds in a general way, as one might expect, to his four stages of the history of salvation; indeed, the latter is only the former writ large. What he sees is a process unfolding in stages, not in a continuum, certainly, for salvation is not man's doing, but a dialectic between God and man leading from one stage to the next.

(1) Augustine views the initial situation of each human life as one of potentiality for good, not of fatedness for sin (at least one reason for his strong insistence on this is that he is still very much occupied with his polemic against Manichaeism). The soul is not yet all that it can become (or all that it would have been had Adam not sinned), but its shortcomings are to be taken as an admonition to change for the better, and the first step that must be taken, corresponding to the transition from the situation prior to the law to that under the law, is to acknowledge one's *ignorance* of what ought to be done and then to seek after instruction (*De lib. arb.*, III, 22, 65). And even when men do not react appropriately and seek instruction, God in many ways calls upon them to return, through both the external law and his inward address to the heart (III, 20, 57).

(2) Man "under the law" makes proper use of his knowledge of God's requirements when he comes to the discovery that they cannot be fulfilled by his own powers. This is the specific locus of what Augustine calls "difficulty," *willing* without being able to *accomplish* (*De lib. arb.*, III, 18, 51–52; 22, 65). The proper outcome is man's seeking of divine aid (*adiutorium*) in order to achieve what is required.

(3) What makes the transition from existence "under law" to existence "under grace" is *faith*. Augustine understands faith in the Pauline way, setting it in contrast with works, though he also notes that faith does not displace works entirely; good works are required, but faith is the beginning, and good works will follow from it (*Exp. ad Gal.*, 19). Toward what is faith directed? Augustine answers, again in Pauline fashion, that it is directed toward *grace*. The term "grace" seems to be used consistently to designate *a new way of salvation*, one based upon forgiveness and thus offered to man without consideration of prior merits. Sometimes the term refers to the free and merciful character of the divine decision lying behind the offer; sometimes to the death of Christ, because of which the offer can be made without regard to sins (*De div. quaest.*, q. 68, 3); sometimes to the gospel through which the decision is communicated to man ("*admonitio vocantis Dei*" [*Exp. ad Rom.*, 9]); and sometimes as the new "time,"

6+

the new dispensation in human history in which this way of salvation is offered.[31] The offer is not new in every respect, for Augustine follows Paul in saying that many men in the time of the law and before it believed in the promises of God; nevertheless it takes full effect only with the completion of the earthly work of Christ.

Grace, then, is the offer of a definite way of salvation; it is preached in order that men might believe, and it is received through faith (*De div. quaest.*, q. 68, 3). *Another* term, "*adiutorium*," is reserved to designate the inward aid that is given *after* man believes, enabling him to begin doing the good works required by the law. The distinction is not merely terminological. Intervening between these two divine acts of *gratia* and *adiutorium* is the decision of faith, man's own decision to believe the promises of God and to rely upon divine help, forsaking the attempt to gain salvation by himself; and aid is given *only* to those who respond to the gospel with faith. Faith is the proper culmination of man's struggle with his natural weaknesses, his ignorance of the good, and his painful failure to do the good even when he knows and wills it; faith is, indeed, the *only* exit from the human predicament, for it is the renunciation of all attempts to achieve salvation by oneself and the acceptance of an offer made graciously by another. The struggle against sin can now become successful with the infusion of love by the presence of the Spirit, for man will not only will but do what is good.[32]

(4) The struggle against sin is not completed during the present life; man is not yet *in pace*. Nevertheless Augustine does view the Christian life "eschatologically," for there is already a possession of the goal in the "inner man," which is the "first fruits" of salvation. Augustine thought that Paul's expression "the first fruits of the Spirit" in Romans 8, 23 referred not to the Holy Spirit but to the spirit or mind of man (an understandable

---

[31] This is the meaning of the expression "*gratia fidei*" (*Exp. ad Gal.*, 3, 15, 19), as Janssen (*Die Entstehung der Gnadenlehre Augustins*, p. 122, n. 114) has pointed out, for it is made more explicit in *De div. quaest.*, q. 61, 7, where Augustine speaks of "*tertium tempus quo fidei christianae gratia data est.*"

[32] It may help the cause of "ecumenical theology" to note the similarity of this analysis of justification to the one Newman worked out on the basis of his reading of the theologians of the Church and a fresh study of Paul, in his *Lectures on the Doctrine of Justification* (1838).

confusion, for Paul uses πνεῦμα in both ways), but he interpreted it in a genuinely Pauline direction, linking it with its context in Romans 8. Thus the highest part of the soul, the mind or spirit, is the first offering man makes to God, reaching out in faith, hope, and love beyond the situation of mortality in which believers, in common with all men, still groan in travail, but with this difference, that they do it with eagerness, "intent on the things that lie ahead" (Philippians 3, 13), awaiting the resurrection in which the body as well will come to share, for the first time, in the benefits of their adoption as sons.[33] Therefore though grace and faith belong to the third stage, the *adiutorium* given by the Spirit really belongs to the fourth, for it is not transitory but it is, on the contrary, a foretaste of the peace of God, and the only change that will be undergone is an increase of love and awareness and enjoyment of God and an extension of the Spirit's control into all aspects of soul and body.

The entire dialectic of finite spirit with which Augustine has been operating, the interplay between the shortcomings of man as he is and the possibilities that lie before him, moves toward and terminates in the gift of the Spirit:

Man's Creator is to be praised at every point, for he gave him the capacity to rise from these beginnings to the highest Good, and aids him as he advances, and completes and perfects his advance. . . . That it cannot instantly fulfill the duty it recognizes means that this fulfillment is another gift which it has not yet received. . . . By its very difficulty it is admonished to implore for its perfecting the aid of him whom it believes to be the Author of its beginning. Hence God becomes dearer to it, both because it gains existence not from itself but from his goodness, and because by his mercy it is raised to happiness; for the more it loves him from whom it derives its existence, the more surely it rests in him and enjoys his eternity more fully (*De lib. arb.*, III, 22, 65).

Augustine has come almost to the point of formulating an insight about man which will become increasingly important to him and will then pass into the later theology of the West,

---

[33] See Jean Pépin, "'Primitiae spiritus.' Remarques sur une citation paulinienne des 'Confessions' de saint Augustin," *Revue de l'histoire des religions*, CXL (1951), 155–202; Aimé de Solignac, "Primitiae spiritus," *BA*, XIV, 552–555; and for Augustine's interpretation of the whole context in Romans 8, Thomas E. Clarke, *The Eschatological Transformation of the Material World according to St. Augustine* (Woodstock, Md., 1956).

that of the "double gratuity" of beginning and completion, mere existence and the movement toward beatitude, or, as he will put it much later, nature and grace (*De civ. Dei*, XII, 9).[34] What he says about man's fulfillment rests on a distinction between man's own powers and the divine aid which supplements them: God not only creates man freely, without need or obligation on his part, but he also overcomes the instability and self-contradiction of finite life and brings man to fulfillment with the further gift of the Spirit, again without need or obligation, and if man fails to seek or accept this gift the loss will be his and not God's (*De lib. arb.*, III, 16, 45).

What we find emerging in the various writings of this period, then, is a clear-cut framework for the analysis of the relation of man to God, more precisely, of human freedom to divine sovereignty and initiative. Augustine attempted to take proper account of both, for he was simultaneously completing a systematic work on free choice, directed against the Manichaeans, and grappling with the biblical theme of salvation by grace; he was fully aware of the problems involved, and it is not hard to understand why he later defended himself so vehemently against the insinuation that he had reversed his position in the years following these writings. Indeed, the framework of his analysis was not even worked out for the first time in dealing with the Pauline corpus, for all the components from which a doctrine of free will and grace could be assembled were being prepared during the preceding years. Löhrer has a useful chapter on the earlier development of Augustine's understanding of grace, and he points out that a consistent pattern is followed even in the works written in Rome, or certainly in those written in Thagaste: man has a capacity for turning toward God and knowing God intimately, and when he responds to the divine call in the act of conversion he is given the aid by which to accomplish God's will (*capacitas, vocatio, conversio, opitulatio*).[35] Such passages are incidental and probably manifest not Augustine's own independent reflections but the standard assumptions of the Christian community; it is difficult to imagine, in fact, what other assumptions *could* have

---

[34] See chapter 4, section 2, below.

[35] Löhrer, *Der Glaubensbegriff des hl. Augustinus*, pp. 233–241, and the entire chapter, pp. 224–268.

been held by people convinced, as they were, of both the freedom of the will and the need of divine aid. But this pattern increasingly became more firmly fixed and more fully elaborated after Augustine encountered Ambrosiaster's commentaries on Paul.

What really changes is not his understanding of the dynamics of the will or of the character of salvation but his awareness of the context *beyond* man's own life, namely, the history of salvation and especially the work of Christ. It is to this last that we must now turn, for Augustine now views "grace," the offer of a way of salvation without regard to preceding merits, as having been made possible by the death of Christ in behalf of sinners (*De div. quaest.*, q. 68, 3), and for the first time in his career as a Christian thinker he has gained a clear conception of the nature of the redemption effected by Christ.

4. THE CROSS

One of the points at which Ambrosiaster had the most lasting effect on Augustine's thought is the doctrine of redemption. It is well known that this doctrine has undergone a longer and more uncertain development than most. The view prevalent among the Church fathers was the so-called "ransom" theory, according to which the death and resurrection of Christ represent some kind of transaction with, or deception of and conquest over, the devil. But Anselm forthrightly criticized the notion that the devil had any rights over man and instead worked out the view that the death of Christ repairs man's relationship with God by making satisfaction for sins. This view, in one variant or another, has been assumed by most Catholics and Protestants since that time to be authoritative, and it was even given dogmatic status in the Calvinist churches.

Augustine clearly holds to the ransom theory of redemption. But in this matter as in others his thought attracts more than ordinary interest, for he did not merely repeat the general consensus of churchly teaching but thought the problem through again. I am not sure to what extent his view is unique; to make a proper judgment about that a detailed study of the Greek fathers would be necessary. But he *does* indicate how the ransom motif can be made into a creditable theory still worthy of the attention of theologians.

Much of the work had already been done before him by Ambrosiaster in the course of his study of the Pauline corpus. To him the key passage (for he alludes to it repeatedly) is Colossians 2, 13–15:

And you, who were dead in trespasses and the uncircumcision of your flesh, God has made alive together with him, having forgiven us all our trespasses, having cancelled the decree against us with its legal sentence; this he took from our midst, nailing it to the cross. Having disarmed the principalities and powers he made public spectacle of them, triumphing over them in himself.

The *chirographum*, the sentence decreed against the descendants of Adam, is taken to be bodily death, the punishment for Adam's sin. The devil has power over man's mortal body, and he is free to use its fears and desires for the purposes of temptation. But what the devil has gained in Adam and in all those who succumb to temptation is lost in Christ (Ambrosiaster makes direct use of Irenaeus with his correlations between Adam and Christ). When the sentence is "affixed to the cross," sin is overcome and the powers who have gained control over man are conquered "in Christ." How? Ambrosiaster's acquaintance with Roman law suggested an answer (in his version, at least, the ransom theory is just as "forensic" as several other theories of redemption). An accuser, though he is heard as long as he can prove the guilt of those he accuses, runs the risk of being held culpable of false accusation (*In Rom.* 7, 4). The devil is led into precisely this predicament by his *zelum*, his jealously of the Redeemer who was teaching men to become acceptable to God by renouncing the devil (*In II Cor.* 5, 22; *In Rom.* 4, 23). The powers have put to death someone in whom no guilt could be found, and because they became guilty in the use of the very authority by which they had held guilty souls in bondage, the bond of guilt which held men ("sin," but in a complex sense) has been broken—not universally, but for all those who adhere to the one "in whom" (in whose case) the powers have been made guilty, all those who bear the sign of the cross in which they were conquered (*In Col.* 2, 13–15; *In Rom.* 8, 3).

This is essentially the view that Augustine came to hold. In his earliest statement of it (*De lib. arb.*, III, 10, 31) it goes this way: the devil, having tempted the woman and caused her and her husband to fall, had a just right of possession over them and their offspring, for he gained them and kept them in his power by fair means, working upon their minds and hearts through persuasion and evoking their free consent. But the devil, who held men justly, was also overcome justly. He had rights over those men who consented to the temptations of concupiscence and were thus held guilty before God; but he did not have rights over the Second Adam, who lived without concupiscence and did nothing deserving death. When the devil slew the righteous one he lost his rights, not over all men, for they still consent to temptation and are justly held, but over all those who adhere in faith to the one whom the devil slew unjustly, having no rights over him.

Two features of this theory have often given offense: the suggestion that the devil has rights, and the notion of a ransom paid to the devil. With respect to the former, Jean Rivière (who has made the only full-length study of Augustine's atonement doctrine) points out that this first statement of the doctrine is set within the context of a larger discussion of the providential ordering of the world.[36] (My own suspicion is that this one paragraph was inserted into a section written earlier, as furnishing support for, even a more convincing version of the position already stated there.) The question of the third book of *On Free Will* is why the will turns away from the higher good. Augustine does not rest with the answer that the will is exercised freely and that its defection as such has no reason or cause; beyond that, he argues that the perfection or plenitude of the universe *requires* that there be creatures who are free and who, because they are finite, have the possibility of either adhering to God or falling away from him (III, 5, 13; 12, 35; etc.). And when they do sin there is an appropriateness about the consequences, an appropriateness which, though it is derived from divine wisdom, is now rooted in the very nature of things (III, 9, 24–27; 11, 32; etc.). When Augustine comes upon Ambrosiaster's theory of sin and redemption he sees it as a verification of the framework he has

[36] *Le dogme de la Rédemption chez saint Augustin* (Paris, [3]1933), pp. 48–54.

already worked out, stressing the sequence of cause and effect, free action and its consequences, in all temporal affairs; and in turn he will be inclined to formulate the new theory of redemption in terms of relationships of *ius* within the finite order (not abstract justice so much as de facto right, permission, concession, appropriate to each case). Events are allowed to take their course through the interaction of finite agents and the unfolding of consequences, all of it within the framework of a divine justice which has granted this degree of freedom and allows the consequences of sin to be at the same time its punishment.

The second problem is the notion of ransom or price (*pretium*), which to some later critics suggests an amicable transaction between God and the devil. It is apparent, however, that the metaphor is used not to suggest a complete scenario but to highlight two parallels, which in this case stand at some distance from each other: there is a deliverance from captivity, and it takes place according to the standards of justice or right governing the relation between two parties. What intervenes is not, however, a mutually advantageous agreement but an overstepping of the bounds by one party, almost a *hamartia* of the sort familiar to classical tragedy: the devil, through an excess of zeal, exercises his rights in an improper way, and because of this *abus de pouvoir*, as Rivière often puts it, he forfeits his rights over those who adhere to Christ.[37] In his sermons Augustine often uses the familiar patristic imagery of a tricking of the devil, with the humanity of Christ functioning like the bait in a mousetrap (*esca in muscipula*); but this is only a picturesque illustration. Certainly Augustine never wished to suggest that the devil was ignorant of the economy of salvation; his own view was that the demons, though they were deprived of all intimate knowledge of God's purposes, overhead the disclosures made to the patriarchs and prophets and thereby were able to devise counterfeit rituals and revelations, close enough to the true way of salvation that even the faithful sometimes confuse them (*De Trin.*, IV, 17, 23).

It would be more accurate, then, to think neither of an amicable transaction nor of deception on God's part but of an open confrontation with the forces of evil. And this is at least one feature of the ransom theory that makes it worthy of consideration still,

[37] Rivière, pp. 150–153.

for, unlike the views of Anselm and Calvin and their successors, which locate the focus of redemption in the hidden depths of God and even in the intra–Trinitarian relations,[38] the ransom theory sets it firmly within earthly life, more in keeping with the gospel narratives which present it as a drama played out between finite agents—the forces of evil, the human soul of Christ, the men who stand between them—with tangible problems of religious observance and political policy as counters, with bids made in terms of opposed orientations to life, and the stakes being eternal life and death. One can see why the ransom theory has gained fresh support in the twentieth century in the historical studies of Aulén and the theological reflections of Tillich, for as Tillich says it represents God as participating in the destructive consequences of estrangement and transforming them.[39]

How, then, does Christ conquer evil? First inwardly, of course, by his own sinlessness in the face of temptation and opposition; and this is perhaps what many contemporary theologians have in mind when they use the language of the ransom theory. And that is important, for one essential feature of the theory is the awareness that *mortality*—with all the fears and anxieties and inclinations that follow from man's life as "flesh"—is what gives occasion for sin: as Augustine puts it, the forces of evil have an unrestricted power of tempting and rewarding and slaying in the flesh, a power which cannot really be restrained in the realm of the bodily, though it *can* be resisted in the spirit (*De Trin.*, IV, 13, 17); in this way they have access to Christ as well, first through temptation and then through the arousing of hostility toward him. We might recall, by the way, that the ancient world carried out an extensive "demythologization" of its belief in demons, for after Posidonius almost every Stoic and Platonist philosopher, almost every pagan and Christian teacher assumed that the demons have no immediate access to the mind, as God has, but act only upon the body and the imagination to arouse fears and desires.[40]

---

[38] *Cur Deus homo*, I, 9–10; *Institutio christianae religionis*, II, xvi, 2–3.

[39] Gustaf Aulén, *Christus Victor* (New York, 1951); Paul Tillich, *Systematic Theology*, II (Chicago, 1957), 174–176.

[40] Various sources could be mentioned, such as Cicero, *De re publica*, VI (the dream of Scipio); Porphyry as quoted by Augustine in *De civ. Dei*, X, 9; Didymus, *De Spiritu Sancto*, 60; and Ambrosiaster, *In Rom.* 7, 14. For Augustine's own views see especially *Ep.* 9, 3 and *De ag. chr.*, 1–3.

6*

But to say only that is not to speak to the issue as Augustine formulated it. Something more is involved than the *agon* which is part of the inward life of every man and whose outcome should be the "casting out" of the devil by refusing to yield to temptation (*De ag. chr.*, 1, 1). Augustine was concerned rather with an encounter between Christ and the powers of evil in which the latter were led to forfeit their claims over *other* men. We must ask, then, how he understood and explained this process, how the *mors indebita*, the unmerited death of Christ, cancelled the hold of the powers of evil over those men who would adhere to him.

Augustine assumed, of course, that mortality is the punishment of sin, and since Christ had no sin the forces of evil acted beyond their *rights* over mortal flesh, though not beyond their *powers*, in inciting violence toward him. But what constitutes their rights is not mortality as such but their success in tempting men and holding them under their control. With perfect propriety, therefore, we may leave to one side the traditional question whether, and how, mortality is among the consequences of man's succumbing to temptation (Augustine's own views on the matter underwent various changes), for the central point is that the rights of the community of evil—the deserved bondage of men to evil and their sharing in the common destiny of sinful humanity—extend as far as there is *guilt*; what makes the powers of evil act "beyond their rights" in the case of Christ is that, in their haste to get an opponent out of the way, they have been led to make a false accusation of guilt, whether implicitly (by imposing death, which for Augustine is the penalty of sin) or explicitly, in the accusations and criminal punishment that are part of the narrative of the crucifixion. Jesus dies under reproach; but in this seeming victory of the powers of evil the bond of a common guilt which has kept humanity in one mass is broken through. How? In that here is one situation in which there is an unambiguous contradiction between the accusation and what is deserved. Three things are involved: in his own life Jesus makes an exception to the general rule that human life is held in the bonds of guilt; but in his encounter with the kingdom of evil he is treated as though he also fell under that rule; and thereby the kingdom of evil is discredited and forfeits its claim over those men who adhere to him.

Now I suggest that such a pattern is not unique in every respect: one thinks of the prophets and righteous men mentioned by Jesus himself, who in obedience to God opposed the forces of evil and were often rejected as troublemakers and evildoers, but whose blood discredits and condemns those who rejected them. The difference would be that their case is *not* unambiguous, for it could always be said that they were not without fault themselves, that their deaths were not entirely unmerited, and that their power consisted chiefly in their testimony to the demands and the promises of God. But some such pattern, I suspect, lies at the heart of Augustine's understanding of liberation from the community of guilt: as it attempts to draw all of humanity into itself, by fair means through temptation or by foul means through false accusation, it finds a limit in the faithfulness of the righteous man; its seemingly universal hold is broken, and the achievement can then be appropriated by others.

Augustine continued to hold this ransom theory adapted from Ambrosiaster; aside from incidental statements it is developed at length in *De Trinitate*, both in book IV (about 406) and in book XIII (about 418), and in the *Enchiridion* (about 423). But increasingly it was supplemented by another theme, that of *sacrifice*. Christ was called the righteous priest who offered his own unblemished life to God in behalf of mankind, from whom he received his humanity. The function of this sacrifice was said to be to reconcile men to God, to reunite them with him and overcome the alienation of sin, and it is accomplished by Christ in such a way that, while he "remains one" with the God to whom the offering is made, he is both offerer and offering "in one," and "unites in himself" those for whom the offering is made (*De Trin.*, IV, 14, 19).

Rivière thinks this means that the ransom theory was becoming absorbed by another theory which came to expression only partially in Augustine but was completed by Anselm in his satisfaction theory. He may be right in seeing some anticipations of Anselm's notion of satisfaction in Augustine; if so, Anselm's concepts might be utilized, if it were done carefully, in describing Augustine's theology at this point. But all this need not imply that the thrust of Augustine's reflections was toward the adoption of a satisfaction theory *to the exclusion* of the ransom theory.

Rivière assumes that the ransom motif is made obsolete when the new line of thought is followed out consistently and that its persistence in Augustine's own writings is only a vestige of the past, not a guarantee that he saw it as something indispensable. But it seems to me that the evidence which is gathered and the analyses that are made by Rivière himself suggest something different: that the two motifs coexist quite well in Augustine's theology and do not absorb but supplement each other. Sacrifice, if his analysis of the pertinent texts is at all reliable, is directed toward God and makes up for the *guilt* (*reatus, culpa*) of other men; ransom is an undergoing, at the hands of the forces of evil, of the *punishment* (*supplicium, poena*) that follows from this guilt.[41] Sacrifice, furthermore, is treated by Augustine as an *inward* act of total devotion of mind, heart, and strength (this is discussed with special sensitivity in *De civ. Dei*, X, 5–6), and it is not confined to the death of Christ but pertains to his entire human activity, so that from this perspective even his death is important chiefly as "obedience unto death"; ransom, on the other hand, has to do solely with Christ's suffering a *mors indebita* with the consequence that men are liberated from their bondage to evil, though of course the righteousness of Christ is what makes the accuser lose this case.

What this suggests is that Christ's life of perfect obedience can be treated as a sacrifice which establishes a new relationship between man and God through what scholastic theology called "merit" or "active obedience," and his obedience unto death might also have Anselmian overtones as a "satisfaction" or "compensation" for the past sins of men (a "*hostia pro peccato*," as Augustine says in *De Trin.*, IV, 12, 15); but all of this can be said without forcing upon these functions of his obedience the added burden of being the *sole* explanation of the death of Christ and its significance for men: he can be viewed as the priestly "representative" of men before God, acting in their place to make up what is lacking in their own service of God, without requiring that his priestly activity before God include as one of its necessary components his suffering of the penalty of sin. Augustine, in fact, would have denied that. In his older translation of the Bible, the statement that Christ is the propitiation for sins

[41] Rivière, pp. 175–176.

(I John 4, 10) implied not that he must suffer their penalty but only that he is the *litator*, the offerer, of a sacrifice pleasing to God (*In Joann. ep.*, tr. 7, 9). Then the *death* of Christ, considered not as the final act of obedience but *as death*, the undergoing of the penalty of sin, will be explained not by the demands of divine justice but by the action, indeed, the contingent action (though perhaps with the inevitability of a spontaneous inclination) on the part of the forces of evil when they are confronted by the righteous one. The death of Christ need not have the antecedent necessity postulated by Anselm, for, after all, the task of a theory of redemption would seem to be not to find an antecedent necessity for *every* detail of the redemption but to meditate *a posteriori* on the character and the consequences of what has actually taken place. To be sure, in Augustine's view the ransoming of men by the *mors indebita* of Christ is an essential feature of the redemption, for it is the means by which the devil's right of possession over those who belong to Christ is alienated from him; and Augustine thinks that the actual sequence of events is somehow forseen and planned out in advance, so that God draws evil into defeating itself. Still the whole transaction turns upon the *culpability* and thus the *freedom* of the forces of evil. The death of Christ as such is not to be explained, then, in terms of the demands of divine justice but in terms of the self-defeating excesses of rebellious evil.

If this dual approach to Augustine's theory is correct, the theme of sacrifice indicates the positive aspect of the redemption, Christ's relation to God in behalf of those men who will adhere to him, while the theme of ransom is linked with the negative aspect of cancelling the devil's rights over them. What this suggests for the understanding of the whole question of justification is that the real obstacle is not the honor or justice or wrath of God himself, for God is ready to take men back into his company on the basis of their faith in the divine promises or in the righteousness of Christ, but the train of consequences within human life following upon sin; these have a de facto claim upon men, consistent with divine equity itself, keeping them implicated in the community of evil and preventing their entry into the company of God until two things happen: until some other and stronger claim upon them comes into effect, *and* until a sufficient reason is found for cancelling the prior claim. The former is accomplished in the righteousness of Christ, the latter in the forfeiture of their claim by the powers of evil; and both are involved in justification, for freedom from accusation by, and implication in, the society of evil is just as important as being attracted toward and placing one's trust in the righteousness of Christ.

This is the point of contact between Augustine and Luther, and Luther's insights about the "accusing conscience" may help to indicate what is essential to the ransom theory of Augustine and, before him, Ambrosiaster. It has already been pointed out that the theory is set in a forensic framework and uses legal vocabulary, for it assumes a cosmos of right, not might. The ransom theory is "dramatic," to be sure; but the drama is more that of the courtroom than that of physical combat. What makes it more dramatic and less mechanical than the forensic theories of atonement put forward since Anselm's time is that the setting is not the divine court, with God as sole judge, but an interpersonal situation in which all parties are capable of seeing the force of the arguments, in which the powers of evil can be silenced by reminding them of their blunders, and in which the human mind and heart (which is the forum of judgment that finally counts in each individual life) can assess the counter-claims and, rejecting the voices of accusation and despair, attach itself to the righteous one and follow in the way of discipleship. There are passages in Augustine which sound the same chords as Luther, most notably this one from the *Confessions* (IX, 13, 36) in which he is describing his mother's last wishes:

She desired only that remembrance of her be made at the altar where she had worshiped day by day, for she knew that at it we receive the sacred victim by whom the handwriting against us was erased; by whom the enemy, who is always reckoning up our failings and seeking to convict us, was conquered, not being able to find any fault in him; and in whom we as well conquer. Who can return to him his innocent blood? Who can repay the ransom with which Christ purchased us and delivered us from him? Your handmaid bound her soul to the sacrament of that ransom with the bonds of faith. Let no one tear her away from your protection; let not him who is at once lion and serpent bar the way, either by force or by guile; for she will answer, not that she has no debt to pay, lest she be convicted and taken into custody by the cunning accuser, but that her debts are cancelled by Christ, who cannot be repaid the price which he paid for us when the debt was not his to pay.

Here Augustine is close to the Pauline and Lutheran theme of the sinister function of "the Law," God's demand for men which still stands over them but which, after sin, only gives certainty of condemnation when they rely upon it for their security and can then be exploited by the forces of evil with God's permission and even as the executors of his "wrath." The problem is for men to be transferred out of this legal relation to God, which is now effective only for damnation, to a new relationship based on "grace," the forgiveness of sins and the righteousness of Christ. The difficulty is not, however, that God is prevented by his own justice or wrath from acting for men's salvation (this is the false problem injected by Anselm, and then by the Reformers, though it was by and large avoided by the scholastic theologians), but that when God in his sovereign mercy acts to establish a restored fellowship of men with himself there must also be some "just" way by which those men can be detached from the community of evil to which they "justly" belong. It is precisely at this point that Augustine, following Ambrosiaster, clarifies a point that remains vague in Paul, is stated too much along Anselmian lines by Luther, and is completely overlooked by most other theologians.

If we want to give a just characterization of Augustine's view of redemption, we must recognize that he finds in it various aspects which are really distinct and which resist being driven into a single framework of explanation. In his writings there seem to be four irreducible aspects to the work of Christ[42]:

(1) In his earthly activity as *revealer* and *example* he makes God known to men, proving his love, demonstrating his humility, but also leading the perfect human life even in the face of opposition: these themes, that Christ has an effect upon men's minds and affections through his words and deeds, are found in Augustine's writings from every period.

(2) In his inward devotion and total obedience he is the *reconciler*, making a sacrifice "for sin" as the priestly representative

[42] This is a modification of the classification worked out by Portalié, *DTC*, I, 2, cols. 2367–74.

of the race in the sense that he compensates for the shortcomings of other men.

(3) He is the *redeemer* who by undergoing an undeserved punishment discredits the forces of evil and ransoms men from their solidarity in guilt.

(4) Finally there is an ecclesial and eschatological function as *pioneer* and *head* of a redeemed humanity. This is the framework of the fourth book on the Trinity (3, 5–6; 13, 16–18), where the purpose of the incarnation is said to be the renewal and reunification of mankind. The single death and resurrection of Christ is, so to speak, reduplicated in its significance for other men, for they are subject to the *double* death of both soul and body and have need of a double resurrection. Consequently Christ's death and resurrection is both a *sacramentum* of the current death and renewal of the inner man and an *exemplum* of the future death and resurrection of the outer man. In the latter there is a literal correspondence between Christ and his followers, who are not to fear those who kill the body but are to fill up what is lacking in his sufferings in order to gain resurrection and become as he is. The former is a figurative correspondence; the bodily death and resurrection function in this case as an efficacious *sign* of something else, and certain features of the gospel narratives are taken to have *only* this meaning: the cry of dereliction on the cross, or the *"noli me tangere"* of John 20, 17 (the *non tangere* is a refusal to know Christ after the flesh and a raising of one's attention above, to the right hand of the Father where one's life is hid with Christ).

Augustine's approach to the knotty problem of redemption, then, is to divide and conquer. And this is really the practice of many later theologians as well, especially when they are operating in a doctrinal rather than a speculative context. The scholastics habitually listed a number of different aspects of the work of Christ, drawing together all the theories that had been championed by individuals; and the practice is worth continuing if one can find, as Augustine did, the real divisions between these various aspects.

5. Predestination

One aspect of Augustine's study of the Pauline epistles has yet to be mentioned, and it comes last because it is the one point at which a major shift took place in Augustine's thought. His understanding of free will and divine aid changed little from the time of his earliest writings into the period of the Pelagian controversy. But it is different with the problem of election which Paul discusses in Romans 9 through 11.

In the writings that come from the period 394–396 (the exposition of the questions on Romans, the unfinished commentary on Romans, and question 68) Augustine follows Ambrosiaster: election is a choice which God makes among men, and since it would be unjust if he arbitrarily gave preference to some, the choice must be based upon some difference between them, foreknown by God; and that difference is one of "merit." This position does not contradict the Pauline doctrine of salvation by faith rather than works, for the merit which God foreknows is that of faith, not of works, that of man's desiring to do the will of God and looking for divine aid, not his accomplishing it. The merit of faith is simply man's response to the preaching of grace, accepting the divine offer of aid and renouncing independent efforts of his own. Grace is offered freely to all men; its reception in faith is their own act; then the aid of the Holy Spirit is given to them, and if they remain in the company of the Spirit (which is again their own doing) they will inherit eternal life on the basis of their good works (*Exp. ad Rom.*, 60). (This is the reason for his consistent distinction between *gratia* and *adiutorium* in these writings: grace is offered freely to all, without distinction among them and entirely apart from any consideraton of merits, while the divine aid which follows upon the reception of this offer presupposes the merit of faith.) Even the element of "merit" in faith should not be misconstrued, for Augustine points out that faith is made possible only by the call; one can take credit for coming when he is called, but he cannot take credit for being called, and it is the call which "effects" the decision of faith (*De div. quaest.*, q. 68, 5).

Romans 9–11, with its reflections on Jacob and Esau, Israel and the Church, is first interpreted in the light of these assumptions. It is apparent that Paul spoke in these chapters of God's foreordination of events and of his "hardening" of certain men, of their being drawn by the potter from the same clay (the *massa luti*, the common mortality which all inherit from Adam [*Prop.*

ad Rom., 62; *De div. quaest.*, q. 68, 3]) but being molded into either vessels of wrath or vessels of mercy. But the differentiation is thought to be based on foreknowledge of their hidden merits, and in order to explain why these merits are sometimes well hidden Augustine postulates a call that is issued, it seems, to all men, sometimes inwardly, sometimes externally through words or visible signs, given sometimes to individuals and sometimes to whole peoples, all according to the mysterious ordering activity of God (*De div. quaest.*, q. 68, 5–6). Such ideas have not been at all unfamiliar to Augustine, but they are now brought to bear in support of the essential equality of opportunity for all men.

The reversal in Augustine's understanding of election is not hard to pinpoint, for it occurs between the first and second replies to some questions of Simplicianus, written in 396 or 397, after Augustine had become a bishop but probably before the elderly presbyter had succeeded Ambrose as bishop of Milan. The first question is concerned with Romans 7, and that passage is interpreted in the same fashion that we have seen earlier: the law is given not to abolish sin but to make it known, to prepare man to receive grace by demonstrating to him both his guilt and his inability to accomplish the good that he wills, his need, therefore, of both the forgiveness of past sins and the infusion of *caritas* for the accomplishment of what is good (*Ad Simpl.*, I, q. 1, 7). Augustine still thinks that the one thing that remains to free will, despite its need of forgiveness of past sins and aid in overcoming the habit of sinning, is to turn in supplication to God, seeking the power to fulfill the law (q. 1, 14).

In question 2 the basic pattern remains the same (the change should not be overdramatized): grace is still the call issued to man either outwardly or inwardly, and it is received by faith, but faith is only "conception," not yet the "new birth" which will come with the infusion of the Spirit in baptism (q. 2, 2). The only change is in Augustine's understanding of predestination. He reads in Romans 9 that Jacob was loved and Esau was hated "when they were not yet born and had done neither good nor evil" (Romans 9, 11). As a result he is now persuaded that election to grace (or the refusal of mercy) comes *prior* to any decision on man's part. Whether a man believes or does not is decided by God, and he quotes I Corinthians 4, 7: "What do you have that you did not receive?" Man receives from God, then, both the act of willing and the power to do what is willed, the former through the call, the latter through the infusion of love (q. 2, 10 and 12).

But Augustine must then explain how faith can be man's own act and yet be called forth by God. For the first time he puts forward the doctrine termed "effective calling" in Calvinism or "efficacious grace" in Catholic theology: a *vocatio effectrix* is what brings forth the response of faith, and the reason that "many are called but few are chosen" is that those on whom God has mercy, and they alone, are called *congruenter*, in a way suited to their condition (*"quomodo scit ei congruere, ut vocantem non respuat"*)—and then Augustine plays on words to suggest the perfect harmony between an efficacious calling and a free response, for just as the calling agrees with the one who is called, his response is an agreeing with and an accommodating to (*congruere* and *contemperari*) the one who calls (q. 2, 13).

This explanation is in keeping with Augustine's general theory of volition: the willing or not willing (*nutus*) is our own, but we cannot will anything at all unless something comes before the mind delighting and attracting the affections, and what will come before the mind is not always within our own power, for it is something that "comes to us" (*occurrit*) and is "presented" (*visum*) to the mind (q. 2, 21–22; cf. *De lib. arb.*, III, 25, 74). This theory of willing on the basis of what "occurs" to us has been assumed in all of Augustine's writings from *De ordine* on. What is new is not that faith depends upon the call of grace, but that the call is not issued to all with the same force, and whether or not a man believes is dependent upon the character of the call.

Such a theory of grace must require as its corollary some explanation of the destiny of the others, those who are called but not chosen. It must be that they have not been called congruently or efficaciously, and this circumstance is ultimately derived from God's "hating" them, or rather their sin, or "hardening" them, and this is nothing else than his deciding not to have mercy on them (*nolle misereri* [q. 2, 15]). It is not that God is unjust to these and just to the others, but that he is just to these and merciful to the others; according to a hidden "equity" some men, in just punishment, are abandoned to their sin so that its consequences can unfold and take their full course, while others are rescued by divine mercy.

Though all of this takes place within the framework of divine justice, the real *explanation* of this outworking of the consequences of sin, it is to be noted, is the nature of the finite process itself, *not* the mysterious counsel of God; the latter explains only the mercy given to some. Consequently the metaphor describing the human race as a single lump of clay from which vessels of honor and dishonor are shaped gains new importance. Augustine had already used it to describe the solidarity of the race in the consequences of the sin of Adam, but the possibility of escape had been held out to those who freely responded to the call of grace. Now he says that only those who have been shown a special mercy are called out of it. Thus the net of earthly consequences is drawn tighter. But how? There is not yet a doctrine of original sin. But Augustine now begins to think of man as being captured by his first sin and becoming increasingly accustomed and addicted to them.[43] This is the meaning of the statement (q. 2, 20), usually misinterpreted along the lines of Augustine's later doctrine of original sin, that "carnal desire, reigning in man as a punishment for sin, has drawn the whole human race together into one and the same *conspersio* (a moistened lump of clay), because the original guilt has permeated throughout (*originali reatu in omnia permanante*)."

The changed interpretation of predestination and grace could have come in part from the pressure of internal difficulties, for Augustine at the close of question 68, probably written in 396, faced the difficulty that men are sometimes said to have been called while they were still in the womb or even while they were still in the loins of their father (q. 68, 6). But Pincherle has shown that the decisive influence was Tyconius' *Book of Rules*, specifically the third rule concerning faith and works.[44] The parallels between the second reply to the questions of Simplicianus and Tyconius' discussion of faith and works are striking. Both of them use such texts as I Corinthians 4, 7 ("What do you have that you did not receive? And if you received it, why do you boast as if it were

[43] Athanase Sage, "Péché originel. Naissance d'un dogme," *REA*, XIII (1967), p. 212. This view, he suggests, should be called not *péché originel* but *péché d'origine*, sin "from the beginning" of each individual life.

[44] The work has been edited by F. C. Burkitt (New York, 1894).

not a gift?"), I Corinthians 1, 31 ("Let him who boasts, boast of the Lord"), and Ephesians 2, 8–9 ("By grace you are saved through faith, and this is not from you, but it is the gift of God, not because of works, lest anyone boast"). These are precisely the texts mentioned by Augustine many years later in his retrospective analyses of the development of his understanding of grace (first in *Contra duas epistulas Pelagii*, then in the *Retractationes*, then in *De praedestinatione sanctorum* and *De dono perseverantiae*, finally in the unfinished work against Julian).[45] In those writings Augustine stresses the crucial importance of I Corinthians 4, 7 upon his own thinking, and he says that it came to him as though by divine revelation (*De praed. sanct.*, 4, 8). But he makes no mention of Tyconius. Instead he connects this text with Cyprian's *Testimonia*, where, indeed, it does appear. But Pincherle points out that Cyprian did *not* understand the text in the sense given it by Augustine, and by Tyconius before him; it may be that Augustine's recognition of this fact led him to stress the authority of the *apostle* rather than the father.[46]

Why is it that Augustine suppresses the influence of Tyconius? Partly because of his concern in the debates with the Pelagians to prove the antiquity and catholicity of his own views, a concern which led him increasingly to make extensive citations of Greek and Latin fathers in order to prove, against the charge of innovation, that his doctrine had ecclesiastical authority.[47] And if this makes Augustine appear too cynical, Pincherle also suggests another reason for the failure to mention Tyconius: that he was unknown beyond Africa, and since Augustine was writing for a wider public he remained silent about him where he might have acknowledged the insights of another dangerous figure, such as Origen, who was better known.[48]

The influence of Tyconius, in fact, is acknowledged obliquely during that same period, late in Augustine's career, for he added a long section to *De doctrina christiana* in 426 to bring it to completion and in one passage (III, 33, 46) mentioned the Pelagian controversy in connection with Tyconius' third rule. Augustine is gentle in his judgment of Tyconius, who, he says, did not

[45] See the analysis of the passages in Pincherle, pp. 175ff.
[46] Pincherle, p. 178.
[47] Pincherle, pp. 179, 187.
[48] Pincherle, p. 188.

write with precision because the Pelagian heresy had not yet arisen. And it is certain that Augustine did read the *Book of Rules* in 396 or 397 while writing the third book of *De doctrina christiana*, and what is said in a letter (Ep. 41) written about this time to Aurelius, the bishop of Carthage, suggests that he broke off writing the work at the point where, thirty years later, he began to discuss Tyconius' rules because an acknowledgment of the influence of a Donatist might have compromised him.

When Tyconius and Augustine are compared, it is evident that Tyconius did *not* furnish the crucial propositions but only confronted Augustine with some texts from the Pauline corpus which changed his understanding of the contrast between faith and works, promise and law; the end product was Augustine's own, derived from his earlier convictions and perplexities. But what Augustine learned with Tyconius' aid had such an impact that it constitutes the major turning-point in his thought. All that he had worked out concerning the freedom and bondage of the will, the call of grace and its reception through faith and the infusion of love, came to be seen in a new light; it was not so much modified as brought to what seemed to be a fitting conclusion in the conviction that the will is so bound by custom that it cannot free itself, cannot even receive the promises of grace and seek divine aid, but must be called forth by a divine invitation that is suited to the particular situation of each man, that is issued, therefore, by a providence which has watched over the details of his life from the beginning. This is the new understanding of man—and of himself in particular—to which Augustine found himself directed by his reflections on grace, and it gave, I suspect, the most intimate impulse toward the fresh examination of himself and his own past that he carried out with such originality in the *Confessions*; it also supplied the insights which enabled him to take up again, confidently and successfully this time, the more speculative tasks at which he had earlier tried his hand in the uncompleted commentary on Genesis. And perhaps his new role as a bishop gave him both the obligation and the liberty to undertake intellectual activities of greater scope. In many ways, then, a period of apprenticeship was ended and Augustine at the age of 42 was ready to stake out the ground for the building of a theological edifice which would have the stamp of his own artistry on it.

PART TWO

The Master

CHAPTER 4

Exploration (397–410)

ALL THE INDICATIONS suggest that a major turn came in Augustine's thought at some time in 396 or 397 with his arrival at a fully Paulinized understanding of grace and the bondage of the will. He broke off *De doctrina christiana*, wrote the *Confessions*, projected a *De Trinitate* in which he would attempt to defend and to understand the doctrine of the Church, elaborated a comprehensive cosmology, at once philosophical and religious, within which to interpret the entire creaturely realm (first at the end of the *Confessions* and then in the long Genesis commentary which is the repository of most of his philosophical reflections for over a decade), and revised his evaluation of the Platonists as a result of fresh encounters with Porphyry's anti-Christian polemics. A continuity in his interests and his basic assumptions extends from 397 until about 410 or 411, when a host of new influences began to pour in upon him.

Something of a stage-setting for this period is probably to be found in his work *On Christian Instruction*, written, he says, in the time just after becoming a bishop, thus in 396. The work is important because it operates on two fronts simultaneously, revealing something of Augustine's concerns with both, for it is on the one hand an examination of exegetical method, making use of the tools of classical culture, and on the other a critical scrutiny of that culture and an attempt to draw out the best in it and displace the rest with the heritage of biblical religion. Both fronts must be considered together if the work is not to be misconstrued and Augustine's real concerns are to come to light, for he never wishes to approach either the Bible or classical culture without the other.

Marrou in his classic study has underlined the cultural import of Augustine's change from a "philosophical" to an "ecclesiastical" milieu. Augustine, who had earlier identified himself with the world of classical literature and philosphy and shared its goals even when he thought they could be attained only by following the way indicated by Christianity, now affected ignorance of and distaste for classical writers, in the typical ecclesiastical manner, lest he seem to recommend classical culture in its entirety, including its mythology and its spectacles.[1] He retained his lively interest in dialectic and rhetoric, but now they were put to practical use as tools for studying the Scriptures and persuading men to follow their teachings.

By way of putting the matter into perspective Marrou suggests that the Christians were attacking not culture as such but its decadence and sterility in post-Hellenistic times, and under such circumstances their cultural asceticism may even have represented the true humanism. Their criticisms should not be over-dramatized, he thinks. After all, they knew only the *one* culture of Greece and Rome and remained immersed in it despite their attacks on it; their actual function (and perhaps their conscious aim as well) was to evaluate and correct an existing culture, not to destroy it or to construct a new one.[2]

Augustine is quick to acknowledge the value of much that has come from classical culture: its social institutions, its historical narratives of past events, its descriptions of the natural world, its practical arts with their ability to channel physical processes, and above all the rational disciplines of dialectic and mathematics which lead the soul beyond the changeable world (*De doct. chr.*, II, 19, 29—39, 59). But these are to be rigorously controlled; they are not to become ends in themselves but are to be put in the service either of man's practical needs in the conduct of life or of the interpretation of Scripture (II, 39, 59). He adopts, for a time, Ambrose's theory that whatever is good and true in Plato's philosophy was learned from Jeremiah when they were both in Egypt (II, 28, 43) and even more audaciously expresses the

---

[1] Marrou, *Saint Augustin et la fin de la culture antique*, pp. 346–347.
[2] *Ibid.*, pp. 352–355.

opinion that whatever is of value in the writings of the pagans can also be found in the Scriptures, with much more besides (II, 42, 63). He goes to the extent of recommending the compilation of glosses on Scripture so that Christian readers will not have to study anything more than is necessary (II, 39, 59). It is easy to see why Augustine's remarks were taken by the medieval glossators and commentators to be a prescription for understanding everything in function of the imagery of Scripture, so that the latter becomes the only fixed point of reference and all of nature and history is dissolved into a symbolization of its truths. But that was not Augustine's understanding of the matter. He was too vividly aware of what classical culture had achieved, quite independently of the biblical heritage, and too vividly aware of the cognitive status of its empirical reports and rational deductions, to fall into that kind of particularism and authoritarianism; his approximations to it were a passing fancy, though unfortunately an influential one.

A more reliable indication of his actual assumptions is found in the comparison, derived from Irenaeus (*Adv. Haer.*, IV, 30),[3] of the rational disciplines and the ethical investigations and the monotheistic aspirations of classical culture with the gold of the Egyptians, to be taken from them as from unjust possessors and put to proper use by the new Israel (II, 40, 60). What he had in mind was a vital process, never completed and never to be taken for granted but continually to be enacted anew, of bringing every thought into captivity to Christ (II Corinthians 10, 5), of "leaving the society of pagans under the leadership of Christ"; and this meant not merely fleeing Egypt with the stolen booty but "observing the Pasch," that is, devoting all these things to God in love (II, 40, 60—41, 62). Far from devaluing classical culture, Augustine intended to exalt it; he thought that this episode during the Exodus was a *figure*—a mere foreshadowing— of a far more momentous occurrence in the transformation of classical culture by the Greek and Roman Christians (II, 40, 61). The Gentiles have a certain status in *Heilsgeschichte* because of their sciences and their philosophy (cf. *Conf.*, VII, 9, 15); this is the glory of the Gentiles, just as the glory of Israel is that from

---

[3] Berthold Altaner, "Augustinus und Irenäus," *Theologische Quartalschrift*, CXXIX (1949), 165–168 (*KpS*, pp. 197–200).

them come the covenant, the law, the promises, and the Christ. The difference is that the heritage of the Gentiles, unlike that of Israel, is not transmitted in an uncorrupted form and must first be corrected by the authority of Scripture.

What Augustine actually championed, and even more clearly practiced, was not a narrow biblicism but an ongoing encounter between philosophical reflection and careful study of the biblical text. This means that his thought can be taken as a prime illustration of the pattern that H. Richard Niebuhr termed "Christ transforming culture."[4] The transforming power comes from the instruction given in revelation, the new self-understanding aroused by the gospel, the new motivations infused with *caritas*. But there must be something already there to be transformed. And it is evident from the character of Augustine's achievement that the outcome of the transforming process is dependent upon both the classical and the biblical heritage; without the one or the other it would not be what it is. Augustine may not have been even dimly aware of the extent to which he was reading the doctrines of classical science and philosophy into the biblical text, for the practice was a standard one and his was a historically unsophisticated age; he thought that he was discerning, with the aid of secular knowledge, truths hidden in the text from the first. But on either interpretation of the matter, his or our own, what he was doing had the character of a "correlation" between general human experience and the particular insights of the people of God, and Tillich is right, I think, in saying that the actual practice of any great theologian is not to follow slavishly the letter of Scripture or the conventional doctrines of the Church but, while taking them altogether seriously, to think them through again with the aid of the best knowledge and critical reflection of his time.[5]

We shall find that this problem of relating revelation and culture dominates Augustine's thoughts during a succession of daring explorations. But we shall also encounter a number of striking changes of attitude that occur within the space of a decade, and it will be our task to try to discern their causes.

---

[4] H. Richard Niebuhr, *Christ and Culture* (New York, 1951), pp. 206–218.
[5] Paul Tillich, *Systematic Theology*, I (Chicago, 1951), 59–66.

1. SELF-EXAMINATION

In *De doctrina christiana* Augustine was brought to think seriously about the contributions of classical culture, the tension of its more licentious and idolatrous features with Christianity, and the final convergence of all that is true and good in human culture with the biblical revelation. But his reflections break out of the theoretical genre and become autobiographical in the *Confessions*, where observations on the educational process, the vocational aims, the amusements and the passions of late Roman society occupy an important place. It is notoriously difficult to discern the scheme of organization of the *Confessions*, let alone Augustine's motives in undertaking the work,[6] but there is merit in Pincherle's suggestion that, along with whatever else it may be, it is a kind of sequel to *De doctrina christiana* and that the writing of the latter work was interrupted because he found a better vehicle for investigating the same problems.[7] It may be that Augustine, in writing of Cyprian and Lactantius, Victorinus and Optatus and Hilary, and the many still living who had fled Egypt (*De doct. chr.*, II, 40, 61), began to think of himself, of his debt to Cicero and Plotinus and many others, but also of the influence of classical culture in drawing him into the mire and holding him there, and felt impelled to reconsider, in the light of his new discoveries about grace, both the course of his own life and the character of the culture that had shaped his thoughts and ambitions.

The writing of the *Confessions* was probably occasioned by a combination of internal and external factors—his new renown as a bishop, inquiries about his earlier life, attacks on his integrity, his own reflections on classical culture, his new understanding of grace, all of them together requiring a massive reexamination and reinterpretation of his own life. Whatever the relative weight of the various motives, the *Confessions* function as a kind of first *Retractatio*. Toward the end of his life, in 426 and 427, Augustine looked back over his entire literary output and "reconsidered" the things he had said and the influences to which he had consented. But that reconsideration was not the only one he under-

---

[6] For a survey of some of the discussion of this question see Solignac, *BA*, XIII, pp. 26–36.

[7] Pincherle, p. 194.

took. Repeatedly he was led to reconsider his life and opinions, and it seems that the works in which he does this—scattered passages in the Cassiciacum dialogues, perhaps *On True Religion*, certainly the *Confessions*, some aspects of *On the Trinity* and *The City of God*—are his most original. He "put more of himself" into them, not only in that he worked at them with a greater intensity and made more direct use of introspection, but in that he disclosed in them, covertly or by name, the influences that left a permanent impress on his thinking. Such writings disclose the broad continuities in his life, the problems to which he repeatedly turned his attention, each time with new subtlety of insight and accuracy of conceptualization. Karl Jaspers has pointed out a similarity between Augustine and two modern figures, Kierkegaard and Nietzsche (he is also aware of their differences, of course, but the similarity is still striking): all of them "thought with their blood," in a highly personal way; each time they came to a problem it was examined afresh, and they were not afraid to change their minds, nor were they afraid of small inconsistencies in thought and expression, for they knew that it was all held together in the unity of their own life; and finally, all of them were led to reflect upon the changing course of their own thought and reexamine their literary productions. [8]

The *Confessions* is one of those works which deserve being read sentence by sentence in the original, guided by a detailed commentary of the sort that has yet to be written or by a teacher able to hear all its resonances, for this work which, read casually in translation, often seems a commonplace expression of an all too familar piety is really a carefully textured work of art in which almost every sentence is laden with reflections of biblical language and of Augustine's own philosophy and theology. It is not just an autobiographical record of the past. It is an attempt to *interpret* that past with the aid of his current convictions, many of which are in continuity with his earlier writings—the use of the parable of the Prodigal Son to interpret his own career, for example, anticipated in the *Soliloquies*, I, 1, 5 ("*recipe fugitivum tuum, Domine, clementissime Pater*"), and its neo-Platonist analogue in the theme of the wandering and returning of the soul in a journey of the affections—but all of which are set in a different light by his newly

[8] Karl Jaspers, *The Great Philosophers*, I (New York, 1962), 213–214.

acquired understanding of the bondage of the will and its liberation by the efficacious calling of God. This means that studies of the *Confessions* must of necessity fall into different genres: some are concerned to get back to the events narrated, some are focused upon the framework of interpretation imposed at the time of writing, some study the literary artistry of the narrative.

Augustine claims not to falsify the record: "There you see me as I was," he will write later in Epistle 231. Nevertheless he does not attempt to evoke the experiences of the past in a disinterested, "aesthetic" fashion; he describes and interprets them, often frankly "editorializing," from the perspective of the present, and this is an essential part of the undertaking:

I want now to recall the abominable things I did in times past and the carnal desires that defiled my soul, not because I value those sins, but because I value you, my God. For love of your love I shall retrace my wicked ways (the recollection of them is bitter, but I do it in order to savor your sweetness, a sweetness which does not deceive but is secure and brings lasting joy), and I shall gather myself together again following the dispersal of my affections which tore me apart when I turned away from you, the only Unity, and lost myself in multiplicity (II, 1, 1).

It is not accidental, then, that Augustine should recall the past in God's presence, under the form of prayer, for the coherence of his life in the past, present, and future is supplied by God; the *reality* of the past is to be discovered not through reliving the feelings and the assumptions of times long vanished, but through heeding the instruction that comes through revelation and recollecting the past in constant encounter with God.

But it is precisely because of his belief that God has supplied continuity throughout and that revelation has given the key to the interpretation of the whole story, that Augustine wants us to see the *way* and not merely the *goal*. He is not retracing his steps merely in order to ask forgiveness for what he has been. He thinks that it will also help to reveal something of the true character of man's life before God. And yet what it discloses is not one simple pattern. Several different patterns emerge, tangled together.

1. Most apparent, perhaps, is the theme of wandering and homecoming. Augustine, looking back, senses that he has always been immersed in evil. "Where and when was I ever innocent?"

he asks (I, 7, 12). We should remember that his thought about the origin of man's bondage to sin is now in transition. He must come to grips with the Pauline conception of man, which sees in Adam the origin of mortality and of sin itself. Where he had assumed the preexistence of the soul (though with no great conviction), he now views it as only one hypothesis among others and gives to the theoretical question of the soul's origin a position far inferior to the practical question of its destiny and the measures man is to take in view of that destiny (De lib. arb., III, 20, 55—22, 63).

Augustine tries, nonetheless, to discover when and how the bondage to sin originates. He points out the peccadilloes of infants (I, 7, 11), and thinks that infants are different from adults not in being any more innocent but in lacking the abilities to carry their selfish inclinations into effect. Throughout the discussion Augustine still assumes that the situation of the soul is determined by its own attitudes and decisions, sometimes not fully conscious, to be sure, but clearly its own. The mortal body furnishes the occasion for sin, but it does not do away with the soul's essential freedom, and the individual soul bears responsibility for becoming captured by too great familiarity with and affection for earthly affairs. Robert O'Connell has marshalled impressive evidence that throughout the *Confessions* Augustine utilizes the Plotinian theme of the "fall" of the soul and various kinds of imagery drawn from it.[9] And yet Augustine must be taken seriously when he says that he holds the question of the *preexistence* of the soul open. The imagery of the fall must be considered ambiguous, then, open to various interpretations. And what seems most likely is that it is used in such a way that it does *not* imply preexistence but rather describes the character of infantile experience. Augustine's theory is no longer that the origin of sin is in the preexistent soul's nostalgia for the body. But he has not yet come to a doctrine of original sin. His theory at this time is rather what Athanase Sage has termed "sin from the beginning" (*péché d'origine* in contrast to *péché originel*): because of the mortality of the body which is the consequence of Adam's sin there is an inclination toward sin, a temptation which is acted upon in the

<hr />

[9] "The Riddle of Augustine's Confessions: A Plotinian Key," *International Philosophical Quarterly*, IV (1964), 327–352.

first personal act of an individual; from then on he becomes increasingly entangled in sin.[10]

Augustine finds it hard to say much about his experiences as an infant. But what he recalls of his boyhood years reinforces the sense of having been lured away and immersed in an evil milieu. He was drawn into the "bitter sea" of a humanity united in only one purpose, the seeking of temporal happiness on earth (XIII, 17, 20). He speaks of the "tides of temptation" which beat upon him during his youth (I, 11, 18). Even the educational system conspired against him; for when languages were taught, it was with the aid of the epic poems of Homer and Vergil, in which the deceit and lust of the gods were glorified.

We are carried away by the stream of social custom, and who can withstand it? Will the torrent never dry up? How much longer will it sweep the sons of Eve down to that vast and terrible sea which can scarcely be crossed even by those who climb up on the ark of the cross? (I, 16, 25).

And there is the famous sentence at the beginning of book III, used by T. S. Eliot in *The Waste Land*: "To Carthage then I came, where a cauldron of unholy loves sang all about my ears." What a man loves will determine the character of his life. But love can be directed toward anything at all, and Augustine, looking back, finds that his life was wanton and futile; he had freedom, but it was a "fugitive's freedom" (III, 3, 5).

He was aware of what we call cultural conditioning, and he saw its moral and religious import. Of course he believed that man is always a sinner; but he felt that a man's location in history is important to the shaping of his life. The temptations and the sins are not always the same, for the cultural milieu will present different inducements and different possibilities. And Augustine was able to discern this fact because he himself had made such a perfect adjustment to his culture: he had been born in a modest social position, with a mother who was as ambitious for her son as she was pious; he had sought and gained the approval of his culture, rising through the channels that were available to young men with energy and ability. The values of classical civilization lured him, and he wandered into the far country.

[10] Athanase Sage, "Péché originel. Naissance d'un dogme," *REA*, XIII (1967), 219; 223–233.

But why should it be that Augustine thinks even the years of wandering and distraction worth recalling? It is not only because they are instructive about the nature of man's alienation from God. In a strange way they even make a contribution of their own.

2. There is, then, something of the idea of *felix culpa*. Even sin contributes to the total scheme of things, for when men make a bad use of the freedom which God has created, God is able to make a good use of their evil wills. Somehow even the darkness has a function in relation to the light.

What is it about man that makes him rejoice more at the salvation of a soul for which all had despaired, or at the deliverance of one that has been in great danger, than when hope has never been lost or when there was not much peril?

Why is it that in our part of creation there is this alternation of defeat and progress, of hurt and reconciliation? Is this the rhythm that you gave to the world when, from the highest of the heavens to the lowest things of earth, from the beginning to the end of the ages, from the angel to the worm, you allotted appropriate places and times to good things of every kind and to all your righteous works? (VIII, 3, 6 and 8).

When Augustine describes the history of the human race, despite its evil, as a harmonious song made up of antitheses, or as a chiaroscuro painting, he does not intend to gloss over the seriousness of evil or to suggest that God is in any way responsible for sin. On the contrary, he has a sense of dynamic process through it all. Men sin on their own account and strive against God; but God is able to override the evil loves and actions of men and make them contribute to the accomplishment of his own purposes. And Augustine sees that kind of providential guidance in his own life, as when he speculates that his own ambitions and the enticements of other men were the means used to draw him from Carthage to Rome and closer to the circumstances which would contribute to his conversion (V, 8, 14ff.).

3. But there is even more than this. Perhaps most interesting about Augustine's account of himself is that he sees running throughout his life a straight line of development, a constant growth. For despite his moral uncertainty, he made steady intellectual and psychological progress. Something good was emerging even in the midst of evil. His life was not only the Yin and

Yang of wandering followed by homecoming; it was also a steady journey toward wisdom. From this perspective the *Confessions* follow the typical form of the novel, describing the education of a young man, his movement from innocence to experience, his initiation into the realities of life, his gaining of maturity.[11]

This theme of steady progress and growth is not immediately apparent in the *Confessions*, for Augustine expends most of his efforts in suggesting that the time before his conversion was "lost time":

I was compelled to memorize the wanderings of someone named Aeneas, while I was oblivious to my own erring ways, and to lament the dying Dido, who killed herself for love, while all the time I was dying in the midst of these things, far from you, o God my life. And I was so miserable as to bear it all without shedding a tear (I, 13, 20).

Nonetheless Augustine acknowledges that he did learn to use the Latin language elegantly—and eloquently—from his study of the *Aeneid*. His classical education helped him to unfold his potentialities and bring them to full exercise. And the crucial event, of course, was his reading of Cicero's *Hortensius*, which fired him to search for integrity and true happiness, whatever they might be. Classical culture also assisted him throughout his search, bringing premature resolutions under criticism and finally giving him a glimpse of the Promised Land itself.

But homecoming is something else again. Augustine describes the way in which, even after he was convinced of the goal to pursue, he was unable to will wholeheartedly to seek it. He inquires, in retrospect (VIII, 9, 21), why this strange phenomenon, this *monstrum*, occurs: the mind is obeyed when it commands the body, but not when it commands itself. The ability to will is in man, and if he were to resolve fully to turn to God he could do it, for all that is needed is an act of will: in this case to will is already to do. And yet, when the mind orders itself to make this act of will, it does not carry out its own command. The problem, of course, is half-heartedness; the command is given hesitantly, with uncertainty, without the whole will. As it turns out, then, it is no *monstrum*, no strange phenomenon; it is quite simple:

---

[11] See especially Anne Brunhemer, "The Art of Augustine's Confessions," *Thought*, XXXVII (1962), 116–117.

the will is divided, partly willing and partly not willing, perhaps willing three or four or five conflicting things. This division of the will against itself is no mystery, needing to be explained, for example, in Manichaean fashion in terms of conflicting principles of good and evil. It is quite understandable as a sickness of the soul (*aegritudo animi*), and the sickness is that of ambivalence and vacillation. Augustine describes it almost clinically in his *Exposition of the Epistle to the Galatians* (ch. 54) written a few years earlier: when we are faced at the same time by carnal custom and by the demands of righteousness, and have a certain liking (*dilectio*) for both of them, we may be drawn for a moment by fear toward one of them more than the other, but quite unwillingly; or if there is equal fear or anxiety on both sides, then we pause, weighing them both, pulled both ways by the fluctuating loves and fears; but in neither case will there be decisive action.

This sickness of the soul, this dividing of the will, is not, Augustine says, anything that man would wish upon himself. It is not something that he *does* so much as something that he *suffers*; it is not *sin as such* but the *punishment* of sin. Acts which are first committed freely are punished by addiction to those same sins. The misdirecting of the will leads to taking pleasure in what is willed, and then one becomes accustomed to it, and familiarity soon becomes necessity (*Conf.*, VIII, 5, 10). Augustine finds it incredible that man should be thought at every moment of his life to have the same degree of indeterminate freedom, as though nothing had ever happened. The fact that man exists in time is constitutive of his being; he is shaped by his accumulated decisions, his whole existence is affected by the loves which draw him in this direction or another, and then he will no longer be in a position to act *de novo*, with the freshness of a new beginning.

This was Augustine's situation just prior to his conversion. As Courcelle has pointed out in his discussions of the *Confessions*,[12] Augustine represents himself as Hercules at the crossroads, confronted by women beckoning him along divergent ways— Continence with her numerous sons and daughters, calling him toward the life that he knew to be integral to the proper pursuit of wisdom; but also his former mistresses, to whom he was still attached by strong memories and affections. He knew, he

[12] See chapter 1, section 2, above.

says, the step that he wanted to take; and yet the closer he came to it, the more he shrank from it. Why? Because of the power of "custom," such familiarity with a pattern of behavior and such emotional attachment to it that he could not think of himself without it and consequently could not cut himself loose from it (*Conf.*, VIII, 11, 26; cf. the discussion of the adhesive power of love, and its effect upon the life of the mind, in *De Trin.*, X, 8, 11).

The impasse is resolved, as we have seen, not in his giving way to a flood of tears and throwing himself down under the fig tree, not in his hearing the words, "*Tolle, lege*," but in his reading of the Scriptures and having them speak directly to his condition; and I have argued that this presentation of the matter, while not necessarily untrue to the facts, is shaped by his fresh theological conviction that man is converted by being called in a way "congruous" with his individual needs.[13] His will, he believes, has always been free in principle; but it remained in bondage to its own misdirected affections until it was "called forth" by a divine summons (IX, 1, 1).

The whole process, both of slipping into bondage and then of discovering the way to be taken and being liberated for it, is quite credible in human terms, and Augustine devotes much effort to analyzing his own experience as accurately as possible and interpreting it in the light of his philosophical and theological convictions. Must we not say that the literary and rhetorical power of the *Confessions*—extraordinary even among the works of Augustine—is due to his tenacious resolve neither to let his own experiences stand at face value, unexamined, nor to accept any interpretation of his life which could not be supported in some way by those experiences; his insistence, then, that both fact and interpretation be brought together and fused and assayed in the crucible of restless inquiry in direct encounter with God?

2. COSMOS AND HISTORY

Augustine, like most of the fathers, took a special interest in the creation narrative for the reason that it furnished Christians, living in a cultural atmosphere much concerned with origins and

[13] See chapter 1, section 2, above.

causes, an authorized *Peri archōn*, and one which had striking parallels (at least as they invariably read it) with the best of Greek philosophy. Augustine came back to the opening chapters of Genesis again and again—in his early work on Genesis against the Manichaeans (388–389), in his unfinished literal commentary (393–394), in the closing books of the *Confessions* (401), in the long commentary on Genesis (begun about 402), and in books XI and XII of *The City of God* (417), each time building on his earlier insights and elaborating them further, always proceeding, to be sure, with an air of inquiry and acknowledging the possibility of alternative interpretations, but with a basic confidence that he was moving in the right direction and with a steady crystallization of his views.

Though his exegesis may seem fantastic and far-fetched to the modern reader acquainted with more historically disciplined methods of interpreting a text, what he attempted to accomplish is not really alien to our own aims in exegesis and in theology, for he tried, first, to pay scrupulous attention to the text in all its details (and though he was able to work only with a Latin translation, it preserved faithfully the many grammatical and conceptual peculiarities of the Hebrew original) and, second, to bring revelation and the best of the science and philosophy accessible to him into fruitful encounter—not anticipating that revelation would be merely a confirmation, in more popular language, of rational knowledge (for Augustine was prepared to find that revelation upset many of the precipitate judgments of the philosophers), yet confident, on the other hand, that the deliverances of revelation, when reflected on with the aid of the best of natural knowledge, would yield a superior and perhaps even more reasonable philosophy.

Judged according to his own aims and in the light of the knowledge, both of the book of Scripture and of the book of nature, available to him, Augustine's achievement is astoundingly successful. He succeeded in giving (probably for the only time in the entire history of exegesis, for what it is worth) a satisfactory interpretation of the opening chapters of Genesis as they stand, with all their perplexities. Though it will not convince those who are aware of the difference between the Yahwist and the Priestly writer and the possible backgrounds in the earlier religious history of the Near East, they will be in a position to see the massive obstacles Augustine had to overcome in giving a unified interpretation to those chapters. And he not only respected the text as it stood; he was able to bring his own scientific and philosophical questions to it and come back with a plausibly restructured cosmology and metaphysic. In this he ranks with Philo and Origen, and he probably surpasses them in both thoroughness and steadiness. It is striking how far he goes beyond one of the major works of the generation preceding him, the commentary on the Hexaemeron by Basil of Caesarea (a work which he himself used in the translation of Eustathius). Basil's exegesis is straightforward, quite unlike Augustine's penetrating and imaginative procedure, and it is far more antagonistic to the suggestions of the philosophers. Augustine gained a few useful insights from that work, to be sure; but they are among the few instances of Basil's taking scientific and philosophical problems seriously.[14] Augustine is much more inclined than Basil, in defending the Bible, to refrain from too hasty an assertion of the power of God and instead to acknowledge the problems and wrestle with them by reasoning philosophically, in the manner already demonstrated by Origen. It is only later, in *The City of God*, that he begins to invoke divine omnipotence and the authority of Scripture (in part, perhaps, because the tide was now running against Origen).

We have already seen the outlines of Augustine's exegesis beginning to take shape in the unfinished commentary on Genesis written during his early years in Hippo.[15] He began to apply the Plotinian doctrine of "spiritual matter" to the angels, thinking it corroborated by the language of the creation narrative, and this theme is what furnishes continuity to all of his subsequent ventures in exegesis. Though he proceeds cautiously, with constant questioning and conjecture, he is convinced of the basic rightness of his interpretation and moves steadily ahead elaborating it.

In the twelfth and thirteenth books of the *Confessions* the outlines are sketched clearly for the first time. The heavens and

[14] See Berthold Altaner, "Augustinus und Basilius der Grosse," *Revue bénédictine*, LX (1950), 17–24 (*KpS*, pp. 269–276).

[15] See chapter 3, section 1, above.

the earth of the first verse are respectively the spiritual and the corporeal creation. The angels who adhere to God are called a heaven above the visible heavens, or the house of God, or the true Jerusalem, because God dwells within their minds, both as the primary object of their knowledge and as the animating principle of their wills (similarly Augustine in his sermons on the Psalms often calls human souls, the elect within the earthly Church, a "heaven"[16]).

Following this summary statement in verse 1, Augustine thinks, the narrative goes on to indicate the factors that have contributed to the production of an ordered cosmos: the "material" principle, which is formless matter in the case of the corporeal world, indeterminate and wavering life in the case of the spiritual creation; the "formative" principle, the divine Word; and the "dynamic" principle, the basis of rightly directed movement and the guarantee of continuity, the Holy Spirit. If the formless earth of verse 2 should be, following the interpretation of verse 1, the matter from which the whole corporeal world was made, then the obscure deep must be spiritual matter, the changeable, groping, unstable life which created minds would have led if left to their own resources. But materiality is not left to itself; the Spirit hovering over the deep represents the generosity of God by which things not only are given existence but are led to the highest and best mode of being of which they are capable by being joined to the formative power of the Word.

The first utterance of the Word is, "Let there be light"; the first thing to be created, that is, fully formed, is the light of the first day. Augustine has a perfectly consistent solution to the vexed question what this light, created before there were any luminaries in the skies, might be: it is, he suggests, God's calling upon the spiritual creation to turn toward himself and, by adhering to God and contemplating him without cessation, to be illuminated by the eternal Wisdom and become fully "formed."

As theologians since Peter Lombard have recognized, the discussions of the light of the first day are the chief locus of Augustine's doctrine of nature and grace, the distinction between

---

[16] For citation of the numerous passages where this identification is found, see Fulbert Cayré, *Les sources de l'amour divin. La divine présence d'après saint Augustin* (Paris, 1933), p. 84, n. 4.

what finite spirit can become on the basis of its own resources and what it can become through the gracious activity of God. I have tried elsewhere to analyze in detail Augustine's views on this topic, views which, because they are expressed in such a veiled symbolism and in the form of commentary rather than theological exposition, are easily misconstrued if they are not overlooked altogether.[17]

Augustine had long since known that finite spirits must turn toward God as the fullness of being both out of a realistic assessment of themselves (for they cannot cut themselves off from the whole, as though they were equal to God) and for the sake of perfect happiness (for this can consist only in the possession of that which will not pass away); he had also come to see the Spirit as the principle of right orientation and stability, the basis of the love for God and the adherence to God by which lasting beatitude can be attained. But it is only now that he explicitly formulates the "double gratuity" of beginning and fulfillment (though he was feeling his way toward it in *De lib. arb.*, III, 16, 45; 20, 56; 22, 65). At the beginning of the thirteenth book of the *Confessions* he states that the illumination of the angels is not their own accomplishment and that it is given to them not out of necessity or need on God's part, nor as a matter of right or of exigency on the part of creatures, but as a gift. The gift presupposes the existence of a recipient, but both the creation of a being capable of receiving the gift and the giving of the gift that is to be received are gratuitous acts on God's part. The hovering of the Spirit over the waters is interpreted as an attestation to God's sovereignty over the world and his benevolence toward it, and thus a denial of any indigence in God or any dependence upon the course of finite events for the completion of his own nature (*Conf.*, XIII, 1, 1; 3, 4—4, 5; *De Gen. ad litt.*, I, 7, 12).

What is it that grace adds, over and above the nature of intelligent creatures? It is not a new destiny, that of gaining full happiness in the vision of God, as it is for many of the scholastic theologians, for Augustine assumes from start to finish that this is the *only* destiny suited to man and that it follows from his nature as an intelligent being. Nor is it a new set of powers for the attainment of a destiny toward which man strives but is incapable

---

[17] Eugene TeSelle, "Nature and Grace in Augustine's Expositions of Genesis I, 1–5," *RA*, V (1968), pp. 95–137.

of reaching, for Augustine assumes that the mind, by its nature, is set in relation to the eternal Word and is capable of immediate intuition of God, though he thinks this impossible when the mind is dulled by sensual affections; he readily acknowledges that the Platonist philosophers have been able to catch a moment-ary glimpse of God before again falling away, not being able to endure the brilliance of the divine light. The insufficiency of nature lies not with the capacity of the finite mind but with the instability of the finite will, and the function of the grace of the Spirit, when it is offered, is to overcome this instability of the will by arousing and sustaining the fervor of love and thus bringing its powers to full and persistent exercise.

Still following the pattern worked out a few years earlier in connection with the conversion of man, Augustine thinks of the process in four stages:

First there is "spiritual matter" with its formlessness and fluidity, in other words, the indeterminacy of finite life, capable of apprehending and being formed by the Word, yet intrinsically unstable, always threatened by the possibility of flagging in its zeal or being distracted by other concerns.

Second, there is the "*Fiat lux*," the divine call issued to spiritual creatures so that they will turn toward God. This cannot be interpreted as a mere announcement that adherence to divine Wisdom is the sole basis of true happiness; more than that, it must be an *invitation* and a *promise*, offering something new to the ones addressed, a *destiny* and with it a *task* to be fulfilled. What is offered, in a way analogous to the grace given to sinful men, is the assistance of the Spirit in seeking and remaining in the divine presence. But this assistance is conditioned upon the free act of conversion.

Third, then, there is conversion on the part of the finite will. It is called forth by the divine invitation, but it is genuinely the act of the creatures themselves.

Finally the will, having responded to the invitation, is enkindled and sustained by the gift of the Holy Spirit infusing *caritas*, which is identical, it will be noted, with the unambiguously good exercise of the will:

In your Gift we rest; there we enjoy you. Our "place" is our rest. Love bears us there, and your good Spirit delivers us, lowly though we are, from the doors of death. In good will we come to peace . . . . My "movement" is my love; by it I am borne, to whatever place I am borne. By your Gift we are kindled and borne aloft; burning with your fire, onward we go toward the peace of Jerusalem. There good will shall so install us that we shall will nothing else than to remain there eternally (*Conf.*, XIII, 9, 10).

The terminus of this pilgrimage of the spirit is the unceasing vision of God. It is made possible by *caritas*, the steady adherence of the will to God; but it is not identical with *caritas*, for love, however intense, remains a mere desire apart from its fulfillment in the possession of that which is desired, and the "possessing" in this case is through knowledge (*De civ. Dei*, XII, 9). In contemplation the creaturely mind, possessing divine Wisdom through knowledge and thereby participating in it, "becomes light." It is only in this unceasing contemplation of God that finite life finds perfect stability and rest; the intrinsic mutability of finite life is neutralized (*cohibetur*) in possessing the eternal God and possessing him with the certitude that this possession will not come to an end (*Conf.*, XII, 9, 9; 11, 12; 15, 19). This inhibition of temporality, it should be noted, is not so much physical as existential (it is not "behind" but "in" consciousness and freedom): the concern of finite spirit with the problems of its own existence is brought to a satisfying resolution, so that it finds joy in God and is distracted by no fond memories or bitter regrets concerning the past, no hopeful anticipations or restless wishes concerning its own unending possession of happiness. Even here Augustine stresses the grace of divine faithfulness, supplying continuity where creaturely mutability might still call beatitude into question (Augustine, unlike Aquinas, thinks that it is possible for a finite will to fall away from even the unmistakable good of the vision of God).

Augustine does not use the term "grace" in connection with this topic during these years, though he applies it later (*De civ. Dei*, XII, 9) and it is obviously pertinent to his analyses. To what exactly would it refer, given his usage at the time? Primarily to a decision of God concerning the destiny of intelligent creatures, a decision whose background in God's freedom is symbolized by the hovering of the Spirit over the waters and whose completion is symbolized by God's seeing that the light was good.

What stands between is the issuance of the call, "*Fiat lux*," and, following upon the response of conversion, the infusion of the Spirit. In both the beginning and the completion, Augustine thinks, God's initiative and the perfect gratuity of his action are stressed by the biblical narrative: in the Spirit's hovering over the waters and the giving of the invitation, the initiative is taken in order that finite life might be changed for the better through conversion and adherence to God ("*ut fieret*"); in God's seeing that the light is good, in other words, in the adherence of intelligent creatures to God with the aid of the Spirit, the initiative is taken in order that it remain what it has become ("*ut maneat*" [*De Gen. ad litt.*, I, 5, 11; 8, 13]). In the case of the angels the gift of the Spirit leads directly to beatitude, for their decision to respond or not is all-or-nothing, while in man there is a time of pilgrimage and testing before lasting happiness is attained; but in either case it is clear that Augustine thinks of grace as leading in the end to the perfecting of finite life by its stabilization and full formation in God.

When Augustine wrote the closing books of the *Confessions* in 400 or 401 he had forged his interpretation only through the first five verses. The rest of the creation narrative was treated as an allegory of the earthly life of the people of God, very much like that which he had worked out ten years earlier in the commentary written against the Manichaeans; and he even thought that there were textual indications that it *should* be interpreted figuratively (*Conf.*, XIII, 24, 37). Whether he also thought of his interpretation of the first five verses as allegorical is uncertain. In any case the last part of book XII (23, 32ff.) is a discussion of the problems of biblical interpretation, and it is important as a disclosure of Augustine's own exegetical assumptions and procedures in dealing with perplexities such as those encountered in the creation narrative. He views the logical obscurities and the grammatical peculiarities of the text as an open invitation to the reader to penetrate beyond the surface in seeking its "meaning." He thinks that a passage like the creation narrative has a kind of multi-dimensionality; it can be construed in a superficial way without gross distortion in more primitive ages and among simple people, but the inquiring mind will want to face up to and follow through every paradox, confident that the labyrinth was constructed by the divine author to lead to meanings which are at first only latent. Taken literally by the simple, the words are a "nest" in which faith is nurtured; but on further meditation they appear as a "leafy orchard" filled with hidden fruit (*Conf.*, XII, 27, 37—28, 38).

Such a method of interpretation is commonly found in manuscript-oriented religious communities (it is characteristic not only of patristic and medieval Christian exegesis but of rabbinic exegesis and can doubtless be paralleled in other cultures). It has many similarities with the dominant method of literary interpretation in the twentieth century, and this is not surprising, for it is one way of taking a text seriously—indeed, the only way when historical studies, which might cast light upon the background of the text and the meanings of the words, are undeveloped and when the text is honored for what it says and is not viewed as an expression of human experiences or a symptom of social or psychological tensions.

Augustine, without ever forsaking the allegorical method (indeed, he considered it a matter of faith [*De Gen. ad litt.*, I, 1]), decided a few years after writing the *Confessions* to undertake a literal commentary on the opening chapters of Genesis, interpreting them not as a figure of the economy of salvation but in their "historical" sense as an account of things done. In the process he made much use of physical and metaphysical speculations, doubtless hoping to show that reflection undertaken within the sphere marked out by revelation and faith can defeat learned but proud men even at their own game.[18] He acknowledged that non-Christians know much about the natural world on the basis of experience and reflection, and it would be foolish if Christians were to become "delirious" and make irresponsible use of biblical passages, not understanding their true meaning, and thereby exhibit their ignorance in the presence of learned men. The real harm, he says, would be not that these over-zealous Christians would be held in contempt, but that educated men, whose salvation the Church seeks, might reject "our authors" (the writers of the Scriptures) as *indocti* (*De Gen. ad litt.*, I, 19, 39).

---

[18] For this aspect of Augustine's interests, see Marrou, *Saint Augustin et la fin de la culture antique*, pp. 374–377, 455–456, and Pépin, *Théologie cosmique et théologie chrétienne*, pp. 406–422.

The accusation of Porphyry that the apostles were ignorant men always irritates Augustine; he glories in it when moral courage and the gaining of salvation are in question (*De Trin.*, IV, 18, 24), but he rejects its implications when the truth of the biblical revelation is in question. The problem is that educated men, seeing that Christians say erroneous things about matters in which they have knowledge, might infer that what is said about the resurrection of the dead and eternal life is also false; he does not want Christianity to suffer undeservedly the fate that Manichaeism deservedly suffered with him by making claims that conflicted outrageously with natural knowledge. He has confidence that whatever has been discovered about the world on the basis of reliable evidence cannot be inconsistent with the Bible, and, on the other hand, that where secular writers *are* clearly inconsistent with the Bible they can be proved, or at least believed, to be wrong, for Christ possesses (in the words of Colossians 2, 3) "all the treasures of both wisdom and knowledge, *sapientia* and *scientia*" (*De Gen. ad litt.*, I, 21, 41).

The point immediately at issue in this discussion concerns the waters above the firmament. Origen had decided that the natural order of the elements requires the interpretation of these waters above the firmament as a covert reference to the angels. Basil, in the commentary which Augustine now had in his hands, attacked this exegesis and offered the view that the "firmament" is not something solid and resistant but quite simply the region of the atmosphere, which we often call the heaven, and in which there are indeed waters which fall in rain or snow (*Homilies on the Hexaemeron*, III, 8–9). Augustine now ignores Origen's interpretation, kicking away the ladder by which he had reached his theory of spiritual matter, reports Basil's (*De Gen. ad litt.*, II, 4, 7), and lends his support to another view (not his own, for in the unfinished commentary, 8, 29, he reports it as the opinion of others) that there are waters even above the atmosphere in the form of minute particles of ice, and that these explain the slow thirty-year orbit of Saturn, contrasting so drastically with the one-day orbit of the astral heaven just beyond it.

In neither this passage nor any other is Augustine engaged in original scientific speculation. But he manifests his confidence that the biblical faith can stand with the best of secular thought, and his posture is altogether undefensive; he has respect for the work that has been done, and if he does not stand in exactly the same place as the philosophers, at least he is not opposed to them. Like the Augustine of the early years after his conversion, he seems to feel the excitement of reason's quest and wishes to take part in it, though in a believing way. For a time (probably between 402 and 405, when he had few interruptions and was was able to work steadily on *De Trinitate* and the Genesis commentary[19]) there is a pure joy in intellectual inquiry of the kind that Augustine does not always manifest. It is a period devoted in large part to what he himself called *scientia*, the knowledge of created things, in contrast to *sapientia*, the seeking and contemplation of eternal things (*Ad Simpl.*, II, q. 2, 3; *De Trin.*, XII, 14, 23 and 15, 25; XIV, 1, 3). It is authentic *knowledge*, not belief or opinion, and it is made such by the element of rational certainty in generalization and inference.

But all of this does not mean that he has turned to pure speculation about the cosmos and lost his interest in human history and its relation to the beginnings of things. Indeed, from that period come both the overview of human history in *De catechizandis rudibus* and the defense of the Catholic Church in *De baptismo*. Furthermore, it is evident that the calling of the angels in the "*Fiat lux*" is the archetype of human history, both in the founding of the heavenly City, the ultimate destination of the saints, when a portion of the spiritual creation responds to the divine call, and in the fall of the demons who will draw the human race into their sphere of influence. But Augustine has not yet made that connection in the explicit way that will form the theme of *The City of God*. The two cities still belong to human history alone; the retrojection of their origins to the angelic realm at the beginning of time is only gradually being worked out. What is more important for Augustine's thought during these years is that the founding of the heavenly City, as God's first and highest conferral of order beyond himself, sets the context within which all else in the natural world and in human history takes place. Thus the *cosmological groundwork* is being laid for what he will later say about the history of the human race and about the focusing of all events upon the pilgrimage of the saints toward the

[19] Mellet and Camelot, *BA*, XV, 562.

heavenly City. It is these cosmological dimensions, not alien to the history of salvation but rather broader than and inclusive of it, that Augustine proceeds to explore in the creation narrative.

Once he began to follow out his singular interpretation of the opening verses of the creation narrative he seems to have been struck repeatedly by its potentialities for elaboration into an entire cosmology along Platonist lines. Since the ancient world-view was shaped primarily by the discovery of the mathematical regularity of the movements of the heavens, it is not surprising that the rule of the cosmos by angelic beings was of greatest importance to Augustine, as it was to other ancient men. The oddities of ancient science and mythology (and though it is hard to say where to draw the line between them, there *is* a distinction) should not obscure for us the metaphysical principles at work in Augustine's discussion; we must first follow him the whole way and understand sympathetically his picture of the world, and only then attempt to detach from it any insights that may be immune to the collapse of ancient cosmology.

Augustine notices that the narrative repeatedly utilizes a curious three-stage formula: "God said, 'Let there be'"; "and so it was made"; "and God made". His explanation is that every created thing is first made, so to speak, in the eternal uttering of its idea in the Word of God; then in the knowledge which the angels have of the thing, still to be created, in its idea within the Word; and only last in its finite actuality (*De Gen. ad litt.*, II, 6, 10—7, 15). This does not mean that the angels are the mediators of creation; God is the sole creator, the one who makes things in their separate existence. But Augustine thinks, on the basis of the text and because of his own philosophical proclivities, that no creatures beneath the angels were created "without their knowledge" (*De Gen. ad litt.*, IV, 22, 39). This introduces a kind of symmetry into the entire creative process, since the angels themselves have been brought to full actualization through their own knowledge of the divine Word, and its explains why the clause "and God made light" is absent in the narrative of the first day alone, for it would have been redundant (*De Gen. ad litt.*, II, 8, 16). Knowledge, according to the Plotinian ontology which is the basis of Augustine's interpretation of the opening verses of Genesis, is constitutive of the full actuality of an intelligent being; and Augustine soon found corroboration in Scripture, where man is said (Ephesians 4, 23–24) to be renewed and become a new man through his knowledge (*agnitio*) of God, his conformation with the Image of God (*De Gen. ad litt.*, III, 20, 30–32).

The culminating achievement in this train of thought is Augustine's interpretation of the six days, each with its evening and morning (*De Gen. ad litt.*, IV, 21, 38—35, 56; *De civ. Dei*, XI, 7). He has noticed that the text speaks not of "the first day" but of "one day" (Hebrew does not differentiate between cardinal and ordinal forms for the number one, and this peculiarity was faithfully transmitted in the Septuagint and in the early Latin translation). This curious expression reinforces another biblical passage (Ecclesiasticus 18, 1) which, in Augustine's translation, says that God created all things *simul* (the original says *altogether*). Creation does not take place in six days, then, but is completed in the first moment of time.

What, then, are the six days? Nothing more is said of them than that they consist of evening and morning. Augustine, perhaps totally unaware of the cycle of the Hebrew day, and in any case assuming that any natural day must be terminated rather than begun in the evening, had the far more imaginative idea that the unusual sequence (first evening and then morning) symbolized a dimming and brightening, a declination and ascent, in the attention of the angels.

For a first exercise to get one's reflections moving in the right direction (*De Gen. ad litt.*, IV, 22, 39—23, 40) one can think of the days as a rapid survey of all the realms of creation: the evening which concludes each day is the angels' looking in turn at each realm (first themselves, then the firmament, and so on) as it is completed and stands forth in its own being, the outcome of God's creative intention, yet inferior to what it has been (and remains) in the divine ideas; the morning which follows is their referring of these various creations, already completed and already known in their own being, to the praise of the Creator; and the new day reaches its full brightness in their looking to the divine ideas to see what is next to be created.

But the angels' knowledge transcends a temporal succession of this sort. All the days are *simul*. Therefore the succession of days is to be converted into an abiding *structure* (*De Gen. ad litt.*, IV,

24, 41ff.) based on the contrast between the comparative dimness of the knowledge of created things in themselves and the unobscured lucidity of the knowledge of those same things in God's ideal projection of them as they should be. The angels' knowledge, dominated as it is by an unbroken contemplation of God and the divine ideas, always remains "day"; but they also know created things as they are in themselves, and this looking downward is "evening" (only a comparative dimness in relation to noontime knowledge, not a darkening, for it is never night, there is never a knowledge of created things to the exclusion of a knowledge of the Creator); and the proper *relating* of these two modes of knowledge by referring all knowledge of the creature to the glory of the Creator is "morning." All the days are simply a reiteration of the *one* day, the perfect lucidity and unity of the angelic community which is God's first creation (IV, 31, 48), and this reiteration is to be understood not as a temporal succession but as a properly articulated knowledge, an *ordinata cognitio* (IV, 23, 40) of the whole of creation according to the distinctions between its various realms, coming full circle in the seventh day, an unending day without evening, with the enjoyment of God as the ultimate end. To those who might think that all of this is a far-fetched allegorization Augustine retorts, What is a more *proper* and *literal* meaning of light than the divine Understanding and a perfect creaturely participation in it? (IV, 28, 45).

The one day and the shifting hues of evening and morning are understood noetically. But this does not mean that it is merely theoretical in character. Its significance is finally a *practical* one, and with cosmic import, for the angels, though they are associated with the creation of the world only as specially privileged observers, are brought into its administration as the chief agents of the ruler. (This distinction between creation and administration comes to Augustine from Cicero and ultimately from Posidonius, who also influenced Philo and the Eastern fathers.) The entire discussion of daytime, evening, and morning knowledge is framed by a broader concern with the angels' cosmic role, and it is only this that holds it all together.[20] If *the angelic community*

---

[20] For an especially detailed discussion of this entire aspect of Augustine's thought see Odilo Lechner, *Idee und Zeit in der Metaphysik Augustins* (Salzburger Studien zur Philosophie; Munich, 1964), chapter 4.

itself, at least as it participates in divine Wisdom, is characterized as "day," then the only reason for bringing in the rest of creation and assigning to each realm a "day" of its own is that the angels are *present to* all these realms, in one way at their creation and in another way in their administration.

The term "*praesentia*" (or its verb form "*praesentare*") occurs repeatedly in chapters 21 and 35 of book IV, and its importance in a neo-Platonist metaphysic is underscored by its frequent use in Plotinus' discussions of soul (*Enn*. IV, 3). "Presence" in that context is the proper mode of relation of soul to body, remaining sovereign over it and not being drawn into excessive involvement with it; and the angels' presence to the corporeal world follows this prescription. They are present to created things in accordance with their twofold knowledge of them, first looking to the ideal patterns of them in the divine mind and only on that basis looking to them as they are in themselves, with their own places in the texture of events. To their daytime knowledge of God's purposes for the world is added an evening knowledge of the ongoing process of the actual world, but the latter is always referred back to the Creator and there is a constantly renewed awareness of the divine plan—this is what characterizes the angels' mode of "presence" to the temporal process they administer.

It is even their mode of presence to themselves in the guidance of their own lives. Their awareness of their own being in its differentiation from God (the evening of the first day) is immediately referred to the praise of the Creator. But there is not only that, for it would still involve too great a distancing from the Creator. If the angels become light, it is because they have immediate knowledge of God and of the divine ideas, including the ideas according to which they themselves have become fully formed. Thus they know themselves *primarily* in the ideas within God's mind and only secondarily in themselves as distinct from God, with an evening knowledge that never becomes night but is always dawning into day again (IV, 32, 50).

What Augustine means is not, I think, that they have a better knowledge of their own *actuality* through God than through themselves; he always assumes that created minds are self-transparent, capable of knowing their own being immediately. Here, as in other passages concerning the divine ideas, he is interested in them as "practical" ideas, antecedent to the fact and looking prospectively toward it, plans for things to be done, standards which ought to be followed in making judgments and decisions. It is in this sense, then, that the angels look beyond themselves for a proper "idea" of themselves: without self-assertiveness, which would only narrow their perspective, they ask what they are to be within the whole and according to the Wisdom that presides over the whole. It is a theme already present much earlier in his thought, derived originally from Plotinus; and it will come to be extended to Augustine's anthropology as well when he writes the last books of *De Trinitate*.

All of this holds a certain interest to contemporary philosophy because of a similarity to Heidegger's tactic of approaching the problem of "being" through man, so that man's existence is the "light" that illuminates all of being to whatever extent it can be illuminated. But in contrast to Heidegger (and to Rahner, who in *Geist in Welt* pointed up the similarities with Aquinas' theory of knowledge) Augustine gives it a special twist, for it is not finite spirit as such that illuminates being and is the shepherd of being, but God himself, and man will be the sought-for light and guide to just the extent that he allows himself to reflect the light of God.[21]

This "practical" relevance of the divine ideas is also the key to Augustine's interpretation of the opening verses of the Fourth Gospel, worked out probably in 406 (*In Joann. ev.*, tr. 1, 16; *De Gen. ad litt.*, V, 13–15; *De Trin.*, IV, 1, 3). He decides in favor of a rather crotchety punctuation: "All things are made through him, and without him nothing is made. What is made is life in him, and the life is the light of men." It means, he says, that all things, even those that are not living in themselves, are life in the divine ideas, where they are united, harmonious, vital; where they have a mode of subsistence which is higher and truer, being eternal and immutable; where all things are, as Augustine will put it later in *The City of God* (VIII, 4), *serta, certa, recta*— connected, certain, correct. All of this follows from Augustine's ontology. But it does not mean that according to his ontology

---

[21] Some interesting suggestions are made by Rudolf Berlinger, *Augustins dialogische Metaphysik* (Frankfurt, 1962), p. 52, and Lechner, *Idee und Zeit*, pp. 178–182.

the finite reality of things is to be scorned, for the divine ideas themselves are focused upon those things that are to come into being. There is always a certain tension between the being of things in themselves, which is inferior to divine being, and the divine ideas, which, though they are superior to the created things, are nevertheless oriented toward their realization. The tension is to be resolved not by fleeing to the eternal and forsaking the temporal altogether but by setting them in their intended relationship; and Augustine credits the angelic city with having accomplished precisely this, looking to finite things and becoming engaged in the temporal process without forsaking the eternal but constantly referring all these concerns back toward the eternal. It is only in God that all things are "life"; but this liveliness of all things in the divine ideas is the light of men (and of angels) and they are to consult it in their dealings with the corporeal world and in the conduct of their own lives.

Although Augustine always bases happiness upon the possession of God alone, so that one is not made any happier by the addition of finite things nor any less happy by their absence (*Conf.*, V, 4, 7), the same total renunciation is *not* characteristic of his approach to what lies outside the question of happiness. He is not so "otherworldly" as to suppose that spirit can entirely forget the cosmic process, for it has not only its own body but responsibilities for the administration of the corporeal world and cannot rest before the eschatological harmony of all things is achieved. This responsibility, Augustine thinks, is quite appropriate to its place within the total scale of being; it is even fulfilling ("*propter ipsos*," "*bonum est eis*"), for in thus serving God with an awareness of all his aims for the world and for human history spirit finds its true freedom (*De Gen. ad litt.*, V, 19, 37).

In the third book of *De Trinitate* Augustine develops the parable of a righteous man whose soul is a "throne of divine Wisdom," a man all of whose actions are done in obedience to the divine law to which he listens in his heart. All that he does will have no other cause, therefore, than the divine will. This will be true not only of his actions but even of the things that he suffers. Say that he is ill. However the physicians diagnose his ills in terms of body chemistry and other proximate causes, their ultimate cause will have been his obedience to divine

Wisdom, which has led him to exhaust himself in works of love. And the same will be true of all those things done by others who are somehow under his supervision, even when not all of their acts are as wise or as righteous as his own (*De Trin.*, III, 3, 8). Augustine then extends this parable first to a household, then to a state, and finally to the celestial city. This last, of course, is the inner court from which the entire cosmos is administered, descending through the various levels of soul and of matter.

Nothing visible or sensible occurs which has not been either commanded or permitted in this inmost hall, invisible and intelligible, of the supreme Emperor, who assigns, according to his indescribable righteousness, rewards and punishments, retribution or favor, throughout the magnificent and immeasurable republic of the whole creation (*De Trin.*, III, 4, 9).

The divine mind, omnipresent yet undivided and undispersed, is the focal center of the entire cosmic process in which all is coordinated. The ideas in the divine mind are the "causes" of all that occurs, *not*, however, if the parable is to be relied upon at this point, in the sense that they are the *sole* determinant of the process, but more along the lines of Plato's contrast (*Phaedo*, 97c–98c) between *causes* and *conditions*, the former being understood as aims and plans within some mind, the latter as the non-mental circumstances which must be taken into account by mind (in *De civ. Dei*, V, 9, Augustine argues that "efficient causality" belongs only to those beings which act intelligently and voluntarily). And Augustine never thought that God's is the only mind shaping the course of events. In his earlier writings he adopted Plato's and Plotinus' notion of an *anima mundi*, a world-soul which contemplates the purely ideal realm held within the divine mind and translates it into temporal movement (*De imm. an.*, 8, 14; *De mus.*, VI, 14, 44 and 17, 58; cf. *Retr.*, I, 11, 4). During the first years in Hippo he began to shift that same function to the angels, for he seems to have been captivated (as Newman was after reading some of the same works[22]) by Origen's theory that authority over the different portions of nature and human society is distributed among the various angels, who administer the world in God's behalf, and among

[22] Newman, *Apologia Pro Vita Sua*, part III.

the demons, who are thrown into the realm of gross matter but retain a limited freedom of action (*De lib. arb.*, III; *De div. quaest.*, q. 79).[23] It is this intensely pluralistic and open model of the cosmos that is elaborated in detail in the Genesis commentary and later in *The City of God*.

Though this particular doctrine has since fallen out of fashion, the intuitions it expresses are not alien to us. It is a representation or an interpretation of one of the possible ways we have of experiencing and living in the world, and the same intuitions can be worked out in our own day in more evolutionary terms. Though Augustine's knowledge was less rich and more confining than our own, he could have spoken, with William James, of a concatenated or "strung-along" rather than a consolidated or "block" universe. What is of most interest about the ancient cosmology of spiritual powers—what convinced thinking men that it was required by what they knew of the world—is that it sees finite processes (at least on earth, where change is all too apparent) as the educing or evolving of new combinations out of matter, not by iron necessity alone, not by chance alone, not even by God alone (though all must be taken into consideration), but chiefly by intra-mundane agents that can exploit the potentialities already latent within it. This is what the angels do in obedience to divine wisdom, so disposing the elements that the preconditions are set up for the most advantageous development of things. But the demonic spirits are also able to turn the potentialities of matter to their own purposes, not without restriction, but still with much leeway in the lower parts of creation to which they have been exiled, much as condemned criminals, laboring in a mine, can still make use of air and fire and iron (*De Trin.*, III, 8, 13). This is the explanation Augustine gives of the miracles of the Egyptians and the Magi and others: the demons, having a more accurate knowledge than men of the potentialities of matter, and a sharpness of perception and a swiftness of movement that enable them to assemble the components and apply the causes more rapidly, are able to accomplish

---

[23] Altaner, "Augustinus und Origenes," pp. 34–35 (*KpS*, pp. 245–246), notes the sudden entrance of this motif and suggests that its source is Origen's twenty-third homily on Luke, translated by Jerome and available after 390. It must be said that the doctrine contained in this homily is quite sketchy; Augustine would have to fill in many details for himself.

impressive things and draw men into their sway (*De Trin.*, III, 7, 12—9, 18).

If we want the closest analogue in our own day to this ancient cosmology of spiritual powers it is to be found in what many heralds of "secularity," theistic and non-theistic, are saying today about man: that he has awesome and godlike powers for the transformation of his world and ought not to await direct divine intervention but must accept his own responsibility and act decisively to change the world for the better. Such thoughts are not foreign to Augustine himself, for that matter: in many of his discussions of pain and misfortune, those things that Leibniz called "natural evil" but Augustine, rejecting his Manichaean past, refused to call evil in any sense, he views them as a challenge to man to acquire knowledge of the workings of nature and put it to constructive use. His illustrations often seem to be derived ultimately from the edifying discourses of the Stoics: We are like visitors to a forge, surrounded by unknown implements; we feel resentful if we are hurt in falling against a furnace or a sharp tool, but the smith knows the usefulness of each one of them, indeed, it is only with their aid that he can do his work (*De Gen. c. Man.*, I, 16, 25–26). The venom of scorpions is poisonous, but it is not evil in itself, for it can be put to medicinal use by someone who knows its properties (*De mor.*, II, 8, 11–12; *De civ. Dei*, XI, 22). For the rest, Augustine urges men to live according to a pluralistic view of the world and simply appreciate the intricate structures and the well-adjusted behavior of all things, without reference to the inconvenience or discomfort they may occasion us (*De civ. Dei*, XII, 4).

Given this view of things, the success of created intelligence in guiding the temporal process from within will be based not primarily upon unusual physical powers of its own but upon its ability to understand and exploit the potentialities implanted in matter by God himself; these include not only the various qualities of the elements but the "seeds" which are operative in the reproduction and development of plants and animals.[24]

[24] The most recent and most extensive discussion of Augustine's own doctrine is Albert Mitterer, *Die Entwicklungslehre Augustins im Vergleich mit dem Weltbild des hl. Thomas von Aquin und dem der Gegenwart* (Vienna, 1956). The historical background is traced in Hans Meyer, *Geschichte der Lehre von der Keimkräften von der Stoa bis zum Ausgang der Patristik* (Bonn, 1914).

There is nothing mysterious or even unusual about Augustine's doctrine of seeds, spelled out in *De Trin.*, III, 8, 13 and more extensively in books V and following of the Genesis commentary. It is probably drawn from some doxographic summary of the classical Stoic doctrine, overlaid perhaps with a Pythagorean emphasis upon number. The seeds are minute bodies knit together from water under the formative influence of incorporeal *rationes seminales*, different for each species (*De Gen. ad litt.*, X, 20, 35ff.; *De civ. Dei*, XXII, 14). What the ancient philosophers tried to explain with the aid of this theory were, first, the phenomena of reproduction and development, in which a large organism grows from a seed which is not only much smaller but is not at all isomorphic with it (phenomena explained today in terms of the genetic key encoded in DNA molecules, not far from what they suspected); and, second, the putative phenomenon of spontaneous generation, in which maggots and other creatures develop, seemingly without parents, out of organic or even inorganic matter. Ancient men thought, sometimes on the basis of careful observation and sometimes on the basis of rumor, that spontaneous generation was widespread, and this led them to postulate the presence of seeds throughout earthly matter, somewhat like Leibniz' omnipresent monads; the earth is "pregnant" with them (*De Trin.*, III, 9, 16). Our more pale version of this is, I suppose, the discovery of microorganisms nearly everywhere in various states of dormancy or virulence. All told, the reproduction and development of living things and their assimilation and transmutation of matter are striking instances of "genesis." The attempt was made to explain such phenomena not by invoking mystery or chance but by positing some genetic key within nature itself, having the capacity to guide development and exploit the potentialities of dead matter.

Augustine, who had long held this theory on philosophical grounds (cf. *De ver. rel.*, 42, 79), found it confirmed by what we now call, on the basis of documentary analysis, the second creation narrative. What he read, in a somewhat garbled and misconstrued but for the most part literal translation of the idiom of the original Hebrew, was this:

When day was made, God made heaven and earth and every green tree of the field *before it was on the face of the earth*, and every plant of the field *before it grew*, for God had not yet caused rain to fall on the earth, and there was no man to till the earth. And a fountain arose from the ground and watered the whole face of the earth (*Genesis*, 2, 4–6).

He assumed, then, that in the original act of creation at the first moment of time only the heavenly bodies and the outlines of land and sea were brought into visible shape, but not the growing things on the earth; they were "created," to be sure, but only *virtually*, in their *causes*, that is, in the seeds by which they would subsequently be consolidated as organisms. And this is quite appropriate, he thought, for it takes *time* for living organisms to develop (*De Gen. ad litt.*, IV, 4, 10). The fountain rising from the ground and watering the earth—the *whole* earth, not Eden alone—refers, he thought, to the initiation of organic growth after the original creation, the knitting together of living bodies when the maternal earth (*parens terra* [V, 23, 44]), which supplies most of the components for bodily growth, was fertilized by the primordial seeds, which are formed from water (V, chapters 7–12, 23). These seeds are the same ones that continue to operate in the reproduction of living things, though with some differences: the visible seeds with which we are acquainted are already organisms and have been produced by previously existing plants and animals, while the original seeds were more minute, only one component of our visible seeds, and they gave rise to developing organisms without having come from parents.

Though Augustine's scenario of the creation has certain external similarities with the evolutionary theory and has played a role in liberating Catholic opinion from resistance to evolutionary thought, it is not evolutionist. It would have been had he made the outcome of the original creation merely a set of potentialities for the rise of living matter (the "potentiality" of methane, ammonia, and carbon dioxide to form simple amino acids); but that would have been a denial of the *finishing* of the whole work of creation at the first instant, and instead of it he asserted that the genetic control-mechanism was fully constituted from the first. His theory was actually framed in an anti-transformist spirit, in order to guarantee the fixity of species in the face of such difficulties as spontaneous generation, in which living organisms seemed to arise from dead matter.

The temporal course of the world is the deployment and

interaction, then, of the various conditions and causes created at the first moment—the elements, the seeds of living things, the angelic powers. Augustine is especially concerned during this period to locate all radical creative action of God at the beginning, to such an extent that he underplays the more spectacular aspects of miracles and, somewhat in the fashion of many modern thinkers, defines the contrast between the "natural" and the "miraculous" as one between accustomed events whose causes are usually apparent and unusual events whose causes are often hidden (*De Gen. ad litt.*, VI, 13, 25—14, 26; *De Trin.*, III, 6, 11; *In Joann. ev.*, tr. 8, 1; tr. 9, 1). His tendency is to stress the marvel of every seed. Miracles are happening every day in the coming into being of new lives. But carnal men let their understanding be chained by the expectations built up through repeated experience; and when they are accustomed to seeing repeated occurrences they do not think them worthy of serious consideration. The function of miracle is therefore to break the web of familiar patterns and so startle men by the "unaccustomed" character of the event that their attention is drawn toward the God who is attested everywhere (*Serm.* 241, 1; *Ep.* 102, q. 1, 5–6). But even miracles, it will be noted, are wrought not immediately by God but through the angels in accordance with his instructions (this is the argument of the whole of book III of *De Trinitate*).

For all his stress on the difference between creation and administration and the operation of finite causes in the latter, Augustine is not in danger of leaving God idle in the heavens. Everything that occurs takes place within the framework of God's care. But his problem is to differentiate between God's direct and indirect influence, and he has a number of distinctions which cut across each other and seem to reflect a progressive clarification of his thoughts.

(1) Most simply there are two ways in which God can influence things, the one immediately and from within the being (*intrinsecus*), the other from without (*extrinsecus*), through the mediation of created things which apply physical or imaginal stimuli or supply the materials needed for growth (*De Gen. ad litt.*, VIII, 25, 46—26, 48).

(2) But slightly earlier in the same writing there is another differentiation according to the "dual operation of providence,"

the natural and the voluntary (VIII, 9, 16–17; 23, 44—24, 45). In the case of some things, God acts through the inevitabilities of natural processes; in the case of others he influences the course of events through free agents, who act sometimes in a morally neutral way (agriculture, the crafts), sometimes in obedience to divine command (the angels' participation in the administration of the cosmos, men's participation in the history of salvation), and sometimes rebelliouslly (the activities of demons and sinful humanity).[25]

(3) The oldest division, and the vaguest, is between preservation (*continere, substituere*) and governance (*gubernare, regere, administrare*). The former is a sustaining of whatever level of substance, form, or appetition has been reached, while the latter is a further directing of the course of events, sometimes inwardly and sometimes externally.[26]

If there is any consistency among these distinctions, they can be put into an order something like this:

PRESERVATION	INTRINSIC	EXTRINSIC
NATURAL	Preservation of all things rational and irrational	Divine guidance of the nexus of physical causes
VOLUNTARY	Inward illumination of rational creatures and infusion of grace	Human labor Angelic administration Symbols and rituals in the history of salvation
		Permission and over-ruling of evil

GOVERNANCE

There is one apparent exception to the rule that all divine administration of the world is through finite causes, for in an often-cited passage (*De Gen. ad litt.*, IX, 18, 33–35) Augustine says that God reserved to himself certain acts in the history of

[25] Cf. Gotthard Nygren, *Das Prädestinationsproblem in der Theologie Augustins. Eine systematisch-theologische Studie* (Göttingen, 1966), pp. 207ff.
[26] See the analysis of texts in Stanislaus J. Grabowski, *The All-Present God: A Study in St. Augustine* (St. Louis, 1954), p. 142.

salvation and did not implant their causes in the world. But as he himself indicates this only means that such acts belong not to "natural" providence, operating through the inevitabilities of the material world, but to the other, the "voluntary" providence, in which there is a direct commerce between God's will and finite minds, for the history of salvation consists of miracles and theophanies executed by the angels, who know God's hidden purpose, and of God's own inward action upon human minds (cf. VI, 15, 26).

In every case divine influence is exerted, then, in accordance with the natural capabilities of created things and through a sequence of finite causes. There are open spaces within the temporal process, but they are filled not by an unmediated intervention of divine power but by God's instruction and encouragement of finite agents in accordance with their capacities ("*pro suo modulo*," as he often says). Augustine thus avoids—to put it in the language of a more modern philosophical concern—a "mythical" conception of God's activity, that is, imagining him as one being or one factor among others within the spatio-temporal realm. He does not "do" things in the same manner as the causal agents we see around us, and wherever it seems that he "does" things in this way it turns out to be the work of intermediate agents.

This, I think, is the fundamental consideration in, and certainly the lasting importance of Augustine's view that God, being eternal, does not act temporally. In precisely this context (*De Gen. ad litt.*, VIII, 20ff.) he engages in a fresh consideration of the problem. He does not want to deny God's immediate influence upon the temporal process, everywhere but especially upon finite spirits. But God is not *in* the temporal process as a finite agent is. A finite agent (a "soul" of any sort) is able to act upon matter only by becoming in some way "commingled" with it so that its own incorporeal *intentio* or *nutus* can be translated into corporeal movement (VIII, 21, 41–42). Very much in the fashion of Plotinus' Psyche, the angels are the intermediaries between time and eternity. Because they can act within the temporal process without losing their knowledge of God's purposes they are given super-vision over all those portions of creation which are incapable of apprehending God—matter, irrational life, spirits darkened by sin—though each level of soul also has its own degree of spontaneity and some kind of immediate relation to God (VIII, 24, 45).

When immediate divine influences are strictly limited to those that can be "intrinsic" to finite reality—that is, those that are based upon finite capacities and lead them to some new actualization, as in the formation of matter, or the consolidation of bodies, or the sustaining of vitality, or the illumination of minds—then not everything is possible at every time. The capacities of the finite must be respected, and that means that some things can be accomplished only in a more roundabout way, through other finite agents and not immediately. This, of course, is the function of the angels. Though it is impossible to suppose God intervening directly in the manner of an intra-mundane agent, such agents, distinct from God, are available and play an indispensable role.

Augustine, because of his general metaphysical principles, had good and convincing reasons for asserting the existence and the exalted role of the angels; and if, because of a change in our understanding of the cosmos, we are not capable of making the same affirmations, something important has gone out of our cosmology. The same metaphysical principles concerning the influence of God upon the world may prevail (indeed, the similarity of Augustine's views to many currents in modern philosophy and theology is striking). But precisely because of the importance assigned to intra-mundane causes, the abdication of the angelic powers at the apex of the hierarchy of finite causes leaves a vacuum. The course of events must be more erratic and halting; progress must occur more slowly and painfully, for there is no unifying and organizing principle within the cosmos itself. What there will be, then, is an evolution of living forms toward man, and then an evolution of man's dominion over the earth in the direction of greater capability and, it may be, toward greater righteousness, so that he comes to fill the role formerly assigned to angelic powers.

Precisely such a restructuring of the entire picture of the world and its relation to God is what has gone on, with great anxiety, in the nineteenth and twentieth centuries. That it need not be alien to the tradition of theism in the West, or even to Christian theology, the achievements of men like Whitehead and Teilhard have shown; but even though the metaphysical principles may be fundamentally similar to Augustine's, the details will be different and everything must be thought through again, for now it is in and through man that the physical world is unified by understanding and led toward a single harmonious goal.

3. THE TRINITY: FIRST ATTEMPTS

The approaches to Augustine's Trinitarian doctrine have been drastically re-routed by careful chronological investigations, for if Chevalier is correct the project of writing a work *On the Trinity* was expanded and recast after 413 when Augustine came into contact with some Eastern statements on the Trinitarian problem, and books V-VII, which contain his theory of the Trinitarian relations, come only after that date.[27] If those books do come so late, then we must readjust our understanding of the whole course of Augustine's Trinitarian speculations, for what is best known about them, the use of psychological analogies from human experience, depends upon the theory of relations which he derived from Eastern sources. Though it is in keeping with his earlier tendencies, it is not his own independent contribution. In the past it was often pointed out that Augustine discussed the psychological analogies only after working out a doctrine of the Trinity based on Scripture and dogma; but even those who said this the most ardently were hardly prepared for to discover how massively it applied to the course of his thought.

Augustine may have had intimations of the direction to be taken, for in the *Confessions* (XIII, 11, 12) he discusses man's being, knowing, and willing (*esse, nosse, velle*), all of them distinct yet interpenetrating in one inseparable life. He begins by discussing them in terms of Trinitarian *ontology* of the sort long familiar in his writings.[28] But the possibility of a Trinitarian *analogy* is at least raised when he projects these three aspects of

[27] Irénée Chevalier, *Saint Augustin et la pensée grecque. Les relations trinitaires* (Fribourg, 1940), pp. 15–28. Further refinements of chronology have been given by Anne-Marie La Bonnardière, in *Recherches de chronologie augustinienne* (Paris, 1965).

[28] See chapter 2, section 2, above.

human life toward God himself. Du Roy points out[29] that this is the first time Augustine attempts to understand the "immanent" Trinity within God; previously he had been concerned only with the Trinity in relation to the triadic structure of finite reality. He suggests that it may have been Augustine's becoming a bishop that required him for the first time to consider seriously and to defend the Nicene doctrine of three persons in one substance.

Whatever the reason, he began writing a work on the Trinity about 401. For many years, however, nothing at all was done with possible psychological analogies to the Trinity. Indeed, very little was done by way of scrutinizing the Church's dogma in the way we have come to think typical of doctrinal theology. We should not suppose that his original project was anything like the final product, therefore. There were too many false starts, too many new discoveries, and the record in Augustine's letters and the *Retractationes* indicates that he had much trouble with the work before it was finally released to the public.

For an understanding of Augustine's Trinitarian thought during the years when he began the work, we must limit ourselves to the first four books, and even within them we must exclude those portions which were added later, especially a long section in book II (up through 7, 12).[30] We must be cautious, furthermore, in approaching book I, a collection of biblical testimonies and rules for their interpretation. Although most of the materials could well belong to the first draft of the work, the book as a whole appears to have been thoroughly rewritten. The driving, magisterial rhythm, the use of the Vulgate in biblical citations, the extensive command of biblical texts, especially from the Fourth Gospel, and the interest in looking up the readings found in Greek codices, all tend to indicate that it is a late product, probably coming from the period between 418 and 420. To our list we can add book VIII, however, which for a number of reasons is to be assigned to this earlier period. But that is all. The usable material is radically diminished, and most of the familiar landmarks followed in the conventional discussions of *De Trinitate* are removed. We must start over again and piece together the materials from the period, supplementing them

---

[29] *L'Intelligence de la foi en la Trinité*, pp. 435–436.
[30] La Bonnardière, pp. 172–173.

from the Genesis commentary, which was progressing much more steadily, and from the sermons.

Usually we find that there is little more than a continuation of motifs that had already been present much earlier. The Word is still called the Form or Image or Likeness of the Father, "equal" to him in every respect, whereas creatures are unlike him and gain their similarity to God through participation in the Word (*Conf.*, XIII, 2, 3; *De Gen. ad litt.*, I, 4, 9—5, 10). Many years later Augustine will exploit this contrast to move from the formative conversion of creatures, who are other than God and whose formation involves a "composition" of matter and form, potentiality and actualization, to the formative conversion which takes place within the "simplicity" of God when the Word is generated through God's self-knowledge (*De Trin.*, II, 1, 3; *De civ. Dei*, XI, 10). But Augustine has not yet seen the way toward such a theory of the generation of the Word, for he has not yet discovered the importance of *relation*. The closest he comes to it is in his discussions of the *verbum cordis*, the "conception" of something which we form within our minds and then express in audible words. This contrast between "what we want to say" and our outwardly "saying" it was a commonplace in Stoic logic, and Augustine knew of it in a purely philosophical way, without applying it to the Trinitarian problem, in his *De dialectica* written in 387.[31] He first used it in a Trinitarian context in 393 (*De fid. et symb.*, 3, 3-4), following the practice of many earlier ecclesiastical writers. The point is that in any external act we have some inward plan which is held in the mind and guides the whole operation; similarly the divine Word is the counsel through which all things are created (*In Joann. ev.*, tr. 1, 9-10). And an examination of this internal process of conceiving already takes him some distance toward a doctrine of the Word, for the conception or internal word is purely the result of a mental act of *thinking*: "As your mind is spirit, so the word which you conceive is spirit and remains within the conceiving activity of the heart, within the mirror of the mind." Similarly, then, the divine Word is the "*locutus Deus*," and the uttering of the Word is a conceiving activity that remains within God and all

[31] B. Darrell Jackson, "The Theory of Signs in St. Augustine's *De doctrina christiana*," *REA*, XV (1969), 19-22.

of whose components are of the same substance as God (*In Joann. ev.*, tr. 14, 7).

But even such rudimentary speculations have no part in what remains of the original *De Trinitate*; it is rather a painstaking examination of problems preliminary to the attempt to understand the inner life of the Trinity. The purpose of book I is to make use of the "*canonica regula*" of the Church in interpreting those passages of Scripture which seem to imply that the Son is inferior to the Father (*De Trin.*, II, 1, 2). The rule is really twofold, for there are some passages designed to suggest that the Son is less than the Father "according to the form of a servant," i.e., in his humanity, while there are others designed to suggest that he is derived from the Father though equal in nature. All of this could have been carried out at the time the work was first projected, for the "*regula catholicae fidei*" is mentioned as early as question 69 (about 495), in the course of a discussion of the text, "Then will the Son also be subjected to him who subjected all things to him" (I Corinthians 15, 28), and with the same two points: that when the Son is spoken of as being less than the Father it is to be taken to refer to his humanity, except where the reference is clearly to his divinity, and then a distinction between Begetter and Begotten must be what is meant (*De div. quaest.*, q. 69, 1). It is thus an anti-Arian rule for exegesis which Augustine could easily have learned from writers like Hilary or Ambrose. Much of book I may have been written about 400, then; but the book as we have it has been overlaid with later materials.

If the highly developed doctrine of the missions and theophanies of the persons which opens book II is to be dated about 418,[32] then the next secure base of operations is the inquiry into the problem of theophanies and the question of the visibility or invisibility of the Son and Spirit which begins at II, 7, 13 and occupies the rest of books II through IV. Augustine sets out to examine three questions (cf. II, 7, 13; III, 1, 4): which persons were manifested to the patriarchs before the incarnation of the Word and the pouring out of the Spirit; whether the manifestations were newly created or were angels sent for this purpose; and whether the Son and Spirit were "sent" prior to the incarnation, and, if so, how this sending differs from that which took place later.

[32] La Bonnardière, pp. 94–95, 111.

It is a sign of the relatively undeveloped state of theology in the West that Augustine started out from the classic problem of earlier Trinitarian thought, the view, held by the Apologists and retained by the Arians but rejected by the Church at large, that the Word and Spirit are visible and that it was they who appeared in the theophanies. Although he was writing well after the Council of Nicaea and the fuller development of its doctrines by the Cappadocians he was not yet fully apprised of their views. He was not placed in the position, therefore, of reproducing and defending a fully formulated, standardized dogma; of necessity he must laboriously retrace the development of the Trinitarian doctrine for himself, with the aid of a few writers like Hilary and Didymus and Ambrose, thinking through the problems piecemeal and only later discovering the decisive clues furnished by the Cappadocians.

In his opening discussion of the theophanies (II, 8, 14ff.) Augustine is in direct encounter with one of the monuments of earlier Trinitarian thought, Tertullian's *Adversus Praxean*, for he explores much the same series of theophanies in the books of Genesis and Exodus.[33] His own view, opposed to Tertullian's, is that the theophanies are always mediated by created things which signify the invisible and intelligible God. They do manifest God "as he is"—the three figures who appear to Abraham in Genesis 18 even manifest the Trinity—but never "properly," only "significtively" (II, 17, 32). The theophanies are thus a specialization of the more general pattern of manifestation suggested in Romans 1, 20: though sinful man is unable to apprehend God immediately, he can know him through visible things, and this is his *only* way of return to God. Augustine thinks that the theophanies are always executed by angels, "bearing the person of God" (III, 10, 19), as a number of statements in the New Testament and the frequent use of the expression "the angel of the Lord" in the Old Testament narratives would indicate. Sometimes the angels appear and act in their own ethereal bodies, sometimes they utilize bodies drawn from the terrestrial world; and it is in order to explain the latter—and the miracles of demons as well—that he draws upon the Stoic theory of "seeds," probably well before his discussion of the same topic in his

[33] Schindler, *Wort und Analogie*, pp. 110, 140.

Genesis commentary (*De Trin.*, III, 8, 13—9, 19). Thus the biblical narratives can be accounted for in a rational way in accordance with his general cosmology, and in turn his cosmology is shown to have direct relevance to the history of salvation.

The discussion that is theologically most interesting comes in the fourth book, when he asks in what way the Son and the Spirit can be "sent," and how their visible sending, narrated in the New Testament, differs from their appearances to the patriarchs, which were only signs.[34] First, they are said to be sent by the Father not because they are inferior to the Father but because their being is derived from the Father; the "missions" of the persons are thus a proper reflection of the intra-Trinitarian relations. And Augustine has a realism about the missions which was lost in the Middle Ages. The term "mission" refers, he says, not merely to the Word's *becoming flesh*, for this would imply nothing more than that the "man" was sent, but to the Word's being sent *in order to become flesh*. And the term can be applied not only to the incarnation but to *all* those occasions on which the Word makes himself present to the servants of God, dwelling with angels and holy souls. Here Augustine is referring not to theophanies, for these are only figurative, not proper "sendings" of the Word, but to all those cases in which there is an immediate indwelling of the Word, in his own person, within finite minds, all those cases to which it would be appropriate to apply the text, "*in animas sanctas se transfert, atque amicos Dei et prophetas constituit*" (Wisdom 7, 27). In all such instances there is a sending and coming of the Word in order to be "with" and "in" created minds. What makes the incarnation unique is not that there is a sending and coming of the Word, but that the sending and coming is in order to become man, to assume the man into unity of person with himself (*De Trin.*, IV, 20, 27).

This discussion is very much in keeping with the whole tendency of Augustine's Trinitarian theology, and it serves to indicate how badly it has often been misunderstood. Augustine could take a realistic view of the missions because he did not suppose that the "inseparability" of the operations of the three

[34] For Augustine's doctrine and its background in Hilary and Ambrose, see Jean-Louis Maier, *Les missions divines selon saint Augustin* (Paradosis, XVI; Fribourg en Suisse, 1960).

persons implied a complete lack of distinctions among them. But while he thought that their operations are distinct in *all* of God's works, a "mission" of one of the persons involves something further—a coming to intelligent creatures in order to be heard and received by them, so that they might in turn be "with" God through knowledge and love. It means, to take up the challenge issued in our own day by Karl Barth,[35] that it is quite possible to speak of the unincarnate Word, the Λόγος ἄσαρκος, entirely apart from any movement toward the incarnation, and still have a gracious presence of God, for Augustine thought that the incarnation of the Word, like other sensory means of communication, was needed only because of sin, and apart from sin finite minds sustained by the Spirit would be able to apprehend the Word immediately (in the Genesis commentary [I, 17, 32] the same verse from the book of Wisdom is used of the illumination of the angels following their conversion to God). What constitutes a mission, then, is always the sending of a person of the Trinity to intelligent beings in order to have an influence, through their minds, within time and to lead them into God's own life. What differentiates the two kinds of mission is that in the one case the Word is apprehended "from time," in their transcending themselves and looking toward God, while in the other the Word dwells within Jesus of Nazareth "in the fulness of time." In both cases the Word is sent, but only in the incarnation is he sent "into this world" to be experienced sensibly through a human life linked to him; in the other case finite minds, so to speak, go "out of this world" (*De Trin.*, IV, 20, 28).

The visible mission of the Holy Spirit is not the assumption of an intelligent creature, as in the incarnation, but only a temporary manifestation in a dove or the tongues of fire (*De Trin.*, IV, 20, 31–32; *In Joann. ev.*, tr. 6, 3), a passing sign of permanent gift of the Spirit to those who are Christ's. Augustine does not see how these could have been produced directly by God, without the cooperation of some intelligent being within the created world; thus the angels are again given a crucial role in the theophanies in keeping with Augustine's principle that God, for the sake of good order, relates himself to the realm of matter only through

[35] Karl Barth, *Church Dogmatics*, IV/1, 52; IV/2, 33–34.

soul—the angels, the human mind of Christ, men with their arts and sciences, perhaps other animate life with its spontaneous actions as well.

All of this, it will be noted, is a doctrine of the Trinity based on Scripture and on the rational operations of analyzing and inferring. But Augustine also strives to gain a more *immediate* understanding of the Trinity, and the attempt is recorded in book VIII.

The eighth book on the Trinity was probably written before books V through VII. Though its prologue attempts to establish a continuity with those books, book VIII itself reflects none of the themes worked out in them. And though its conclusion (10, 14) is usually thought to suggest than an analogy to the Trinity within the finite mind has been discovered, within the book itself there is no attempt to find such a finite trinity; Augustine even states that the divine Trinity is unique and that there are *not* any other trinities (5, 8). The prologue suggests, accurately enough, that Augustine is now concerned to go beyond a doctrine worked out on the basis of authority and seek a direct understanding of its contents. But what is it that the book attempts to understand? Not the problem of essence and relation, as the first paragraphs suggest, but rather the divine essence itself and the three persons who share it equally. It is hard to say how much of the introductory passage on the overcoming of the imagination (from 2, 3 on) is from the original version; but in keeping with that theme he is concerned throughout the book with the general problem of rising in contemplation to the divine nature, and to the persons individually.

There are four attempts, all of them modifications of one attempt, becoming increasingly complex in the face of the obstacles that are met. First there is the attempt to reach God directly, in his eternal being, by negating and dropping away one misconception after another in the expectation of gaining at last a direct vision of the Truth. But the mind is repulsed because of its lack of preparation.

Then a second attempt is made, this time not through a frontal assault but by a *via remotionis* or *eminentiae*, taking the finite perfections of being and goodness which meet us in our experience and removing their limitations. It is based on Romans 1, 20, and throughout there is a play on its phrase "*intellecta conspicere*," glimpsing God by understanding the things that are made. But the whole pasaage is finally Plotinian in inspiration and rhythm:

There is *this* good thing and *that* one. Take away "this" and "that," and look at Goodness itself, if you are able; thus you will see God, who is good not by possessing another good but as the Good of all good.

There would be no changeable goods unless there were an unchangeable Good. So when you hear of "this good thing" or "that one," which could change and then would be called not good, if you are then able to glimpse, *without* those things which are good by participation, the Good by participating in which they become good (for you are aware of it *at the same moment* that you hear "this good")—if, I was saying, with these things set aside, you can glimpse that which is good in itself, then you will glimpse God (*De Trin.*, VIII, 3, 4–5).

The path goes through the finite, but that does not make it any less an *inward* way, for the focus is upon the inward activity of judging whether something finite is good, and the *notio ipsius boni* (VIII, 3, 4), our intuition or "notice" of Goodness itself, is the standard according to which this judging is done.

This way is more suitable than the first, for it is an attempt to grasp God not in his naked deity but as he is reflected in finite effects. But a complication ensues.[36] Though the Good can be apprehended in this way, the problem is to *adhere* to it, and only the pure in heart can endure God's presence. The preparation for this vision will be through purification in love, and to accomplish this is the prerogative of Christianity. Even the simple, who, unlike the philosophers, have not apprehended God directly, can be prepared through a love based upon faith, and the more contemplative spirits as well must follow the same path.

The requirement is a familiar one in Augustine. What he now attempts is a discovery of God even on the basis of faith, hope, and love, eschewing the more dramatic ways. His point of departure

---

[36] I question du Roy's view ("L'expérience de l'amour et l'intelligence de la foi trinitaire selon saint Augustin," *RA*, II, p. 438, n. 102) that the sections now to be discussed (4, 6—6, 9 and 9, 13) are later than the rest of the book. They do constitute an excursus, but one necessary and integral to the development of the argument, adding a complication but not negating what has been said, indeed, leading toward the next stage.

is the principle, commonplace in ancient philosophy, that nothing is loved which is not already known in some way. God is loved on the basis of faith. But faith itself involves knowledge, not in the giving of assent as such (for this is based upon authority) but in understanding, through the resources of general experience, what is proposed for belief. But what is it in our general experience that forms the basis of belief in the unseen Trinity? The answer leads back once more toward Augustine's own theory of judgment. Much that we "know," as he points out, is non-sensory and is not a part of our own actuality (even an unrighteous man can know what righteousness is). Somehow, then, we perceive norms or demands present to our minds. Consequently faith, hope, and love have a somewhat more delimited role, as it turns out, than might appear at first glance (VIII, 9, 13); they are not our only means of access to God, for we are aware of the way men *should* live. The point, rather, is that in the life of the people of God men have *actually* lived in this way, and to believe, on the basis of historical reports, that they have so lived makes our awareness of God clearer, makes our love for the good firmer, and gives us hope that we also might follow the same way of life.

The Christian religion thus intensifies man's vague apprehension and love of the eternal Form of righteousness. But finally Augustine places the stress not upon the *apprehension* of this Form (for it remains vague even in the believer) but upon *love* for it. It is in the act of love that God is experienced most intensely by man while he is still in pilgrimage, and Augustine lights upon the theme of the First Epistle of John (4, 16 and 20) that God is love, and he who abides in love abides in God; thus, he concludes, the man who loves even his neighbor will experience *his own act of love* and, in it, *God* as its animating source.[37]

How can Augustine avoid sentimentality and a confusion of the divine and the human? He engages in a kind of transcendental analysis of the act of love in order to see what it involves. In this act, he points out, man is present to himself, both in being aware of his own love and in freely willing ("loving") this act

---

[37] "*Dilectio*" is the term consistently used in the earlier Latin translation of the epistle, and it is preserved in most passages in book VIII, though it is overlaid by the Vulgate's "*caritas*" in the quotation of I John 4, 16 in VIII, 8, 12.

of love. An act of will is primarily intentional, directed toward some object; but it is also self-referencing, for it wills (and in this case rests in) itself. Therefore in loving one's neighbor, whom one can see, one also loves the act of love with which one loves. Now it can be *caritas* only if it has an object appropriate to *caritas* (VIII, 8, 12), and the brother or the neighbor is such an object. And yet this by itself still is not sufficient. Finally an act of will is made *caritas* only because the brother or neighbor is loved for the sake of the Form of righteousness, either because he already embodies it or because it is hoped that he will come to embody it (6, 9; 9, 13). Man's own act of love is what he experiences most immediately; but its "formal object" or "horizon" of willing is the Word, and only because of that can the love in question be "from God," indeed, God himself.

This explains why Augustine thinks that the experience of love can be an experience of the whole Trinity (VIII, 8, 12), and why the triadic structure of love mentioned at the end of the book (10, 14), involving one who loves, one who is loved, and love itself, is intended to apply to the divine Trinity and not, as it is usually asserted, to a triad within man.[38] How he can derive the entire Trinity from the act of love is explained in a contemporaneous discussion of the same theme (*In Joann. ep.*, tr. 7, 6), where Augustine states that "*dilectio*" refers both to the divine nature, for "God is love," and to the Holy Spirit, for "love is of God"; consequently the Holy Spirit, whose *proprium donum* is love, can be called *Dilectio ex Deo*. Love based on the Holy Spirit as the divine Gift is, so to speak, the point of coincidence between God and man; that which is loved is the Word, apprehended at least dimly; and the Father is then the subject of this love, distinct from man but taking him up into his own activity in a way compatible with the nature of finite mind.

The notion of an "experimental knowledge" of God through love, as the Franciscan theologians will later put it, is found in earlier writings (*De doct. chr.*, II, 41, 62; *Conf.*, VII, 10, 16 and X, 30, 40), and most notably in one passage toward the end of the *Confessions* (XIII, 31, 46):[39]

---

[38] Du Roy, "L'expérience de l'amour," pp. 436–440.
[39] The theme is explored in Franz Körner, "Deus in homine videt," *Philosophische Jahrbuch*, LXIV (1956), pp. 166–217.

8*

Those who see your works through your Spirit see you in them. Therefore when they see that these things are good, you are the one who sees
that they are good; and whatever things are pleasing because of you,
you are the one who is pleasing in them; and whatever things please
us through your Spirit are pleasing to you within us.

The eighth book on the Trinity may be an attempt to develop this
earlier insight. But fresh encouragement has come in the mean-
time from a passage in Scripture which Augustine had previously
overlooked, the fourth chapter of the First Epistle of John.

The suspicion that the eighth book was written earlier than
books V–VII is borne out in another document in which the same
theme of immediate experience of God as *Dilectio* appears, the
sermons on the First Epistle of John.[40] It appears suddenly in
the seventh sermon on the epistle, as he wrestles with the new
ideas found in the fourth chapter: that God is Love, that love is
from God and that he who loves is born of God, that love of
God is bound up with love of one's brother. Then it disappears
just as quickly. Augustine will continue to say that a man is
immediately aware of his own act of love (*De Gen. ad litt.*, XII,
6, 15), but this phenomenon will be exploited for nothing more
than to illustrate the way in which something can be known
immediately, through itself and not through an intermediary,
by its presence to the mind; the act of love will be no more
privileged than the act of faith, which will be used in the same way
as an illustration of immediate knowledge (*Ep.* 147, 4, 9, also
written about 413).

The prologue of the sermons on the epistle states that Augustine
had just preached a series of sermons on the Gospel according to
John, and Mlle. La Bonnardière's judgment is that these must be
the first sixteen of the sermons or *tractatūs* on the gospel, trans-
cribed during delivery and then edited by Augustine himself.
It can be shown convincingly that these first sermons on the
gospel belong to the same period as the sermons on the Psalms
of Ascent (the 119th through the 133rd in the Greek and Latin
numbering); in fact they were delivered in alternation, according
to the requirements of the lectionary, and a theme which arises

---

[40] The correlation has already been made by du Roy, "L'expérience de
l'amour," pp. 428–429, and *L'Intelligence de la foi en la Trinité*, pp. 431–432,
though he seems wrong in dating book VIII early, about 400 or even before.

from one book will be reflected in the sermons on the other, in regular sequence. Maurice Le Landais has worked out a detailed table of the likely order of the sermons and their dates in the Church calendar.[41] They begin shortly before the feast of St. Crispina on December 5, which is mentioned in the sermon on Psalm 120, and continue through the Paschal season. Le Landais follows the usual chronology, which places them between 413 and 415, but Mlle. La Bonnardière's method of dating passages by a study of the Scriptural texts that are used places them between 405 and 410, and an analysis of the calendar suggests the winter and spring of 406–407.[42] Since the suggestion that God can be experienced in man's own act of love is seemingly limited to one short period, it seems probable that the eighth book on the Trinity comes from this period, thus from the late spring or the summer of 407, following the sermons on the epistle.[43]

All the evidence confirms this hypothesis. That these sermons are earlier than book XI of the Genesis commentary is proved by their undeveloped interpretation of the statement (John 8, 44) that Satan "did not stand in the truth" (*Enarr. in Ps.* 121, 3; 131, 14; 133, 1; *In Joann. ev.*, tr. 3, 7; 5, 1; 8, 15; 14, 2). Augustine takes a view of Satan which he will soon call into question, for he makes use of Isaiah 14, 12 ("*Lucifer qui mane oriebatur, cecidit*") and says that Satan was called Lucifer because he was first radiant with reflected wisdom but then became dark because he did not remain in the Truth (*In Joann. ev.*, tr. 3, 7; *Enarr. in Ps.* 120, 5). Soon Augustine will be more strongly inclined toward the opinion that the devil *never* stood in the Truth, and he will interpret the Lucifer passage as applying more to the devil's

---

[41] Maurice Le Landais, "Deux années de prédication de saint Augustin," *Études augustiniennes* (Théologie, XXVIII; Paris, 1953), p. 35.

[42] La Bonnardière, pp. 48–50.

[43] The seventeenth sermon on the Fourth Gospel does pose a problem, for it alludes to the *dilectio* theme (tr. 17, 8), though only briefly, and in the course of making the different point that by loving one's neighbor one purifies oneself for the vision of God. I agree with Mlle. La Bonnardière's judgment that this sermon and those following it come from a period later than the first sixteen. Why, then, the allusion to the *dilectio* theme? It may be that Augustine was reminded of it by looking into his earlier writings on the Trinity, for these sermons exhibit far greater interest than the earlier ones in the Trinitarian problem and reflect a more developed understanding of the Trinity. Indeed, they were probably called forth by the Arian challenge of 418.

human entourage, especially those who have first been within the people of God (*De Gen. ad litt.*, XI, 23, 30—24, 31). Another indication of an early date is the absence of a biblical text which might have reinforced his assertion that God can be experienced in man's own act of love. The passage in which Paul says that man becomes "one Spirit with God" (I Corinthians 6, 17) is entirely absent in the eighth book on the Trinity, but it does appear in book VI (3, 4; 4, 6; 8, 9) and in *Ep.* 147, 15, 37, and much later in book XIV, 14, 20.

What our investigations show is that the original *De Trinitate* was a fragmentary enterprise, without the unified plan that scholars have thought he had from the start. Perhaps it was at some time during these years, while he was struggling to piece together a more comprehensive doctrine of the Trinity, that he wrote the famous passage which is included (together with summary material which comes from a later time) in the prologue to book III:

I would have them believe who will that I would rather occupy myself with reading than with writing more things to read, and if they will not believe it, let them give me something which would answer the questions, my own and those of others, whose weight I must bear because of my office in the service of Christ and my ardor in the defense of our faith against the waverings of carnal and animal men; then they would see how easily I would restrain such activities and how gladly I would put up my pen.

He goes on to say that the works on this question which "we" have read (the Latin world? his own circle?) are not widely diffused, and not enough skill in the Greek language is current "among us" to make works in that language widely known; he is sure that he has exhausted the few translations that are available.

But I cannot resist my brethren, whose rights over me make me their servant, when they ask me to obey their altogether laudable desires in Christ and employ my tongue and pen—the two-horsed chariot which *caritas* urges on in me. And I must confess that in the process of writing I have learned many things which I had not known before. Therefore let not my labor be deemed superfluous if it reaches the eyes of the leisured or the erudite, for it has been indispensable to many men who have neither leisure nor erudition, among whom I number myself.

About 413 he was to discover new vistas opened up by the Greek fathers, and only then would he be able to draw the work into a unity and move toward an unforeseen conclusion.

4. The Shadow of Porphyry

One feature often noted in the *Confessions* and subsequent writings is the vigor of Augustine's attacks on the Platonists, those proud philosophers who scorn Christianity and claim to be able to make their own way toward salvation. Augustine still considered himself a Platonist and utilized the writings of the philosophers; but there was now a marked ambivalence in his attitudes toward them, and a sharp discrimination between the useful contributions they had made and the final bankruptcy of their orientation.

At some time during those years Augustine must have become acquainted with Porphyry's attacks on Christianity in his work *On the Philosophy from Oracles*. The shock waves can be clearly discerned in 400, when Augustine wrote *On the Agreement of the Evangelists*. This work, in which for the first time he utilized, for scholarly purposes, Jerome's new "critical translation" of the gospels, was directed chiefly against the Manichaeans' exploitation of the inconsistencies in the gospel accounts, which he had already aired a year or two earlier in *Against Faustus*. But Augustine says in the *Retractationes* (II, 42, 1) that the first book of the work was in answer to those who, though they pretend to honor Christ as an exceptionally wise man, refuse to believe the New Testament writings because they were set down not by him but by his disciples, who erroneously thought him divine. And within the work itself (*De cons. ev.*, I, chapters 13–15) he mentions that the Platonists claim to know of books written by Jesus, in the form of epistles to Peter and Paul, concerning the magical arts by which he did his miracles: thus it is alleged that Jesus himself, far from denying the pagan gods, cultivated them. From what Augustine says about Porphyry in *The City of God* it is evident that he was the cause of this sudden flurry of activity; but how much earlier than 400 his influence was felt is less certain. Since the discovery of the anti-Christian animus of this leader of neo-Platonism brought about some major changes in Augustine's thinking, we must devote some attention to the character of his attacks on the Platonists and ask when and how it was that Porphyry "cast his shadow between Plotinus and Augustine."[44]

Careful study of the quotations in *The City of God* and elsewhere makes it possible to get some idea of Porphyry the opponent of Christianity.[45] On one side he was highly critical of pagan religion and said that ignorance and vice could not be removed by the mysteries but only by the divine hypostases themselves (*De civ. Dei*, X, 23 and 28). And yet he was caught in a dilemma. He recognized that it is given to only a few to reach God by the path of immediate contemplation of the divine Nous, and, lacking any confidence in Christianity, he had to counsel the multitude to follow the way of the mysteries and magic; yet he himself viewed this way as insufficient, for according to his own theory it was capable of purifying only man's imagination, not his mind. In his book *On the Return of the Soul* he enunciated the famous precept, "*Corpus est omne fugiendum*": one who wishes to attain lasting beatitude must transcend the corporeal altogether, even the imaginal, and worship the Father in the pure sacrifice of intellectual contemplation; in that way alone is it possible to escape definitively from the cycle of reincarnations in which the soul rises to the astral heaven but is drawn downward once more. Porphyry, according to a number of passages in Augustine (*Serm.* 241, 4–7; *De civ. Dei*, X, 30; *De Trin.*, XIII, 9, 12), was embarrassed by the standard Platonist doctrine of an unending cycle of reincarnations, leaving beatitude to return to the miseries of this life once more, and held out the possibility of enduring beatitude with the Father, though only for those who succeeded in dying to the body, purifying their souls of all interest in its affairs.[46]

Augustine points out that the same Porphyry who in his letter to the Egyptian priest Anebo raised some embarrassing questions about ritual and theurgy, in his work on the return of the soul settled for the second-best, knowing that a purely inward worship is only for the few, and advised those who could

[44] Paul Henry, *Plotin et l'Occident*, p. 91.

[45] See especially Pépin, *Théologie cosmique et théologie chrétien*, pp. 418–461; O'Meara, *Porphyry's Philosophy from Oracles in Augustine*; and Hadot, "Citations de Porphyre chez Augustin."

[46] Pépin, *Théologie cosmique et théologie chrétien*, pp. 434–442.

not live intellectually to go to the theurgists for purification by way of the imagination (*De civ. Dei*, X, 11 and 27). But it may be that Augustine is not making an effort to assess Porphyry's views fairly. Without doubt Porphyry recommended theurgy only as a *penultimate* way, as a preparation for the inward worship which alone leads to lasting happiness. It is true that Porphyry linked ritual and divination with the evil demons, especially "the one who is called *Fallax*," the Deceiver (*De civ. Dei*, X, 11); and Pierre Hadot, very much in continuity with Augustine's attempt to catch Porphyry in an inconsistency, thinks that the philosopher changed his views. It may be (as Hadot thinks) that Porphyry in the early work *On the Philosophy from Oracles* freely used the products of divination but later, in *On the Return of the Soul* and the letter to Anebo, rejected his earlier enthusiasms.[47] But it is also possible that Porphyry's views can be made consistent with the aid of a distinction which he himself certainly made between the good and the evil spirits. In the only passage Augustine cites under the title of *The Philosophy from Oracles* (*De civ. Dei*, XIX, 23, 4) Porphyry says that the Hebrews rightly prohibited commerce with the evil *daimones* of the air and with the lesser spirits of the earth while they venerated the heavenly gods and, most of all, God the Father; and Porphyry adds that this is what the heavenly gods themselves have commanded, urging that the soul be turned toward God and not toward themselves. But uninstructed and impious men did not heed their commands and served the *daimones* in a way incompatible with the proper worship of God. The sequel indicates, implicitly at least, the difference between the two modes of worship, for he says that God the Father of all has need of nothing ("*nullius indiget*"), but it is good *for us* when we worship him through righteousness and purity and the other virtues, when life itself is made a prayer by seeking God (thus purifying the soul), and imitating him (thus deifying the soul by directing all its affections toward him).

What characterizes true worship, then, is that it does not bring men under bondage but, because of the generosity of God (and of the celestial gods), leads them toward fulfillment. The demons, on the other hand, attempt to draw men under their

[47] Hadot, "Citations de Porphyre chez Augustin," pp. 226–229.

power. They accomplish this chiefly, it seems, through divination, and the fact that their oracles are fulfilled makes men give them credence. Porphyry carefully worked out a theory of the way in which they are able to predict the future, and it indicates (if nothing else did) that he placed the demons in a different class from the higher gods, for according to him they do not have a knowledge of the ideas in the divine Nous but either calculate the future effects of present causes or announce projects of their own which are fulfilled because of their power over men's passions and over the lower portions of the cosmos.[48]

Augustine may in fact have plagiarized from Porphyry even while criticizing him. Twice in contexts related to problems raised by the philosopher (De cons. ev., I, 35, 53; De Trin., IV, 18, 24) Augustine quotes from Plato's Timaeus (29C): "As the temporal is to the eternal, so faith is to truth."[49] The point he wants to make in both passages is that men, weighed down with earthly loves, are incapable of reaching the eternal and can be purified only through belief, and belief is bound up with the temporal in two ways: it concerns human life, which is mutable, and it is directed toward verbal accounts of temporal events. What makes it likely that Augustine acquired this passage at second hand is the fact that it is used as an isolated slogan, with no awareness of its meaning in the context of Plato's dialogue (namely, that one must tell a story in order to describe appropriately the origin and destiny of a temporal universe),[50] for its purpose here is to support an anagogic theory of religious symbols. This is not totally foreign to the dialogue itself, I grant, for Plato was suggesting that the men of old had transmitted beliefs which were worthy of credence, but the *anagogical* use of the *Timaeus* cosmogony and other religious traditions comes to be regularized only in the middle Platonism of Albinus and Nemenius. To Augustine the anagogical function of religious symbols has a Christian

---

[48] O'Meara, *Porphyry's Philosophy from Oracles in Augustine*, pp. 143–145.
[49] *Ibid.*, pp. 106, 166, n. 2.
[50] This is, in fact, Augustine's own more usual view of the nature of belief (that it concerns the past and future course of the world, beyond the range of immediate experience), and it is even developed at length in proximity to one passage in which *Tim.*, 29C is used (*De. Trin.*, IV, 16, 21), but it is not bound to it by any logical ties and the point being made is quite different; therefore Augustine's theory of belief probably comes from Varro.

meaning, of course, based upon his own earlier reflections (many of them already influenced by neo-Platonism). But such a theme could also be found in Porphyry, where it would be related to his own belief in the revelations made through the various cults and oracles, starting where man is and leading him toward the divine through a process of purification. If Porphyry does differentiate, as I have argued he does, between the demons, who deceive man, and the celestial gods, who do not seek honors for themselves but promote the worship of the Father, then he could give a place to theurgic initiations which conduct men into the divine presence, where the divine Nous then completes the process. Augustine, to be sure, disputes Porphyry's faith that the oracles have come from the divine realm; nevertheless his own conception of the way of salvation has many similarities to that of the philosopher.

Augustine was not disposed to respect Porphyry's scruples in this matter, however, both on principle, for Christian tradition with almost complete unanimity classed the Greek deities among the fallen angels, and for polemical reasons, since Porphyry had attacked the Christian religion as a worship of demons and Augustine, never one to lose debating points, turned the accusation around and suggested, though with great sorrow, that he was the one who was really under the sway of the demons. Porphyry, it seems, stood in a poignant situation. In his native Syria, if Eusebius is to be believed (*Ecclesiastical History*, VI, 19), he was acquainted with Origen and his strongly Platonist brand of Christianity during his early years, but was frightened away by the persecutions which broke out while he was still a youth. He seemed to desire a universal way of salvation of the sort that Christianity claimed to be, but he said that if there was such a way it had not yet come to his attention (*De civ. Dei*, X, 32). Augustine suspected that he had considered Christianity only to reject it; he saw the persecutions and thought it was soon to die out, and concluded that it could not be the universal way. But he retained a certain longing for some elements of Christianity, and even more for the monotheism of the Old Testament (Porphyry, like Posidonius before him, had high regard for the God of Israel), and took into his philosophy such Jewish and Christian doctrines as the creation of matter from nothing and the everlasting salvation of the soul.

His ambivalence made him, so to speak, one of the first "rationalist" Christians or semi-Christians, though the Chaldaean Oracles which he utilized suggest that he was anticipated in this by the second-century Platonist, Julian the Theurgist, who compiled them. According to *The City of God* (XIX, 23) Porphyry quoted with approval an oracle of Apollo to a man who had asked what God he should worship in order to win back his wife from Christianity: the reply was that she was demented beyond hope, worshipping a "dead god" who had been executed by a just sentence, and the oracle concluded, "The Jews apprehend God better than the Christians." Again, there is an oracle of Hecate to the effect that Jesus had a pious soul, but is wrongly worshipped, for he merely shares an immortality common to all pious souls. When asked why Jesus had been condemned, the oracle answered that he had misled other men *fataliter*, by the decree of the gods, who willed that he should be the occasion of error to many souls not destined for salvation; but this should arouse not resentment against him but pity for the folly of the Christians (XIX, 23). Porphyry's view of Christianity, then, is that it is not the hoped-for way of salvation for all men, but that Jesus was a most wise and righteous man whose soul, like all righteous souls, was exalted to lasting beatitude, though without resurrection of his body, for any union of the soul with the body would be inconsistent with true happiness. The New Testament writings were considered to be largely fiction; the Christian religion, a cult of demons masquerading as a worship of the Son of God, with Peter, a practitioner of magic arts, the chief culprit (*maleficus* [*De civ. Dei*, XVIII, 53–54]).

At what time does Augustine indicate an awareness of this anti-Christian Porphyry? Perhaps about 390, at the time he wrote *On True Religion*, though the lack of any specific response to the details of his criticism of Christianity is puzzling.[51] If we leave this possibility open, we must then ask when Porphyry's attack on Christianity, if he knew of it earlier, next registered on Augustine's sensibilities, this time evoking a more agitated reaction.

One possible clue might be the indictment of the Platonists issued at the end of book VII of the *Confessions* (20, 26—21, 27), where Augustine says he thinks it fortunate that he read the books

[51] See chapter 2, section 3, above.

of the Platonists first, and only then the writings of the apostle Paul, for it showed him the difference between "presumption" and "confession," between glimpsing the goal in the distance but not being able to arrive at it and traveling the one road that actually leads there. But the presumption of the Platonists need not be anything as explicit as Porphyry's attempt to gain purification by his own powers, apart from the Christian religion, though the latter *is* meant in two later passages, coming from about 406, which use the same figure of the way and the goal (*De Trin.*, IV, 15, 20; *In Joann. ev.*, tr. 2, 2–4). All that Augustine says in the *Confessions* is in keeping with what can be gathered about Augustine's situation at the time of his conversion, especially as it was clarified in his talks with Simplicianus,[52] and need not be an after-image of some fresh insult from Porphyry.

But one feature of Augustine's remarks about the Platonists has often been taken to be clear proof of the impact of Porphyry, certainly by the time Augustine wrote the *Confessions*, and, if the narrative has any historical value, as early as the spring of 386. That is his use of Romans 1 against the Platonists.[53] He applies to them the statement (Romans 1, 21): "Knowing God, they did not honor him as God or give thanks" (*Conf.*, VII, 9, 15; VIII, 1, 2). Even to say this is to pay them a left-handed compliment, for he contrasts them with others, mentioned in Wisdom 13, 1, who have no knowledge of God at all (*Prop. ad Rom.*, 3; *Conf.*, VIII, 1, 2). But continuing his indictment he applies to them the rest of the passage in Romans, even accusing them, it would appear, of idolatry and the worship of creatures rather than the Creator. Since Porphyry is far more vulnerable than Plotinus to such accusations—especially the Porphyry of the *Philosophy from Oracles* or perhaps of *On Abstinence*—these passages are important for judging which works of Porphyry Augustine read, when he read them, and what effect they had upon his thinking. What we shall find, however, is that the Porphyrian hypothesis is far less secure than it seems at first glance.

---

[52] See chapter 1, section 2, above.

[53] O'Meara, *The Young Augustine*, pp. 143–155; Goulven Madec, "Connaissance de Dieu et action des grâces. Essai sur les citations de l'*Ép. aux Romains*, I, 18–25 dans l'œuvre de saint Augustin," *RA*, II (1962), pp. 273–309.

The first important passage (*Conf.*, VII, 9, 15), coming at the conclusion of a list of the things he read and the things he did *not* read in the books of the Platonists (since the wise of this world, though they know of the Word, refuse to learn from Christ in his humility), says:

> Therefore I also read there the travestied glory of your incorruption, changed into idols and various images, the likenesses of corruptible man and birds and animals and reptiles—that Egyptian food, clearly, for which Esau lost his birthright, for it was the head of an animal that your first-born people worshiped as though it were you (*pro te*), returning to Egypt in their hearts and bowing down their souls, the image of God, before the image of a calf that eats hay. These things I found there, but I did not eat of them, for it pleased you, Lord, to take away from Jacob the reproach of being the second-born, so that the elder should serve the younger; thus you have called the Gentiles into your inheritance. I came to you from among the Gentiles, and I set my mind upon the gold which you had willed your people to carry away from Egypt, for it was yours, wherever it was: thus you said once to the Athenians through your apostle that "in God we live and move and have our being" as some, even by their testimony, had said; and the books which I read belonged most assuredly to that gold. But I did not set my mind upon the idols of the Egyptians, which are served using your gold (*de auro tuo*)[54] when they change the truth of God into a lie and honor and serve the creature more than the Creator.

The Platonists are represented, then, as the Egyptians, whose food Augustine refused to eat but whose gold he stole in the fashion of the Israelites. It has often been thought that the mention of Egypt is explained by Augustine's knowledge that Plotinus came from there, or that Egypt was the epitome of all that was striking about the pagan religion which fascinated Porphyry. But the Egyptian food and the gold and the idols are all spoken of metaphorically. The concrete language about animal forms is required by the Pauline text (Romans 1, 23), but Augustine interprets it, as we shall see, rather less tangibly. And it should be noted that the calf is *not* called golden—gold is spoken of in a

---

[54] This is an instrumental use of *de*, often found in Augustine. A number of examples from the *Confessions* (among which this passage is not included) are listed in Clement Hrdlicka, *A Study of the Late Latin Vocabulary and of the Prepositions and Demonstrative Pronouns in the Confessions of St. Augustine* (Washington, 1931), pp. 168–169.

very different connection. The idols are served "using your gold"; it is not that the idols are made of gold but that the gold is used in serving *real creatures*. Thus the passage is more complex than it appears, and two distinct motifs converge in it.

The metaphor describing doctrines as food is found elsewhere in the *Confessions* in connection with the Manichaeans, and it is even embroidered by calling the external media of communication through speech or writing "dishes" (III, 6, 10; V, 3, 3). There the food is identified with the imaginings of Manichaean mythology, which cannot satisfy because they are nothing; they are worse than the visible sun and moon, which are at least real, and they are worse than the fables of the poets, which are not alleged to be true (III, 6, 10). The equivalent theme of the changing of the glory of the incorruptible God into the likeness of corruptible men, based on Romans 1, 23, is first found in the address *On Faith and the Creed* (7, 14), delivered in 393. At that time Augustine already associates it with the religious use of the imagination, and he says that we are not to imagine God as having a right or left side, or sitting with his knees bent, lest we fall into the sacrilege condemned by the apostle; for if it is an abomination to set up an image of God in a Christian temple, it is all the more an abomination to set up such an image in the heart, which is the true temple of God. The Egyptian food must have to do, then, with a bondage to phantasmata which the Platonists should have been able to avoid but to which Augustine accuses them of succumbing despite all their precautions. Perhaps what he has in mind is their acceptance of the pagan myths as vehicles of philosophical truth.

The other motif, that of the "spoiling of the Egyptians," was a commonplace in the Church to describe its utilization of the best of Greek learning as truth ultimately derived from God. The Platonists and other philosophers have gained a knowledge of God, and though they have misused it the gold is still God's own and can be exploited by the people of God. The first use of the theme of "spoiling the Egyptians" is in *De doct. chr.*, II, 40, 60, and there we can see more clearly the force of the antithesis between the Egyptian food, which Augustine refuses altogether, and the gold which is expropriated because it really belongs to God. Just as the Egyptians had many valuable things which the people of Israel detested and avoided, but had other valuable things which they took with them to put to better use, so, he says, the teachings of the pagan philosophers, most notable among whom are the Platonists, contain not only vain imaginings and burdensome practices which Christians ought to avoid, but many truths—the liberal disciplines, moral precepts, even truths concerning the one God—which are like gold and silver dug from the mines of divine Providence, which operates everywhere, but misused in the worship of demons (cf. *Enarr. in Ps.* 46, 6; *Serm.* 197, 1; *De un. bapt.*, IV, 5–6).

The two themes are quite distinct. Men can be misled by their *imaginations* and project them upon God; and men can know God and yet worship creatures (*real* creatures, not idols, which are mere imaginations). If we wish to see all this spelled out more clearly it can be found in the *Confessions*, V, 3, 5, where Augustine is reflecting on the aberrations of the men who have gained a knowledge of astronomy—the astrologers, certainly, but perhaps the philosophers as well, both Stoic and Platonist. They have thought too highly of themselves, Augustine says; supposing themselves "exalted and lucid like the stars," whose paths they can trace, they have in reality fallen to the ground with darkened hearts. Then follows the analysis (and I punctuate not according to the printed editions but as the logic of the passage seems to require):

They say many true things about the created world, but they do not seek the Truth, the Creator of these things, with reverence; therefore they either do not find him or, if they do find him, they do not honor him as God or give thanks. They become vain in their thoughts and think themselves wise, attributing to themselves what belongs to God; as a consequence they (a) attempt, with the most misguided blindness, to attribute to God the illusions (*mendacia*) that they find within themselves, projecting them upon God, who is Truth, and thereby changing the glory of the incorruptible God into the likeness of corruptible man and birds and animals and reptiles (Romans 1, 23), and (b) convert the truth of God into a lie (*mendacium*), worshipping and serving the creature more than the Creator (Romans 1, 25).

Idolatry thus has two distinct aspects. It may be the constructing of phantasmata and projecting them upon God (this is a line of analysis growing out of neo-Platonism and present in Augustine's thought from the first); or it may be the worship of creatures (and this, as we shall see, is based on Varro's philosophy of religion). In both cases there is a confusion of divine truth with lies (not falsehoods, for *mendacium* is a far stronger term than *fallacium*). But in the one the movement is from the imagination toward the divine, giving divine status to something which man has concocted within himself, while in the other the movement is from a valid knowledge of the divine to some perversion of the proper service of God. When there is only the former, the situation is described by Wisdom 13, 1, which speaks of the vanity of men who do *not* know God, even on the basis of the good things they see around them; when there are both of them together, he applies Romans 1, 18–25, which describes men who are able to follow the indications everywhere present in the created world and rise above them to a knowledge of God himself, but who then misuse their knowledge and are plunged back into the same situation as the others (*Prop. ad Rom.*, 3; *Conf.*, VIII, 1, 2). In the latter case, that of men who know God but do not honor him as God or give thanks (Romans 1, 21), the aspect of enslavement to the imagination is expressed by their exchanging the glory of the immortal God for images resembling mortal man or birds or animals or reptiles (Romans 1, 23), while the aspect of misuse of the knowledge of God is expressed by their exchanging the truth of God for a lie and serving creatures rather than the Creator (Romans 1, 25).

Augustine began to use this passage from Romans more frequently and to direct it against the Platonists not after reading something new of Porphyry's but after reading Ambrosiaster's commentary, which suggested to him the broader import of the passage. Men think themselves wise, this writer says, when they investigate the orbits of the planets and the qualities of the elements; and they excuse their neglect of God by thinking that they can rise to him through these created things, as one gets to a king through his courtiers, while all that they are doing in reality is to transfer the name of God to created things and worship their own fellow servants rather than God himself (*In Rom.* 1, 23). Then follows the explanation of this phenomenon, a kind of "logic of idolatry," following the clues given by Paul in Romans 1, 25: to "change the truth of God into a lie" is to ascribe the term "God," which has truth when it is used with proper reference, to wood and stone and metal, which have their own true or appropriate names, different from God's. It may not be that God is directly denied; but because lying is a deliberate confusion of the true and the false, it is a lie to use the name or attributes of God with reference to creatures. Then the true God is being rejected *de facto*, and the creature is worshiped more than the Creator. And in all of this it is men's knowledge of God that makes them inexcusable, liars and not only in error (*In Rom.* 1, 25).

Augustine now elaborates this theory of idolatry with the help of Varro's philosophy of religion, preserved in *The City of God*, VII, 5–6. Varro had said that the men of old erected statues and other images as a visible reminder of that which can only be apprehended with the mind. He even gave it a Posidonian twist, for Posidonius had used this line of analysis to criticize the idolatries of Greek civic religion, arguing that images only "decrease awe and increase error," and had suggested instead that the true icon is the whole physical universe, through which God is to be approached not with the eyes but with understanding; philosophy therefore is the true "mystery," giving access to the World Soul and to all its parts.[55] Augustine, always alert to subtleties which might serve his polemic, uses this Posidonian theme in *The City of God* to twit Varro, who reproduced it in his writings but did not have the courage to reject civic religion entirely: on your theory, Augustine says, it would have been better for the ancients to worship without any icons at all; and in any case, he adds, this Stoic theory even at its best really concludes to a World-Soul which is bound up with all things, not to a Creator (VII, 5).

That precisely these themes were of concern to Augustine at an earlier time as well is proved by a number of his sermons against idolatry, preached in 399 or soon after, at the time the imperial edict of Honorius began to be enforced in North Africa.[56] A number of times Augustine paraphrases the philosophical justification of the use of images: that it is not the image

---

[55] Samuel Blankert, *Seneca (Epist. 90) over natuur en cultuur en Posidonius als sijn bron* (Amsterdam, 1940), pp. 190ff.

[56] La Bonnardière, *Recherches de chronologie augustinienne*, pp. 158–164. She mentions especially *Enarr. in Ps.* 113, sermo 2, and *Sermo* 197; also *Sermo* 62, *Enarr. in Ps.* 76, 15, and *Enarr. in Ps.* 96, 11.

itself, but the reality it signifies, that is being worshiped. The Stoic coloration of this theory enables him to attack it despite its sophistication; he needs only to point out that the thing signified by the statute of a deity is some part of the world, such as the earth or sea or sun, or at best the numinous power at work in it, and not God the Creator. His argument, then, is that the use of images, even when given the benefit of the doubt and interpreted *in meliorem partem*, is an attribution of deity to parts of creation and thus a transformation of the truth into a lie.

The date of his interest in this motif can be pushed back even farther, to 396, for in *On Christian Teaching* (III, 6, 10—7, 11), in the context of a warning that the sign not be mistaken for the thing signified, he adds that it does no good to say that the statue of Neptune is a sign of something else, for it refers only to the sea; therefore the only suitable conclusion of that argument is that *neither* the sign nor the thing signified should be worshiped. By contrast with the Stoics he takes the case of Israel, which properly observed many rituals even when their meaning was not known, for these rituals signified the redemptive deeds of the Creator and through them men's worship was properly directed.

The outcome of these investigations into Augustine's understanding of Romans 1 is that it is impossible to say, on the basis of the passage in book VII of the *Confessions*, that Augustine was reacting specifically against Porphyry the devotee of mythology and theurgy. The meaning of Augustine's language, despite appearances, is far more "spiritualized" than that. His indictment is the subtler one that the Platonists, though they have apprehended the Truth of God, have been led through their pride farther into dependence upon images (at least to the extent of studying the traditional myths and acquiescing in the idolatry of popular religion), and thereby they have been serving creatures rather than the Creator, at least *de facto*, since the referent of the pagan myths and idols is the natural world.

There is nothing in book VII of the *Confessions*, furthermore, to indicate that Augustine yet had any thought that the Platonists were under the sway of the demons. His theory of myth and idolatry remains Varronian. But a change can be seen in book X of the *Confessions* (41, 66—42, 67). Speaking in his own person, but probably as a representative of the universal situation of fallen man, he says that he had glimpsed God's splendor but was not able to approach it, and in order not to lose God he wanted to possess, along with God, a lie (*mendacium*); as a consequence he lost God as well, for God does not share his place with a lie. He utters a cry that comes out of the general human situation:

Who can reach God?...Whom will I find who can reconcile me with God? Should I have recourse to angels? With what prayers and rituals?

Many people, trying to return to God but not being able to accomplish it by themselves, have turned, so he hears (from Porphyry?), to angels, and then have desired visions, and then have become prey to illusions. Thereupon Augustine gives his full diagnosis, once more following the pattern of Romans 1 but without its language: men who, instead of submitting humbly to God, were puffed up with pride and sought after knowledge attracted the fallen angels to themselves, for they resembled them at heart; these powers of the air masqueraded as angels of God, and proud men were much impressed by them because they had no fleshly bodies, but the magical practices through which men had commerce with these powers and by which they thought they could become purified only furnished the means by which they were deceived by the demons and brought under their hold. The devil, promising to be a mediator of salvation, is only the deceiving mediator (*fallax mediator*) of death, and this is the deserved punishment of men's sin. The sudden entry of this analysis of religion into Augustine's writings, following so soon after his extensive use of the quite different theory of Varro, would seem to indicate the influence of Porphyry in the intervening time.[57]

[57] Of the sermons listed by Mlle. La Bonnardière (note 56 above), only two (*Enarr. in Ps.* 113, sermo 2, and *Enarr. in Ps.* 76) fail to mention any themes that could have come from Porphyry, and even they mention Paul's statement (I Corinthians 10, 19–20) that pagan sacrifice is a commerce with demons. Sermon 197 (said to have been preached on the Kalends of January, thus at least half a year later than the iconoclastic council in Carthage) has an extensive discussion, quite similar to *Conf.*, X, 41, 66–43, 68, of the problem of proud men who attract the Deceiver to themselves and are falsely promised a way of purgation. *Enarr. in Ps.* 96, 12 insists that holy men (such as Paul and Barnabas in Acts 14) and holy angels do not want to receive worship but direct all honor toward God; if men out of caution want to give reverence to the spirits, either good or evil, his answer is that those who worship God alone need fear nothing from either group—certainly an echo of Porphyry's complex reflections.

Books I through IX of the *Confessions*, the more "autobiographical" portions, were probably written in 397. But it has often been thought that books X through XIII were written later, since Augustine mentions (X, 3, 4) those who have read the earlier books; and the whole work could have reached completion at any time between 398 and 401.[58] If Augustine read Porphyry's *Philosophy from Oracles* between the writing of book VII and of book X, the theory of two separate periods of composition would be supported. And since Augustine still adhered to the Varronian theory of religion in some of the sermons preached at the time of the Council of Carthage in May of 399, it would appear that he read Porphyry only after that date, and wrote the last books of the *Confessions* about the same time as the first book of *On the Agreement of the Gospels*, that is, about 400, pouring his discontent into the latter and utilizing Porphyry's insights in the former.

During the period from about 400 to 405 (while he was working on the early books of *On the Trinity* and the Genesis commentary) Augustine does not seem to have been greatly disturbed about Porphyry. He took a sanguine view of philosophical activity, refraining from attack upon the philosophers and even thinking quite "rationalistically" himself, as we have seen, expecting perhaps to beat the philosophers on their own ground. It may be that the kind of cosmological speculation in which Augustine engaged, paying much attention to the work of angels and of demons, owes something to the challenge Porphyry presented. And it is certain that one of his motives in writing the Genesis commentary was to vindicate the Scriptures in the face of the attacks of learned men.

But he was not uncritical in his attitude toward Porphyry. Perhaps the most representative sampling of his thoughts during those years can be gained from a series of three sermons (numbers 240–242 in the editions) preached on three successive days after Easter in defense of the resurrection of the body.[59] Porphyry is

[58] For a survey of the question see Solignac's introduction to the *Confessions*, BA, XIII, 45–54.

[59] These sermons should be dated about 403 or 404. Some features definitely place them not far from 400—the concern with the truth and consistency of the gospels (240, 1), the view that bodily corruption is the only consequence of man's sin (240, 3), the statement that the Platonists are "better" than other

mentioned three times by name and is once called "the most bitter enemy of the Christian religion" (*Serm.* 241, 7). The doctrines reported are unmistakably his: the soul is immortal; the cause of its sorrows is to be located in an earlier life when it dwelt in the company of the stars until a desire for bodily things drew it downward; the only way to escape this cycle in which provisional beatitude is followed by another fall is to observe the precept, "The body is to be shunned altogether."[60]

Augustine met Porphyry on the field of rational argument. He considered, first in these sermons and then in a number of other passages through the years, the problem posed by Porphyry: that the resurrection of the body is incompatible with the lasting happiness of the soul (these passages, in chronological order, are *Serm.* 241, 7; *De civ. Dei*, X, 29 and XII, 20; *De Trin.*, XIII, 9, 12; *De civ. Dei*, XIII, 16–18 and XXII, 26). In all these passages we find, usually quite explicitly, an interweaving of three motifs: Porphyry's precept to "flee the bodily altogether," with the purpose of purifying the soul and ultimately reaching lasting beatitude, *permanere cum Deo* (*De civ. Dei*, X, 29); Porphyry's consequent denial of the Christian doctrine of the resurrection of the body, that of Christ or of any other, as incompatible with beatitude; and Augustine's refutation of this Porphyrian principle from the doctrines of Platonism itself. For against Porphyry he can cite Plato's view that the gods have ethereal bodies in the heavens (and it should be noted that Augustine's understanding of the resurrected body was that while it is material it is not corruptible but is like the ethereal bodies attributed by Plato to the stars [*Sermo* 241, 7; *De civ. Dei*, X, 29 and XXII, 26; *Retr.*,

---

philosophers (240, 4; 241, 1–3), the suggestion that the stars are animated (241, 8; cf. *De Gen. ad litt.*, II, 18, 38), the interest in the order of the elements (242, 6, 8ff.), the well-developed theory of mediation (240, 5; cf. *Conf.*, X, 41, 66–43, 68; *De cons. ev.*, I, 35, 53), and the interest in the idolatry of the Egyptians (241; cf. *Serm.* 197, 1). Some other features push the date somewhat later—the interpretation of miracle (241, 1; cf. *Ep.* 102, q. 1, 5–6; *In Joann. ev.*, tr. 8, 1; *De Gen. ad litt.*, VI, 13, 25–14, 26), and the discussion of the problem of the initial beatitude of souls (or demons) which later fall: if they forget their past miseries and are unaware of their coming fall, they are happy through error, not through unending possession of God (241, 5; cf. *Ep.* 73, 7 to Jerome, written in 403–404).

[60] For a resolution of the seeming inconsistencies between the view reported in these sermons and what is known from other sources about Porphyry, see Pépin, *Théologie cosmique et théologie chrétienne*, pp. 434–442.

I, 4, 3]); and he quotes the famous passage on the eternity of the world from Plato's *Timaeus* (41A–B), in which the Craftsman addresses the heavenly gods (I follow Augustine's text):

Consider those works of which I am the Father and Maker [this excludes particular corporeal things, which are the work of the gods, but it includes the gods themselves, with their corporeal bodies, and the corporeal world as a whole]. Although what has been bound together can be dissolved again, only an irrational will would wish them to be unbound. Because you have come into being, you are not immortal and indissoluble; nevertheless you will not be dissolved, and death cannot touch you, for no hazard is stronger than my own purpose, which is a greater bond for your endurance through time than those natural bonds with which you were bound together when you came into being.

This passage is utilized against Porphyry in all the passages mentioned, and is usually quoted at length. Augustine quotes it in Cicero's translation, and this has led most scholars to list the *Timaeus* among the philosophical works which Augustine read. But O'Meara has already pointed out that the most extended passages from the *Timaeus* in Augustine's writings appear in contexts related to Porphyry, and he suggests that the dialogue was given a prominent place in Porphyry's *Philosophy from Oracles* and as a consequence held a special interest for Christian writers: both Arnobius and Aeneas of Gaza, in the context of discussions based on Porphyry, mention the same passage.[61] Though O'Meara still assumes that Augustine read the *Timaeus* in Cicero's translation, I believe that the evidence indicates that he knew only a few passages and that these can be traced to works in which they were quoted. His knowledge of this passage probably came, then, from Porphyry's *Philosophy from Oracles*, and he simply used one passage in the work to refute another. He himself as much as says this in *De Trin.*, XIII, 9, 12, where he tries to show that Platonism, and especially Porphyry's own modification of it, implies the Christian doctrine of resurrection: the Platonists had said that the soul is caught in a cycle of attaining to beatitude and then returning to the miseries of this life; those who were embarrassed about this doctrine (*viz.*, Porphyry)

[61] O'Meara, *Porphyry's Philosophy from Oracles in Augustine*, pp. 146–148, 166, n. 2. See also Hadot, "Citations de Porphyre chez Augustin," p. 216, n. 47, where he attempts to show that it comes not from the *Philosophy from Oracles* but from *On the Return of the Soul*.

thought that the soul could attain to endless beatitude, but without a body; but because of the beliefs they themselves hold about the eternity of the world, they refute their own doctrine ("*ipsi redarguant*") about the nature of the soul's beatitude. And in *De civ. Dei*, X, 29, Augustine suggests that Porphyry quite inconsistently advises men to flee the body but believes the world to be a huge animal, held together by the World-Soul.

If it was in Porphyry's *Philosophy from Oracles* that Augustine first encountered the Platonist teaching that the steady purpose of the Craftsman is the bond of continuity for the heavenly gods and for the whole material world, there is a tantalizing possibility that Porphyry supplied to Augustine precisely that element in Platonism which is most akin to biblical thought and which is found in the *Timaeus*: the vivid sense of temporality and the problem of its relation to eternity (29C), the suggestion that the world originated in time (or, if not this, at least the awareness that it is constantly changing and that any element of order has been introduced by intelligent purpose), its explanation of creation as resulting from God's lack of envy (29E), the joy of the Craftsman at the perfection of the universe (37C), and his address to the gods, promising that his steadfast will would preserve the ordered universe from the threat of dissolution (41A–B).

The similarity between these features of the *Timaeus* and the interpretation Augustine gives of the creation narrative in the closing books of the *Confessions* and in the opening books of the Genesis commentary is striking. Although Augustine had long since drawn a contrast between that which changes and that which abides, and had seen that the former can gain stability only through adherence to the latter, and had even made the Holy Spirit the animating principle of this right ordering of the dynamic element in the world, it was only about 400 that all of these began to be drawn together into a unified cosmology.

I do not intend to over-dramatize the change. It is precisely its subtlety and its appropriateness to what Augustine had already been saying that support the suspicion that a work by Porphyry may have occasioned it. Augustine could not have read the *Timaeus* prior to 400, for there are no echoes of it. And it is doubtful that he read it then, or at any later time, for his use of it is too fragmentary, even on the supposition that he passed over the difficult mathematical and physical speculations contained in the dialogue. Some passages are only alluded to, or are used as isolated catch-phrases when their immediate context might have been useful for Augustine's purposes. Thus the most decisive argument against Augustine's having read the *Timaeus* is an argument from privation, from his ignorance of certain passages which he might have used and which might have been more valuable than those passages he did use. The presence of passages from the *Timaeus* in his writings can be accounted for by his reading of doxographies or philosophical discussions in the Platonist tradition, for they are in every case widely known, even commonplace passages.[62] What best explains the unobtrusive entry of these motifs into Augustine's writings, even before he thought to cite the *Timaeus* for polemical purposes, is that they had already been taken up and reworked by Porphyry in the context of his own philosophical speculations, probably early in his career when he would still be classifiable as a "middle Platonist."[63] When Augustine encountered them they were already in a form quite compatible with his own Platonism,

---

[62] A check of *The City of God* indicates that comparatively few passages from Plato's dialogue are utilized:

(a) Several concern the passage (*Tim.*, 31B–32B) which calls fire and earth the elements at the extremes, air and water the elements which join them together (*De civ. Dei*, VIII, 11 and 15; XXII, 11). These could come from a doxography or from some ecclesiastical writer.

(b) Several point out, only in passing, that Plato called the astral spirits "created gods" (IX, 23; X, 31, XII, 25; cf. Serm. 241, 8).

(c) Several cite the statement (*Tim.*, 29E–30A) that the cause of God's creating the world is that he was good and did good works. Cicero's translation is *not* used.

(d) Mention is made of God's joy at the perfection of the universe (*Tim.* 37C) in *De civ. Dei*, XI, 7. It is uncertain whether this is in Cicero's translation, for there is a lacuna in the manuscripts.

(e) In *De cons. ev.*, I, 35, 53 and *De Trin.*, IV, 18, 24 there is a quotation from Cicero's translation of *Tim.*, 29C: "*quantum enim ad id quod ortum est aeternitas valet, tantum ad fidem veritas.*" I have argued above, following suggestions of O'Meara (pp. 106, 166, n. 2), that this was found in Porphyry.

(f) This leaves only *Tim.*, 41A–B, cited at length in a number of passages, which I have argued is derived from Porphyry again.

[63] The interest of middle Platonism in the problem of temporality and its overcoming by divine purpose is highlighted in Dörrie, *Porphyrios' "Symmikta Zetemata,"* pp. 171–172. The lasting interest of Porphyry in this aspect of the *Timaeus* cosmology, and his identification of the Demiurge with the World-Soul, is discussed in Theiler, *Porphyrios und Augustin*, p. 15, and Beutler, "Porphyrios," cols. 304–305.

shaped as it was by Varro and by Plotinus and by other works of
Porphyry; they stimulated him to look for new dimensions in the
biblical text, and in the process his own theological position
was drawn into a unity for the first time, though without any
drastic reversal of his earlier convictions.

Porphyry appears to have played a dual role in Augustine's
intellectual development. He brought to Augustine's attention
some features of the Platonist tradition which he had previously
overlooked; and these were the aspects of Platonism most in
keeping with biblical modes of thought. Thus he reinforced
Augustine's confidence that the most reasonable philosophy
could be found in Scripture, and the reading of Porphyry's
Philosophy from Oracles may have been the immediate occasion of
Augustine's turning again to the creation narrative, first in the
closing books of the *Confessions* and then in the Genesis commentary, in an attempt to trace that true philosophy. But
Porphyry the opponent of Christianity brought to Augustine's
attention, far more forcibly than ever before, the tension between
the Platonist and the biblical conceptions of the cosmos and of
the destiny of man.

And yet the situation is a curious one. For about five years
Augustine was fully aware of Porphyry's anti-Christian sentiments
and responded to them with reasoned argumentation. Suddenly
he mounted a different attack on Porphyry, probably in 406, both
in book IV of *The Trinity* and in the second sermon on the Gospel
according to John, preached in December of that year.[64] What
rankles him most about the philosophers, of course, is that they
scoff at the resurrection of the body. But now he strikes at them
with greater intensity, and with arguments that are more *ad
hominem*. He thinks they are not qualified to speak on the question
of resurrection. They are better than the other philosophers, to
be sure, when it comes to understanding the unchangeable
being of God through the things that are made. But this does not
mean that they are also to be consulted about the temporal course
of the world and its future destiny; that lies beyond the range of
historical reports, and even the Platonists are unable to inspect

[64] For the dating of the earliest sermons on the Gospel of John, see Le
Landais, "Deux années de prédication de saint Augustin," p. 35, and La
Bonnardière, *Recherches de chronologie augustinienne*, pp. 48–50.

the eternal ideas in which God has planned it out (*De Trin.*, IV, 16, 21—17, 23). And their pride not only makes them incapable of the contemplation of God; it leads them to despise the only way of access to it, the death and resurrection of Christ (*De Trin.*, IV, 13, 18 and 17, 23; *In Joann. ev.*, tr. 2, 4). And in the sixth book of the Genesis commentary (VI, 9, 15–17), which probably comes from that same period,[65] he decisively rejected for the first time the Platonist doctrine of the preexistence of the soul, whose possibility he had entertained for many years; and in explicit opposition to those who thought that the diversity of men's fortunes is due to their merits from a previous life, he now asserted, again for the first time, a doctrine of hereditary sin based on the biblical statement (Psalm 50, 7 [51, 5]) that man is "conceived in iniquity."

What occasioned such a change of strategy? Pépin thinks that Augustine was made aware of Porphyry's later work *Against the Christians*, not directly, for it had been suppressed by the Imperial officials, but through Eusebius and probably through other channels.[66] What these other channels might have been is suggested by an episode with personal overtones that took place about this time. A presbyter in Carthage had written to him reporting the objections to Christianity put forward by some *illuminati* in Carthage to a mutual friend of theirs whom they had been trying to persuade to become a Christian (*Retr.*, II, 57). His answer to these objections is contained in the letter to Deogratias (number 102 in the editions), which could have been written at any time between 406 and 410. Augustine knew that five of the objections came from Porphyry, and the second is

[65] Some parallels between the different writings of this period may be noted:

	De Gen.	In Joann. ev.	De Trin.
"that which is made is life in him" (John 1, 4)	V, 13–15	tr. 1, 16	IV, 1, 3
pride of the philosophers		tr. 2, 2–4	IV, 10, 13–17, 23
"conceived in iniquity"	VI, 9, 16	tr. 3, 12; 4, 10	
six ages of the world		tr. 9, 6; 15, 4	IV, 4, 7
"mystery of faith" (I Timothy 3, 16)	V, 19		IV, 20, 27

[66] See the entire discussion of Porphyry in Pépin, *Théologie cosmique et théologie chrétienne*, pp. 418–461. It seems to me that he argues far too strongly for an influence of *Against the Christians* on Sermons 240–242 (pp. 433–442), for nothing unique to that work is reflected in them.

9+

seemingly ascribed to his work *Against the Christians*. He professed incredulity that the great Porphyry, whose works he knew, could have said such things (*Ep.* 102, q. 4, 23; *Retr.*, II, 57). It may be that the episode (if it took place as early as 406) helped to tip the balance.

And yet the fact that a basic shift was taking place in Augustine's whole conception of man, involving some matters which belonged strictly to intramural debate among Christians, suggests that his turning against the philosophers might have been the effect not of some fresh insult to the faith from their side but of the stronger pull of doctrines incompatible with those of the philosophers, drawing his thoughts at last into a different orbit. And a more complete survey of his ideas at the time indicates that this is indeed what happened.

5. THE OLD ADAM

The writings which come from the period about 406 (if the dating we have used is correct) testify to a major transition in Augustine's thought. He unambiguously rejected the Platonist doctrine of the soul's preexistence, at least so far as it implied that the soul's present state is the result of its actions in a previous existence, in favor of the view that all men, even newborn infants, are involved in the common destiny of the human race, entirely apart from their own decisions. In the sermons on John he says that man is born with a *tradux peccati et mortis*, an offshoot of the sins of the parents, and it is characterized especially by concupiscence (*In Joann. ev.*, tr. 3, 12; 4, 10). In the fourth sermon on the First Epistle of John (tr. 4, 11) he spells it out even more fully:

Adam was created by God, but when he consented to the devil he was born of the devil, and all whom he begot were like himself. We are born with desire, and even before we add our own guilt we are born of that damnation.... Therefore there are two births, that of Adam and that of Christ, the one casting us down to death, the other raising us up to life; the one bearing with it sin, the other freeing us from sin.

He makes the famous statement, which was to become the center of so much controversy among the theologians, that "no one achieves anything by himself except falsehood and sin" (*"nemo habet de suo nisi mendacium et peccatum*" [*In Joann. ev.*, tr. 5, 1]); and in the sixth book of the Genesis commentary (chapters 35–39) he says, more strongly than at any time before or afterwards, that man completely *loses* his participation in the Word, the Image of God, through sin. And if any doubt about Augustine's views remains, his letter to the bishop Boniface (*Ep.* 98), usually dated 408, states explicitly that infants have guilt because of the carnal will of another and that this guilt is taken away in baptism.

The remedy for man's situation is a dependence upon God far more radical than anything Augustine had yet suggested. Man is worthy only of punishment; grace is given freely, not as a reward for merit, and it is given not because of anything man has already become but in order that he become something different (*In Joann. ev.*, tr. 3, 8). There is even a rather "Lutheran"-sounding passage in the sermon on Psalm 122 (n. 3): pride is a looking to oneself, a taking pleasure in what one already is; but the only true security consists in taking pleasure in God:

But who is it that takes pleasure in God? The one in whom God takes pleasure [by infusing *caritas*]...He takes pleasure in you, so that you might take pleasure in him. But he cannot take pleasure in you unless you are displeased with yourself. If you are displeased with yourself, direct your gaze away from yourself. If you look at yourself truly, what you find will displease you and you will say to God, "My sin is always before me." Your sin is always before you in order that it will not be before God; and you refuse to be before yourself in order that you might be before God.

This stress on justification does not diminish the other element of sanctification, and the latter is still seen as indispensable to salvation; though Augustine insists that grace is given freely and in mercy, he sees eternal life as a reward given in justice to a life led under the influence of grace. Still, the reward is not technically a reward given to human merits; it is a reward given to grace, *praemium gratiae*, and eternal life is a crowning not of human merits but of God's gifts (*In Joann. ev.*, tr. 3, 9–10).

There remains a tension, therefore, between what man is and what he should be. Augustine wrestles with the apparent contradiction between two statements in the First Epistle of John: that "he who is born of God does not sin" (I John 3, 9) and that "if we say we have no sin, we are liars" (I John 1, 8). The former, he says, applies to the central orientation of the heart in *caritas*, the root from which good works spontaneously proceed, the latter to the lesser sins which no one, as long as he lives on earth, can help committing daily, but which are covered by love and are remitted through saying the petition in the Lord's Prayer (*In Joann. ep.*, tr. 5, 1–7). The conflict within the believer continues throughout his life, and Augustine frequently draws a contrast between his present situation and the future completion of the process of salvation: the believer is saved, purified, perfected even now, but still only in hope (*in spe*), not yet in reality (*in re* [*Enarr. in Ps.* 123, 2; 125, 4]). This contrast between *spes* and *res* is not entirely new in Augustine's writings. It is based, of course, upon Paul's statement (Romans 8, 24–25):

In this hope [of the redemption of our bodies] we were saved. Now hope that is seen is not hope. For who hopes for what he sees? But if we hope for what we do not see, we wait for it with patience.

Augustine understood the eschatological tension expressed in Romans 8 much earlier,[67] and he formulated the contrast between *spes* and *res* about 398 (*C. Faust.*, XI, 7). But now it is applied not merely to the problem of mortality and weakness but especially to the problem of continued *sinning*.

The reason for this intensified stress upon original sin and the unmerited character of grace and the continued reality of sin even in those who are being renewed—well before the outbreak of the Pelagian controversy, it will be noted—is that Augustine is now engaged in polemic with the Donatists, the African sect that was insisting upon moral and spiritual purity in the Church and claiming that the Catholic bishops had long since lost any continuity with the pure Church of the apostles. In many passages in these sermons the Donatists are mentioned, as though they are still a force to be reckoned with and are the focus of much controversy.[68] And on one occasion Augustine remarks, apropos

[67] See chapter 3, section 3, above.
[68] For a discussion of these passages see Le Landais, "Deux années de prédication," pp. 63–67, and Paul Agaësse, in the introduction to his translation of the *Commentaire de la première épître de S. Jean* (Sources chrétiens, LXXV; Paris, 1961), pp. 24–28. It will be noted that both authors assume a later date, but their discussions reveal nothing that is inconsistent with the situation about 406.

of the question whether sin continues in the believer, that schisms are found not among those who continually depend on Christ as their advocate or propitiator for daily sins but among those who say, "*We* are righteous, *we* justify the ungodly" (*In Joann. ep.*, tr. 1, 8).

Precisely that was the leading question in the controversy with Petilianus, carried on between 400 and 403 (book II was written before news had arrived of the death of Anastasius, the bishop of Rome, in 402) and preserved in three long books by Augustine. Petilianus had asserted that a new birth in baptism can come only from a "source" (namely, the one who baptizes) which is itself pure. Throughout his reply Augustine not only hammered at the internal weaknesses of the Donatist argument—the problem of the person who is baptized by someone who only feigns righteousness, or the observable fact of differences in spiritual gifts between the baptizer and the baptized—but developed the alternative position that when the human minister baptizes externally with water it is Christ himself who baptizes inwardly with the Holy Spirit; and he supported this emphasis upon Christ rather than the human administrant by constantly quoting such biblical texts as "Cursed is he who trusts in man" (Jeremiah 17, 5) or "It is better to trust the Lord than to put confidence in man" (Psalm 118 [117], 8).

It was in controversy with the Donatists that Augustine first began to qualify his own perfectionism with an awareness of the continuing actuality of sin and the need of incorporation into Christ, to qualify his praise of the moral achievements of the apostles and martyrs and ascetics of the Church with an acknowledgment that the Church, though it is properly the community of the elect, will always have unworthy members mingled into it. It is not that he acquiesced in the sins of nominal Christians, either out of despair or out of opportunism; the familiar laxity of Western Christendom, shared by both Catholicism and Protestantism, is the outcome of medieval developments. In Augustine's day the Church maintained high standards of behavior and enforced its penitential discipline strictly.[69] The conflict

---

[69] See F. Van der Meer, *Augustine the Bishop*, pp. 382–387; Anne-Marie La Bonnardière, "Pénitence et réconciliation des pénitents d'après saint Augustin," *REA*, XIII (1967), 31–53, 249–283; XIV (1968), 181–204.

between the Donatists and the Catholics was not one between rigor and laxity so much as one between a sacramental theory based upon the transmission of the charismatic qualities of men and a sacramental theory based upon divine gifts symbolized by and conveyed through human actions; or, more broadly, between a perfectionism which expected the Church to be without spot or blemish while still on earth and a realism which rejected that expectation on several counts—the continuing reality of sinfulness, the need of a righteousness which comes from a source beyond man himself, and the obvious futility of the hope of making a definitive separation of the wheat from the chaff at any time prior to the last judgment, in other words, as long as human judgment can be in error and as long as time remains for apostasy or for amendment of life.

Most of this was worked out by Augustine in the course of his controversies with the Donatists. But he derived some aid and comfort from the authoritative figure in the African Church, Cyprian; and at one point especially the influence of Cyprian seems to have been decisive. Debate with the Donatists would not, by itself, have generated a doctrine of original sin. The source of that doctrine in Augustine seems to be Cyprian, not so much in any of his specific statements but in what was implied by many of his statements. In Augustine's later writings against the Pelagians (especially *C. duas ep. Pel.*, IV, 8, 21—10, 28) he discloses which passages in Cyprian were important to him in connection with this theme, and they are found chiefly in the letter to Fidus on the baptism of infants (*Ep.* 64), the commentary on the Lord's Prayer, and the *Testimonies*.

Augustine engaged in an extensive study of the writings of Cyprian and of the records of the whole controversy leading up to the Council of Carthage in 256 while writing his work *On Baptism*, running to seven long books; this was begun about 400 and probably took several years to finish. The *Testimonies* are not utilized there, however, and the motifs with which we are concerned do not yet appear. But texts drawn from the *Testimonies* do play a large role throughout the polemic against Petilianus, written not much later. In the *Testimonies* (III, 54) Cyprian utilizes Psalm 50, 7 (51, 5) and I John 1, 8 to prove that "no one" (seemingly including infants) is without sin. In his work on the

Lord's Prayer (chapter 22) he uses I John 1, 8 to prove that there are "daily sins" which the Christian needs to have forgiven. And the exhortations to put trust in God rather than in man (Psalm 118 [117], 8 and Jeremiah 17, 5) are used together in the *Testimonies* (III, 10). It seems likely, then, that Cyprian supplied the materials with which Augustine constructed his new understanding of man.

But one other factor which may have nudged Augustine away from Platonism should be considered. This is the controversy over Origen which was precipitated in the East by Epiphanius and led within a few years to an imperial rescript against Origenism and the deposition of Chrysostom as patriarch of Constantinople in 404. Just what Augustine knew of the controversy is uncertain. Probably he never read Origen's *De principiis*, which was the occasion of most of the criticisms; what he knew about the work was gained at second hand, especially from Orosius' *Commonitorium*, sent to him much later, in 414. But Origenism was a *cause célèbre* in the West during the papacy of Anastasius (399–402), who ratified the condemnation of its errors in the East and sent a letter (quite uninformative, however, about the details) to the bishop of Milan and perhaps to others as well. And during these years Augustine was engaged in correspondence with Jerome, one of the leaders of the attack upon Origen; Jerome mentioned (in *Ep.* 68 in the Augustine corpus) that he was sending to him a copy of his reply to Rufinus (probably the first two books of the *Apology*) and would send the completed reply (probably the third book) when he could. This would be in 401 or 402. That Augustine received the *Apology* is proved by his expression of pain at seeing such a bitter quarrel between two men who had been such close friends in the past (*Ep.* 73, 8) and his mention of Jerome's attacks on Origen and Didymus (*Ep.* 82, 23).

The three books of Jerome's *Apology* consist of little more than personal invective. They say very little about Origen's doctrines or what is objectionable in them—except on two points uncomfortably close to Augustine. Rufinus had refused to decide between three views of the origin of the soul: that it is transmitted through generation, that it is newly created at conception, and (Origen's view) that all souls were created at once and sent at the appropriate time into bodies (*Apol.*, II, 8; III, 30); Jerome clearly assumes, however, that Origen's view is out of the question and that creationism is the standard view of the Church (II, 10; III, 28). In addition, Jerome disapproves of Origen's belief that the original body with which man was created, and the body in the resurrection, are without sex and even without the limbs that man bears while he lives in gross matter (*Apol.*, II, 5). It is possible that Augustine was drawn up short by these remarks and rethought his own views, which on both counts had been very close to Origen's.

Whatever the circumstances that occasioned it may have been, Augustine did change his conception of man's primitive state. Previously he had taken the view that man was created with an ethereal body and was not subject to death and had no sexuality until after his sin, when the body became gross, earthy, more like the animals. But in the sixth book of the Genesis commentary (VI, 19, 30—29, 40) he reversed his position: Adam's body was *not* the same as the body the saints will receive at the resurrection, for he had immortality only in the sense that his animate body would have been changed into a spiritualized body had he not sinned; he was mortal, but had a *posse non mori*, a possibility of immortalization as the reward of faithfulness.

These remarks take the form of an extended reflection on Paul's contrast (I Corinthians 15, 42–50) between what men have been in Adam and what they become in Christ: the first Adam became a "living being," a body animated by a soul; the last Adam is resurrected with an imperishable "spiritual body." Now this passage plays an important role in Irenaeus' *Against the Heresies* (V, 9–13), which Augustine had in hand.[70] It would seem that Augustine consulted this work and took up the problematic formulated by Irenaeus (V, 12, 5): In what sense is man's redemption in Christ a *restitutio in pristinum*, a restoration of what man was intended to be in Adam? Augustine's own answer is somewhat more precise than that given by Irenaeus, but it is a faithful representation of his views. There is a *restoratio in pristinum* only with respect to the mind, which is renewed through knowledge of God and according to his Image (Augustine makes use of the same biblical texts, Colossians 3, 9–10 and Ephesians 4, 23–24, that were suggested to him by Irenaeus). With respect to the body, however, there will be a *renovatio in melius*, for man was

---

[70] See Altaner, "Augustinus und Irenäus," pp. 162–172 (*KpS*, 194–203).

created "animal" and is to be raised a "spiritual" being. Augustine thus discovers an alternative to the Platonist and Origenist understanding of man which he had been holding, and one with greater authority within the Church.

The influences discussed thus far are literary. One other factor, this time a direct personal influence, may have been the decisive one. About 405 Paulinus, a deacon of Milan who had been secretary to Ambrose, came to Africa and settled in Carthage. He was still there during the Pelagian controversy; indeed, he took the lead in the proceedings against Caelestius in 411, acting as prosecutor in the diocesan trial held in Carthage, and in 417 he prepared the official *libellus* against the Pelagians in the negotiations of the African Church with Rome.[71] It is likely that Paulinus brought with him all of Ambrose's works when he moved to Africa, and that from about 405 onward Augustine was in a position to consult them, as he did repeatedly during his later controversies with the Pelagians.[72] In view of the demonstrated aggressiveness of Paulinus' personality it is not difficult to imagine that as soon as he arrived in Africa he began to exert some pressure on Augustine to conform more closely with Ambrose's clearly-stated teaching that Adam's sin is transmitted to all his descendants. Years later, when accused of "innovation" in putting forward the doctrine of original sin, Augustine replied,

My instructor is Cyprian, . . . my instructor is Ambrose, whose books I have read, and whose words I have heard from his own lips, and through whom I received the washing of regeneration (*C. Jul. op. imp.*, VI, 21).

In his concern to prove that he has followed the teaching of the Church he doubtless telescopes the influence of Ambrose's writings with his personal influence; whatever Augustine, looking back, thought he received from Ambrose's instruction, he did not hear it at the time as a doctrine of original sin. Such a doctrine does appear about 406, however, and in a form that owes much to Ambrose. Augustine's statement, already quoted, that man achieves

---

[71]The letter is to be found, in the midst of other papal documents, in *CSEL*, XXXV, 108-111.

[72]Giuseppe Ferretti, *L'Influsso di S. Ambrogio in S. Agostino* (Rome, 1951), p. 38.

9*

by himself only falsehood and sin (*In Joann. ev.*, tr. 5, 1) bears strong verbal similarities to several passages from Ambrose's lost exposition of Isaiah[73]; and the view that sin is transmitted through desire and copulation comes directly from Ambrose.[74]

Thus a decisive change in Augustine's career as a theologian occurred at this point, about the year 406. Until then his views had been shaped chiefly by the spirit of Greek philosophy as conveyed through Plotinus and Porphyry and some exegetical works of Origen. Now he turned against some of the most characteristic doctrines of the Platonists and looked to the writers of the Church. The circumstances, as we have seen, were complex, and it is difficult to say what relative weight the different factors might have had. But they conspired to cast doubt on the views that had been dear to Augustine the philosopher, and as he reflected on the problem he came steadily closer to the position that would be characteristic of Augustine the teacher of the Church.

The years between 407 and 410 are very nearly unknown territory in Augustine's intellectual life. He was at work on the Genesis commentary, and he was busy trying to bring the controversy with the Donatists to a close with a decisive victory for the Catholic Church and its friends in the Imperial court. But aside from that we know little of his activities. The *Retractationes* mention no major writings, and scholars who have tried dating the extant sermons have been unable to place many of them in these years. Perhaps it was a time of intellectual reorganization, if not disorientation, and those with a flair for psychology might find it significant that in 410 Augustine's health failed and he spent some time resting at a villa near Hippo (*Ep.* 98, 8; 109, 3; 118, 34). While he was there he received word of the sack of Rome. A period spent in relative isolation had ended in exhaustion; a new period full of stimulation from the broader world had begun, and it would lead to the full maturation of Augustine's theology.

[73]See the fragments in Ferretti, pp. 91-92, based on the edition by Ballerini (reprinted in *CC*, XIV, 405-408).

[74]Ferretti, pp. 66-73.

CHAPTER 5

Integration (411–418)

WE COME NOW to another clearly delineated period in Augustine's thought, marked off by the rise of fresh interests—the undertaking of the apologetic task of writing about the destiny of the Roman Empire and simultaneously the polemical task of evaluating classical civilization in all its aspects; the use of the theme of the two cities as the overarching principle for organizing and interpreting the entire historical process; the continuation of his speculations on the Trinitarian doctrine, with more success this time because of the hints supplied by the theologians of the East; and the defense and elaboration of his earlier convictions about sin and grace following the challenge issued by Pelagius and others. These years mark the climax of Augustine's theological career. For the first time he can truly be called a "systematic theologian"; his earlier investigations are brought to some kind of resolution, and his treasures, both old and new, are exhibited in the massive syntheses of *The Trinity* and *The City of God.* It was not only a time of completion and summing up, of course, for new and serious problems were posed by the sack of Rome in 410 and the influx of wealthy refugees into North Africa, bearing with them unsettling questions about the fate of the Empire and new formulations of Christian doctrine. But these do not seem to have alarmed Augustine; they seem to have acted more to catalyze his already developing reflections than to call his assumptions into question. Following more or less accurately the order in which these problems came to his attention, let us begin with the debate over classical civilization and the Pelagian controversy, then turn to the topics of the Trinity and its analogues in human life.

1. The Two Cities

We cannot enter into a detailed analysis of *The City of God*, for that would be a vast enterprise of its own. Many of its themes have already been aired, however, for it is often a summation of Augustine's convictions, worked out in the preceding decade, about matters philosophical and theological. But Augustine's magnum opus must at least be acknowledged with a place of its own in a survey of his thought!

The immediate occasion of the writing of *The City of God* was the sack of Rome and especially the anxious or scoffing questionings about it on the part of men whose whole life was bound up with the Empire and its values, men like Volusianus, who began to suspect that the Christian ethic of turning the other cheek was incompatible with the needs of political life (*Ep.* 136, 2), or more hostile spirits who insinuated that it was curious that the Empire had prospered under its traditional religion and was disintegrating only with the establishment of Christianity. On this latter score Christians found themselves mousetrapped, for in 382 the Altar of Victory had been removed from the Senate in Rome, and at that time Symmachus warned against neglecting the gods; the controversy went on through the years and in 410 was still fresh in everyone's memory.

Without the rise of such problems, Augustine might never have written *The City of God*. But he was well prepared for the task, and it represents not a new line of reflection but the continuation of some old ones. It is conceivable that he might have undertaken something like it even without the stimulus of a political and religious crisis. He had already engaged in a critique of the idolatries of classical religion and of the religious philosophy represented by Porphyry, topics which occupy much of the first ten books of *The City of God*; and we have seen how important a source of information it is about influences upon Augustine's earlier thought. His own speculations had already led him to reflect, furthermore, upon the founding of the heavenly City from which the cosmos is administered and toward which the faithful strive during their earthly pilgrimage; upon the position of the fallen angels; and upon the influence of both these societies upon the course of human history—all of which are the concern of the twelve books that make up the second part of the work.[1]

Augustine probably projected *The City of God* in 412, and in the Genesis commentary (XI, 15, 20) he announced his intention to write a lengthier work about the two societies which arise from two contrary loves. The first ten books, containing his polemical reply to the paganizers and the doubters, were finished quickly, probably by 415. The second part took longer: the four books dealing with the origin of the two cities were written perhaps between 415 and 418; the four dealing with their course through history, between 419 and 421; and the four dealing with their destiny, between 421 and 426. Given the complex scheme it is not surprising that the work can be approached from a number of angles—as a polemical work or an apology directed to the situation following the sack of Rome,[2] or as a massive philosophy or theology of history[3]; as an analysis of political ideology and the political situation in antiquity,[4] or as a source of principles which can still guide the political and moral theory, and the ecclesiastical policies, of later generations[5]; as a recommendation to accept the actual character of political life[6] or as an invitation to change it for the better.[7] The fact that something of a case can be made for each of these interpretations suggests that we should not have too narrow a conception of the scope of the work.

[1] For the development of the theme, see A. Lauras and H. Rondet, "Le thème des deux cités dans l'œuvre de saint Augustin," *Études augustiniennes* (Théologie, XXVIII; Paris, 1953), pp. 99–160.

[2] John Neville Figgis, *The Political Aspects of S. Augustine's "City of God"* (London, 1921).

[3] Heinrich Scholz, *Glaube und Unglaube in der Weltgeschichte* (Leipzig, 1911); Joseph Ratzinger, *Volk und Haus Gottes in Augustins Lehre von der Kirche* (Münchener Theologische Studien; Münich, 1954).

[4] Franz Georg Maier, *Augustin und das antike Rom* (Tübinger Beiträge zur Altertumswissenschaft, XXXIX; Stuttgart, 1955).

[5] Gustave Combès, *La doctrine politique de saint Augustin* (Paris, 1927).

[6] Herbert A. Deane, *The Political and Social Ideas of St. Augustine* (New York, 1963), and, to a lesser degree, Figgis.

[7] Charles Howard McIlwain, *The Growth of Political Thought in the West* (New York, 1932), pp. 154–160; J. Straub, "Augustins Sorge um die regeneratio imperii," *Historisches Jahrbuch*, LXXIII (1953), 36–60.

What I want to focus upon here is the way Augustine the philosopher and bishop and theologian relates himself to the rough and tumble of political life. This will involve us in what is perhaps the chief systematic problem that arises from the work, how the opposing cities of God and of the devil are embodied in the pilgrim Church and the empirical state, and what orientation can be given to political life.

It is obvious that the two cities spring from contrary loves and have diverse destinies. The one city is "heavenly," the city of the angels who contemplate the face of God and the destination of the saints on earth; the other city is "earthly," belonging to the realm into which the evil angels were thrown and in which men satisfy themselves with earthly values or allow themselves to be deluded by false ways of salvation. And Augustine thinks that the history of the human race is dominated in general by the fallen angels; the only significant exception—significant because embodied in communal forms and not left to isolated individual lives—is found in an anticipatory way in Israel (as an earthly nation, but symbolic of the heavenly City) and in a fully explicit way in the Church (still engaged, however, in pilgrimage toward the goal).

How the political order fits into this broader pattern becomes clear toward the end of book XIX. Here, as once before in book II (chapter 21), Augustine examines Cicero's definition of a republic as a commonwealth, an assemblage united by a community of interest and a common acknowledgment of the right. Cicero had already used this definition to show that many societies are not proper polities at all, for there is no such common loyalty, no such justice (*De re publica*, III, 31). Augustine argues that *no* societies, not even that of the Romans, can satisfy that definition, partly because an empirical survey indicates that they have not acted in accord with what anyone would call justice, but in the last analysis because true justice or rectitude consists chiefly in giving God his due; according to this standard it is only the people of God, now spread among all the nations, that can be called a true people (*De civ. Dei*, XIX, 23, fin.). But Augustine has ready at hand an alternative definition of a republic (and since it appears, quite casually, as early as *Ep.* 138, 2, 10, written in 412, it may be that it was not worked out by Augustine himself in the light of the difficulties he found with Cicero's definition, but was drawn from another writer, perhaps Varro): a people, a city, a republic, is quite simply an assemblage bound together by *concordia*, by agreement in the things they will love (XIX, 24). *What* they happen to love remains a variable.

The practical political question is, then, What is the range of that variable? At one end, clearly enough, it can include the values of rubber bands and military dictatorships. At the other end it could conceivably reach as far as to make Augustine a clericalist, one who supposes that the Church can enable the state to become a true state for the first time.[8] In one passage (II, 19) he does concede that, *if* all the rulers and all the peoples were to become Christians and heed the precepts of the Christian religion, earthly society could become felicitious. But he knows very well that many men do not listen and are drawn instead toward vice. Both there and in book XIX he clearly states that true peace and justice are enjoyed by the Church only through faith and hope; the *only* true society or commonwealth is the City of God in the heavens (II, 19; XIX, 20 and 27).

Thus Augustine's expectations for political life were not high, partly out of despair over the likely course of human events, partly because of the more vivid attraction of another goal, the heavenly City. To him earthly tasks could not have ultimate significance, for it was not easy to see how the building of the earthly city could make much difference to the final outcome. As he looked at human affairs Augustine was overcome by a sense of fleetingness and mortality. The dead are succeeded by the dying (V, 14). And instead of feeling exhilaration at the possibility of having some influence upon the course of events long after his own death he thought that *homo moriturus*, man fated to die, should not be overly concerned about the régime under which he lives as long as he is not required to act in an immoral or impious way (V, 17).

Such a vision of human life, however shortsighted it may be, delivered him from the fanaticism that will undertake anything for the sake of a desired goal. His discussions of war are pervaded by a disconsolate awareness of its miseries and a bitter contempt

[8] The most forceful modern argument in favor of this interpretation is by McIlwain.

for those who think it noble and glorious: "Tear off the disguise of wild delusion and look at the naked deeds; weigh them naked, judge them naked" (IV, 14). Under such scrutiny the achievements of the Roman Empire do not stand up well, and through the centuries readers of *The City of God* have been held fascinated by his provocative language: empires, if they lack justice, are nothing but robber bands, *latrocinia*, and the former differ from the latter not through the avoidance of cupidity but through the addition of impunity (IV, 4); the Romans may boast about the expansion of their Empire, but a sober evaluation indicates that it was achieved at too great a cost and has accomplished little good (V, 17); it would have been better if the multiplicity of peoples had been left alone to pursue their own ways of life in freedom (IV, 15).

This is what has been called, quite appropriately, Augustine's political realism, by which is meant a refusal to hold illusions about the nature of political life, a willingness, on the one hand, to make use of the methods that are effective in the real world, but at the same time an exercise of restraint growing out of a sense of the limitations of the political process. Involved with it is a non-utopian, non-eschatological conception of human history, a readiness to accept what already is, to take what comes, and not to be surprised if there are disappointments.[9]

And such an attitude does characterize at least a good part of Augustine's responses. To be sure, we should not be too facile about this. Earlier in his life as a Christian he was attracted by the heroic lives of the apostles and martyrs, disobedient both to sacred traditions and to civil authority, and he wrote that laws should be obeyed only if they are in accord with eternal law (*De lib. arb.*, I, 6, 15; *De ver. rel.*, 31, 58). But these are theoretical utterances. In his own life Augustine seems always to have been nothing else than an obedient citizen, and in his activities as a bishop he never opposed Imperial policies but, if anything, shifted his own attitudes to accommodate to them.[10]

[9] A good case for this view of Augustine is made, though finally I think it is overdrawn, in Deane, *The Political and Social Ideas of St. Augustine*, especially pp. 66, 117–118, 137–138, 219–220.

[10] For the details of his changing views on the policy to be taken toward the Donatists, see Combès, pp. 352–409, and Deane, chapter 6.

It is true that Augustine had good theological reasons for his political realism. Doctrinally, Donatism and Pelagianism posed much the same challenge. In both cases what we have is an earnest perfectionism calling for purity in the Church and in individual lives, pointing to corruption in the ruling classes, and exhorting men to live according to the law of Christ in all their affairs. Certainly they did not live up to their own profession. But Augustine's objection to them was not only that they were hypocritical or deluded about themselves. It was that no man can lead a perfect life, however sincerely he tries.

But from the *social* point of view both Donatism and Pelagianism, in their different ways, represent an attempt to hold on to the Church of the earlier centuries, a Church which did not countenance compromise with the spirit of the age and which anticipated with equanimity remaining in the position of a minority. And in both cases Augustine's support was thrown on the side of toleration for human shortcomings, not so much in private morality (for the Church of his day had stern disciplinary standards) as in a broader structural way; by resisting too close a scrutiny of the actions of the Church and the Empire and the implications of their mutual involvement, Augustine helped open the way to the absorption of semi-pagans, among both the aristocracy and the populace, into the Church and an easy alliance of throne and altar.[11] Augustine's behavior in both cases demands a careful examination.

Probably it does disclose a tragic flaw in his personality, for unlike Ambrose he was not prepared to stand up against civil authority. There is a problem here, and if it has been faced at no other time it must be faced today, when our knowledge of human motivations makes it possible and our awareness of political problems makes it necessary. The anguished reactions of humane spirits to Augustine's political behavior are probably more to be trusted than the indifference or defensiveness of ecclesiasts. The failings of the man are not trivial, for the legislation he supported, and the arguments he put forward, which

---

[11] See especially John Morris, "Pelagian Literature," *Journal of Theological Studies*, n.s. XVI (1965), 26–60, and Peter Brown, "Pelagius and His Supporters: Aims and Environment," *Journal of Theological Studies*, n.s. XIX (1968), 112–114.

continued to be honored long after the legislation had lapsed, have had an enormous effect on the history of the West. If they do express a limited style of life, then they lose that much more of their hold.

A certain submissiveness, perhaps even cowardice in political matters is one side of Augustine. And yet it should not be enlarged out of proportion. He was not ready to acquiesce unreservedly in the unpleasant realities of political life. Part of his legacy is an insistence that force be used by civil authority according to norms of justice. And though he could see no final value in political life and was dismayed at the mutability and the sinfulness permeating it, he was able to think at a *proximate* level about the positive aspects of the justice and peace achieved in the political order. He could do it because there is a fruitful *ambiguity* about political life and the political virtues.

What is crucial to the proper understanding of his political attitudes is his theory that the ordinary virtues, the inclinations and skills men display in dealing with earthly affairs, are finally dominated by the ultimate value to which they are "referred," the horizon within which all is desired, the fundamental motivation and commitment of the will. Therefore they can be judged under two aspects, one ultimate and one merely proximate. Augustine thinks of the civic virtues as authentic shadows or offprints of true virtue (esp. *Ad Simpl.*, I, q. 2, 16); through them men are led to acts of great moral heroism, and their fruit is civic harmony. Because of these virtues Rome became great, and it happened through divine providence, for it is proper that earthly virtue be rewarded with earthly gain. But that is all. In earthly success they have their reward. Civic virtue is not a sufficient ground for eternal salvation; indeed, its chief motivation, a desire for glory, runs counter to the true virtue which wills everything out of love for God, the true *pietas* which is the foundation of genuine order (*Ep.* 138, 3, 16–17; *De civ. Dei*, V, 14–21; XIX, 25).

Therefore the Church, which is allegorically Jerusalem ("vision of peace," the city that still looks toward Zion, the full "contemplation" of God), is in exile within the earthly kingdom, allegorically Babylon (which means "confusion"). But the policy she follows in her life under exile—worth noting afresh in our own day, with its new Diaspora of the Church—is the one outlined by the prophet Jeremiah (chapter 29): to build homes and dwell in them, to plant gardens and eat their produce, to marry and have sons and daughters, and to seek the welfare of the earthly city, for Jerusalem also shares in its peace even though it is a mere earthly peace.[12] And what Augustine had in mind was not a mere acquiescence in the necessities of sinful humanity. He thought of political life as a *good*—indeed, perhaps the greatest of temporal values, since it seeks to establish conditions of earthly peace based on earthly harmony and justice; the pilgrims toward the eternal City ought therefore to share in its earthly peace and contribute to it (*De civ. Dei*, XV, 4; XIX, 17 and 26).

Just how far was Augustine prepared to carry that cooperation with the life of the earthly city despite his expectation that it would never lead to a complete transformation of its life? If we wish to see his spontaneous answer to that question—not before but after the disillusioning events of 410—we will find it in his letter to Marcellinus (*Ep.* 138), written in 412, which contains *in nuce* the argument of *The City of God*.

When Augustine learned of the fear of people like Volusianus that the Christian ethic was incompatible with the needs of political life, his first impulse was to argue that it *does* have historical viability. If turning the other cheek is politically naïve, he argues, then the men under whom Rome became great were similarly naïve, for he can quote Sallust to the effect that they would rather overlook an injury than punish the offender, and Cicero to the effect that they forgot the wrongs done to them. If these things are praised as a record and a recommendation of political virtue when they are read in the Roman authors, it shows that Christianity, if it were really heeded, could strengthen the commonwealth even more. For what holds every society together is a harmony of interests, and this can be accomplished better under monotheism than under polytheism, better through love than through selfishness. Augustine thinks that such harmony can be achieved in two ways, working together. The Christian ethos may function in a purely private way, through

---

[12] *De cat. rud.*, 19, 31–21, 38; sermons on the Psalms of Ascent, and also on Psalms 64, 136, and 138; and *De civ. Dei*, XIX, 26 (cf. Lauras and Rondet, "Le thème des deux cités," pp. 115ff.).

patience and forgiveness, demonstrating how temporal things ought to be valued less than eternal. It may also function publicly, for the magistrate has the obligation of correcting men for their own welfare, establishing peace, removing opportunities for self-seeking and violence, and fostering the conditions most suitable for virtue, deeds of mercy, and the sharing of goods with the poor (*Ep.* 138, 2, 9–15).

Thus Augustine thinks that the historical viability of the Christian ethos has already been proved, in part by the civic virtues of the old Romans of the Republic, but chiefly by the spread of Christianity throughout the world and the political success given to those emperors who were the champions of orthodox Christianity, Constantine and Theodosius (*De civ. Dei*, V, 25–26). One of the most neglected aspects of Augustine's political thought (partly because it is usually construed in a narrowly ecclesiastical way, partly because the most important texts lie outside *The City of God*) is his belief that in the Christian era prophecy was still being fulfilled. To those who might think that the history of salvation ended with Christ and that nothing of significance can happen afterward, he would answer that much has happened and perhaps still more is yet to happen. This is especially strong in the little work *On Faith in Things Not Seen*, probably written about 400, in which, following a discussion of the nature of belief, he suggests that many *indicia*, many evidences in confirmation of belief, are to be found in the life of the Church. At the time of the prophets none of the things they foretold had come to pass; then some of them were fulfilled in Christ, others in the Church, and others are still to come (3, 5—7, 10). In the spread of the Church throughout the world he sees the only adequate fulfillment of the promise to Abraham (Genesis 15, 5) that his descendants would be as numerous as the stars in the sky and the only adequate realization of Christ's worldwide rule. In the adherence of rulers to the Church, and in Theodosius' decree against idols, he again sees the fulfillment of numerous visions in the prophets of the ideal future in which the nations would acknowledge the God of Israel and idolatry would be cast down. And he points out (*C. litt. Petil.*, II, 42, 210–213; *In Joann. ev.*, tr. 11, 14) that rulers have a unique ability to serve God, for only they have the power to remove idols and forbid blasphemy. (The political justice of this is beyond question to him, for he views pagan religion as both irrational and morally unhealthy[13]; when it is consumed in the flame of a true sacrifice of love for God, it is a sign of the spiritual maturing of the race.)

Now passages like these could be used for nothing more than a justification of an all too familiar clericalism and triumphalism. And it is true that Augustine was encouraged by the many signs of Christianity's political success and thought it a good thing. But he obviously saw it as more than the triumph of a humdrum institutionalism. His rationale is worth noting, even though he may have misused it to give ideological support to oppressive and shortsighted policies; for in the spread of Christianity and its influence on the governing powers he felt the tremor of a fulfillment long hoped for and still in the making. And though this fulfillment belongs to the time of the Church and is focused in the Church, its *importance* can be assessed properly only when one looks to the hopes that were projected long before the Church and whose scope extends well beyond the confines of the Church alone. What Augustine had in mind is not millenarianism, which he rejected after adhering to it briefly during his early years in Hippo, nor a theocratic dominance of Church over society; he anticipated not a perfect triumph over the kingdoms of this world but an altogether believable influence upon them, probably fluctuating as rulers and peoples come and go, and in it all he could still see a fulfillment of the prophets' hopes for the improvement of the conditions of life on earth.[14]

It may well be that this was an interpretation of the time of the Church and of its influence upon political life that Augustine held for only a brief period of optimism between, say, 400 and 410, when his expectations were sobered and he saw ill fortune as a real possibility for the Christian world. But however diminished his hopes may have become, all of this remained, nonetheless, a part of the framework of his understanding of the time of the Church. In *The City of God*, books XVII and XVIII, he discusses a number of Old Testament prophecies of an age of righteousness

[13] See Combès, pp. 332–345.

[14] For the contrast between Augustine and more sanguine writers like Eusebius, see Theodor E. Mommsen, "St. Augustine and the Christian Idea of Progress: The Background of *The City of God*," *Journal of the History of Ideas*, XII (1951), 346–374. The points of similarity are by and large ignored.

and prosperity. Many of them are applied to Christ, and many to the eternal City; but some are applied to the time of the Church, and Augustine seems still to believe that the Church not only can cooperate with the kingdoms of this world (for that is simply the result of their bearing some vestiges of justice) but can make an impact for the better upon their life.

What we emerge with after an examination of Augustine's own political principles is probably neither a policy of maintaining an ecclesiastical domination of society (for this ignores the tension between what the Church strives to be and what can be realized within the political order), nor a mere acquiescence in the "realities" of political life (for this will be either too despairing or too cynical), but the counsel that the Church pursue her own way of life in faithfulness to her own calling, sometimes making common cause with others who have a sense for secular justice, sometimes bringing the demanding criteria of the City of God to bear upon the social order in rebuke for the compromises that are often accepted as a matter of course. It is misleading to read the story of the two cities as a parabola connected to eternity at both ends, in their origins and their diverse destinies, but suspended in another environment, that of the purely relative and proximate, throughout their historical course. Augustine wanted to introduce an element of ultimacy into earthly life itself, to show men that, for all its complexities and all its changing fortunes, it is permeated with motivations whose import even now is spiritual life or death; and though the question of strategy was a difficult one for him as for us, he wanted to argue that the Christian ethos, formed as it is by eternity, does have a viability in earthly affairs, demonstrated sometimes by its faithful testimony in the face of opposition and—who can tell?—sometimes by its success in influencing the shape of events.

2. MAN'S BONDAGE AND LIBERATION

The most famous controversy in Augustine's career as a theologian, and the one through which he had a direct influence upon the development of Christian doctrine, was that carried on with Pelagius and kindred spirits between 411 and his death in

430, when he was still at work on a refutation of the latest writings of Julian of Eclanum.[15]

But increasingly it appears that Pelagius was not the father of the movement that came to bear his name. Marius Mercator, one of the earliest historians of the movement, said that its source was Rufinus the Syrian, who came to Rome at the time of Anastasius and from whom Pelagius then got his ideas; and according to the minutes of the local council held in Carthage in 411 (reported by Augustine in *De pecc. orig.*, II, 3, 3) Caelestius said he had heard the transmission of sin denied by the holy presbyter Rufinus, who stayed with Pammachius in Rome. Since Pammachius was a friend of Jerome's, it is possible that the man in question was the same Rufinus who was a member of Jerome's monastery in Bethlehem and was sent to Milan and Rome in 399 to represent his case against the Origenists. A *Libellus de fide*, an extensive statement of the Christian faith addressed to an unnamed bishop of Rome, survives under the name of Rufinus. It manifests a concern to oppose the errors of "the wicked Origen" and has a long refutation of the Arians, utilizing arguments from Gregory Nazianzen's third and fifth theological orations. Most important for our purposes, it attacks those who teach the transmission of sin and the damnation of infants, and asserts that the baptism of infants is not for the remission of sin but to confer on them participation in the kingdom of God. It has often been thought that the work must have been written in opposition to Augustine, on the theory that he was the first person to teach original sin in any explicit way; but Refoulé has demonstrated that Augustine's very first attack on the "Pelagian" heresy, the first thirty-four chapters of the first book of *On the Merits and the Remission of Sins*, consists of a refutation of the *Libellus de fide* of Rufinus the Syrian. It would seem, then, that

[15] On Pelagius and the course of the controversy see Benjamin B. Warfield, "Augustine and the Pelagian Controversy," printed as an introductory essay in the American edition of the *Select Library of Nicene and Post-Nicene Fathers* (1887) and reprinted in *Studies in Tertullian and Augustine* (New York, 1930), pp. 289–412; Friedrich Loofs, "Pelagius und der pelagianische Streit," *Realencyclopädie für protestantische Theologie und Kirche*, 3. Aufl., XV, 747–774; Georges de Plinval, *Pélage. Ses écrits, sa vie et sa réforme. Étude d'histoire littéraire et religieuse* (Lausanne, 1943); *Essai sur la style et la langue de Pélage* (Fribourg en Suisse, 1947); Robert F. Evans, *Pelagius: Inquiries and Reappraisals* (New York, 1968).

original sin and the baptism of infants for its remission were older and more widespread ideas than they appear at first glance, and Rufinus and Pelagius and their followers were trying to defend what they believed to be the authentic Catholic teaching against what appeared to them a dangerous trend in certain circles of the Church.[16] Probably the germ of the controversy was the now undisputed fact that differing explanations of infant baptism were held in the East and in the West.

Pelagius and some of his followers were among the refugees who fled from the Goths and sailed to Africa, but Pelagius himself soon went on to Palestine and was not personally the center of the controversy for some time. Caelestius was the one who triggered the crisis when he applied for ordination as a presbyter. He refused to withdraw six theses which collided with the traditions of the African Church; the theses were condemned by the local clergy of Carthage, and Caelestius was excommunicated as a heretic. And when he went to Rome, he was condemned there as well.

The theses in question were (1) that Adam was mortal and would have died whether he sinned or did not sin, (2) that Adam's sin affected only himself, not the human race, (3) that the law leads men to the kingdom of heaven as much as the gospel, (4) that there were sinless men even before the advent of the Lord, (5) that infants are born in the same state as that of Adam before his sin, and (6) that Adam's sin and death do not cause all men to die any more than the resurrection of Christ causes all men to rise (*De gest. Pel.*, 11, 23; *De pecc. orig.*, 11, 12). Now this is *not* Pelagius' view of the matter, nor Rufinus'. They did not think that Adam would have died a natural death even without sinning, or that infants are born in the same state as Adam prior to his sin. They thought that the sin of Adam was the cause of death as it is now experienced, though they did not think that sin or guilt is transmitted along with death. And Augustine was always aware of the differences among the various spokesmen for the movement. He knew that Pelagius, when accused of heresy in Palestine

[16] For a careful analysis of the *Libellus de fide* and a discussion of its authorship, see Berthold Altaner, "Der Liber de fide, ein Werk des Pelagianers Rufinus des 'Syrers,'" *KpS*, 467–482; for its date, F. Refoulé, "La datation du premier concile de Carthage contre les Pélagiens et du *Libellus fidei* de Rufin," *REA*, XI (1963), 41–49.

in 415, denounced the statements read out from the Carthaginian proceedings and from Caelestius' apologia. But his opinion was that Caelestius was only stating openly what Pelagius had kept concealed (*De pecc. orig.*, II, 6, 6), and a major portion of his polemic against Pelagius is designed to prove that Pelagius falls under the same condemnation as Caelestius and that he had escaped it only through duplicity (this is the argument of *On the Deeds of Pelagius* and *On the Grace of Christ and Original Sin*).

But *was* Caelestius in fact a faithful disciple of Pelagius, or of Rufinus, who took their views to the logical conclusion? There is much to indicate that the movement was more diffuse, a confluence of varying ideas and concerns, not always consistent with each other. A study of the literature of the movement seems to indicate, for example, that one body of writings often thought to have come from Pelagius is the work of a man who had arrived recently from Britain, was fired with enthusiasm for this earnest type of Christianity while in Rome, and then fled, perhaps in company with Caelestius, to Sicily, where the extant writings were produced.[17] In 414 Augustine corresponded with a man in Sicily who reported that some Christians there were teaching doctrines similar to those of Caelestius and inferring from them what we would call a "sectarian" view of the Church—that a rich man must sell all that he has in order to enter the kingdom, that no oaths ought to be taken, and that the Church ought to be without spot or blemish in the world (*Epp.* 156–157).[18]

Despite the complexity of the affair, and despite his rather tentative approach to it at the beginning, not knowing that it was to develop into a major dogmatic dispute, Augustine was never disposed to treat it subtly. To him Pelagius and Rufinus were as great a danger as Caelestius. Though they could make a more plausible case to be teaching Christian doctrine, they still excluded all the points that Augustine had come through the years to think essential, and with sure reflexes he reacted against them.

Augustine might well have been more patient, for the points under dispute had often taken him years to resolve. He himself

---

[17] Morris, "Pelagian Literature," pp. 41–43.
[18] See Morris's sensitive analysis of the social protest of the writer and his gifts as a satirist (*ibid.*, pp. 45–51).

had once dismissed the problem of infant baptism with an almost mocking gesture of despair (*De quan. an.*, 36, 80), and then had decided that all infants, baptized or not, share the same middle state (*De lib. arb.*, III, 23, 66); he had supposed in his earlier years as a Christian that it was at least possible for a man to live with perfect virtue and happiness; he had been willing to entertain theories of the origin of sin in individual lives quite at variance with the doctrine of transmitted sin, and though in 412 he could assert that it had always been held by the Church and by all churchly writers (*De pecc.*, III, 5, 10—6, 12), he himself had arrived at that conviction only a few years before, in 406; he, like Pelagius, had felt the influence of Ambrosiaster's interpretation of Paul, which saw man as capable of discovering his need, seeking divine aid, and deciding for it when it was offered, and Pelagius could quote tellingly against the later Augustine the Augustine of *On Free Will*. But instead of patiently explaining the course of his own discoveries, he took it to be a matter for confrontation and attack at the doctrinal level. Occasionally he did assume the posture of reasoning together, and such passages are the most tranquil and lucid to later readers. But he exhibited a conviction and a passion about the affair from the first. He claimed to be responding in a fraternal spirit, avoiding the mention of names in order to spare their feelings and make it a matter of issues rather than personalities; but he announced at the same time that he would not spare their written statements, hoping that they would be brought around by the force of argument and by fear of condemnation before it became necessary to proceed formally against them (*De nat. et gr.*, 7, 7; *De gest. Pel.*, 22, 46—23, 47).

The vigor of his reaction might be explained in personal terms. Perhaps Augustine saw in Caelestius and Pelagius his own earlier self which he had now outgrown and toward which, having the wisdom of hindsight, he could feel by turns resentful and scornful. That is a hypothesis to be explored by every means at our disposal. But we should also consider an alternative possibility. Perhaps Augustine knew from the start that Caelestius and Pelagius were of a different spirit; that he had never been a "Pelagian," despite the similarity among the statements made, because he had always taken the human predicament seriously—the gap between its aspirations and its reality, the delightful allure of earthly beauty and the powerful hold of custom and affection, the pulling of the will in many directions at once by the multiplicity of values pouring in upon man—and to him the teachings of the Pelagians seemed flat, ignorant of the complexities of the human heart, "moralistic" in the pejorative sense.

Too often the difference between the teachings of the Pelagians and those of even the mature Augustine is miscalculated. When one really sets to work outlining the two positions it becomes apparent at how many points they are similar, at least at the propositional level: they want to affirm the capacity of man to respond to God, the demand of total obedience, the power of custom in holding man back, the pivotal role of the gospel and of other inducements presented to the mind, the freedom of man's response to them, the role of divine aid in sustaining devotion. The conflict does not really concern any of these points about the mechanics of the relation between free will and grace. Augustine is not any less concerned than Pelagius to give a role to the human will throughout the process, and Pelagius knows just as well as Augustine that the Pauline epistles make grace the crucial factor through it all. And yet it is obvious that at every point they understand these things in opposing ways.

As soon as Augustine read the profession of faith of Rufinus the Syrian, and learned of the condemnation of Caelestius in Carthage, and looked up Pelagius' expositions of Paul, he knew how much he disagreed with them. They were suggesting that sin is transmitted from Adam not by propagation but by imitation; Augustine reaffirmed the doctrine of original sin and the corollary that it is sufficient by itself, without any personal sins, for the damnation of infants, though with the mildest penalties. They were concerned to safeguard man's freedom to obey what God commands; Augustine agreed that man is responsible for his own acts, but pointed out that narrow desires and anxieties may prevent the full exertion of the will that is needed to do the good (*De pecc.*, II, 3, 3). They assumed that salvation and damnation are based upon man's free decision; Augustine, though he agreed that God does not work salvation in man as though he were a stone or an animal devoid of reason and will (*De pecc.*, II, 5, 6), saw in the fact that one infant is baptized and another is not, that one man turns to God and another does not—and often in marked contrast to all that one might predict on the basis of virtue or native ability—a manifestation of the mysterious counsel of God in predestination, giving grace freely and without regard to human merits (*De pecc.*, I, 21, 29—22, 32). They seemed to be implying that man can become righteous, or at least progress steadily, by his own powers; Augustine, though he thought as before that the decisive factor in the conversion of the will is the presentation of attractive new possibilities which appeal to man's freedom and draw it forth, was convinced that the will to do good could be carried into execution only with the aid of the Holy Spirit. Thus at every point he found these men opposing the teachings of Scripture and the traditions of the Church, and whatever their intentions may have been, he reacted to them as to heretics and innovators.

But this did not prevent his engaging in a more dispassionate analysis of the problems they had raised, more as a theologian than as a defender of the faith, stepping back to formulate the questions at issue and to think them through in a connected way. Perhaps the most constructive aspect of the Pelagian controversy is that Augustine steadily clarified his own views and transmitted to later generations, together with his harangues against the opponents of grace, a series of detailed analyses of the problem of grace and free will, not always systematically coherent but capable of stimulating later theologians to continue his work.

There is a remarkable continuity in his sense of the problem. Later on he would state the three points of controversy as (1) original sin, (2) the gratuity of grace, its being given without regard to merits, and (3) the *de facto* universality of sin among men, including the regenerate (*C. duas ep. Pel.*, III, 8, 24 and IV, 2, 2; *De don. pers.*, 2, 4). Similar questions are already raised in the earliest treatise against Rufinus and Caelestius, in the second book of *On the Merits and Remission of Sins* (I list them in the order of inquiry): whether it is possible for a man to be without sin during the present life, and whether there actually have been men living without sin; whether it is possible for any man, except Christ, to be without sin from the beginning of his life; and why it is that men sin and, correlatively, why it is that some men do turn toward God.

At first Augustine was willing to affirm, with the Pelagians, that it is at least *possible* for a man to live without sin, given free will, which is commanded to obey God, and grace, which can bring forth a good exercise of the will. And he was ready to acknowledge that some sections of Scripture might be read as asserting that there had been men who led sinless lives, as long as this is credited to God (*De spir. et litt.*, 2, 3; 36, 66). But his own judgment was that all men have sinned, and continue to sin even after being reborn. Here he was able to build on convictions long since arrived at, for he knew from his reading of Paul that there is an ongoing warfare within man's life, and he had already faced, in the First Epistle of John, the apparent conflict between the assertion, "He who is born of God does not sin" (I John 3, 9) and the other assertion, "If we say we have no sin we are liars" (I John 1, 8), applying the former to the central orientation of love, the latter to the lesser sins which are effaced by love (*In Joann. ep.*, tr. 5, 1–7). He could now affirm, very much in continuity with what he had said earlier, that the saints are praiseworthy not because of sinlessness but because of their continuing awareness of their sin and their striving, in hope, for a perfection that will become a reality only after death (*De pecc.*, II, 13, 20—16, 24; *De spir. et litt.*, 36, 65).

But whatever the answer to the question whether men might attain to perfect righteousness *at some time* during their life on earth, he denied that they could lead a perfect life *from birth*. It would have been possible if Adam had not sinned, for his mind would have been given perfect stability and all the functions of soul and body would have been subordinated to its direction (*De pecc.*, I, 16, 21; II, 22, 36). But sin disrupts this harmony, and its effects are transmitted through generation; concupiscence —insubordinate, disorderly desire—remains even in the righteous and is transmitted to their children, and though its guilt is removed in baptism, it continues to tempt men throughout their earthly life.

When it comes to the question why men sin, and why some men then turn toward God, Augustine recognizes, on the one hand, that it would be difficult to explain the fact of sin if God were the author of all men's acts, and, on the other, that it would be difficult to explain the fact of obedience if God merely created the will and from that point on everything were from man

himself (*De pecc. mer.*, II, 18, 28–30; *De spir. et litt.*, 33, 57–59).
He puts both explanations together, then: the finite will is the
source of sin, God is the source of the good act. The will itself
is a *media vis* (*De spir. et litt.*, 33, 59), one of those "natural
goods" which can be used either for good or for evil (*De pecc.
mer.*, II, 18, 30; cf. *De lib. arb.*, II, 18, 47—20, 54), though this
does not mean that it can remain in the middle, for it becomes
either good or evil when it issues forth in decision. Its exercise
for evil is the result of either ignorance of what is good or a
failure to take delight in the good even when it is known (*De
pecc. mer.*, II, 17, 26); the corresponding effects of grace are the
instructing of the mind with "certain knowledge" and the
strengthening of the will with a "victorious delight" (*victrix
delectatio*) in the good (*De pecc. mer.*, II, 19, 32). By the latter
Augustine means the infusing of love by the Holy Spirit, so that
the more intensely God is loved the more reliably man will take
delight in doing the good (*De pecc. mer.*, II, 17, 27). Thus the
good act is from God, and Augustine can quote, as he did earlier
in the second reply to Simplicianus, Paul's rhetorical question,
"What do you have that you did not receive?" (I Corinthians 4, 7).

Augustine does not intend to deny the freedom of the will at
any point in the process. "Grace does not nullify free will," he
says, "but rather establishes it, and the law is not fulfilled unless
it is freely willed." But the way is a more complex one than the
facile exhortations of Pelagius imply. Augustine furnishes a
"catena" drawn from Scripture:

Through the law comes knowledge of sin;
through faith comes a seeking of grace to oppose sin;
through grace comes the recuperation of the soul from the disease of
    sin;
through the health of the soul comes freedom of the will;
through freedom of the will comes love of righteousness;
through love of righteousness comes the fulfillment of the law
    (*De spir. et litt.*, 30, 52).

The point that is omitted early in this catena—the rise of faith,
which is the critical transition in the whole process—is explained
later, in a passage once more reminiscent of the reply to Simplicianus:

The act of willing by which we believe is to be credited to a divine gift, not only because it arises from the free will which was created with our nature, but also because God acts upon us, in order that we might will and believe, by the suasions of the things we perceive—either outwardly, by the exhortations of the gospel, where even the commands of the law accomplish something if they so warn man of his infirmity that he seeks the grace that justifies through faith; or inwardly, where no one has control over what shall come into his mind. But consenting or not consenting to these suasions is the act of the will itself. Since God acts with the rational soul in these ways in order that it might believe (for it would not even be able to believe anything with its free will if there were no suasion or call which it could believe), it follows that God effects even the will to believe, and in all things his mercy goes before us, though the consenting or not consenting to the call of God, as I said before, is still the act of man's own will. This does not invalidate the saying, "What do you have that you did not receive?" (I Cor. 4, 7) but confirms it, for the soul cannot receive and possess the gifts mentioned there except by consenting. Thus *that which* it is to receive and possess is from God; but the *receiving* and *possessing* is the act of the one who receives and possesses (*De spir. et litt.*, 34, 60).

He does not mean to suggest that man's consenting or not consenting to the divine call is determined by his own decision. Clearly he holds to predestination at this period as much as he did at an earlier time and as much as he will in the later controversies with the Pelagians, and he doubtless assumes what he asserted earlier, that those who are predestined are called "efficaciously," in a way that is "congruent" with their condition. Therefore when he says that the consenting or not consenting is man's own, he cannot mean that man himself decides the issue with what the scholastics would call "freedom of exercise," the freedom to act or not to act, for the act of the will is evoked by the persuasive quality of the call, and this is something that does not lie within man's power. He means rather that the response, or the lack of responsiveness, is still irreducibly man's own. The human mind and its affections are open, to be sure, to realities and values beyond itself, and it is not always in a posture of indifference toward them; but however strongly the mind is drawn toward something, or however hesitant it may be, still the resulting act comes from within the mind itself. The mind is not a mere function of stimuli coming from beyond itself; its responsiveness is internal to itself, and the character of its responsiveness is affected from within, whether by the conservative power of custom or by the converting power of delight in new values to be sought.

All of this, developed in *On the Merits and Forgiveness of Sins* and *On the Spirit and the Letter*, represents Augustine's first, almost spontaneous reaction to a quarrel that had taken place in Carthage and in which he had not been directly involved. What he said at this time came almost entirely from his own resources; very little new reflection was needed. And it all seemed to be only an episode, a momentary disturbance. Augustine went on to other problems; though he kept attacking the Pelagians in sermons and letters, he was occupied with other matters. During the next few years (between 412 and 415) he finished the last books of the Genesis commentary, recast and expanded his work on the Trinity, and delivered his mature judgment on the politics, religion, and philosophy of the classical world in the first ten books of *The City of God*.

The controversy might have passed into oblivion if Pelagius himself had not reopened it with a treatise *On Nature*, seemingly directed against some points Augustine had made. Pelagius was ready to bracket the factual question whether men have actually led sinless lives, for he recognized that this is open to dispute, and wished to focus attention instead upon the more philosophical question whether men *can* lead sinless lives (*De nat. et gr.*, 7, 8). And of course his answer was affirmative. He was willing to concede that this ability may be qualified by the addition, "by the grace of God" (10, 11). But by grace he seemed to mean nothing more than the creation of man's natural powers, and the giving of the law, and the forgiveness of sins. He did not think of grace as a liberation of the will from bondage or an aiding of the will to accomplish what it could not otherwise accomplish; Pelagius assumed that in all men the capability to lead a sinless life (*posse non peccare*) remains what it was in Adam, for it belongs to human nature and cannot be lost.

It was in debate with Pelagius—first with his treatise *On Nature*, then with a treatise *For the Freedom of the Will*—that Augustine's thought began to develop further. In defending his own position Augustine was forced to reflect extensively upon the meaning of the crucial term "nature" which Pelagius had injected into the discussion (and it is apparent that the problem of "nature" was understood on both sides as a problem of man's *posse*, his usable active powers, as Augustine states repeatedly [*De nat. et gr.*, 45, 53—51, 59]).[19] Pelagius had taken a position which seemed at first glance to be entirely credible: human nature remains the same, and *posse non peccare* is part of the equipment which belongs to man by the necessity of nature and cannot be lost; although the exercise of this *posse* depends upon free decision and thus may never come about, the *posse* will issue into action whenever man chooses. Pelagius had set up a neat distinction, then, between the *necessity of nature*, which always includes an ability to act, and *willing*, which is always exercised freely and is then brought to effective completion in doing what is willed.

Augustine replied by citing facts from experience which destroy that distinction as a credible philosophical position. On the one hand there is an aspect of "necessity" even within the free activity of the will, for whatever we will, it must in every case be willed for the sake of some value; on the other hand what the will commands is not always carried into effect, for the activities of a finite agent are conditioned both by external circumstances and by internal modifications of its own being. With such widespread evidence in many other fields of human activity, there is no reason to deny the same thing when it comes to man's relation to God.

The question, then, is whether the possibility of leading a righteous life, free from sin, belongs inseparably and inamissibly to man's nature. To Pelagius it does. To Augustine it does not; on the contrary, man's nature is susceptible of a change for the worse: "nature can be perverted" (*De nat. et gr.*, 51, 59). But he recognizes that it is not enough merely to assert this on the basis of some Pauline texts or arguments from general experience; some account must be given of the way in which human nature can be changed for the worse. He acknowledges the force of Pelagius' query how sin, which is not substantial but accidental, could alter and weaken human nature, and he answers with an

---

[19] For a fuller discussion of this problem see François-Joseph Thonnard, "La notion de 'nature' chez saint Augustin. Ses progrès dans la polémique antipélagienne," *REA*, XI (1965), 239–265.

analogy: to refrain from eating food is accidental, but it affects the substance, for it is an abstention from something that is needed for the healthy functioning of the body, and the consequences can even be irreversible, weakening the body to such an extent that it is no longer able to take food. It will be noted that the understanding of finite beings here expressed is intensely relational, for while the distinction between substance and accident is acknowledged to be meaningful in all discourse about finite things, it is not interpreted as setting up a barrier between an unchanging "thing in itself" and merely external relations with other things. Through accidents, substance is related to substance. Substance is itself dependent upon other beings for sustenance and growth; and the relatedness is all the more intense in finite spirits, whose being is open to the entire field of reality and whose perfect fulfillment is to be found only in the knowledge and love of God (*De nat. et gr.*, 20, 22).

Because of the intrinsic mutability and relativity of finite spirit Augustine's use of the term "nature" acquires a certain complexity. At times it is used in such a way as to be equivalent with the category of substance, expressing the being and continuity and self-identity of the subject throughout all its changes of state, and this remains good despite the perverse orientations that are taken (*De nat. et gr.* 55, 65; *De civ. Dei*, XII, 3). But the term "nature" is also applied, with equal propriety, to the variety of concrete states in which the same substance (or, in the case of the human race, the same species) may find itself from time to time. Nature in this sense is not substance alone but concrete being, having specific possibilities for action which are already shaped by the posture it takes toward its wider situation. As soon as there is activity there is some definite mode of relation to other beings, which then has consequences for its own future possibilities of action. And yet the changes of state, however drastic and however lasting, remain "accidental," destroying nothing of the "substantial" being. Vice is "in" nature; it is not an "evil nature" (*De gr. Chr.*, 19, 20).

All of Augustine's discussion of the nature of an intelligent being, whether in the first or the second sense of the term, finally comes to a focus in volition, which is the controlling center of mental life. The problem of nature as it was debated during the

Pelagian controversy is the problem of *posse facere*, and this turns out to be, in the last analysis, nothing other than a problem of willing. Even the contrast between willing and doing, derived from several Pauline texts, is not between distinct faculties but between two dimensions of the life of the will. It is one thing to have the wish or the momentary intention to follow a course of action, but it is another thing to carry the intention into effect through wholehearted application of one's energies over a span of time. Thus even the problem of "nature," of *posse facere*, is a problem that must be understood from an existential perspective. The debility of sinful man, then, is a problem within the will, arising from the power of custom and affection in the case of personal sin, from the temptations of concupiscence in the case of original sin.

The fact that it is linked with free will does not make it any less a problem involving "nature"—and in both senses of the term—for Augustine is interested in the aspect of *necessity* that is found even within the free exercise of the will. He denies that freedom can ever have the complete arbitrariness ascribed to it by Pelagius. But he does not thereby make freedom an illusion. He is concerned only to point out certain constant traits of all willing. However malicious it may appear, willing is always for the sake of some *value*, though that value may be insignificant or inappropriate. And however foolish or disastrous his course of action may be, a man cannot will something which appears to him to be contrary to his own *happiness*, though his understanding of happiness may be shortsighted and influenced by the passions of the moment. These are constants that belong to the nature of willing wherever it is found. But constants, inevitabilities, necessities can arise through the free decision of the agent as well, especially when this decision involves a fundamental orientation either toward or away from God. To Augustine such a decision is so momentous that, by the nature of the case, it can be exercised only under certain conditions. It can be exercised by intelligent creatures in the freshness of their creation, but sinful humanity is not in a position to exercise it prior to the offer of redeeming grace.

It is to be noted that Augustine does not deny that an indeterminate *possibilitas utriusque partis*, as Pelagius had put it, a freedom for decision, is presupposed by the actual willing and doing of either good or evil. The question is whether this possibility endures. Pelagius had stated eloquently that the *possibilitas utriusque partis* is always present as a fertile root from which either flowers or weeds may issue forth, according to the choice of the man who is its gardener. The eloquence turns out to have been singularly unfortunate, however, for Augustine can retort that when the Lord speaks of fruit-bearing trees they are characterized as either good or evil, and when Paul speaks of roots which sprout forth he mentions only cupidity, the root of evil acts, and *caritas*, the root of good acts (*De gr. Chr.*, 18, 19). And this is not said on the spur of the moment, as a rhetorical trick; the contrast between *caritas* and *cupiditas* has been his accustomed way of speaking for many years (*De lib. arb.*, I, 4, 9–10; *De div. quaest.*, q. 35 and q. 36). He puts forward an alternative image: the root or source of action (or, to change the figure, the center of gravity of human life) is not to be sought in an indeterminate *possibilitas utriusque partis*, but in the fundamental orientation that is actually taken by each man, either *caritas* or *cupiditas*. The possibility of decision, around which the debate has revolved, is affirmed; but it is related not proximately but remotely to the actual behavior of men, with the fundamental orientation of the will intervening. In other words, the possibility of decision is not itself the root of action but is susceptible to being tipped toward one root or the other, *capax utriusque radicis* (*De gr. Chr.*, 20, 21).

In addition to the "necessity" intrinsic to the nature of all willing, then, there is also a further "necessity," a determination to a definite horizon of possibilities marked out by the fundamental orientation of the subject. Willing, wherever it is found, is freedom within a certain horizon of necessity; and the difference between true freedom and bondage is not that between arbitrariness and constraint, but that between responsiveness to authentic value and self-will. There is always free choice, says Augustine; but it is not always *good* choice: the horizon of choice may be marked out by an evil orientation, and then it is only what Paul calls freedom from righteousness; but if the horizon of choice is marked out by obedience, it is true freedom from sin (Romans 6, 20–22).

In this way Augustine is able to explain how the will can truly be in bondage because of concupiscence and long familiarity with sin, how, even though it is the sufficient cause of its own sin and bondage, it cannot return to righteousness without the entrance of another factor from beyond itself which will not only call forth the desire to do good but sustain its activity and prevent further sin (*De nat. et gr.*, 23, 35; 26, 29). The point that he is concerned to make is that it all takes place in accordance with the nature of man—even with the nature of man as a freely willing being. Augustine had been sure of these things through introspection; he knew the dynamics of the will from his own experience of vacillation and ineptitude, and it all fitted coherently with the philosophy he had learned from the Platonists and the biblical message. From the start of the controversy he had been able to recognize a contrary understanding of man and of salvation, and he moved against it with vigor. But the debate proved constructive even for Augustine. Because of it he was challenged to state his position more accurately, and in new ways; and some of the more thoughtful writings produced in the course of debate have repeatedly stimulated later thinkers to look more deeply into the dynamics of human life and the broad continuities that shape it.

The climax of the Pelagian controversy came in 417 and 418. At first it seemed that the Pelagians were on the way to being cleared by the new pope, Zosimus, of the charges made against them. But the Africans wrote to him saying that the case had been tried and the judgment given must remain in force. And in order to forestall any unfavorable ecclesiastical decision they also made use of their influence at the Imperial court. Augustine wrote his tract *On the Deeds of Pelagius* at this time, while the case was still in the balance, and in it he took special care to publicize the alarming social teachings of Caelestius and his unknown Sicilian follower and made them out to be a natural consequence of the theology of Pelagius. The government, which did not care greatly about the theological problem in dispute, acted quickly against an apparent threat to the social order. The Imperial documents were directed against Caelestius, not Pelagius, and he was accused not of heresy but of being a "disturber of the peace" who had organized a faction in Rome and distributed secret pamphlets.[20] Then the Church, finding its hand forced, also acted on the doctrinal issue, and those who would not submit were banished. Among the rebel bishops was Julian of Eclanum, a brilliant and aggressive Italian who fled to the Greek East and from there continued to attack Augustine and the Africans. But the continuation of the controversy under the leadership of Julian, and its influence on the development of Augustine's thought, belong to a later chapter.

3. THE TRINITARIAN RELATIONS

The heart of Augustine's doctrine of the Trinity is found in books V through VII of *De Trinitate*. He argues there that God, remaining one in substance, is three because of the mutual relations of paternity, generation, and procession. It has usually been supposed that these books constitute one of Augustine's more original contributions to theology and that they were written comparatively early, between 400 and 405. But an important study by Chevalier showed that they were not written until 413 or 414, since Augustine's writings up to that time contain nothing of his doctrine of relations, and that this doctrine, far from being Augustine's own contribution, was suggested by Eastern writers on the Trinity. In a letter at the end of 413 (*Ep.* 151) Augustine said that he intended to read ecclesiastical writers on the topic, and in another letter written in 413 or 414 (*Ep.* 148, 2, 10; 10, 15) he mentioned that he had already read opuscula by Ambrose, Jerome, Athanasius, and Gregory. During the next few years he worked through these insights and extended them in a study of the psychological analogies to the Trinity in man, and in 416 or 417 at the latest he sent the first twelve books to Aurelius of Carthage (*Ep.* 173).

Though he made no effort to discover the exact source of these new insights, Chevalier drew special attention to Gregory Nazianzen's third theological oration (number 29 in the whole series), directed, like Augustine's discussion, against the Eunomian

[20] Morris, "Pelagian Literature," pp. 51–54.

brand of Arianism (*Or.* 29, 16; *De Trin.*, V, 3, 4), and to Didymus' work on the Holy Spirit.[21] Subsequent study has served to confirm Chevalier's suggestions. The knowledgeable patrologist Berthold Altaner, though critical of Chevalier's lack of interest in tracing specific sources, builds upon his findings; he confirms the suspicion that Gregory's third theological oration is a crucial source, and that Didymus' work had been in Augustine's hands as early as 393.[22] There are still difficulties to be resolved. Rufinus translated nine of the orations of Gregory Nazianzen about 400; but the third theological oration is not among them.[23] Augustine must have used it, however, for it is the only source from which he could have drawn his discussion of the question whether the Son is begotten willingly or unwillingly by the Father (*De Trin.*, XV, 20, 38; *C. Serm. Ar.*, 1, 2).

Gregory's crucial insight for the development of the Trinitarian doctrine seems to have come as he set about answering the Eunomians' argument that whatever is said of God must be said according to substance, not according to accident. If the Father is ungenerated, they had argued, this must be said according to substance, and consequently the Son, who is generated, must be different from the Father in substance. Gregory saw that the only solution was to transcend the opposition between substance and accident and speak of relation ($\sigma\chi\acute{\epsilon}\sigma\iota\varsigma$ [*Or.* 29, 16]). What he had in mind was the relationship of parent and offspring, which involves both an identity of nature and a distinction between begetter and begotten; thus "unbegottenness" is not a characterization of the essence of God but of the relation of the Father to the Son, and the begetter and the begotten must be both distinct (because of their relation) and of the same nature (*Or.* 29,

[21] Chevalier, *S. Augustin et la pensée grecque*, pp. 141–159.

[22] Altaner, "Augustinus, Gregor von Nazianz und Gregor von Nyssa," *Revue bénédictine*, XLI (1951), pp. 54–62 (*KpS*, pp. 277–285); "Augustinus und Didymus der Blinde. Eine Quellenkritische Untersuchung," *Vigiliae Christianae*, V (1951), pp. 116–120 (*Kps*, pp. 297–301).

[23] The following orations were translated by Rufinus:

1 = 2	4 = 41	7 = 35
2 = 38	5 = 26	8 = 16
3 = 39	6 = 17	9 = 27

The Latin text of Rufinus' translation has been edited by Engelbrecht in the *CSEL*, vol. XLV. The Greek text of the five theological orations (27–31 in the whole series) has been edited by A. J. Mason (Cambridge, 1899).

10–12). He also notes, however, that the relationship of generation in finite life is transitory, coming into play for a time and then ceasing to have reality after the offspring has become a distinct being, while in God there is neither beginning nor cessation of a real relation between begetter and begotten (*Or.* 29, 5).

With these suggestions—most important ones, but not fully worked out by Gregory—Augustine set to work speculating for himself. Perhaps for the first time in many years he consulted Aristotle's *Categories* in order to get some light on the distinction between substance and accident and on the general problem of "predicamentals," the things that are said of God (it will be noted that his first concern is with *logical*, not metaphysical analysis, asking about the *meaning* of the language we use about God and attempting to get beyond the often misleading grammatical forms of that language).

An accident, he notes, is always a changeable feature of finite things, or, if it is a permanent characterization of a finite thing, it still belongs to something that has come into being and can perish again (*De Trin.*, V, 4, 5). God cannot have accidents in either sense, for he is not changeable. But this does not imply that everything must be said of him according to substance, as the Eunomians had argued. Relation must therefore be lifted out of the set of categories applicable to finite being alone, for the relations among the persons of the Trinity, since they are not changeable, are not *accidents* (*De Trin.*, V, 5, 6).

A similar transformation must be accomplished in the case of the category of substance, for this also was worked out by Aristotle in the course of an analysis of finite being and was treated as the correlate of accident; that is to say, if there are accidents, there is a substance in which they inhere and which is the vehicle of change. It is obvious that the term "substance," understood in this sense, can be used of God only *abusivē*, catachrestically or improperly (*De Trin.*, VII, 5, 10; the source is probably Didymus, *De Spir. Sanct.*, 38). Therefore Augustine prefers the term "*essentia*," "being itself," in theological contexts because it escapes the limitations of the categories which apply to finite being. Thus "essence" and "relation," both of them used in a new sense, are the terms with whose aid Augustine will try to gain a clearer understanding of the Trinity.

The difference between Father, Son, and Spirit, as Augustine notes repeatedly, is not one of essence but one of mutual relation alone. He argues at length in books V and VI that all terms which do not imply relations among the persons are to be taken to apply to the divine nature which they share, thus to all three persons equally—and these include not only terms like "divine," "good," "great," "eternal," "omnipotent," but even terms like "just" or "wise" or "holy" which are often associated more closely with one or another of the persons but which pertain nonetheless to the divine essence shared by all three persons. And of course all these perfections are really identical with each other in the simplicity of the divine essence.

In book VII Augustine confronts a puzzle. He wants to say that the mutual relations of the persons do not bring any further perfection to the divine nature or fulfill anything that is lacking in the individual persons (VII, 1, 2—2, 3). For example, God does not become wise through his self-relatedness; he is already wisdom itself, prior to the mutual relations. Only in that way can the simplicity of God's nature be preserved; if God were not already wise but became wise through the Word, the latter would be a quality bringing him to perfection, and there would be a composition between his essence and the perfecting quality. Therefore Augustine must conclude that each of the persons, individually, possesses all of the divine perfections "in himself" and not through his relations to the others.

Let us notice what this seems to suggest when we think in terms of our ordinary experience and language (VII, 1, 2 and 6, 11). A relative term ("father of," "master of," "friend of," "neighbor of") always presupposes a being which becomes related to another being; thus there is a real distinction between the mutual relations of these beings and what they are in themselves. There is in addition a further distinction between those beings and the essence which they share (Abraham, Isaac, and Jacob are all men). If this line of thought is followed, it will mean that a distinction must be made between the divine essence, and the three persons as they are in themselves, and their mutual relations.

But Augustine resists making that inference. God's essence, to begin with, is not abstract and generic. If anything, it is more

10*

comparable to the one ingot of gold from which three statues are made. And yet it is not divided up in that way. Each of the persons possesses the divine nature in its fullness and is not anything less in himself than what he is together with the other persons (VII, 6, 11; cf. VI, 7, 9). Each person is substance, and the *same* substance as the other persons (VII, 1, 2).

Therefore Augustine's view is that it is *one and the same thing* to be the Father, or the Son, and to be God (VII, 1, 2 and 6, 11). There can be no real distinction between the "being" of God and the "subsisting" of the persons, as the language of the Greeks might seem to suggest. The terms "person" and "hypostasis" must refer, then, to the one divine being insofar as it is related to itself in three ways (cf. VII, 4, 9—5, 10). Instead of differentiating between essence and subsistence and relation, Augustine makes them continuous; indeed, the terms "person" and "hypostasis" are interpreted in such a way as to collapse all of these notions, drawn from finite experience, into one, which is then referred to the self-related being of God.[24]

If this remains uncertain in books V–VII, whose concerns are chiefly logical, it is confirmed by Augustine's later speculations, coming between 418 and 420. The clearest statement is found in the opening section of book II (1, 3), probably written quite late: the Son, by seeing the Father, *is* the Son, for his being begotten by the Father consists in nothing else than seeing the Father. The same understanding of the Trinity is found in the eighteenth sermon on the Gospel according to John (tr. 18, 20), which uses the same biblical text as the passage from *De Trinitate* (John 5, 19–20) and is placed by Mlle. La Bonnardière around 418.[25] Here Augustine first calls for introspection in order to observe that the human mind can "see" within itself, without the senses, and then suggests that the same kind of inward self-relatedness, the "see-

[24] A major portion of Chevalier's book (pp. 37–86) is devoted to showing that Augustine had difficulties with his Trinitarian doctrine that are solved only by the Thomist doctrine of subsistent relations. It would seem, however, that the difficulties are not as great as he suggests. Augustine clearly puts forward a doctrine that is in all essentials the same as the Thomist, namely, that there are "real" relations (*ST*, I, q. 28, a. 1, corp.), that they "constitute" the persons (q. 30, a. 2, ad 1), and that they are mutual relations of the divine essence itself (q. 29, a. 4, corp.).

[25] La Bonnardière, *Recherches de chronologie augustinienne*, pp. 94–95, 111.

ing" and "hearing" mentioned in the passage from the Fourth Gospel, is what constitutes the Son: the Son *is* this seeing and hearing, his very being is his seeing and hearing of the Father. The same identification of the Word with seeing is also found in Sermon 126 (n. 15), which comes from the same period.

This is the Plotinian doctrine of a formation and actualization that takes place through knowledge, now purified of any suggestion that there is potentiality within God and therefore safely applicable to God for the first time. The solution had always lain before Augustine's eyes, for Plotinus (*Enn.* V, 1, 7) wrote: "The One is not Nous. How then does it beget Nous, except through turning toward itself and seeing? This seeing is itself Nous." But Augustine needed to devote extensive reflection to the whole problem of conversion and the formation of a mental "word"; and though he had long possessed all the resources for coming to this conclusion he appears to have been hesitant to state it until he had explored, exhaustively it seems, the nature of the human analogue which he wanted to apply to God and the modifications which must be made before it could be so applied. The analogue was explored in books IX through XI of *De Trinitate*, probably written between 415 and 417, and the contrast between the composite perfections of the finite mind and the simplicity of the divine mind was outlined in book XI of *The City of God* (chapters 10, 25–28), written about 417. Augustine was then in a position to explain how the Trinitarian relations, without adding any perfections to God or actualizing any underlying potentialities (for they are instead the deployment of the perfection which his being already possesses, growing out of fullness rather than emptiness), can still constitute something new and distinct, beyond the perfection of his essence considered by itself.

There we see the importance of the analogies to the Trinity developed in books IX–XI and then in book XIV. Though they owe much to the relational doctrine of the Trinity and could not have been elaborated without it, they contributed in turn to the completion of that doctrine of the Trinity, furnishing a pilot project in which Augustine could test various conceptions of intra-mental relationships on a more observable level before he ventured his final assertions about God.

4. THE TRINITY IN MAN

In books IX through XIV of *The Trinity* Augustine investigates
various analogies between the human mind and the divine
Trinity. Perhaps the origin of these reflections can be seen toward
the end of book VII, where he notes that the sensual man is not
able to think except in terms of space and quantity, by means of
images. In order to be purified of this limitation of mind, he goes
on, one must first *believe* in the Trinity on the basis of Scripture.
But Scripture also says that man is the image of God—and now
Augustine rejects the Alexandrian identification of the Image
with the Word, interpreting the "*ad imaginem nostram*" of Genesis
1, 26 to mean that man himself is to be an image of the whole
Trinity. He still takes the "*ad*" seriously: man can become more
like or more unlike God, and he is to be renewed through a
closer imitation of God.

At the beginning of book VIII, in an introduction probably
written later than the body of the book, he says he is seeking
to discern God *with the mind*, that is, without imagining him
under the forms of space and time. Thus he now sets out on a
more inward way, dealing with the same realities as in books I
through VII and following the same rule of believing where
understanding fails, yet seeking understanding so far as it is
possible. The anagogy of book VIII, written earlier, is inserted;
but then he goes on to the analogies as such.

The anthropology develops along two lines. One of them is
based upon the doctrine of relations which had been suggested to
Augustine by the Eastern writers on the Trinity; he analyzes the
phenomenon of self-relatedness in man and works out a theory of
self-related substance. The other is based upon the Plotinian
doctrine of formative conversion, and he works out a theory of
the mind's conversion toward itself and its becoming formed
through conceptualization in the *verbum mentis*. These two lines
of inquiry, while distinct, support each other, for the character
of mind as necessarily and constantly related to itself serves to
illustrate Augustine's theory of substance and relation in the
Trinity and helps to explain how *unity* can remain in the midst
of self-relatedness, while the process of inquiry and reflection,
conceptualization and evaluation, serves to illustrate his under-

standing of the subsistence of the Persons and helps to explain how a genuine *triad* comes into being. In man these two aspects are sundered from each other: his self-relatedness is not yet a fully articulated conceptualization; the mind can know and love itself confusedly or erroneously, and proper conceptualization finally rests on something more than his own being. In God they coincide. Thus it is easier to analyze them in man than in God, though the task is at the same time more complex.

The discussion of the mind revives a problem which has been encountered at an earlier stage[26]: the question whether the acts of thinking and willing are properties of one or another physical element, or of atoms, or of the brain or the blood, or of the harmonious cooperation of bodily matter. Augustine acknowledges the difficulty of the question; refraining from dogmatic argument, he defines the question and analyzes the data piecemeal.

The question is whether mental acts are properties, accidents, of something else, whether it be the body or its equilibrium or some element within it (*De Trin.*, IX, 4, 5; X, 10, 15). His argument on the negative side is that the accidents are inappropriate categories with which to designate acts having intentionality. An accident "inheres" in the particular body which it modifies, while intentionality "goes outside" the subject, whether the relation is to oneself or to something beyond oneself. Acts of knowledge and love would seem to be designated more appropriately by the category of substance. And his argument on the positive side is that, whatever uncertainties or even misconceptions we may have about the *nature* of mind, the mind knows its own *being* with a convincing immediacy, not through images but through its inward presence to itself; and to know something with certitude is to know its substance (X, 7, 9; 10, 16). As Charles Cochrane has put it, mental experience "is not rendered in the slightest degree more intelligible by being translated into terms other than itself, especially into terms of physiology."[27]

These arguments are logical in character, and not too much should be claimed for them when we recall the metaphysical qualifications with which Augustine hedged his statements about

[26] See chapter 2, section 1, above.
[27] Charles N. Cochrane, *Christianity and Classical Culture: A Study of Thought and Action from Augustus to Augustine* (New York, 1944), p. 404.

the mind's experience of itself. Mental acts are *in* man, as part of the life of the soul, but they are not identical with or exhaustive of his being; we say that they are "his" acts, and that it is he who acts "through" them, but we do not say of man, as we do of God, that he *is* his acts (XV, 22, 42–43). Because human *being* is not already *knowing*, the latter, even when it is constant (as in the case of self-awareness), is always the actualization of a potentiality. Man remembers or knows or loves himself only through his relation to himself, whereas Augustine believes that in God, because he is wise and loving by his nature, each person remembers and understands and loves by himself, not through another (XV, 7, 12; 17, 28). If the relations of the mind to itself involve potentiality and actualization, and if this process arises immediately from the being of the mind itself, this means that the mind is pervaded by *potentiality*; thus it would be meaningful to speak of "potencies" of the mind, as long as the stress was placed not on their difference from the substance of the mind but on their immediate and intrinsic rise from the mind.[28]

In God there is no potentiality, no compositeness. But there *is* relation. This means that relation is an analogical notion which has a greater generality than the contrast between the composite and the simple, the potential and the perfectly actual. In God the triadic relation is not a "synthetic" process giving God something more than he had before, in Plotinian and Hegelian fashion; rather the Trinitarian relations arise out of God's perfection and are the overflowing of what he is essentially and absolutely, and relation does not compromise simplicity. On the human level, however, mind, for all its self-transparency, is characterized by potentiality; it is *task*, *Existenz*, a vitality and an openness which is not yet knowing and willing, and the latter acts are brought about only through mind's relatedness to itself and to other things. When we say that acts are ours and that we act through them, but find ourselves unable to say that we *are* our acts, this suggests that man himself is to be found more on the side of potentiality than of actuality, more in looking than in seeing, more in seeking than in possessing. If we may state it in terms of a metaphysical analysis with which Augustine would be sympathetic, distinctions can be made between (1) the "being" or "substance"

[28] Cf. Schmaus, *Die psychologische Trinitätslehre*, pp. 272–277.

of the mind, (2) its "potentialities," only formally distinct from it, (3) its actual relations to itself in remembering, understanding, and willing, really distinct from the mere potentiality, and (4) a further deployment of the mind in reflection and conceptualization about itself.

The purpose of Augustine's investigations is not to get an exact terminology—too much effort has often been devoted to repeating his numerous triadic formulas—but to understand the nature of substance and relation in the mind. His initial attempt is phrased in terms of *mens, notitia sui, amor sui*, but he finds this a false triad, for it supplies only mind as the substance and its two relations of self-knowledge and self-love (IX, 4, 4). A more proper triad is then put forward: *memoria sui, intelligentia sui, voluntas sui*. The point that he wants to make in all of this is stated clearly in book X (11, 18): each of the mental acts can be considered either substantially, as rooted in the agent (and under this aspect all of them coincide in one life or mind or substance) or as a relational act (and under this aspect they are distinct from each other and can be spoken of only insofar as they refer beyond themselves to each other).

Let us try to characterize the understanding of the mind that is being expressed here. The mind has an unmediated memory and knowledge and love of itself. These acts are *preconceptual*, but they are not unconscious or merely potential; there is an actual self-relatedness. And they are something more than the immediate and non-relational feeling of "self-awareness" often spoken of by contemporary philosophers, for Augustine understands them as genuine *relations* which differentiate the mind into remembering and the life which is remembered, knowing and the life which is known, willing and the life which is willed. Though he knows that experience is filled with data drawn from sensation, indeed, that the mind of an infant is only gradually fanned into flame by the stimulation brought to it (*De Trin.*, XIV, 5, 7; *Ep.* 187, 8, 26; *De civ. Dei*, XXII, 24, 2), still he thinks of these modes of self-relatedness as *immanent to each mind*, and the mind's presence to itself is their sufficient cause.

It will be noted that for Augustine the mind is actuated not primarily by its relation to the "forms," as in Plato, nor by its relation to sensible things, as in Aristotle, but by its relation *to itself.*[29] If the activity of the mind were viewed as primarily *theoretical*, this would be quite unsatisfactory, for it would bottle up the mind within itself. Augustine's analysis succeeds because his perspective is *practical* or *existential*—the mind is present to itself not in self-contemplation and self-enjoyment but in an active way, remembering and anticipating its own life, experiencing its own freedom and the responsibilities that go with it, consciously willing its own actions. Its presence to itself does not close it off from other beings or from the future.

But the matter is complicated by the fact that we can know ourselves with varying degrees of explicitness and accuracy, and we often say that we are seeking knowledge of ourselves. What do we assume in saying that? Augustine argues that we would not even be able to seek unless we knew what we were seeking (IX, 12, 18; X, 1, 1—4, 6). But there are various ways of knowing what one is seeking: one may know it by analogy with others of its kind, or by report, or by previous experience; one may know it as an idea alone; one may know it by inference from something already known; or one may simply be seeking the knowledge itself, as a human activity (X, 2, 4). But none of these ways of "knowing what one is seeking" is applicable in the case of the mind, and Augustine's answer is that the mind seeks knowledge of itself because it is already aware of itself through presence to itself. He puts forth a version of his character-istic argument from presupposition: even if the mind were un-known to itself and were seeking itself, it would nonetheless be aware of itself as not knowing and still seeking; therefore it is impossible for the mind to be ignorant of itself (X, 3, 5).

Although his usage has been undifferentiated throughout book IX, Augustine now begins to reserve the term *"nosse"* to desig-nate the mind's knowledge of itself through self-presence. From this irreducible self-knowledge come the acts of seeking (*studere*), thinking (*cogitare*), and conceiving (*verbum gignere*) through which the mind tries to gain a more precise and explicit understanding of

[29] Zepf, "Augustinus und das philosophische Selbstbewusstsein der Antike," *Zeitschrift für Religions- und Geistesgeschichte*, XI (1959), 116–117, 122–123, 131–132. The preparatory role of Porphyry is pointed out by Dörrie, *Porphyrios' "Symmikta Zetemata,"* pp. 187–221, and Pépin, "Une nouvelle source de saint Augustin," *Revue des études anciennes*, LXXXI (1964), 103–105.

itself. The mind *always* knows and loves, remembers and under-stands and wills itself (X, 12, 19; XIV, 7, 9—10, 13; XV, 15, 25). This is a self-possession which is more constant and more basic than our fleeting acts of attention to ourselves and our changing conceptualizations of ourselves. The latter are "adventitious" to the mind (XIV, 8, 11); but there is a self-relatedness in which the mind is *not* adventitious to itself (XIV, 10, 13).

The one triad, then, is a necessary "structure" of the mind, following from its presence to itself. The other is a dynamic process that must be played out in time. What sets the human mind apart from the divine Trinity is that it is changeable and can be related to itself in varying ways, and in order to explicate this phenomenon Augustine takes the Plotinian schema of conversion and formation, detaches it from its exclusive connection with the relation of human potentialities to God, and generalizes it as a model for describing the dynamics of the mind in all its aspects, as it relates to itself and to external things as well as to God.[30] The triad of immediate self-relatedness is the more "inward" and the more "certain" (X, 10, 16); but the process of concep-tualization is both the more crucial for man's destiny and the more hazardous.

The function of the *verbum mentis* is not to acquaint man with himself (for he is already present to himself) but to give him a definite "image" of himself. In man, whose mind is both finite and mutable, this involves a venture, whereas God's relation to himself is always a true Word and a right self-affirmation in the Spirit. Man, being limited, is not identical with the rule of truth and goodness, and any definite conception of himself will be selected out of a wide range of possibilities; this is done through an act of judgment (at least implicit) which also involves, by the nature of the case, an act of approbation on the part of the will (IX, 8, 12—11, 16).

The doctrine of *verbum* should not be understood too narrowly, for the term applies not only to explicit conceptions but to vaguer images of oneself (and of other things as well); what makes it an inward "word" is not that it is conceived intellectually (for it may not be purely intellectual; the "word" of Carthage is the

---

[30] See especially David J. Hassel, "Conversion-theory and 'Scientia' in the 'De Trinitate,'" *RA*, II (1962), p. 391.

remembered image, and the "word" of Alexandria, a city which Augustine has never seen, is the imagined picture [VIII, 6, 9]) but that there is approbation—valuation and decision, bringing definiteness where there had been indeterminacy in one's mental processes (IX, 8, 13—10, 15). Men always have *assumptions* about themselves, even without explicit reflection or conceptualization, and whenever they are ready to act on the basis of these assumptions they have a *verbum mentis*.

How do these assumptions arise? The mind becomes attached to things which it loves (external things, persons, social customs or expectations or aims) with such "adhesive" force that it cannot think of itself without them and eventually supposes itself to be like them (X, 5, 7—7, 9). The problem is not that the mind has lost its immediate self-knowledge (Augustine stays by his assertion that nothing is more present and more knowable to the mind than the mind itself), but that the mind has become so attached to things other than itself that it "con-fuses" itself with these accretions (X, 8, 11).

Augustine goes on in books X and XI to undertake a complete phenomenology of formative conversion, not only as it takes place in self-definition but in all the processes of temporal experience. He works out a triadic theory of conceptualization, applicable at every level of the life of the mind, for in all experiences—whether in sense perception or the remembrance of past experiences or thinking about one's present self—there is a triad consisting of the *content* of intuitive experience (the thing that is known or remembered), the act of *cogitating* or *attending*, by which the mind is directed toward the content, and the *conformation* of the mind to the content by forming an "image" or "conception" of it (XI, 4, 7). In all these cases, as Augustine says, the "word" or "likeness" of the thing can be said to have been generated by it, for thought is given form by the contents of intuition or memory (XV, 10, 19). The word is "knowledge from knowledge," or a "saying what we know" (XV, 11, 20), in the sense that the contents, already known by intuition or memory, shape an articulated thought which strives to be true, that is, conformed to the thing itself.

The fact that a man can have "misconceptions" about himself indicates the relevance of the Delphic injunction, "Know thyself"; and Augustine catches something of its original meaning: it does not imply that the mind is unknown to itself, but it commands the mind to reflect about itself and live in a way suited to its nature—which also means in obedience to the divine law under which it stands (X, 5, 7; 9, 12). While the mind's "word" about itself might be based upon its immediate experience of itself, or upon generalization about human life, or upon social opinion, valid self-definition takes place only in the light of divine Truth, the norm according to which all judgments are made; and the fact that approbation on the part of the will is also involved suggests that a proper self-affirmation can come only from being pervaded by divine Love and referring all finite values to the Creator (IX, 6, 9—7, 13). This is very much in continuity with Augustine's earlier assertions, that the human spirit, though it is luminous to itself in the immediacy of self-knowledge, can make suitable *judgments* about itself only in the light of eternal Truth and in agreement with divine Love (cf. *De ver. rel.*, 39, 72), or that the angels in a sense know themselves better in God than in themselves (*De Gen. ad litt.*, IV, 32, 50), or that a good will consists in loving according to the Form of righteousness, by the power of the Spirit (*De Trin.*, VIII, 6, 9 and 9, 13; *Conf.*, XIII, 31, 46). The mind, while remaining firmly rooted in its own life, must at the same time look "ecstatically" to God for a proper definition of itself and its tasks and its destiny.

Though it is easily overlooked through fascination with the many triads within man, this is the main line of argument in *The Trinity*, appearing at the very beginning of the quest for understanding (books VIII and IX), furnishing the occasion for the other investigations, and reappearing throughout the later books. It is crucial, for example, to the understanding of Augustine's later interpretation of the *imago Dei*. After about 412 the mind's *capacity* for participation in God is often called the image of God, whereas before that time man is said to bear the image of God only so far as he actually *participates* in the Word through intuition. But the change should not be over-dramatized, for it is chiefly terminological. Augustine had never denied that man is *capax Dei*, and that this capacity, however deformed and obscured it may be by sin, cannot be entirely lost; but now this capacity is dignified by being identified with the *imago Dei*. And the change in terminology does not compromise Augustine's theocentrism in the least. He still says that man becomes fully "formed" neither in his immediate self-knowledge nor in any conceptualization of himself, however adequate to the reality it may be, but only in obedience to, and finally in immediate intuition of the Word (XIV, 14, 18 and 19, 26; XV, 16, 26). It is true that he sometimes describes the triadic structure of self-presence as an "image" of God (X, 12, 19; XIV, 8, 11; 14, 20). But he seems to prefer to say that the mind is *not* the image of God in *every* respect, but chiefly in its capacity to remember, understand, and love *God* (XIV, 4, 6; 8, 11; 12, 15; 19, 25). The problem is perhaps clarified in book XV, where Augustine explicates Paul's statement, "We see now through a mirror, in an enigma, but then face to face" (I Corinthians 13, 12). The mirror is man himself, the image of God. But Paul's use of the term "enigma," which in Greek grammar describes an obscure allegory, suggests that the vision through the image is not easy (XV, 9, 16). This is both because there are numerous *dissimilarities* between the divine and human triads, pointed up at length (XV, 10, 17—23, 43), and because it is necessary not only to know the mind but to know *that it is an image* and "refer" what is known to the God whose image it is; otherwise we will see only the mirror (XV, 23, 44). And lest this seem to lapse into a merely inferential way toward God, Augustine then asserts in his typical fashion that the Light has always been present as the basis of all the reliable judgments that the mind has made about itself, and that the only reason it has not been seen clearly is the impurity and weakness of the mind (XV, 27, 50). Thus the divine presence surrounds man's way. The Light is the basis of the awareness even sinful men have of truths and values, and it is always there to be "remembered," not as though recollecting something from the past but by becoming aware of a presence to which they have been "oblivious"; when they receive the aid of the Spirit they are enabled to obey and are brought to full beatitude (XIV, 15, 21).

There is, then, a continuous way leading from the mind toward the divine Trinity. It begins with the quite indeterminate existence of the mind itself, a "life" ready to become aware of continuities through time, an "eye" ready for seeing, a "heart" ready to give affection. What falls most constantly within its scope is its own being and activity; it remembers and knows and affirms itself. But that does not fill the whole horizon of its attention. It is aware of other beings, and it is capable of thought and speech; it must make judgments and come to some definite conception of these other things, and of itself, and of its proper relation to them. Thus the center of gravity in human life is not the intimate relationship of the mind to itself but this task of judging and deciding within the wider field of reality in which man is set. It is a task that is left to the mind itself; the norms may be supplied by the secret presence of the Word, but there is room for error and perversity. As a consequence the mind loses sight of God, and is fascinated by temporal things, and cannot think of itself apart from them. It must be accosted within that realm and be led first to *belief* in invisible things; then gradually, it becomes capable of arriving at an immediate *experience* of them. That which is experienced first, Augustine thinks, is the love borne along by the Spirit; but as understanding grows, the mind becomes more accustomed to divine things and enters into more intimate commerce with the Word. The fulfillment that is antici-pated is a complete formation of the mind in immediate know-ledge of the Word, a resting in the constancy of God's being and purposes, and consequently an enjoyment of God with the same intimacy as his enjoyment of himself in the Spirit.

After nearly two decades of work Augustine is able at last to draw to a close his reflections on the Trinity and its relation to man. He has set the neo-Platonist speculations on the supreme hypostases and the journey of the soul within a biblical context, and without abandoning any philosophical insights which have seemed right to him—on the contrary, following out every problem and in the process arriving at many new insights—he has been able to find their connections with the characteristic themes of piety and dogma.

CHAPTER 6

Meditation (419–430)

THE YEARS BETWEEN 411 and 418 had been a time of triumph: ecclesiastical and political triumph over the Donatists and the Pelagians, literary triumph over the opponents of Christianity even in the hour of despair, intellectual triumph in bringing his theological speculations to a climax. But the flow of time did not stop, and Augustine discovered, as his philosophy should have predicted, that what is once achieved may not stay in place. His situation became unstable in a number of ways, and the fact that this came on the heels of victory made him react all the more petulantly. His style begins to change markedly about 419. He is no longer the daring freethinker but the submissive servant of the authority of Scripture and Church. This is not altogether unbecoming in a man of sixty-five, and it is excusable in view of his earlier adventurousness. It was a time of settling into the teachings of the Church, some of which he himself had helped to reshape. At its best his manner is meditative, not pressing toward new theses but trying to understand what had been achieved with the mellowed wisdom of old age. But often he is simply dogmatic, rigid, defensive; for he now found himself threatened on almost every front.

Africa, which had been relatively untroubled, now had its turn to experience upheaval as Gothic mercenaries wandered about, bringing with them the Arian Christianity to which their people had been converted a century and a half earlier in the faraway region of the Danube. Arianism, which to the African Church had been a phantom encountered only in catechesis and in the writings of the theologians, now became a living fact. In the summer of 418 someone sent to Augustine for refutation the so-called "sermon of the Arians," a long statement of the Arian faith coming from the old and distant tradition of Ulfila.[1] It must have been about this time that Augustine resumed his sermons on the Gospel according to John after a lapse of many years and with that as his authority elaborated upon the doctrine of the Trinity. From a remark made in one of the sermons (*In Joann. ev.*, tr. 40, 7) it seems that there were Arians for a time in Hippo.[2] During these years he went on through the gospel, preaching the sermons up through number 54, then dictating the rest.[3] He also put the finishing touches on *The Trinity* and released it to the public, perhaps in 421.

But it was not only Arianism that assaulted him. He was accustomed to being looked to as a leader of the Church's intellectual life and he reacted with increasing hostility to disagreement. He learned that an upstart in Mauritania, Vincentius Victor, had written two books on the soul, criticizing Augustine's view that it is immaterial and reproaching him for his uncertainty about its origin. He replied with a barrage—one book to his informant, one to the recipient of Victor's books, and two to the culprit himself, all collected under the title *On the Soul and Its Origin*. Scarcely had this irritant been warded off when a brilliant new spokesman for the Pelagian cause, Julian of Eclanum, emerged, stating the controversy in new terms once more.[4] Augustine had to devote more time to the refutation of the Pelagians, but once again it was a fruitful enterprise, drawing forth further insights. But perhaps most important, Augustine began to receive, if not criticisms, at least puzzled queries about

[1] Manlio Simonetti, "S. Agostino e gli Ariani," *REA*, XIII (1967), 55–84.

[2] La Bonnardière, *Recherches de chronologie augustinienne*, pp. 94–95.

[3] *Ibid.*, p. 87.

[4] François Refoulé, "Julien d'Éclane, théologien et philosophe," *Recherches de sciences religieuses*, LII (1964), 42–84, 233–247, has tried to indicate something of Julian's individuality as a thinker. A careful criticism, forcing some major qualifications of Refoulé's interpretation, has been given by F.-J. Thonnard, "L'Aristotélisme de Julien d'Éclane et saint Augustin," *REA*, XI (1965), 296–304.

his understanding of grace from people within the Church not directly linked to the party of Pelagius; in replying to them, necessarily with a more irenic tone, he began to recognize some problems and perhaps to adjust his views.

We shall concentrate on the main line of intellectual endeavor during this period: his further penetration into the doctrine of grace. Augustine's most original reflections in this last decade involve a concentrating of his attention upon the central articles of faith as they relate to man and a meditating upon their inter-connections and their background in God's purposes—what could be called, if the term is understood with proper breadth, *Glaubenslehre*; for what Augustine was doing has many similarities with, indeed, is in many respects the progenitor of the spirit of much of nineteenth- and twentieth-century theology as seen in Schleiermacher and Barth, Scheeben and Rahner: frankly taking the standpoint of faith rather than neutral reason and then reflecting upon the character of the Christian consciousness, its content, its expectations, asking about the relation of creation to human destiny, the tension between the original possibilities of man and his situation under sin, the character of salvation throughout the history of the race and its relation to the unique position occupied by Jesus. All of these topics are broached by Augustine, and he arrives at a coherent pattern, though it is not as self-consciously unified as it is in Schleiermacher and subsequent theologians. What holds it together is that the entire drama is played out, with a beginning, middle, and end, in the open space between man, with his capacities, his freedom, his entanglement in the irreversible consequences of sin, and God, with his wisdom, his sovereign freedom, his purposiveness.

Augustine's concern with grace and predestination is not a narrow one, and especially in this last decade, when he has to come back to those topics again and again, it becomes clear that they open out into all the other questions of doctrinal theology.[5] In bringing the whole complex of themes together let us follow Augustine's own suggestions, for he thinks that God has acted

[5] In the recent literature on the subject this is a special emphasis of Gotthard Nygren, *Das Prädestinationsproblem in der Theologie Augustins*, p. 275, and F.-J. Thonnard, "La prédestination augustinienne et l'interprétation de O. Rottmanner," *REA*, IX (1963), 270–271.

according to a definite "order," first allowing angels and men to demonstrate what they could do with their freedom of choice (though not without the offer of divine grace), and then, after the rise of sin, showing what he could do with his grace as it took the place of merit (*Enchir.*, 23, 105–107; *De corr. et gr.*, 10, 27—12, 32).[6] We shall begin, then, by looking at the original situation of intelligent life as Augustine conceived it, the role freedom had to play, and the outworking of the consequences of sin. Then we shall examine his understanding of the process of redemption and consider the difficult problem of predestination.

1. Freedom for Grace and the Fall of Man

Augustine always reacted vigorously to the suggestion that he taught what amounted to a doctrine of *fate*. Now it is undeniable that he did hold to something like what is usually meant by fate, for he asserted that the situation of men is affected in crucial ways by factors from beyond themselves, on the one hand the sinful tendencies of the human race, on the other the saving purpose of God. But he refused to accept the term and what it connoted as a characterization of his position. Let us see why.

To him fate meant something quite precise: the doctrine that external occurrences, bodily actions, even thoughts and decisions are determined by the position of the heavenly bodies (*C. duas ep. Pel.*, II, 6, 12), or, more broadly, a universal material determinism (*De civ. Dei.* IV, 33; V, 1 and 8). He dissented from this view on several counts. First, he insisted on the basic freedom of the will, certainly prior to sin, but after it as well; although he acknowledged that decisions may be conditioned by external factors and thought that it is never in a position of total indifference, he still wanted to say that every act of the will comes from within and issues forth not as a mere response to a stimulus but as something done gladly, in keeping with the things that really delight the will, the things that it desires centrally. Second, with respect to the bondage of the human race to sin, he pointed out that it is the outworking of a free act and that it takes place

6 Athanase Sage, "Les deux temps de grâce," *REA*, VII (1961), 209–211.

according to divine justice as God lets the irreversible consequences of the act take their course. Finally, when it comes to the influence of grace upon human life, he insisted that the freedom of the will is not violated but is rather liberated and enabled to accomplish that which is most suited to the character of true freedom.

Augustine wanted to make it clear that much that goes on in the world—defection from God, sinful acts, and the consequences that follow—is not positively willed by God but is merely *known* by him, or, in the case of the consequences of sin, willed only as the penalty for a free act. In many passages he is concerned to argue that God's foreknowledge does not compromise the reality of freedom (*De lib. arb.*, III, 3, 6—4, 10; *De civ. Dei*, V, 8–10)—certainly the freedom of the primitive state, in which fidelity or apostasy is decided by the choice of creatures themselves; but also the freedom that persists in the man bound by sin, for Augustine's view is not that free choice is eradicated in sinful man but that it "suffices only for evil," as he puts it in a famous dictum, and is inadequate for willing the good until it is liberated by divine aid (*C. duas ep. Pel.*, II, 5, 9; *De corr. et gr.*, 11, 31). Let us first look, then, at Augustine's mature understanding of the primitive situation of man and of the consequences of sin.

The earlier controversy with Pelagius over the capacity for sinlessness which both of them attributed to Adam raised a question to which, up to that time, Augustine had not given much thought: In what situation was man first created? He knew that it must be unlike man's present situation in that man was not then in bondage to sin, and salvation would have been based not on the election of some men out of the mass of sinful humanity but on man's free decision between good and evil, between adherence to God and defection from him (this can be seen especially in the discussion of the fall of the angels, and incidentally of man, in *De Gen. ad litt.*, XI). But he also knew that the *posse non peccare*, the capacity for sinlessness, could not have consisted even then in man's own powers alone:

Not even if we were speaking of the whole and perfect nature of man...would it be correct to say that while the *capability* of avoiding sin is not from us [having been created by God as a part of man's nature], the actual *avoidance* of sin is our own—though sinning would be our own; for even then there would be assistance from God, offered, like the light with whose aid healthy eyes see, to those willing to receive it (*De nat. et gr.*, 48, 56).

What he is speaking of here is an aid that is given following a free decision on man's part, to enable him to *carry into effect* what he has willed. But the question also arises whether even the *willing* of what is good can come from man himself without some prior stimulus from God. And it is clear that Augustine assumed such a stimulus. He thought that man was created in a state of "integrity" (*ibid.*), and this perfect harmony of mind and soul and body is credited to God's "grace" (*De pecc. mer.*, I, 16, 21). But in the twelfth book of *The City of God*, written in 416 or 417, he reflects at greater length on this problem. Were the angels who turned to God created without active love for him, and did they then elicit this love by their own choice (though in response to a divine invitation)? That would imply that they made themselves better than God had made them. So he concludes that God does not merely supply the conditions of possibility whereby a creature can then raise itself to a state higher than that in which it left the hand of its Creator; simultaneously with the creation of its nature, and prior to any decision on its own part, a good exercise of the will is conferred by divine operation (*De civ. Dei*, XII, 9). This does not diminish freedom of decision. It really establishes the only set of conditions under which a genuine freedom of decision can exist. Man can either continue to rely upon the aid which is offered, or fall away; and the fact that a favourable decision is *required* of him gives a meritorious character to fidelity and makes defection a permanent disaster. "Man was created upright, and in such a way that he could remain in that rectitude—though not without divine aid—but could go astray through his own choice" (*Enchir.*, 107).

Thus there are two functions of grace in the primitive situation: one an "operating" or "prevenient" grace which establishes man's natural powers in a state of "integrity," with a good exercise of the will and a proper subordination of all other powers to it; the other a "cooperating" or "subsequent" grace which is offered to man and comes into play when he freely grasps this aid.[7]

But all of this is lost through sin. We have already seen that Augustine had held for some time (probably since 406) to a doctrine of original sin. (If the word "sin" [*peccatum*] were to be reserved as a designation for responsible acts, he would be willing to call it a *malum* or *vitium* contracted from the sins of others.) What is transmitted, he thinks, includes not only death and pain but concupiscence, and the latter involves guilt. It may be difficult for modern readers to follow Augustine at this point, but they have an obligation to try at least to understand what he was saying with this notorious doctrine.

In the earlier literature of the controversy—from 412 up through 420, certainly—Augustine does little more than repeat a few basic assertions. Sexuality and procreation were created good and remain good. Marriage has three useful, reasonable, and good ends: the procreation of children, chastity (the quieting of desire in an orderly, faithful way, in marriage rather than licentiousness), and a sacramental bond of union between two persons. He considers the third—taken by itself, with total abstinence from intercourse—to be the model of Christian marriage; but cohabitation for the purpose of producing offspring is entirely proper. If sexual desire is involved, however, it is a sin, though only a venial one since it has occurred within the context of marriage.

His theory is that concupiscence or libido is transmitted because of the element of lust in intercourse. This emphasis on lust could be the expression of Augustine's own personal problems; or it could be based on the biblical text which first convinced him of the transmission of sin, Psalm 50, 7 [51, 5]; or it could be an attempt to give a "rational" explanation of original sin. Sexual desire was striking to him as that area of

---

[7] For a discussion of Augustine's understanding of the primitive state, especially as it appears in the important work *On Rebuke and Grace*, and its relationship to scholasticism and later "Augustinian" movements, see Michel, "Justice originelle," *DTC*, VIII, 2 (Paris, 1925), cols. 2031–33; Charles Boyer, "Le système de saint Augustin sur la grâce," *Recherches de science religieuse*, XX (1930), 501–525, reprinted in *Essais sur la doctrine de saint Augustin* (Paris, 1932), 206–236; Guy de Broglie, "Pour une meilleure intelligence du 'De correptione et gratia,'" *AM*, III, 317–327; Athanase Sage, "Les deux temps de grâce," *REA*, VII (1961), 209–230; Henri de Lubac, *Augustinisme et théologie moderne* (Paris, 1965), pp. 33, 70, 105–108, etc.

human life in which passion farthest outruns the control of reason, and he could not think this "natural" to so exalted a creature as man. It is to be noted, however, that concupiscence, though it consists chiefly of sexual desire, is not that alone, for there are many other ways in which the animal aspects of the soul can escape rational control and tempt man.

The sharp questioning of Julian of Eclanum led Augustine to examine these assumptions more thoroughly. Julian had charged him with holding a Manichaean view of human procreation and instead defended its goodness. Augustine retorted by hinting that Julian was championing uncontrolled sexual desire. But beyond indulging in *ad hominem* remarks Augustine did engage in more vigorous thinking and moved beyond his rather simplistic emphasis on libido.

He made it clear once more that whatever is God's work in the reproductive process is good, and that sin does not affect the biological factor, the "seed" (*De nupt. et conc.*, II, 13, 26; 14, 29). He also stayed by his old assertion that marriage and procreation would have been under the control of reason and devoid of sexual desire in a state of sinlessness. If the good element in reproduction is from God, he reasons, if it is even the same reproductory process that was created at the beginning, then the evil element must be the result of rebellion on the part of finite wills, leading to a corruption of the work of God; the actual state in which men are born comes, then, from these two influences, the creative power of God and the corruptions of sin (*ibid.*, II, 28, 48—29, 50; 34, 57).

This brings to light the assumptions with which Augustine had been operating from the first. It might be accurate to make original sin equivalent with concupiscence, but only if it is seen as something *within the soul* (the argument of *De Gen. ad litt.*, X, 12, 20, in favor of a traducian view of the origin of the soul, is that not the body but the soul is the seat of sin, or rather it is the two of them together, for without the body there could be no carnal delight, yet it is the soul that takes delight). What makes it "sin," involving guilt, is not the fact that there is sexual desire (the animals have this, and it is natural to them) but the fact that there is a *privation* of something else—there is a loss of the soul's adherence to God in love and of the proper ordering of the whole man which would have followed from it. Original sin consists, then, not in concupiscence as such but in the corruption of nature or, more accurately, the loss of the *integrity*, the harmonious *tempering* of human nature. Concupiscence, because it is readily observable, functions as a kind of *sign* of this privation, and the sense of shame which is associated with sexual life is taken to be an awareness of the disorder that has resulted from sin, a sense that one knows a forbidden possibility, an awareness, then, of the lack of harmony between the law in one's members and the law in one's mind (*De nupt. et conc.*, I, 6, 7). Mausbach was probably right when he suggested, in scholastic terms, that while the "material" element in original sin is concupiscence, the "formal" element (what makes it sin) is guilt, and there can be guilt only if the *person* is turned away from God. [8]

Original sin is not biological for Augustine. It does not affect the genetic makeup of man; rather it is a kind of malfunction in the development of the personality. But it *is* associated with procreation, for it is "propagated" from one generation to the next. This is important to Augustine, for he does not think of original sin and its guilt as a mere *juridical* bond, based on a legal unity of the human race in its progenitor. A moral unity of the race must have a real basis, and Adam's descendants participate in his transgression because they have been begotten and born and brought up in disorder (*De nupt. et conc.*, II, 5, 14). And yet Augustine does not think that this is a merely coincidental, *de facto* unity in sin; there is an inevitability about it, moral and natural at once, for he assumes that concupiscence—the animal soul's refusal to obey the mind—is an appropriate punishment for the mind's refusal to obey God, so appropriate, in fact, that it is imposed upon all, even those who are redeemed, for although their guilt is remitted in baptism desire remains active, still tempting them. What makes Augustine insist on this point so strongly is his respect for the reality of temporal events, their irreversibility, their consequentiality. Men are a fragile balance of vitality and spirit; once the balance is lost, they remain bound together through the natural link of procreation, while their personhood makes the disorder of their lives more momentous

[8] Joseph Mausbach, *Die Ethik des heiligen Augustinus*, 2. Aufl. (Freiburg, 1929), II, 185–198.

and gives it the character of guilt. Something like this is at the heart of his doctrine of original sin.

We would say it differently today, for we have a more detailed picture of the history and the prehistory of the human race, and one which makes it difficult to imagine any actual state of obedience to God, devoid of aggressiveness or lustfulness, at some stage called the beginning of the human story. We would locate a perfect harmonization of man's life, if it is realizable at all under earthly conditions, in the future, as a possibility still before us. And in any case we would be inclined to interpret what is "natural" to man somewhat differently. All of this is to be expected, for there are bound to be divergences in knowledge about the world, and less tangible divergences in mental temper, from one age to another.

But at one point we could agree wholeheartedly with Augustine, for he thinks that the actual history of the human race, at least from a time soon after its beginning, has been characterized by disorganization and strife, except where the redeeming work of God has made itself felt. Let us turn, then, to this more concrete question concerning the actual situation of human life.

2. Freedom under Grace and the Salvation of Man

It is only in connection with the work of redemption that we encounter the problem of predestination. The heritage of sin is the result of human freedom, not of divine ordering. Although God by some device could have prevented the fall of angels and men, Augustine thinks, he permitted it out of respect for creaturely freedom and for the sake of the good that could be brought out of it. It is entirely just, furthermore, for men to be left to the consequences of their sin and for their deliverance to be the work of mercy alone.

The question of predestination first arises when it is asked why this or that man is called and assisted toward salvation and another is not. Augustine assumes that it is decided by God. And when the statement, "God wills all men to be saved and come to a knowledge of the Truth" (I Timothy 2, 4) is thrown up against him, he explains it in a non-universalistic way—it means, he says, that no man who *is* saved has been saved except through the will of God, or that some out of all classes and ranks of men have been saved.

It is clear enough that Augustine assumes a choice of certain men prior to any meritorious acts on their part. But the question can still be asked, "Why these and not others?"

At an earlier stage, in Epistle 102, as he reflected on the question (reportedly drawn from Porphyry's work against the Christians) why Christ arrived so late in human history, he put forward an interesting suggestion: leaving out of account, as he says, the mysterious wisdom of God, where there may be a more hidden reason, it could be that Christ appeared and preached his gospel when and where he knew a significant number of men would believe; but, he adds, even in other times some knowledge of God's promises has been given to all those who were worthy of it, those, in other words, who God knew *would* believe, and if men anywhere have lacked such knowledge it is because they would not have believed anyway (*Ep.* 102, q. 2).

This is not a doctrine of predestination on the basis of human merits, strictly speaking; the only merit men have is the entirely *conditional* one that they *would* believe if the conditions were offered, and the only sufficient condition of belief is their being called in a way that speaks to their condition. This view is quite similar to the theory of the Jesuit theologians of the sixteenth and seventeenth centuries. Molina, who knew that Catholic doctrine excluded predestination based on foreknowledge of a human decision made from a position of indifference, suggested that between God's knowledge of what is *actually* done by himself or by others and his knowledge of pure possibility there is a "middle" kind of knowledge, a knowledge of "futuribles," what *would* happen, given the powers and the disposition of the agent, under certain circumstances such as the offer of grace. And then Suárez and Bellarmine added a suggestion about the outworking of that knowledge: to those who are known to be responsive a call "congruous" with their needs is issued to them, and they respond as anticipated.

There is probably something worth considering in this theory, for Augustine held to it for a number of years. But when he was later confronted with it he rejected it as an adequate explanation.

His objection, not altogether just, is that it would mean that men are saved on the basis of merits, and unactualized ones at that (*De praed. sanct.*, 13, 25—14, 29; *De don. pers.*, 9, 23—11, 25). He now places more weight on the good pleasure of God, and over and over he quotes Romans 11, 33: "O the depth of the riches and wisdom and knowledge of God! How unsearchable are his judgments and how inscrutable his ways!"

He considers three possible cases (*De don. pers.*, 14, 35). First, there are the men of Tyre and Sidon, who, it is said, *would* have believed if they had seen and heard Jesus (Matthew 11, 20–24 and Luke 10, 13–15). But here it is a conditional statement contrary to fact, for they did *not* see and hear him. Augustine does not abandon his earlier conception of the way in which men are called; he still says that this statement in the gospels implies that the men of Tyre and Sidon would have been moved to faith "if they had heard words or seen signs congruous with their minds." But God "by a more hidden judgment" (*altiore judicio*) refrained from delivering them out of the mass of sinful humanity.

The second case is that of the contemporaries, the people of Chorazin and Bethsaida, whom Jesus is addressing in the same saying: those who hear the words and see the signs that would have enabled the men of Tyre and Sidon to believe, but still do not believe for themselves. These are the ones whose hearts God "hardens," allowing their sin to take its full course. The men of Tyre and Sidon were not hardened against the call of grace. But it did them no good that they *could have* believed, for they were not predestined, though they will have a lesser punishment—it will be "more tolerable" for them in the day of judgment (*De don. pers.*, 9, 23).

The third case is that of those who are now *unable* to believe, but who, if they are predestined, will have their blindness of mind and hardness of heart taken away, probably by a more inward mode of calling.

And perhaps there is still room for a fourth case, the one that he had earlier proposed, of those who God knows *would* believe and who *are* called in a suitable way.

Clearly Augustine wants to make two points: on one side, that the actual predestining of individuals is finally decided in God's freedom and carried out through his own influence, transcending all the finite preconditions that may be relevant, for he is not compelled to act by even the most plausible of them; but, on the other side, that God's knowledge of the disposition of individuals is not irrelevant, for if they are to be called efficaciously they must be called in a way that speaks to their condition. It is to be noted that in this very work Augustine stresses that the basic *capacity* for faith and love belongs to man's nature, though it is only by grace that it is brought to *exercise* (*De praed. sanct.*, 5, 10). A place for human agency must be affirmed even in asserting the sovereignty of God's own purposes. But that is only a precondition. Though the potentialities for faith and love may be present in man, it is only the effectual calling of those whom God has freely chosen that brings them to actuality. To Augustine the biblical doctrine of predestination is opposed to all those who would say, in one way or another, that grace is given according to man's merits and not according to God's freedom.

As backing for this assertion Augustine can cite a whole range of phenomena. There are the subjective experiences of those who, like Augustine himself, have been drawn into a life of obedience after years of hesitation and who sense that it is due to an influence from beyond themselves. There are, furthermore, the outwardly observable facts of human history: that some men live in places and times beyond the range of the Christian message and the sacraments, and that, even within the sphere of the Church, some infants are baptized before death while others are not, often because of curious coincidences in the web of earthly events. Augustine cannot imagine that these coincidences, so important to the destiny of individuals, are the result of fate or chance; they must be in every case the outcome of a divine disposition of the course of events (*De don. pers.*, 12, 31). To him the salvation of infants, entirely apart from any exercise of their own choice, is one of the most striking instances of prevenient grace and predestination. By the same token it is a perfect case of the influence of external circumstance upon inward destiny.

And this is precisely the point at which the sensitivities of most later readers recoil at Augustine's reasoning. Many Catholic thinkers have said forthrightly that Augustine does not follow the mind of the Church, and the dogmatic position of the Catholic

Church has reversed him. Because of the importance of these later discussions we cannot avoid considering the problem they raise, not in order to overrule the facts in the case but in order to analyze just what judgments Augustine made and where dissent from them is possible.

Benjamin Warfield, whose credentials as a predestinarian Calvinist were impeccable, made an important suggestion toward the end of his classic essay on Augustine and the Pelagian controversy:

It was not because of his theology of grace, or of his doctrine of predestination, that Augustine taught that comparatively few of the human race are saved. It was because he believed that baptism and incorporation into the visible Church were necessary for salvation.[9]

We have seen that Augustine arrived at both of those convictions comparatively late in his career as a Christian thinker; but he did come to them, and firmly. The necessity of incorporation into the visible Church does not, by itself, pose a serious problem. It is true that, against the Donatists, Augustine insisted that all Christians must be drawn together by the bond of peace in the Catholic Church, and he thought that after the completion of revelation in Christ and its proclamation throughout the world all people must belong to the Church to be saved. But that same regulation did not apply to earlier times; and Augustine's principles could be stretched, as they have been by recent theologians, to allow for the salvation of non-Catholics and non-Christians even in the time of the Church. The necessity of baptism for those who die before they have had the opportunity of conversion is a greater problem. And here Augustine was boxed in by his own reasoning. Because of the character of Cyprian's remarks about infant baptism he assumed that its function was to remove the guilt of original sin, and because of his interpretation of original sin he assumed that it was sufficient cause for damnation, without any personal sins being added. Though unbaptized adults outside the sphere of the people of God may be saved by heeding cryptic admonitions from God, infants can be saved only through baptism or its counterpart in Israel, circumcision and membership in the chosen people.

[9] *Studies in Tertullian and Augustine*, p. 411.

This assumption that damnation can result from original sin alone and that deliverance from its guilt can come only through the administration of baptism subjects the destiny of the infant, at least, to the control of external circumstances, what Augustine's opponents called fate and what Augustine, in reply, called the just outworking of consequences and the providential guidance of events by God. It is precisely because the matter is so important—because the destiny of a person is determined by external factors, one way or the other—that Augustine *had* to convince himself that the nexus of finite occurrences is divinely guided: "Often when the parents are eager and the ministers are prepared to give baptism to infants, still it is not given, because God does not choose" (*De don. pers.*, 12, 31). Against all the evidence for the play of natural necessity, and coincidence, and free human activity, he must insist that at least in cases where the destiny of a human being is involved neither fate nor freedom is finally responsible, but divine judgment and providence. This places him in a dilemma theologically: either he must hold to a view of providence as close-textured, tightly ordered by God in every detail, which conflicts with his own cosmological convictions; or he must acknowledge that necessity and coincidence and freedom have at least an accessory role, even though the overarching factor is divine providence, and then it may be difficult to salvage his theory. The only satisfactory way to adjust the problem would have been to do what the later Church did: refuse to base damnation on original sin alone, exempt infants and children, then, from the either/or of damnation or salvation, and restrict the latter to the age of responsibility. This would not conflict with the other things Augustine (and the later Church) insisted on: the fatefulness, the irreversibility, of sin, and the solidarity of the human race, so that later generations are involved in and influenced by sin from the first. But this inevitable involvement in sin would lose its ultimacy and would not be by itself deserving of damnation.

Now all of the foregoing discussion of predestination is rooted, it will be noted, in the question why some infants are baptized and some are not, why some adults are converted and some are not. But Augustine thinks that predestination involves *two* problems—this one of *the beginning of faith*, and another one of *perseverance to the end*, the former based upon prevenient or operating grace, prior to man's decision, the latter upon subsequent or cooperating grace, following upon and supporting man's decision. The two aspects are very poorly put together in his writings. They can be harmonized, but it will be an unstable combination, and I hope to show that what Augustine says in these two different connections actually leads toward divergent theories of predestination.

When Augustine is defending the doctrine of predestination he usually concerns himself with the first, the fact that one person is converted and another is not, that one infant is baptized and another is not. Predestination is viewed, then, as the ultimate explanation of the actual—at least the *observable*—course of events. He sees such and such men entering the life of the Church, or falling away from it again, often in unexpected ways, and he asks why these men were placed at precisely this point in time and subjected to precisely this set of influences so as to will—though from within themselves—good or evil. Augustine assumes that nothing happens without God's knowledge, indeed, without his counsel and will; and predestination is the attempt to give an explanation in keeping with that belief.

But when his readers question him, as did the monks of Hadrumetum and of Marseilles, it is usually to ask whether predestination makes the things with which they have been closely involved in their religious life, rules and exhortations and fraternal correction and prayer, superfluous or meaningless; and then he vehemently insists that it does not. To prove it he engages in an examination of the Christian life and the content of the prayers of the Church, on the principle that the Church has always *believed* and *prayed* in terms of grace and predestination, though its assumptions are now being defended with more explicitness against the new heresy that has arisen (*De don. pers.*, 23, 65).

These two tendencies in Augustine's discussions of predestination could be harmonized, of course, along the lines of the medieval distinction between "predestination to grace," which is carried into effect prior to any decision on the part of men, and "predestination to glory," which is conditioned upon their subsequent faithfulness. This would explain why some men

genuinely respond for a time, yet fall away before they reach
eternal life. Now it may be that Augustine unconsciously assumed
something like this. But it conflicts with his own explicit statements that predestination has reference *only* to those who will
persevere and be crowned with glory. It is just as possible,
therefore, that in these last treatises, written between 426 and 429,
Augustine was on the way toward a different understanding
of predestination than that which he had had previously.

Let us notice the thesis being argued in those treatises, and
the sequence of the argument: (a) both the beginning of faith
and perseverance to the end are *gifts of God*, for they are not
accomplished by man alone and the aid that is given is not merited
by him; (b) if God gives these gifts, then he *knows* that he will
give them, and to whom he will give them; (c) therefore those
to whom he gives these gifts and whom he delivers and crowns
at the end are *predestined* (*De don. pers.*, 21, 54; 17, 42–43; etc.).
In his last writings, at least, Augustine uses terms like "*praedestin-
are*" and "*praedeterminare*" to suggest not a strict determinism
but the *definiteness* of the *plans* that are made. Predestination is
defined as God's foreknowledge of his own actions and his
preparation of the means by which those whom he does liberate
are liberated unfailingly (*De praed. sanct.*, 10, 19; 17, 34; *De don.
pers.*, 17, 41 and 45). It allows a large place for a knowledge of,
and accommodation to, the contingent decisions of free agents,
though predestination goes beyond foreknowledge in that God
also decides upon and foreknows what *he* will do. But God's
ideas are always related to actualities that are to be brought forth,
and in them there is an interpenetration of purposiveness and
intelligent counsel, for if God's will is always the ultimate criterion
of what will be done, it is not isolated from his wisdom and from
his knowledge of finite occurrences.[10]

The fact that men are commanded to do certain things proves
to Augustine that freedom and effort have a role even within the
sphere of grace. Though he assumes that a basic rightness of
orientation in men's lives will come about only as the gift of

[10] See especially Coelestin Zimara, "Das Ineinanderspiel von Gottes
Vorwissen und Wollen nach Augustinus," *Freiburger Zeitschrift für Philosophie
und Theologie*, VI (1959), 272–299, 361–394, and, with special reference to
predestination, Gotthard Nygren, *Das Prädestinationsproblem in der Theologie
Augustins*, which utilizes materials drawn from the writings of all periods.

grace, he expects it then to bear fruit in willing and doing and persevering in the good. The point that is made throughout *On Grace and Free Will* in particular is that everything is the result of grace—but that it must also become human actuality. Augustine even thinks that men ought to pray for the giving of grace, both to others and to themselves, and that prayer and decision and effort are all a part of the process of salvation. He argues, furthermore, that predestination can be taught and preached even to the multitudes, in order to stress that the entire way of salvation is the gift of God; and it ought to be preached not in a fatalistic way, dryly asserting that some who stand will fall and some who now delight in sin will be raised up, but rather with a note of exhortation that those who have not yet laid hold upon grace might do it, and that those who have already believed might so run the race that they will be among those whom God foreknows and predestines to reach the prize (*De don. pers.*, 22, 57–59). He even reflects upon the "logic of preaching" at this point— in speaking of predestination the mood is always to be in the optative, exhorting and promising, using direct address, while in speaking of rejection the third person is to be used and the mood is to be hypothetical: "*If* any are not foreknown and predestined to his kingdom, *then* they shall not persevere" (*De don. pers.*, 22, 61).

The fact that human decisions are taken into account and freedom is not subjected to violence does not mean that the crucial role is played by man and his freedom. The problem, however, is to bring grace and freedom into the proper relation. As man seeks to persevere, he is exhorted to trust more in God than in himself. Augustine expresses surprise that men are inclined to trust their own frailty more than the firm promises of God, and when they object, "I do not know what God intends to do with me," he retorts, "Do you know any better what your own will has in store for you?" (*De praed. sanct.*, 11, 21). To those who think that the preaching of grace will arouse despair at the possibility of salvation, his answer is that despair comes not from trust in God but from trust in the proud and unhappy self (*De don. pers.*, 22, 57 and 62). The proper human response is—we may use Luther's term, for it is also Augustine's—trust, directed, however, not toward the preaching of forgiveness but toward the gift of perseverance. Augustine, like the later Catholic theologians, insists that no one can have assurance of his own salvation, quite simply because he cannot guarantee what he will do in the future; but, like the Reformers, he also wants to assure men that by trusting in the faithfulness of God they can bring themselves into contact with the power that leads toward salvation.

Augustine states repeatedly in these last four treatises that the sons of Adam, unlike the first man, cannot persevere by their own continuing ratification of their relation to God; their changeable wills need to be sustained by a special divine assistance which gives not merely the *possibility* but the *actuality* of perseverance. But in what does this gift of perseverance consist? *Caritas*, love for God, which gives man a *delectatio victrix*, a delight in the good which is victorious over all inducements toward a basic rebellion against God. And this doctrine is not, in fact, a new one; it is not the result of an intensified predestinarianism but one of the affirmations that he had made steadily from an early time. Some of the most important passages are found in the first writings against the Pelagians (*De pecc. mer.*, II, 19, 32; *De spir. et litt.*, 29, 51), and the same doctrine appears long before that (*De Gen. c. Man.*, II, 11, 15; *De serm. Dom. in monte*, I, 12, 34; *Exp. ep. ad Gal.*, 49).[11] Peter is an example of what is needed, says Augustine: he had made grand promises, and yet he denied the Master, because the will to do good, though present, was still weak; but later he became a martyr through his faithfulness, because he was enabled to achieve a "great and robust will," a "great love," a willing that led to the carrying through of what he had willed in the face of every obstacle (*De gr. et lib. arb.*, 17, 33; *De corr. et gr.*, 9, 24).

Augustine states repeatedly that the gift of perseverance is a grace that "cooperates" with men, and their receiving this gift, so that they do persevere, or their falling away is decided *not* by God but by themselves. Those Christians who have turned to God but do not persevere have first deserted God, and it is as a consequence of this that they are deserted by him (*De corr. et*

[11] For a discussion of *delectatio victrix* and some of the later problems in its interpretation see Gustave Combès, *La charité d'après saint Augustin* (Paris, 1934), pp. 8–9 and Appendix II; Etienne Gilson, *The Christian Philosophy of Saint Augustine* (New York, 1960), Part II, chapter 3.

gr., 13, 42). Men can forsake God by their free choice; but if they pray for the gift of perseverance, and the prayer is heard, he will not let them fall away (*De don. pers.*, 6, 10–12). He is speaking, he says, not of the situation of man prior to faith (here there would be different problems) but of believers who have been freed from bondage to sin and are capable of trusting in God (*De don. pers.*, 22, 58 and 60); and whereas the beginning of faith is prepared even for those who do not seek it, the gift of perseverance is prepared only for those who *do* seek it (*De don. pers.*, 16, 39; *De corr. et gr.*, 7, 11). It is especially for them, it seems, that commands and exhortations are issued, for although all men are formally free and thus are responsible for their sins, only these are in a position to obey—but only if they continue to depend upon divine aid; and if they are obedient, they receive the crown of glory. There is still merit, because there are human acts and they are done not without freedom. But, Augustine says, "when God crowns our merits, he crowns his own gifts" (*De gr. et lib. arb.*, 6, 15), and eternal life is "grace for grace" (*ibid.*, 9, 21; *De corr. et gr.*, 13, 41), because cooperating grace has been indispensable throughout.

Now it is clear that the "predestined" (in contrast to the merely "foreknown") include *only those who persevere to the end and are glorified.* Because of the place of freedom and exhortation and effort in their lives (though whatever they accomplish has been aided by grace), their predestination would seem to be based upon God's knowledge of the full course of their lives, with its interaction between human and divine freedom, men freely seeking God's aid, God freely giving it. If so, it would be, to use the language of the schools, "predestination after the foreknowledge of merits"—but only of those merits that *follow* the giving of grace and consist in a steady *dependence* upon divine aid.

It appears that Augustine has, in effect, two theories of predestination. One is concerned with the problem of the *beginning* of faith. Starting from the common situation of all men, bound together in one mass through original sin, his question is why these infants are drawn out of the mass by being baptized, why these adults are drawn out of it by having the gospel preached effectively to them. He respects the historical process enough to know that this question, if it is the *right* question, must be answered

11*

in terms of external factors—the time and place of individual lives, the geographical expanse of the Church, the many coincidences that may make a crucial difference to an individual's destiny. But his other theory of predestination (only hinted at, and then forgotten again) is concerned with the problem of *perseverance* in faith. Beginning from within the Christian life itself, he asks about its dynamics and about the human factors that might affect its outcome. Here we find ourselves in a different atmosphere, one of inwardness and immediacy to God rather than externality and its fateful occurrences. Ultimate salvation depends upon man's faithfulness, freely elicited—yet called forth by grace and sustained by grace.

Starting from the Christian life as the paradigm, it would be possible to develop an understanding of grace and predestination quite different from that usually associated with Augustine— *if* his doctrine of infant damnation were dropped and *if* the biblical view that God wills all men to be saved were taken seriously. This is precisely what the Catholic Church began to do about 850 and continued to do through the middle ages, and it is what many Christian thinkers of all persuasions have done in more recent times. In order to carry through these concerns thoroughly and consistently, one would have to say that redeeming grace, which is indispensable to conversion, is in some way offered to every man prior to any merits on his part, that it somehow makes itself felt and evokes a favorable inclination of man's will, that consent to it is the only reasonable response— and yet consent is not automatic or inevitable, and there is always the possibility that man will fail to respond, perhaps through defiance, perhaps through distraction or negligence or indecisiveness.[12] This would *not* be a hidden form of "Pelagianism" or even of "semi-Pelagianism." With Augustine it would be said that God "prepares" the will, not *after* men believe but *before*, that grace is given not *because* men believe but *in order that* they might believe, that God gives them not only the *capability* to believe but the *will* to believe and the *accomplishment* of all that

[12] The two clearest contemporary statements I have encountered are by Bernard Lonergan (cf. *Insight: A Study of Human Understanding* [New York, 1957] p. 667) and Karl Barth (especially his doctrine of predestination in *Church Dogmatics*, II/2, and his doctrine of evil as the "impossible possibility," developed at length in III/3).

he requires. The point of divergence from Augustine would be this: he thought that operating grace worked infallibly and irresistibly to produce a human act, so that only the elect can be called in a congruous and effective way, while the later theologians would prefer to say that operating grace, though it infallibly gives the *inclination* to act (so that, if the inclination is consented to, the act is credited to God), can still be resisted or simply go unheeded (so that the failure to act is man's own). There is, then, an asymmetry between obedience and disobedience, quite in keeping with Augustine's own principles, and because of it the will, at least when confronted with the possibility of conversion, is not in a position of indifference but must either consent or fail to consent.

What is crucial to such a position is that what is experienced in the Christian life is extended to the situation of all men, at least as a possibility and perhaps often as a hidden actuality as well. If grace is the cause of the conversion of all who *have* believed, this need not mean that it is not also offered to others who, as far as can be seen, have *not* believed; if those who persevere in the Christian life have consented to "operating grace" and continue to rely upon "cooperating grace," then what sets the others apart is that they have not yet allowed the same grace to take effect in their own lives.

Those who wish to reject the other understanding of predestination, as taking effect through the influence of the external environment, should note what an acceptance of this one requires: some conception of God's presence as Redeemer to all men, sufficient for conversion in some form even though it may not be explicitly "Christian"; and at the same time some conception of the way in which external events and symbols, even those which may not be explicitly "Christian," can play a role, for Augustine continues to hold that once man's attention is distracted and dispersed by concern with the finite he becomes incapable of returning to the Light within until he is led to it gently by outward signs. Those familiar with a large segment of modern theology, from Kant's *Religion within the Limits of Reason Alone* to the recent writings of Karl Rahner on the "anonymous Christian," will recognize that the problem is not an outdated one, and that it is not related narrowly to predestination, for it concerns the tension between the *universality* and the *historical particularity* of biblical religion.

I think I have indicated unambiguously enough my judgment that Augustine never abandoned his rather rigid predestinarian position, since he thought it was taught by Paul and other authorities, and he would have been unable to accept any alternative because of his belief in the damnation of unbaptized infants. But I think I have also shown that a *problem* emerges from within his own statements on predestination and that an alternative doctrine is being prepared, however surreptitiously, as he attempts to answer the objections that have been brought against his stated position. It is doubly ironic that during the last decade of his life he continued to hold to a doctrine of antecedent predestination and to think that it is administered through the web of external occurrences, since his thought was moving toward the solution of the two requirements, mentioned above, for any satisfactory doctrine of a universal will of salvation. For it does seem that he came to put greater stress upon internal factors in calling and conversion, thus placing external signs and stimuli in a subordinate position; and he gave considerable attention to the problem of salvation outside the sphere of the Christian Church and affirmed it, if anything, even more emphatically than before. Once more we have proof of the complexity of Augustine's theological activity, his ability to think concurrently along a number of different lines, in each case according to the nature of the problem and the evidence available, and to resist the temptation (if he was even tempted) to achieve consistency prematurely. Let us glance, then, at these two topics; and they form a fitting conclusion to our survey of the development of Augustine's theology, for in a sense they point the way toward later epochs of theological reflection and their solution, in a validly Augustinian way, of a problem that Augustine himself did not solve.

For many years Augustine assumed, as we have seen, that conversion is effected by the presenting of appropriate suasions through the channel of the understanding; the first assistance that is given to the will from within comes with the infusion of *caritas*, and this is given only to those who, responding to the call, have desired to do the good and have sought divine aid.

But it has been suggested repeatedly by the scholars, beginning with Rotmanner in 1897, that from about 418 Augustine began to think of grace as an inward influence from the very beginning of the process of conversion.[13]

The *locus classicus* is a passage in *On the Grace of Christ*, written during the summer of 418 while Augustine was staying in Carthage following the council which condemned Pelagius. He argues, against Pelagius, that instruction is not enough; it must be supplemented by love, and this comes only from the grace which conducts the elect toward glory.

By this grace it is effected not only that we *know* what is to be done, but that we *do* what we know; not only that we *believe* in those things that are to be loved, but that we *love* those things in which we believe (12, 13). This grace, *if it is to be called instruction*, must be so called in such a way that God is believed to infuse it more deeply and more inwardly, with an ineffable sweetness, not only through those who plant and water outwardly but also *through himself*, who secretly gives growth, both exhibiting Truth and imparting *Caritas*. It is thus that God teaches those who have been called according to his purpose, giving them *simultaneously* the knowledge of what they are to do and the doing of what they know (13, 14).

The passage seems to represent one more attempt to trace an inward experience of the Trinity. In the immediate context (10, 11) Augustine cites two passages from the sixth chapter of the Gospel according to John:

No man can come to me unless the Father, who has sent me, draws him; and I will raise him up at the last day. It is written in the prophets, "And they shall all be taught by God." Everyone who has heard and learned from the Father comes to me (John 6, 44–45).

No one can come to me unless it is given him by the Father (John 6, 65).

These texts begin appearing a few years earlier, in *On the Perfecting of Man in Righteousness* (19, 42), written about 416, and Sermon 131, whose date can be fixed very precisely at September 23, 417; but nothing is yet done with them. There is a sharp change, then, in 418. And if the Trinitarian overtones remain debatable in the passage from *On the Grace of Christ*, they are unmistakable in the

[13] For the bibliography of the discussion see Nygren, *Prädestinationsproblem*, p. 98, n. 256.

twenty-sixth sermon on the Gospel according to John, which comes later, but perhaps in the same year. It was delivered in Hippo and was directed against the Arians rather than the Pelagians, and in it Augustine shows more explicitly in what direction his interpretation of the passage had been moving. The Father's "drawing" or "attracting" men (*tractio*) is identified with the revelation that Christ is the son of God, of the same nature as the Father. This revelation comes not through flesh and blood, but through the Father's own instruction, and that instruction is the Word himself, who "is given inwardly, flashes inwardly, reveals inwardly"; while outward words can only plant and water, the inward Light gives increase, for it arouses the desire to partake more fully of eternal Wisdom, and then love and delight and desire are animated by the gift of the Holy Spirit (*In Joann. ev.*, tr. 26, 4–8). The same interpretation is given to the passage in the relatively large number of times it is mentioned in subsequent works from the last decade.

There is no change, I think, in Augustine's psychology. He still assumes that understanding is prior to willing, that the pivotal moment is in the mind's discernment of values which have such an appeal that they draw the will forth, and that the nature of intelligent life would be violated if there were an overpowering of the will without a persuasion of the intellect. But a readjustment is made in his conception of the appeal made to the understanding and, through it, to the will: now the stress is not upon the suitability of the external call but upon the immediate presence of the Word, giving insight into what has been said outwardly and arousing the affections. And a readjustment is also made in his conception of the process of conversion. Previously he had assumed that calling and the infusion of love are separated in time, with the response of faith intervening ("no one is aided unless he himself does something; he is aided if he seeks, if he believes, if he has been called according to God's purpose" [*De perf. iust. hom.*, 20, 43]. Now he stresses their continuity and even simultaneity. The only faith that justifies is the faith that issues directly into love (Galatians 5, 6), and whatever is not from this faith is still sin (Romans 14, 23 [cf. *De gr. Chr.*, I, 26, 27]).

Thus there is a heightened "interiorization" of Augustine's understanding of man's relation to God. It is hardly new, for he had always assumed an inward presence of God and a constant illuminative influence in connection with the Christian life. The external media of communication—words, events, rituals—are not the decisive factor. They do not become superfluous, nor are they merely incidental, for Augustine continues to hold that man is now incapable of directing his attention to the Light within unless he is led to it by outward signs. And yet he affirms that the same redemption is made available everywhere, even beyond the sphere of historical revelation, in one mode or another.

In his letter to Deogratias (*Ep.* 102), written at some time between 406 and 410, he responded to the second question, the one asking why Christ appeared so late in human history when he is alleged to be the only way of salvation, with an expansiveness that went well beyond what the question demanded; far from feeling threatened by the question, he seems to have taken the opportunity to elaborate on his conviction that from the beginning of the world there have always been some men who believed in the Word and lived according to his precepts. There is, to be sure, a difference in times, and with it a difference in signs and rituals, having an increasing explicitness and attracting increasing numbers of men; but it is always the same *fides* and the same *salus*, related to the Word first when he was still to come, then in his flesh, and now, in the time of the Church, as he "fills the world" (*Ep.* 102, q. 2, 11–12). From the beginning, sometimes more cryptically, sometimes more openly, there have been prophets and believers, some of them in the *gens prophetica* of Israel, and some in other nations which have no direct connection with it (for if such people are reported in Scripture, he suggests, why might we not believe that there are others as well?).

Such themes become even more marked in later writings. Augustine affirms that what is now known as the Christian religion is as old as creation and has been adhered to more widely than might first appear (*Retr.*, I, 12, 3). He still keeps to the principle that there is no salvation except through faith in Christ, faith not only in his divinity but in the human achievements of his life, death, and resurrection as well; but in the case of the ancients their faith was in his *promised* humanity and in the Word still to become incarnate, and on that basis the same grace was given by the Spirit (*De pecc. orig.*, II, 24, 29—30, 35).

This is the context in which he broaches the often-mentioned doctrine that what is "latent" in the Old Testament becomes "patent" in the New. Here and elsewhere (*De pecc. orig.*, II, 25, 29; *De nupt. et conc.*, II, 11, 24; III, 4, 7–13) the contrast is used not to suggest a pattern of prophecy and fulfillment but to show how *one and the same* covenant and promise and salvation can be conveyed in different times, first hidden in figures and then openly enacted and proclaimed. Mausbach, like others before and since, suggests that Augustine thereby opens the way to a view of faith that focuses more on the inward posture of trust in God the Redeemer than on a certain set of historical symbols; he finds numerous passages in Augustine's works which hint at the possibility of a "latent" Christianity, in reality though not in name, even outside the history of Israel.[14]

But the fact that grace is offered everywhere does not make the history of salvation in Israel superfluous; and the fact that the same salvation is latent in Israel does not make Christ and the Church superfluous. What is their value? In part it is in supplying a more explicit revelation. But it is chiefly that in the history of salvation something has been wrought by redeeming grace within the sphere of human life itself, something public, furthermore, and made accessible to others through the continuity of traditions and institutions.

Indeed, one of the most interesting developments in this last decade, with its deeper speculations on the mysteries of faith, is the drawing of the whole history of salvation into a single whole, with the gracious God at its source and the incarnation at its focus. Augustine quite systematically makes the incarnation the prime instance of predestination and prevenient grace, the chief actualization of God's saving will. If men are drawn out of their sin by prevenient grace, it is by the *very same* prevenient grace that Jesus was drawn into unity with God and safeguarded from sin even before there was any possibility of human decision on his part (*De praed. sanct.*, 15, 31). Therefore the Pelagians, who persist in saying that grace is given according to man's merit, must say the same thing in their Christology, if they are consistent, and be convicted of adoptionism: they would have to say that Jesus, though born of a virgin and free from sin, made progress by his

[14] Mausbach, *Die Ethik des hl. Augustinus*, 2. Aufl., II, 310–323.

own choice and thereby merited assumption into unity with the Word. But in reality the sequence is just the reverse: the assuming activity of the Word is prior, and because of it Jesus is born of a virgin and has a good will and all the rest (*C. Jul. op. imp.*, IV, 84).[15]

When Augustine describes the incarnation in terms of predestination and prevenient grace, its force is sometimes to stress the contrast between Jesus and other men: though they all have the same nature, there is a difference in the grace given (*De praed. sanct.*, 15, 30). But the differentiation is made for the sake of bringing them all into unity. The same grace, the same Spirit, is given, first to the Head and then to the others (*ibid.*, 15, 31). Jesus is thus the forerunner and the first fruits of the redeemed humanity, and what is said of the others is applicable supremely to him. When, for example, Augustine says that man after sin needs a grace that is, not more gracious, but more powerful than that given to Adam (*"non laetiore…verumtamen potentiore gratia"*), he is referring first of all to the assumption of Jesus into unity of person with the Word, since it is done apart from any consideration of prior merits, but the same pattern is characteristic of redeeming grace generally. Jesus is thus the one through whom, and in union with whom, redeeming grace is offered to all men.

The grace which was given to the first Adam was a grace with whose aid man could be righteous *if he willed*; the more powerful grace given in the second Adam is a grace *by which it is brought about that man wills*,

[15] This is a common theme in his later statements on Christology: "The son of man is assumed not in such a way that he is first created and then assumed, but in such a way that he is created in being assumed (*ut ipsa assumptione crearetur*)" (*C. serm. Ar.*, 6, 8). Augustine thereby anticipates, in a sense, the later doctrine of Leontius of Byzantium, taken over by all subsequent theologians, that the humanity does not have any being of its own *prior to* or *apart from* the Word but has its being *in* the Word by whom it is assumed. But this does not alter what has been said earlier (chapter 3, section 2), that Augustine holds to a Christology of the *assumptus homo*, recognizing a genuine human life, including a human center of consciousness and volition. Indeed, in the same period in which he stresses the prevenience of the assuming activity of God and the absence of human initiative he exhibits, even more intensely than before, an awareness of the place of a human will and a human development in Jesus (van Bavel, *Recherches sur la christologie de saint Augustin*, chapters 5 and 6). The point he is concerned to make in Christology is not, then, that human activity is overpowered or bypassed, but that a gracious divine activity always takes precedence, and the human is what it is because of it.

and wills so strongly and loves with such ardor, that by the will of the Spirit, he triumphs over the contrary will of the flesh (*De corr. et gr.*, 11, 30).

But the differentiation remains, and it is what necessitates the union of the others with Christ (either explicitly or only through hope). Although the same prevenient grace is offered to believers that has taken effect in him, so that they are sustained by it along their way, they still retain the effects of sin and are in need of incorporation into him, to share in the righteousness enacted in his life and the ransom effected in his death. Augustine now makes a more eloquent and more closely reasoned defense than ever before of his own version of *simul iustus et peccator*:

Although the devil is the author and source of all sins, still it is not *every* sin that makes children of the devil, for the children of God also sin: "If they say that they have no sins they deceive themselves and the truth is not in them" (I John 1, 8). But they sin because of that condition by which they are still children of this world, while by that grace through which they are children of God they do *not* sin: "Everyone who is born of God does not sin" (I John 3, 9)....

Baptism, therefore, washes away *all* sins...But it does not take away the *weakness* which the regenerate man *resists* when he fights the good fight but to which he *consents* when, as man, he is overtaken in any fault, rejoicing with thanksgiving on account of the former, but groaning in prayer on account of the latter....The children of God by faith alternately exult over God's benefits and lament over their own evils as long as they are still children of this world with respect to the weakness of this life; but God distinguishes them from the children of the devil not only by the laver of regeneration but by the uprightness of that faith which is active through love, for the just live by faith (*C. duas ep. Pel.*, III, 3, 4–5).

And this is an appropriate point at which to leave Augustine, pilgrim to the last, still striving after the righteousness and peace and joy of the kingdom of God, sobered, when we compare him with the Augustine of earlier years, by a succession of discoveries which made the way seem much more arduous than it had at first appeared, yet all the more confident that the way was safeguarded by the divine Emperor himself (cf. *Conf.*, VII, 21, 27). Reciting the penitential psalms, he finished his earthly journey on August 28, 430.

Augustine the Theologian

AUGUSTINE'S ACHIEVEMENT was acknowledged even by his contemporaries. Jerome, writing to him in 418 (*Ep.* 195 in the Augustine corpus) said,

You are known throughout the world; Catholics honor and esteem you as the one who has established anew the ancient faith (*conditorem antiquae rursum fidei*); and, what is a mark of even greater glory, all the heretics denounce you.

Then he could not help adding that he as well has merited the hatred of the heretics. This testimonial was called forth by Augustine's role in the Pelagian controversy, but not by that alone. It was an age that was in a position to recognize what a contribution had been made by its own thinkers in reformulating the faith on terrain held by classical culture and defending it in the face of new problems. And Augustine left his imprint on the thought of the Church in as massive a way as Origen; perhaps even more than Gregory Nazianzen he merits the title "the theologian." But let us ask in what his virtues as a theologian consist.

What we have seen of his thought indicates that it was not as homogeneous or as original as it is often supposed to be. He was not a solitary figure who singlehandedly altered the course of Western thought through the uniqueness of his personality or the sheer power of his genius. He profited from many thinkers who had gone before, pagan philosophers and Christian theologians. He learned his basic affirmations from them and was often led to modify his views because of them. The primarily *intellectual* character of his thought is demonstrated in the fact that the major turns in his theology are usually precipitated not by personal experiences, however important that factor may be, nor by external circumstances, however compliant with them he often seems, but by his reading something new and being brought face to face with a new problem. Far from going his own way in proud isolation, he was open to the opinions of others—open, indeed, in several ways, which need distinguishing.

Sometimes he found their suggestions indispensable in resolving perplexities that had dogged him for a long time. One thinks of the way the philosophy of Plotinus and Porphyry supplied a view of things to which he was able to give his own assent, based on experiences and reasons of his own, and which he could then go on to develop in his own way; or the sense for the moral heroism of countless figures in the short history of the Church, which impressed him at the time of his conversion and remained a vivid image in his mind; or the theological insights of Gregory Nazianzen, which provided the clue that brought his Trinitarian thought to the natural resolution at which he might never have arrived without assistance. In many cases, then, Augustine made the views of other men his own, gave "real assent" to them for himself, and further developed them in an original way. What we have here is undoubtedly the core of what we mean by "Augustinian" thought, and when it is allowed to express itself freely— as in the *Confessions*, or in many passages in *The Trinity* or *The City of God*—it has a literary and conceptual power that is almost beyond comparison.

Sometimes he could not arrive at certitude, however; despite his interest in a problem and the presence of a large stock of suggestions from others he would remain uncertain, not being able to find the decisive reason for taking one position as against another. The most striking instance is the question of the origin of the soul, certainly a major question to him and to his age, and one to which most men gave a definite, not to say passionate, answer. After giving credence to the Platonist theory, he became increasingly uncertain and finally had to leave it an open question, consoling himself with the thought that, whatever the answer, the soul's destiny is more important than its origin (*De lib. arb.*, III, 20, 55—22, 63; *De an. et eius orig.*, IV, 10, 14).

But often we find that he was influenced by what he himself called "authority." He accepted, especially at the start, the authority of the historians and scientists and philosophers of antiquity, took over their picture of the world (which was, after all, the best that was available, however poorly the information had been gathered and however uncritically it had been sifted), and tried to bring it into harmony with the biblical faith. And he accepted, with increasing fervor, the authority of the Bible and the traditions of the Church and the decisions of its councils, in some instances reversing course with what some might think unconscionable haste, as when he abandoned Origenism once it came under fire, or rejected his earlier rationalism and gave credence to stories about miracles in his own day. But Augustine was a man who took authority seriously, as a matter of conviction, certainly, perhaps also as a matter of necessity; in any case, as a bishop he shared a collective responsibility for the life and doctrine of the Church, and in the spirit of Cyprian and many other pious and wise men he was not prepared to insist upon his own opinions in the face of a great cloud of witnesses.

This acquiescence in authority, the say-so of others, whether in culture or in religion, should not cast doubt on his independence of mind; where he was sure of a point, as a matter of personal conviction, he would stick by it, and even where he accepted the testimony or the convictions of others he made an effort to think the matter through for himself. Its significance is quite different. He was sufficiently aware of the conditions of human knowledge —and we in our more critical age can only second him here—to know that many things, including some of the most important matters, lie beyond the experience of the solitary individual and that one must trust the accumulated experiences and beliefs of civilization or of the people of God. We in our own day have a far greater supply of information about the cosmos and the history of the human race and the vicissitudes of the people of God, together with a far more critical way of assessing it all and bringing it into a unified picture. But we are no less dependent upon the work of others, and we come up against enough surprising facts, enough reversals in theoretical interpretation, to know that it is often just as hard for us to distinguish between duly warranted authority and outrageously shortsighted prejudice. We should be able at least to understand Augustine's own kind of respect for his authorities.

One feature of thought based on testimony is that it is necessarily carried on in the hypothetical mood—its logical character is such that it always means, "This is true, *if* these other assertions on the basis of which I have reasoned are true, *if* this testimony coming from others is reliable"; and usually we are conscious of that to some degree. In such cases we will not find the original insights of a thinker or his deepest convictions by looking directly at the *assertions* that are made; we must look rather at the process of reasoning which intervenes between the premise and the conclusion, or ask in what light the propositions are understood. Consequently it is possible to learn from Augustine's reasoning and appreciate his perspective even where the advance of knowledge has reversed many of his assumptions about the world or where the sense of the Church has rejected some of the things he said about original sin and predestination. Some of the detailed assertions he makes can be abandoned, then, without ceasing to be "Augustinian" in one's thinking, for many of those assertions were made not with the certitude of immediate intuitions but hypothetically, and were given not a "real" but a "notional" assent.

Some such distinction, by the way, is important for the proper understanding not only of Augustine's thought but of his personality, its dynamics and its development, whether in the fashion of conventional biography or following the more penetrating methods of psychoanalysis. It would seem comparatively easy to classify Augustine in the terminology of psychoanalysis, for Augustine was disingenuous enough to disclose much of himself in the *Confessions* and elsewhere.[1] But there can only be a rough-hewn characterization of Augustine the man as long as the biographer or analyst is not in a position to trace the fine details of the images to which he responded (in his exegetical writings and sermons, for example) and the meanings they encode, and especially if he does not have some sense for the "proximity" or the "distance" of each assertion to the center of Augustine's personality. It may well be that his adherence to Manichaeism, or his championing of the doctrines of original sin and predestination, often taken to be revealing manifestations of his inward conflicts,

---

[1] For a recent discussion, see the series of articles in the *Journal for the Scientific Study of Religion*, V (Fall, 1965, and Spring, 1966) by James Dittes, Joseph Havens, Walter Houston Clark, David Bakan, Philip Woollcott, and Paul Pruyser.

will prove to be nothing more than the result of a process of reasoning coherently on the basis of the data and options available. Even where he makes assertions more centrally, it often appears that he came to them more through reflection and insight than through impulse. To the psychologist of religion Augustine poses a challenge, thus far unmet, to try out his theories on the difficult terrain of a life in which emotional intensity was balanced by intellectual rigor, and in which there was a complex interaction among the roles of a seeker after wisdom, a thinker, and a bishop of the Church.

But having noted Augustine's willingness to learn from others and his complexity as a man and as a thinker—having acknowledged, in other words, that he was not always either original or infallible—let us ask more directly about his virtues as a theologian, the reason for his unique stature among Christian thinkers. What suggests itself immediately is his spirit of *inquiry*—his awareness of the problems that lay open before him, his tenacity in exploring all possible hypotheses, his sense for what constituted a satisfactory answer. He thought of himself chiefly as a seeker after understanding; it was to this task that he always returned when he had the time, and it was through theological writings concerned with difficult problems—freedom of the will, the Trinity, the two cities—that he wished to be known beyond the circle of his ordinary responsibilities.

This is not to deny the importance of his exegetical writings or of his sermons; but the former were actually vehicles of theological inquiry (this is especially true of the succession of commentaries on Genesis), and it is often difficult to construe the sermons properly if one does not already have a sense for the overall pattern of his theology at a given stage. Scripture did have supreme authority for him, and it changed his thought in crucial ways from time to time. He took his exegetical activities seriously, furthermore, and repeatedly he engaged in a systematic study of particular passages—the Sermon on the Mount, the creation narrative, the Psalms, the Pauline epistles, the gospels, the Johannine writings—with an awareness of the *diversity* within Scripture, interpreting each writing in a way suited to its literary genre and the meanings he thought it conveyed, sometimes literal (as in Paul), sometimes metaphorical (as in the creation narrative), sometimes allegorical (as in the Psalms). Certainly theologians today ought more often to follow his example in undertaking a careful study of Scripture, and with the same sense for its diversity, disciplined this time, however, by the methods of critical historical study that are now at their disposal.

Yet Augustine cannot be called primarily an exegete, not only according to our own criteria of historical and philological scholarship but according to the criteria applicable in his own age. By those standards Origen, Ambrosiaster, Jerome, Theodore of Mopsuestia, and many others get high marks as interpreters of Scripture. But Augustine was not cut out, by training or by temperament, to be an interpreter; he possessed neither the linguistic skills nor the scholarly patience to accomplish that task, and he never really attempted it. He had begun as a rhetor, not as a grammarian or a logician or a polyhistor; and when his career as a secular rhetor came to an end, it was in response to the lure of philosophy. All his activities were dominated by a concern to engage himself directly with real problems, to inquire into the truth, to convince others, and to persuade them to decide and act in accordance with it.

Augustine's deepest energies were directed, then, toward the theological task. What can we say about his *method* in theology? First, I think that a study like the one in which we have been engaged shows, if we may put it in terms of an ongoing debate in the nineteenth and twentieth centuries, especially in the Protestant theological world, that Augustine was not a "systematic" thinker who drew everything out of a few fundamental principles or followed a rigorously delineated method, but that he belongs, despite the unmistakable coherence of his thought, on the other side, among those thinkers who operate in terms of particular "problems" (*topoi*, *loci*), examining each of them for itself, according to the methods appropriate to it and using whatever evidence is available. He was always concerned with a number of problems concurrently. In some cases they remained open questions throughout his career; in other cases he arrived at his fundamental convictions quite early. But either way they were approached individually, and often the answer given to one question would have only a marginal effect upon his position with respect to another matter. Whether such a procedure is to be recommended unreservedly can remain open. It might be that it leads to eclectic and disjointed thinking, and that Augustine sometimes partakes of those faults. But at the best it gives a proper sense of the wide range of topics that must be considered and the variety of methods that can be used.

Sometimes more needs to be said about this employment of a variety of methods, for it is perhaps Augustine's chief virtue as a theologian and the point at which we stand to learn the most from him today, when we are overly preoccupied with method and often let it inhibit a concern with the subject matter itself. In the fourth book of *On Christian Instruction* he spells out the different rhetorical "styles" that are appropriate to different aims—the precision of the subdued style for exposition or reasoned argumentation, the ardor and seriousness of the moderate style for evaluating and praising and condemning, the ornateness of the grand style for convincing and persuading; and the same variation is to be found in his writings, used quite self-consciously. And just as he cultivated a flexibility of style to suit all occasions, he cultivated a flexibility of mind to suit the diversity of materials. The unity of his thought is not the conceptual unity of a single system but the coherence of a single life animated by a passion for the truth and open to whatever might be learned about the one God and the one complex cosmos over which he rules.

As a consequence Augustine can be called the father and precursor of many different tendencies in Western thought, from the most free-ranging speculation to the most narrow dogmatism. But where his disciples usually followed only a few methods of inquiry, he utilized them all concurrently, often without much mutual influence. An "Augustinian" approach to philosophy and theology can accommodate a number of different perspectives, then, and because they often remain distinct in Augustine's own work it is not difficult to separate them. There will be:

(1) a *natural philosophy* engaged in a study of the world, and its regular patterns and structures, including the dynamics of living things;

(2) a *critical philosophy* that describes the character of such acts as judging and understanding and asks about the conditions of their possibility, leading toward God as the ultimate ground and criterion;

(3) a *phenomenology of finite spirit* with its quests and failures, its false starts and its glimpses of fulfillment, its bondage and its liberation;

(4) a *rational theology* rooted in all these things and perhaps extending (as Augustine thought it did) to some kind of Trinitarian doctrine and a general metaphysic of finite being and its relation to God;

(5) a *doctrinal theology* or a *theology of the history of salvation* based on the data of Scripture and tradition and stressing, in characteristic Augustinian fashion, not revealed knowledge so much as the practical function of events and institutions in the life of the people of God in making salvation present to men;

(6) a *speculative theology* or *Glaubenslehre* engaging in a more individual reflection upon the coherence of the various articles of faith;

(7) an *anagogical* or *mystical theology* seeking a more intimate understanding and experience of the realities known through reason and faith;

(8) an *ethics* focused on the question of the obedient life within the world;

(9) an *ecclesiology* concerned with the nature and the ongoing life of the Church;

(10) a *theology of culture* and a *politics* in which theology and ethics are brought into encounter with the actual character of secular life;

(11) a *logic* and a *rhetoric* concerned with analyzing the problems of meaning and communicability that may arise from any of these enterprises or among them.

All of these disciplines are now being practice in one or another segment of the Christian world. But too often they are practiced in isolation and even set at odds with each other. Not only that. Many of these types of thought have come under suspicion, and there is a timorousness among religious thinkers which allows them to be pushed farther and farther into one or another corner of the intellectual enterprise. The possibility of any rational theology, based in a study of nature and of human activity, is called into question; the biblical story seems dissolved into a multitude of isolated details; the objective reference of religious doctrines is often denied; and all that seems to be left is a set of personal attitudes and experiences. Augustine can perhaps be of help at this point, for his credentials as an "existential" thinker, interested in subjectivity and individuality, are in good order, and he often began with immediate experience; but then he moved outward to make generalizations about the world and about "being" generally, for he was convinced that commitments and beliefs must be brought into relation with whatever can be known about nature and history, perhaps along complex routes of inference, and he was prepared to act according to that policy in the face of all its risks, since much that he said was based, as he knew, on less than adequate information.

It may be too much to expect the grasp of all these disciplines that Augustine achieved; indeed, even by the standards of his age he was a gifted amateur in many fields, innocent of the flood of literature and the mass of technical details that began to overwhelm the specialists in philosophy and the other disciplines in the Hellenistic and Roman periods. But it is possible, at the very least, to cultivate a sense for the full gamut of theology, refrain from elevating one or another method and excluding the others, become aware of developments in the different fields and acquire sympathy with their concerns. And it may be that a breadth of vision like Augustine's will encourage something of the same kind, if not the same degree, of creativity.

If there is any recommendation that emerges from a study of his own procedure, it would be to let all of these diverse enterprises—philosophical investigations, biblical studies, theological reflection, scrutiny of contemporary life and its prospects, logical analyses—go their own way, following their own methods and using the appropriate data, but to resist the temptation to claim dominion for any of them or announce a synthesis prematurely and instead to let them interact and find their own balance within the broad horizon marked out by a deeply motivated search for truth and a passionate commitment to all genuine values.

And if there is any one way in which Augustine's procedure stimulates further thought about the overarching organization of these various disciplines, it is in presenting an alternative to the pattern which has shaped the assumptions of most theology since Thomas Aquinas, according to which reason goes part of the way and revelation then takes over. Augustine instead viewed the doctrine of God, including even the doctrine of the Trinity, as a matter for rational investigation, animated, to be sure, by a religious passion, and helped along its way by Scripture and dogma, but in the last analysis open to understanding. He saw the chief function of Scripture to be *not* that of making God's reality and nature known (though these also are involved) but that of declaring God's intentions for the human race and telling the story of a succession of events in which his salvation took effect within the human communities of Israel and the Church. He seems, then, to give aid and comfort to the approach to Scripture that has been characteristic of recent centuries, with its stress on the human aspects of Scripture and the particularity of its heritage—and at the same time to the attempts of some philosophers (one thinks chiefly of Whitehead and Hartshorne) to carry out extensive reflections on theological problems and to regard God as perhaps the most intelligible of all the realities with which they must concern themselves.

I suspect that the Thomist pattern was appropriate to (and may have been suggested by) the kind of Christian domination of culture that prevailed in a former era. But it may not be at all effective in a world like the one Augustine knew, at least in his earlier years before the alliance of throne and altar was cemented, or a world like the one into which we have been thrust in our own time, a world in which religious authority does not have a commanding position and certitude must come, on one side, from intellectual conviction arrived at in the open competition of ideas and, on the other side, from the vitality and sense of direction of clearly defined religious communities. As we enter a new era, it may be that we will find Augustine a reliable guide.

Bibliography

Alfaric, Prosper. *L'Évolution intellectuelle de saint Augustin. I. Du manichéisme au néoplatonisme.* Paris, E. Nourry, 1918.

Altaner, Berthold. *Kleine patristische Schriften,* hrsg. von Günter Glockmann. Texte und Untersuchungen, LXXXIII. Berlin, Akademie-Verlag, 1967. (Reprints the following articles, among others.)

———. "Augustinus und Irenäus," *Zeitschrift für katholische Theologie,* LXV (1949), 162–172.

———. "Augustinus und Origenes," *Historisches Jahrbuch,* LXX (1951), 15–41.

———. "Augustinus und Eusebios von Kaisareia," *Byzantinische Zeitschrift,* XLIV (1951), 1–6.

———. "Augustinus, Gregor von Nazianz und Gregor von Nyssa," *Revue bénédictine,* LXI (1951), 54–62.

———. "Augustinus und Didymus der Blinde," *Vigiliae Christianae,* V (1951), 116–120.

———. "Augustinus und die griechische Patristik. Eine Zusammenfassung und Nachlese zu den quellenkritischen Untersuchungen," *Revue bénédictine,* LXII (1952), 201–215.

Arnou, René. "Le thème néoplatonicien de la contemplation créatrice chez Origène et chez saint Augustin," *Gregorianum,* XIII (1932), 124–136.

———. "Platonisme des Pères," *DTC,* XII, 2, cols. 2355–59.

Ball, Joseph. "Libre arbitre et liberté dans saint Augustin," *Année théologique augustinienne,* VI (1945), 368–382.

Ball, Joseph. "Les développements de la doctrine de la liberté chez saint Augustin," *Année théologique augustinienne*, VII (1946), 400–430.

Benz, Ernst. *Marius Victorinus und die Entstehung der abendländischen Willensmetaphysik*. Stuttgart, Kohlhammer, 1932.

Berlinger, Rudolf. *Augustins dialogische Metaphysik*. Frankfurt, Klostermann, 1962.

Bonner, Gerald. *St. Augustine of Hippo: Life and Controversies*. Philadelphia, Westminster, 1963.

Boyer, Charles. *Essais sur la doctrine de saint Augustin*. Paris, Beauchesne, 1932.

———. *L'Idée de vérité dans la philosophie de s. Augustin*. Paris, Beauchesne, ²1940.

Broglie, Guy de. "Pour une meilleure intelligence du 'De correptione et gratia,'" *AM*, III, 317–337.

Brown, Peter. *Augustine of Hippo, A Biography*. Berkeley, University of California Press, 1967.

———. "Pelagius and His Supporters: Aims and Environment," *Journal of Theological Studies*, n.s. XIX (1968), 93–114.

Brunhemer, Anne. "The Art of Augustine's Confessions," *Thought*, XXXVII (1962), 109–128.

Buonaiuti, Ernesto. "Pelagio e l'Ambrosiastro," *Ricerche Religiose*, IV (1928), 1–17.

Burnaby, John. *Amor Dei: A Study of the Religion of St. Augustine*. London, Hodder and Stoughton, 1938.

Cayré, Fulbert. *La contemplation augustinienne. Principes de spiritualité et de théologie*. Paris, Desclée de Brouwer, 1927.

———. *Les sources de l'amour divin. La divine présence d'après saint Augustin*. Paris, Desclée de Brouwer, 1933.

Chaix-Ruy, Jules. *Saint Augustin. Temps et histoire*. Paris, Études Augustiniennes, 1956.

Chevalier, Irénée. *S. Augustin et la pensée grecque. Les relations trinitaires*. Fribourg en Suisse, Collectanea Friburgensia, 1940.

Clarke, Thomas E. *The Eschatological Transformation of the Material World according to St. Augustine*. Woodstock, Md., Woodstock College Press, 1956.

Combès, Gustave. *La charité d'après saint Augustin*. Paris, Desclée de Brouwer, 1934.

———. *La doctrine politique de saint Augustin*. Paris, Plon, 1927.

Courcelle, Pierre. *Les lettres grecques en Occident. De Macrobe à Cassiodore.* Paris, Boccard, 1943.

———. *Recherches sur les Confessions de saint Augustin.* Paris, Boccard, 1950.

———. "Propos antichrétiens rapportés par S. Augustin," *RA,* I (1958), 149–189.

———. "Source chrétienne et allusions païennes de l'épisode du 'Tolle, lege,'" *Revue d'histoire et de philosophie religieuse,* XXXII (1952), 171–200.

Dahl, Axel. *Augustin und Plotin. Philosophische Untersuchungen zum Trinitätsproblem und zur Nuslehre.* Lund, Lindstedt, 1945.

Deane, Herbert A. *The Political and Social Ideas of St. Augustine.* New York, Columbia University Press, 1963.

Dörrie, Heinrich. *Porphyrios' "Symmikta Zetemata." Ihre Stellung in System und Geschichte des Neuplatonismus nebst einem Kommentar zu den Fragmente.* Zetemata, XX. Munich, Beck, 1959.

Dorner, August. *Augustinus. Sein theologisches System und seine religionsphilosophische Anschauung.* Berlin, Wilhelm Hertz, 1873.

Duchrow, Ulrich. "'Signum' und 'Superbia' beim jungen Augustin," *REA,* VII (1961), 369–372.

Evans, Robert F. *Pelagius: Inquiries and Reappraisals.* New York, Seabury, 1968.

Ferretti, Giuseppe. *L'Influsso di S. Ambrogio in S. Agostino.* Rome, Pontificia Universitas Gregoriana, 1951.

Folliet, Georges. "'Deificari in otio.' Augustin, Epistula 10, 2," *RA,* II (1962), 225–236.

Fortin, Ernest. *Christianisme et culture philosophique au cinquième siècle. La querelle de l'âme humaine en Occident.* Paris, Études Augustiniennes, 1959.

———. "Saint Augustin et la doctrine néoplatonicienne de l'âme," *AM,* III, 371–380.

Frend, W. H. C. *The Donatist Church: A Movement of Protest in Roman North Africa.* Oxford, Clarendon, 1952.

———. "The Gnostic-Manichaean Tradition in Roman North Africa," *Journal of Ecclesiastical History,* IV (1953), 13–26.

Fuchs, Harald. *Augustin und der antike Friedensgedanke. Untersuchungen zum neunzehnten Buch der Civitas Dei.* Neue philosophische Untersuchungen, III, Berlin, Weidmann, 1926.

Gilson, Etienne. *The Christian Philosophy of St. Augustine.* New York, Random House, 1960.

———. "Notes sur l'être et le temps chez saint Augustin," *RA*, II (1962), 205–223.

Grabowski, Stanislaus J. *The All-Present God: A Study in St. Augustine.* St. Louis, Herder, 1954.

———. *The Church: An Introduction to the Theology of St. Augustine.* St. Louis, Herder, 1957.

Guitton, Jean. *Le temps et l'éternité chez Plotin et saint Augustin.* Paris, Boivin, 1933.

Hadot, Pierre. "Citations de Porphyre chez Augustin (à propos d'un livre récent)," *REA*, VI (1960), 204–244.

Hassel, David J. "Conversion-Theory and *Scientia* in the *De Trinitate*," *RA*, II (1962), 383–401.

Heijke, J. "The Image of God according to St. Augustine (*De Trinitate* excepted)," *Folia*, X (1956), 3–11.

Hendrikx, Ephrem. *Augustins Verhältnis zur Mystik. Eine patristische Untersuchung.* Würzburg, Rita-Verlag, 1936.

Henry, Paul. *Plotin et l'Occident.* Spicilegium sacrum Lovaniense, XV, 1, Louvain, 1934.

———. *La vision d'Ostie. Sa place dans la vie et l'œuvre de S. Augustin.* Paris, J. Vrin, 1938.

———. *Saint Augustine on Personality.* New York, Macmillan, 1960.

Hessen, Johannes. *Augustins Metaphysik der Erkenntnis.* 2. Aufl. Leiden, Brill, 1960.

Holte, Ragnar. *Béatitude et Sagesse. Saint Augustin et le problème de la fin de l'homme dans la philosophie ancienne.* French translation, Paris, Études Augustiniennes, 1962 (first published in Swedish, 1958).

Ivánka, Endre von. "Die unmittelbare Gotteserkenntnis als Grundlage des Erkennens und als Ziel des übernatürlichen Strebens bei Augustin," *Scholastik*, XIII (1938), 521–543.

———. "Römische Ideologie in der 'Civitas Dei,'" *AM*, III, 411–417.

Jackson, B. Darrell. "The Theory of Signs in St. Augustine's *De doctrina christiana*," *REA*, XV (1969), 9–49.

Janssen, Karl. *Die Entstehung der Gnadenlehre Augustins.* Rostock, Carl Hinstorff, 1936.

Jolivet, Régis. *Dieu soleil des esprits ou la doctrine augustinienne de l'illumination.* Paris, Desclée de Brouwer, 1932.

Jolivet, Régis. *Le problème du mal d'après saint Augustin*. Paris, Beauchesne, ²1936.

Koch, Hugo. "Cipriano in Agostino," *Ricerche Religiose*, VIII (1932), 317–337.

Körner, Franz. "Die Entwicklung Augustins von der Anamnesis- zur Illuminationslehre in Lichte seines Innerlichkeitsprinzips," *Theologische Quartalschrift*, CXXXIV (1954), 397–447.

———. "Deus in homine videt. Das Subjekt des menschlichen Erkennens nach der Lehre Augustins," *Philosophisches Jahrbuch*, LXIV (1956), 166–217.

———. *Das Sein und der Mensch. Die existentiellen Seinsentdeckung des jungen Augustin. Grundlagen zur Erhellung seiner Ontologie*. Freiburg and Munich, Karl Alber, 1959.

———. "Abstraktion oder Illumination? Das ontologische Problem des augustinischen Sinneserkenntnis," *RA*, II (1962), 81–109.

Kunzelmann, A. "Die Chronologie der Sermones des hl. Augustinus," *Miscellanea Agostiniana*, II (1931), 417–520.

Kusch, Horst. "Trinitarisches in den Büchern 2–4 und 10–13 der Confessiones," *Festschrift Franz Dornseiff* (Leipzig, 1953), pp. 124–183.

———. "Der Titel Gottes 'Dominus' bei Augustinus und Thomas von Aquino," *ibid.*, pp. 184–200.

La Bonnardière, Anne-Marie. "Le verset paulinien Rom., V, 5 dans l'œuvre de saint Augustin," *AM* II, 657–665.

———. "L'Épître aux Hébreux dans l'œuvre de saint Augustin," *REA*, III (1957), 137–162.

———. "Le combat chrétien. Exégèse augustinienne d'*Éphes*. VI, 12," *REA*, XI (1965), 235–238.

———. *Recherches de chronologie augustinienne*. Paris, Études Augustiniennes, 1965.

Ladner, Gerhart. *The Idea of Reform: Its Impact on Christian Thought and Action in the Age of the Fathers*. Cambridge, Harvard University Press, 1959.

Lauras, A., and Rondet, Henri. "Le thème des deux cités dans l'œuvre de saint Augustin," *Études Augustiniennes* (Théologie, XXVIII; Paris, Aubier, 1953), pp. 99–160.

Le Blond, Jean-Marie. *Les conversions de saint Augustin*. Théologie, XVII. Paris, Aubier, 1950.

Lechner, Odilo. *Idee und Zeit in der Metaphysik Augustins.* Salzburger Studien zur Philosophie. Munich, Anton Pustet, 1964.

Le Landais, Maurice. "Deux années de prédication de saint Augustin," *Études Augustiniennes* (Théologie, XXVIII; Paris, Aubier, 1953), pp. 9–95.

Lewy, Hans. *Chaldaean Oracles and Theurgy. Mysticism, Magic, and Platonism in the Later Roman Empire.* Recherches d'archéologie, de philologie et d'histoire, XIII. Cairo, Institut français d'archéologie orientale, 1956.

Löhrer, Magnus. *Der Glaubensbegriff des hl. Augustinus in seinen ersten Schriften bis zu den Confessiones.* Einsiedeln, Benzinger, 1955.

————. "Glaube und Heilsgeschichte in 'De Trinitate' Augustins," *Freiburger Zeitschrift für Philosophie und Theologie,* IV (1957), 385–419.

Lorenz, Rudolf. "Die Herkunft des augustinischen *frui Deo,*" *Zeitschrift für Kirchengeschichte,* LXIV (1952–1953), 34–60.

Luck, Georg. *Der Akademiker Antiochos.* Bern, Paul Hapt, 1953.

Madec, Goulven. "Connaissance de Dieu et action des grâces. Essai sur les citations de l'*Ép. aux Romains,* I, 18–25 dans l'œuvre de saint Augustin," *RA,* II (1962), 273–309.

Maier, Franz Georg. *Augustin und das antike Rom.* Tübinger Beiträge zur Altertumswissenschaft, XXXIX. Stuttgart, Kohlhammer, 1955.

Maier, Jean-Louis. *Les missions divines selon saint Augustin.* Paradosis, XVI. Fribourg en Suisse, Éditions Universitaires, 1960.

Maréchal, Joseph. "La vision de Dieu au sommet de la contemplation d'après saint Augustin," *Nouvelle revue théologique,* LVII (1930), 89–109, 191–204.

Markus, R. A. "'Imago' and 'Similitudo' in Augustine," *REA,* X (1964), 125–143.

Marrou, Henri Irénée. *Saint Augustin et la fin de la culture antique.* Paris, Boccard, 1938. "*Retractatio,*" 1946.

Mausbach, Joseph. *Die Ethik des heiligen Augustinus.* 2. Aufl. Freiburg, Herder, 1929.

Mitterer, Albert. *Die Entwicklungslehre Augustins im Vergleich mit dem Weltbild des hl. Thomas von Aquin und dem der Gegenwart.* Vienna and Freiburg, Herder, 1956.

Mommsen, Theodor. "St. Augustine and the Christian Idea of Progress," *Journal of the History of Ideas,* XII (1951), 346–374.

Morris, John. "Pelagian Literature," *Journal of Theological Studies,* n.s. XVI (1965), 26–60.

Mourant, John A. "The Augustinian Argument for the Existence of God," *Philosophical Studies*, XII (1963), 92–106.

Mozley, J. B. *A Treatise on the Augustinian Doctrine of Predestination*. New York, E. P. Dutton, 1878.

Nock, A. D. *Conversion: The Old and the New in Religion from Alexander the Great to Augustine of Hippo*. New York, Oxford University Press, 1933.

Nygren, Gotthard. *Das Prädestinationsproblem in der Theologie Augustins. Eine systematisch-theologische Studie*. Göttingen, Vandenhoeck & Ruprecht, 1956.

O'Connell, Richard J. "*Ennead* VI, 4 and 5 in the Works of Saint Augustine," *REA*, IX (1963), 1–39.

———. "The Plotinian Fall of the Soul in St. Augustine," *Traditio*, XIX (1963), 1–35.

———. "The Enneads and St. Augustine's Image of Happiness," *Vigiliae Christianae*, XVII (1963), 129–164.

———. "The Riddle of Augustine's *Confessions*: A Plotinian Key," *International Philosophical Quarterly*, IV (1964), 327–352.

———. "Alypius' 'Apollinarianism' at Milan (*Conf.*, VII, 25)," *REA*, XV (1967), 209–210.

O'Meara, John J. "The Historicity of the Early Dialogues of St. Augustine," *Vigiliae Christianae*, V (1951), 150–178.

———. *The Young Augustine: The Growth of St. Augustine's Mind up to His Conversion*. London, Longmans, Green, 1954.

———. *Porphyry's Philosophy from Oracles in Augustine*. Paris, Études Augustiniennes, 1959.

O'Toole, Christopher J. *The Philosophy of Creation in the Writings of St. Augustine*. Washington, Catholic University of America, 1944.

Ott, W. "Des hl. Augustinus Lehre über die Sinneserkenntniss," *Philosophisches Jahrbuch*, XIII (1900), 45–59, 138–148.

Pépin, Jean. "'Primitiae spiritus.' Remarques sur une citation paulinienne des 'Confessions' de saint Augustin," *Revue de l'histoire des religions*, CXL (1951), 155–202.

———. "Recherches sur le sens et les origines de l'expression 'caelum caeli' dans le livre XII des 'Confessions' de saint Augustin," *Bulletin du Cange. Archivum Latinitatis Medii Aevi*, XXII (1953), 185–274.

Pépin, Jean. "Une curieuse déclaration idéaliste du 'De genesi ad literam' de saint Augustin et ses origines plotiniennes," *Revue d'histoire et de philosophie religieuses*, XXXIV (1954), 373–400.

———. "Saint Augustin et le symbolisme néo-platonicien de la vêture," *AM*, I, 293–306.

———. "Une nouvelle source de saint Augustin: Le Ζήτημα de Porphyre *Sur l'union de l'âme et du corps*," *Revue des études anciennes*, LXXXVI (1964), 53–107.

———. *Théologie cosmique et théologie chrétienne*. Paris, Presses Universitaires Françaises, 1964.

Philips, Gérard. *La raison d'être du mal d'après saint Augustin*. Louvain, Éditions du Museum Lessianum, 1927.

Pincherle, Alberto. *La formazione teologica di Sant'Agostino*. Rome, Edizioni Italiane, 1947.

Plaignieux, Jean. "Influence de la lutte antipélagienne sur le 'De Trinitate' ou: Christocentrisme de saint Augustin," *AM*, II, 817–826.

Plinval, Georges de. *Pour connaître la pensée de saint Augustin*. Paris, Bordas, 1954.

———. "Mouvement spontané ou mouvement imposé? Le 'feror' augustinien," *REA*, V (1959), 13–19.

Ratzinger, Joseph. *Volk und Haus Gottes in Augustins Lehre von der Kirche*. Münchener Theologische Studien. Munich, Karl Zink, 1954.

Refoulé, F. "La datation du premier concile de Carthage contre les Pélagiens et du *Libellus fidei* de Rufin," *REA*, XI (1963), 41–49.

———. "Julien d'Éclane, théologien et philosophe," *Recherches de sciences religieuses*, LII (1964), 42–84.

Ritter, Joachim. *Mundus Intelligibilis. Eine Untersuchung zur Aufnahme und Umwandlung der neuplatonischen Ontologie bei Augustinus*. Philosophische Abhandlungen, VI. Frankfurt am Main, V. Klostermann, 1937.

Rivière, Jean. *Le dogma de la Rédemption chez saint Augustin*. Paris, J. Gabalda, ³1933.

Roy, Olivier (Jean-Baptiste) du. "L'expérience de l'amour et l'intelligence de la foi trinitaire selon saint Augustin," *RA*, II (1962), 414–445.

———. *L'Intelligence de la foi en la Trinité selon saint Augustin. Genèse de sa théologie trinitaire jusqu'en 391*. Paris, Études Augustiniennes, 1966.

———. "Augustine." *New Catholic Encyclopedia*, I, 1041–1058.

Ruch, Michel. "Cicéron et l'Orphisme," *REA*, VI (1960), 1–10.

Sage, Athanase. "Les deux temps de grâce," *REA*, VII (1961), 209–230.

———. "'Praeparatur voluntas a Deo,'" *REA*, X (1964), 1–20.

———. "Péché originel. Naissance d'un dogme," *REA*, XIII (1967), 211–248.

Schindler, Alfred. *Wort und Analogie in Augustins Trinitätslehre.* Hermeneutische Untersuchungen zur Theologie, IV. Tübingen, J. C. B. Mohr, 1965.

Schmaus, Michael. *Die psychologische Trinitätslehre des hl. Augustinus.* Münsterische Beiträge zur Theologie, XI. Münster, Aschendorff, 1927.

Schubert, P. Alois. *Augustins Lex-Aeterna-Lehre nach Inhalt und Quellen.* Beiträge zur Geschichte der Philosophie des Mittelalters, Band XXIV, Heft 2. Münster, Aschendorff, 1924.

Schuetzinger, Christine. *The German Controversy on Saint Augustine's Illumination Theory.* New York, Pageant Press, 1960.

Simonetti, Manlio, "S. Agostino e gli Ariani," *REA*, XIII (1967), 55–84.

Solignac, Aimé de. "Analyse et sources de la question 'De ideis,'" *AM*, I, 307–316.

———. "Réminiscences plotiniennes et porphyriennes dans le début du 'De ordine' de saint Augustin," *Archives de philosophie*, XX (1957), 446–465.

———. "Doxographies et manuels dans la formation philosophique de saint Augustin," *RA*, I (1958), 113–148.

———. Introduction and notes to the *Confessions*, *BA*, XIII and XIV.

Sullivan, John Edward. *The Image of God: The Doctrine of Saint Augustine and Its Influence.* Dubuque, Priory Press, 1963.

Svoboda, K. *L'esthétique de saint Augustin et ses sources.* Brno and Paris, Belles Lettres, 1933.

TeSelle, Eugene. "Nature and Grace in Augustine's Expositions of Genesis I, 1–5," *RA*, V (1968), 95–137.

Testard, Maurice. *Saint Augustin et Cicéron. I. Cicéron dans la formation et l'œuvre de saint Augustin; II. Répertoire des textes.* Paris, Études Augustiniennes, 1958.

Theiler, Willy. *Die Vorbereitung des Neuplatonismus.* Problemata, I. Berlin, Weidmann, 1930.

———. *Porphyrios und Augustin.* Schriften des Königsberger gelehrten Gesellschaft, geistwissenschaftliche Klasse, X, 1. Halle, Niemeyer, 1933.

Thonnard, François-Joseph. "La vie affective de l'âme selon saint Augustin," *Année théologique augustinienne*, XIII (1953), 33–55.

———. "La notion de lumière en philosophie augustinienne," *RA*, II (1962), 125–175.

———. "La prédestination augustinienne et l'interprétation de O. Rotmanner," *REA*, IX (1963), 259–287.

———. "La prédestination augustinienne. Sa place en philosophie augustinienne," *REA*, X (1964), 97–123.

———. "La notion de 'nature' chez saint Augustin. Ses progrès dans la polémique antipélagienne," *REA*, XI (1965), 239–265.

———. "L'aristotélisme de Julien d'Éclane et saint Augustine," *REA*, XI (1965), 296–304.

Van Bavel, Tarsicius J. *Recherches sur la christologie de saint Augustin. L'humain et le divin dans le Christ d'après saint Augustin*. Paradosis, X. Fribourg, Éditions Universitaires, 1954.

Van der Meer, F. *Augustine the Bishop*. Translated by Brian Battershaw and G. R. Lamb. London and New York, Sheed and Ward, 1961.

Veer, Albert C. de. "'Reuelare,' 'Reuelatio.' Éléments d'une étude sur l'emploi du mot et sur sa signification chez s. Augustin," *RA*, II (1962), 331–357.

Verbeke, Gérard. "Spiritualité et immortalité de l'âme chez saint Augustin," *AM*, I, 329–334.

———. "Augustin et le Stoïcisme," *RA*, I (1958), 67–89.

Vooght, J. de. "Les miracles dans la vie de S. Augustin," *Recherches de théologie ancienne et médiévale*, XI (1939), 5–16.

Willis, G. G. *St. Augustine and the Donatist Controversy*. London, S.P.C.K., 1950.

Wytzes, J. "Bemerkungen zu dem neuplatonischen Einfluss in Augustins 'de Genesi ad literam,'" *Zeitschrift für neutestamentliche Wissenschaft*, XXXIX (1940), 137–151.

Zepf, Max. "Augustinus und das philosophische Selbstbewusstsein der Antike," *Zeitschrift für Religions- und Geistesgeschichte*, XI (1959), 105–132.

Zimara, Coelestin. "Das Ineinanderspiel von Gottes Vorwissen und Wollen nach Augustinus," *Freiburger Zeitschrift für Philosophie und Theologie*, VI (1959), 272–299, 361–394.

Indexes

INDEX OF PASSAGES CITED

Scripture

12*

Augustine[1]

[1] Bold-face type indicates pages on which a passage is quoted at length.

[1] Chapter numbering follows *PL*; *CSEL* numbers are in brackets.

Index of Modern Authors[1]

---

[1] This index includes only modern scholars who have written on Augustine or on his setting in antiquity. Modern thinkers with whom Augustine has been compared in the present work are listed in the topical index.

Topical Index

Academics ("New Academy"), 26, 28, 31, 84–86

Accident, meaning of the term, 289–290, 296

Adam, consequences of his sin, 158–159, 180, 192; character of his sin, 160; Augustine's later view of the primitive state, 314–315

Adeodatus, 131

African Christianity, 132–135

Alypius, 42

Ambrose, 30–31, 90, 116, 117–118, 121, 226, 227, 265–266, 294

Ambrosiaster, 157–158, 165, 166, 177, 247–248

Analogies to the Trinity, 117n., 223–224, 299, 300–309

Angels, their state at creation, 202–204, 235–236; their role in the cosmos, 210–213; their knowledge, 208–213; and the Platonist "soul," 214–216, 221–222

Anselm, 131, 169

Anthony, 38, 42

Antiochus of Ascalon, 45, 46, 66–67, 69

Apollinarianism, 146–147, 148–150, 155

Apuleius, 30, 48

Arianism, 122, 226, 227, 294–295, 310–311, 334

Aristotle, 26, 49, 69, 74, 92, 117

Asceticism, 63

Athanasius, 150, 294

Augustine, life, 25–43, 90–92, 131, 132–135, 266, 310–312, 338; early influence of Christianity, 26, 28, 34, 35; his receptivity to Manichaeism, 26–30, 32; his conversion, 38–42, 195–197; his study of Scripture, 26, 35, 118–119, 134, 135–137, 156–157, 197–208; his interpretation of Scripture, 185–188, 197–199, 204–207, 345–346; his theological method, 20–

23, 54–55, 129–130, 130–131, 312, 346–350; the personal element in his thinking, 20–23, 70, 189–190, 197, 342; his varying degrees of certitude about his statements, 342–344; the dates and circumstances of particular works: *On Beauty and Proportion*, 29; *Life in Happiness*, 61–68; *On Order*, 77–78; *Soliloquies*, 59; *On Free Will*, 135, 137, 156; *On True Religion*, 123–126; *On Faith and the Creed*, 135; *Unfinished Commentary on Genesis*, 135, 136–137; *On Christian Instruction*, 185–188, 189; *Confessions*, 25–43, 59, 182, 189–190, 197, 199–204, 251, 256; *The Trinity*, 21, 223–237, 294, 299, 300, 311; *Against the Writings of Petilianus*, 261; *Literal Commentary on Genesis*, 135, 136–137; *Expositions of Psalms 119–133*, 234–236; *Expositions of the Gospel according to John*, 234–236, 311; *Expositions of the First Epistle of John*, 234–236; *The City of God*, 21, 268–269; *On the Soul and Its Origin*, 311; his esteem among his contemporaries, 342; the psychological study of Augustine's personality, 41, 266, 344–345; his contemporary relevance, 349–350

Augustinianism, 145–146, 342, 346–350

Authority, meaning of the term, 27–28, 74–75; its relation to reason, 26–28, 31–32, 73–77; the marks of divine authority, 74–75; its importance to Augustine, 134, 342–344

Auxilium divinum, 162, 163, 177

Baptism of infants, 259, 262–263, 265–266, 279–280, 323–324; differing interpretations of it in the Church, 279–280

Barth, Karl, 156, 229, 312, 330n.